THE MAN
WHO BECAME CINEMA
DILIP KUMAR

PRAISE FOR *MEMORIES OF FIRE: A NOVEL*

'A simple, gripping tale which unfolds across a turbulent period of modern Indian history. The strength of this novel lies in its fascinating mix of complex characters. Through expressive dialogue and eloquent description, Chopra takes his readers on a memorable journey across terrain that is both familiar and surprising'—**Shashi Tharoor, member of Parliament and author**

'*Memories of Fire* is a skilful narrative of events in India and Pakistan in the 1970s and 1980s . . . There are touching and poignant moments and wonderful insights into the Punjabi ethos, a unique and composite culture of its three major religions—Hinduism, Islam and Sikhism. The writer's love for nature also comes through and there are telling descriptions of little-known aspects of north Indian culture . . . An instructive read'—***Outlook***

'*Memories of Fire* is highly recommended to all those looking for rare gems . . . a journey that takes the reader into a charmed world, where the undergrowth drips with nostalgia, touched with strokes of humour . . . It is spicy and informative, a story of our past and present, brimming with anecdotes about our history, people, eccentrics, lovers, scandals—everything that makes for fine reading'—***New Indian Express***

'There is nostalgia for a gentler time as well as bloody descriptions of real-life historical events in this genre-crossing work by author and publishing stalwart Ashok Chopra . . . There is erudition and enough thought-provoking ideas to carry the narrative . . . Aligning religious differences isn't the answer to India's woes, as Chopra shows, tolerance has existed among previous generations . . . Yet, once nationalism raises its ugly head, everything changes . . . It's easier to agree with Chopra that memories encourage a state of reflection—with all its accompanying potential for analysis and solutions. Chopra's purpose is for us to learn from his memories and not to allow the mistakes of the past to be repeated'—*Asian Review of Books*

'The elation of reuniting with friends after a long gap brings back childhood memories and that's precisely what *Memories of Fire* by author and publishing stalwart Ashok Chopra does . . . Based on real-life events, the personalities of the characters in the book are unique and extremely well-built. The account feels to be a mix of nostalgia and detailed background history that is not just entertaining but also very informative and educative. All in all, it's a beautiful combination of humour, history, literature and, most importantly, love and friendship'—*Hindustan Times*

'A historical novel with a sprawling canvas, *Memories of Fire* is publishing veteran Ashok Chopra's first foray into fiction . . . Vivid descriptions of lived experience make the story come alive. Sights, sounds, colour and dashes of earthy humour all spice up the mix. The author draws the reader into the heart of the story and offers generous doses of insight into art, music and literature along the way. Memories of the gentle rhythms of life are as clearly sketched as the storming of the Golden Temple and the brutal violence unleashed on members of the Sikh community in the wake of Indira Gandhi's assassination. Beauty and gore, art and aggression, lust, love, fealty and rebellion—all find a place in the pages of this ambitiously plotted novel . . . The author's impulse to rake up the past springs from his concern for a fractured nation. Motivated by the belief that memory is a "great healer . . . the balm that soothes many a wound", he invites the reader to look back at and reflect upon the past. *Memories of Fire* is as much an ode to love, friendship, religious tolerance and peaceful existence as it is a warning against repeating the deadly and violent mistakes of the past'—*Open*

'*Memories of Fire* stands upright like a giant, straddling storytelling, politics, literature, poetry and more in what seems to be the puny world of fiction . . . The grittiness of the larger picture becomes clearly visible. Between the world of politics and the personal world, the author makes delightful digressions into almost everything else . . . Again and again, there are forays into literature. We are offered a choice of fine ghazals showcasing the beauty of the Urdu language. To see the book purely as a novel would be to undermine its greatness'—*Deccan Herald*

'Ashok Chopra's *Memories of Fire* is a picturesque novel written in such an appealing style that I was transported to my younger days. An extraordinary blend of fact and fiction, it is an essential read, covering a variety of subjects'—*Deccan Chronicle*

'First a publisher, then a writer, Ashok Chopra is nowhere close to stopping . . . [He] might have started writing late but now that he has picked up the pen, he continues to wield it well'—*India Today*

'*Memories of Fire*, set over a span of fifty years in the hills of Shimla and Punjab, does more than just describing and conjuring up the beautiful landscape of mountains and valleys in the region. The author's deep interest in literature, art and culture . . . his knowledge of Indian classical music and its famous exponents . . . his passion for literature are revealed throughout . . . [He] is at his intellectual best when it comes to romance, sex and love'—*Asian Age*

'The most unexpected here [in *Memories of Fire*] is a fine eye for historical detail and great skill in weaving it through the story of five friends whose lives come together after five decades of absence. Through their memories, we share the turbulent, and often bloody, history of the young Indian nation. In this story we see the true character of the region of Punjab before it was divided by religion and language. A sense of community and strong family ties marked this period despite the brief time when madness overtook the people on the verge of independence from colonial rule. Essentially, people were caring and still deeply connected with the past . . . The political parts of the narrative are particularly well-developed and readers would quickly recognize that the histories of the five heroes tell us a lot about the political travails of India . . . Many small nuggets from history, scattered casually around, do make for good reading and are quite informative as well'—*Tribune*

'Ashok Chopra—author, book editor, publisher, columnist and now a novelist—is a man of many facets. A voracious reader with a remarkable memory and the ability to recall what he wants at the right moment, in his novel *Memories of Fire*, he quotes profusely from the works of poets and writers. He grabs your attention from the word go . . . and weaves details skilfully into his narration. No assessment of his novel can be complete without complimenting the writer on his evocative style. Chopra can, for instance, write highly poetic prose about the breath-taking, beautiful Chambal valley, but when descriptions of the Hindu–Sikh riots demand a change of form, his style becomes hair-raising and his narration blood-curdling . . . *Memories of Fire* is a multilayered novel punctuated with contemporary history and it deserves to be read more than once, because one is likely to miss some nuances of narration and description on reading the book for the first time'—*Dawn,* **Pakistan**

'Ashok Chopra sees India and Pakistan as still one seamless entity. That is not to say he does not acknowledge the creation of both countries in 1947. He is too astute for such wishful extremism. He has crossed the border from India to Pakistan and back again all too often to not be reminded every time of the barbed reality of a border that snakes from Kashmir to Kutch. To him the only borders that matter are the borders of his mind, and these are limitless. Chopra belongs to a diminishing genus in India that can still distinguish between Faiz and Faraz, that can appreciate the poignancy writhing in Munir Niazi's lament *"Hamesha Der Kar Deta Hoon Main"*, that can tell whether the khatias are from Lahore's Khalifa Bakery or from some other taste-alike. He belongs to a rare species that can keep abreast of Pakistani politics and Islam without weakening his own religious convictions or his Indianness. His latest book, *Memories of Fire,* is a hexagram of his mind in which his imagination flies from corner to corner, across time, across borders. He speaks through the voices of his forcefully etched characters . . . [His] skill lies in his ability to weave a story that tests the tensile strength of contemporary events and attitudes pulling against traditional determination siding with history . . . Chopra's narrative is grouted deep in sensitivity . . . *Memories of Fire* is undeniably a love story between the author and his characters. For only the deepest and truest of emotions could have created such finely etched images of kinship, camaraderie and enduring friendship. [He] has allowed us to watch them set slowly, gradually in amber' —*Friday Times,* **Pakistan**

Of Love and Other Sorrows

'Ashok Chopra's passionate interest in literature marks this engaging, well-informed account of ten seminal writers who have dealt with the great political, social and moral issues of the twentieth century'—**Manju Kapur**

'Ashok Chopra is a rare connoisseur of literature: eclectic in his tastes and intelligent in his judgements. These essays reveal just how infectious his enjoyment of good prose can be'—**Pankaj Mishra**

'A memorable volume, presenting the major works of "ten modernists" who have made a definitive impact on literature and history. This is a work marked by scholarship [though worn lightly], eloquence and erudition. Ashok has made the narrative eminently readable, thanks to his ability to treat the subject with sincerity and sensitivity'—**Khushwant Singh**

THE MAN
WHO BECAME CINEMA
DILIP KUMAR

ASHOK CHOPRA

EBURY
PRESS

An imprint of Penguin Random House

EBURY PRESS

Ebury Press is an imprint of the Penguin Random House group of companies whose addresses can be found at global.penguinrandomhouse.com

Published by Penguin Random House India Pvt. Ltd
4th Floor, Capital Tower 1, MG Road,
Gurugram 122 002, Haryana, India

Penguin
Random House
India

First published in Ebury Press by Penguin Random House India 2025

ISBN 9780143475842

Typeset in Sabon LT Std by Rakesh Kumar, New Delhi, India

Printed at Thomson Press India Ltd, New Delhi

www.penguin.co.in

MIX
Paper | Supporting
responsible forestry
FSC® C010615

To
Huma and Sanjiv,
whose friendship, though discovered late in life,
is being savoured like old wine
*to add a greater meaning**

and

Atul and Bina,
whose friendship, like vintage wine,
has added many a taste to life

* With apologies to Isabel Allende

'I am writing to please myself,
though there is a feeling in some place in my head,
that this may be punishable. [But] I haven't
written for nothing.'

—Richard Burton[*]

[*] Chris Williams (ed.), *The Richard Burton Diaries* (Connecticut, USA: Yale University Press, 2012).

CONTENTS

Ai humnashinaan-i-mehfil-i-ma
Raftayad wale na az dil-i-maa

(O companion of our mehfil!
You left but not from our hearts.)

—Urfi,
the eminent sixteenth-century Persian poet

AUTHOR'S NOTE

DURING THE NEARLY FIVE DECADES I HAVE SPENT IN THE book world as a publisher–editor, I have published the autobiographies, biographies and memoirs of numerous luminaries associated with the Indian film industry. The biographies, both official and unofficial, include those of Lata Mangeshkar, M.S. Subbulakshmi, Asha Bhosle, Naushad and Pran. Among the autobiographies is the immensely informative and readable autobiography of Anupam Kher: *Lessons Life Taught Me, Unknowingly*. However, the one that I hold closest to my heart is the autobiography by the legendary Indian actor Dilip Kumar: *The Substance and the Shadow*.

This Dilip Kumar autobiography took me twenty-four years to publish, from the first time I met him during the summer of 1990 in Manali, Himachal Pradesh, where he was shooting for Subhash Ghai's *Saudagar* (1991) to the time the manuscript came into my hands and I published it on 9 June 2014, a Monday. (The details are in my memoirs *A Scrapbook of Memories: My Life with the Rich, the Famous and the Scandalous*.)[1]

I had met 'Sahab', as Dilip Kumar was commonly known among his family and friends, a few times during the writing and later publishing of his autobiography. For me, it was always a great pleasure meeting him, as there was much to listen to and learn from. A voracious reader, with an elephant's memory, he was known for his great love for literature and poetry, be it in English, Urdu or Persian. A great orator, anything he read he could easily recall, quote or refer to in his conversations and speeches. After every meeting with Sahab, I came out feeling I had learnt something new, like there was something to treasure for a lifetime.

I recall my meeting with him on Thursday, 24 April 2014. As I was about to leave their sprawling bungalow on Pali Hill, Mumbai, Dilip Kumar's doting wife, the veteran film actress Saira Banu, asked me to meet Sahab. He was taking his siesta. She woke him up despite my protest. 'I have come to take your leave,' I said in Punjabi, a language Sahab and I normally conversed in.

'*Kyun?*' (Why?) he asked.

Then he took my left hand in his, put it on the left side of his chest and asked, 'Can you hear what my heart is saying? It's saying I am always very happy to meet you . . . I love it when you come and will wait for your next visit . . . Please do come soon.' It was straight from the heart. I got a little emotional.

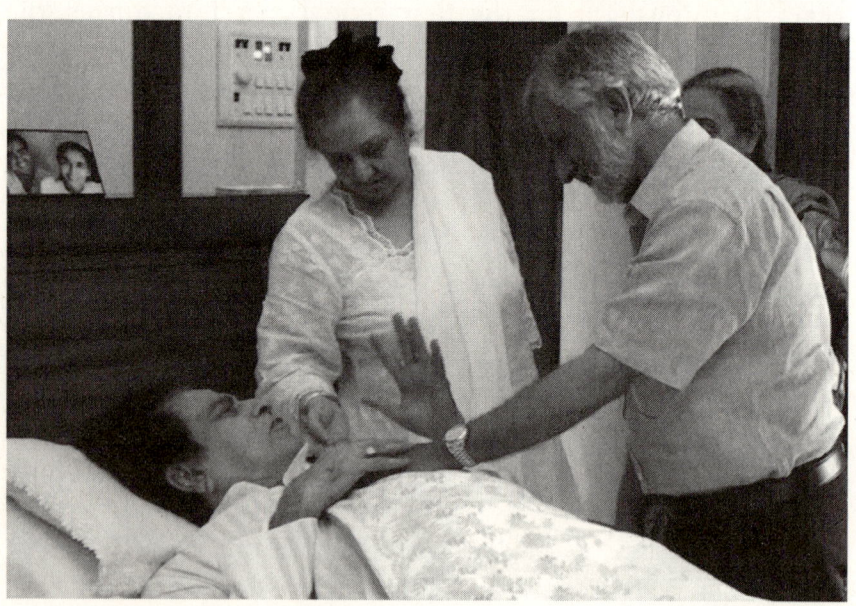

'Yes, I will,' I assured him. 'And I will bring the first copy of your autobiography with me, which will be my *chadawa* [offering] to you.' Then, as I bent down to touch his feet, he put his right hand lightly on my head and planting a warm kiss on my forehead said: '*Khush raho . . . Khuda lambi umar dave*' (Remain happy . . . may God give you a long life). Saira, holding back her tears, said, '*Ameen!*' (So be it!)

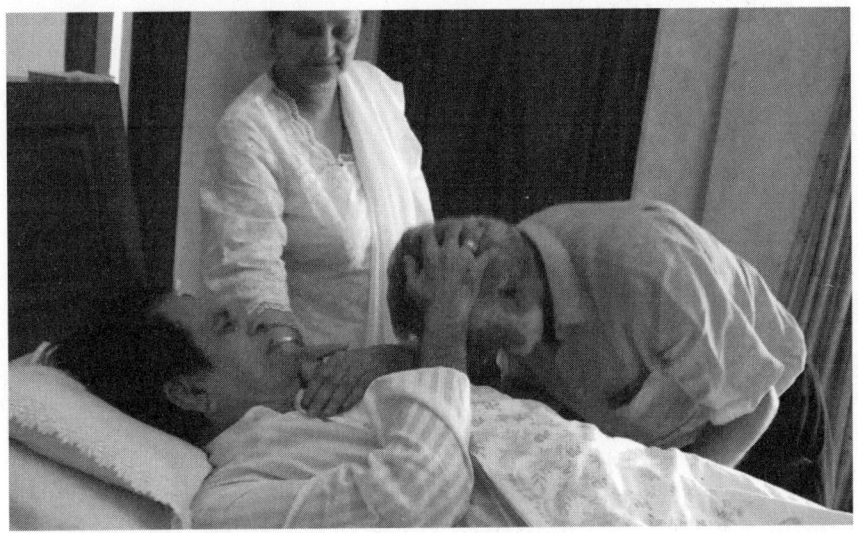

Touching the feet of elders and seeking their blessings in return is a common and an important tradition in many parts of our country. It is considered a mark of respect, a sign of good upbringing. It has been part and parcel of my growing-up years, and I always followed it on meeting and taking leave of Sahab. However, the blessings I received that day from 'The Legend' himself have remained embedded in my psyche to this day. It was a totally different experience for me, an indescribable feeling, an enchanting sensation, which even today evokes layers of emotion in me.

I did meet him on Monday, 12 May 2014, at his home, where he sat with a black-and-white picture of his mother in his lap. Some family members and close friends too had gathered. Saira presented him the first copy of his autobiography. He looked at it, scanned the pages and got somewhat emotional, as did Saira. He smiled, took my right hand in his and kissed it twice—warmly, without saying a word. His silence was very powerful and conveyed a lot more than words could have.

Who knew then that it was to be my last meeting with the one and only Dilip Kumar!

This is not a work of scholarship nor a biography. It is not an academic study nor a thesis on the cinema of Dilip Kumar. It is a kaleidoscopic work. More a summation of my experiences as a film buff with the performances of the legendary actor, through the luminous prism of the galaxy of fifty-seven films he worked in (coupled with the six special appearances he made and one film that never got released) during the six decades of his career in cinema. In comparison to all the big stars, each of whom would have done over a hundred films, fifty-seven sounds somewhat limited in scope and narrow in range. Yet, his oeuvre conveys a reach that is universal and profound, a beauty that is timeless and unparalleled, and the power of the art and craft of Dilip Kumar, which is monumental and transformative. His enduring legacy lies in his unique aura, which, in the words of the French philosopher Gaston Bachelard, is a 'special kind of beauty', a beauty bred and nurtured within the world of cinema, offering future generations of film enthusiasts not just entertainment, information and education but a lens to delve deeper into his films and gain a richer understanding of life, art and everything beyond.

1

THE LEGEND

IN THE GALAXY OF INDIVIDUALS WHO HAVE DOMINATED Indian cinema for over hundred years, quite a few names stand out. They are regarded with awe and reverence, apart from admiration bordering on adoration. There have been many greats, some of whom went on to become icons, some unique, some phenomena and some rare idols too. There was the 'King of Romance' and there was 'The Great Showman'. There was the 'Jubilee Kumar' and there was the one and only 'Superstar'. We have had them all! And yet, today, few remember their names. However, we have had only two legends: Mohammad Yousuf Khan, whom the world knows as Dilip Kumar, and Lata Mangeshkar, often called the 'Nightingale of India'. As the eminent lyricist and screenwriter Javed Akhtar once said, 'Dilip Kumar is remembered even today. And Dilip Kumar will always be remembered.' Yes, many have come, and many have gone. Many *will* come and many *will* go. But, Dilip Kumar, like Lord Alfred Tennyson's famous poem 'The Brook' will go on forever.

And legends are born once in a lifetime!

How does one describe Dilip Kumar? As an institution? Or an icon? As a colossus or a trailblazer? As a thespian or a trendsetter? He was indeed all this and much more. In his encomium, the iconic Amitabh Bachchan, the star of the millennium, who shared screen space with Dilip Kumar in Ramesh Sippy's 1982 film *Shakti*, said on the release of Kumar's

Amitabh Bachchan with Dilip Kumar

autobiography *The Substance and the Shadow* (2014): 'The history of Indian cinema shall in my reckoning be *before* Dilip Sahab and *after* Dilip Sahab, because of his impeccable presence. When you measure a journey, you can never change the milestone. Dilip Sahab to me is that milestone in our film industry. That landmark is permanent, whether you wish to count the miles before, or after it.'

According to the thespian Vyjayanthimala Bali, who acted with Dilip Kumar in seven films, all of them hugely successful: 'His influence on each generation has been such that there is a Dilip Kumar in every successful actor in Indian cinema. Even so, he remains incomparable and unsurpassable. This is because his dedication, honesty and passion cannot be replaced . . . An educated man and a voracious reader of literature from various countries, his subconscious, I feel, is a storehouse of characters he has studied from the works of various authors.'[1]

Despite his somewhat limited body of work (only sixty-three films, inclusive of the six he made special or fleeting appearances in, as quality and not quantity was his watchword), Dilip Kumar held successive generations of viewers spellbound with his phenomenal intensity, exquisite mannerisms, radiant charisma, nuanced dialogue delivery (with subtle variations of tone and cadence), enduring versatility and mesmerizing screen presence. He brought alive, with a rare degree of credibility, every character he portrayed on screen for close to six decades. Be it a boisterous swashbuckler, a rustic villager, a sophisticated urbanite, an irredeemable alcoholic, a Mughal prince, an intrepid freedom fighter or a diehard patriot, to name just a few, he played it with remarkable panache.

No wonder many of his films are now considered masterpieces, to be viewed and studied again and again. They are like gems, shining more with time. It comes as no surprise that he has been the most imitated, as also the most inspirational, actor in Indian cinema.

Dilip Kumar began his career in films with Amiya Chakravarty's *Jwar Bhata*, opposite Mridula Rani in 1944. He was in his early twenties, and a 'raw hand' in an industry that was brimming with a plethora of creative artistes in diverse fields, such as direction, acting, songwriting, scriptwriting and dialogue writing, music and photography. One should remember that at that time, there were no acting schools or institutes, of which there is a proliferation today. He had to make his mark in an arena dominated by well-established stalwarts who were very popular among the masses. Hence, Dilip Kumar had perforce to come up with something new and unique if he hoped to surge ahead. And he did so through a meticulous process of honing his talent, skills and aptitude to perfection. This accomplishment was anything but easy. The process was painstaking, marked by numerous trial-and-error experiments, not to mention a series of setbacks, but he continued on the path assiduously.

With the ever-volatile box office and the acerbic pens of film critics such as the powerful Baburao Patel of *Filmindia*, who was immensely feared and respected, and Clare Mendonça of the *Times of India*, one's future depended on the Friday, when the film was released. That decided if it was a hit or flop. In the initial phase of his career, Dilip Kumar struggled quite a bit to get a grip on the nitty-gritty of the roles he had to play. But through sheer perseverance and resolute determination, he soon mastered the art and craft of the new medium he had walked into and chosen for himself.

His first few films like Amiya Chakrabarty's *Jwar Bhata*, P. Jairaj's *Pratima* or Nitin Bose's *Milan* did not exactly work wonders for him. In fact, sadly, they sank without a trace. However, as the saying goes: failure is the steppingstone to success. Undaunted, Dilip Kumar girded his loins and soon turned the debacles into opportunities. With each passing day, like a keen student, he learnt and imbibed new concepts, ideas, thought processes and techniques from a creative point of view. He was greatly impressed by what is called 'Method acting', which he used effectively to embellish his performances. (More on that in Chapter 3.)

It was with Shaukat Hussain Rizvi's *Jugnu* (1947) that Dilip Kumar made the proverbial breakthrough. The heroine of the movie was Noor Jahan, then an already famous singing star. The rest is history! Dilip Kumar went on to act in a string of films and gradually climbed the greasy pole towards the summit.

Most of his films in the late 1940s and through the 1950s were invariably replete with melancholic and tragic elements, portraying heartbreak and unrequited love. As a result, he was labelled as the 'Tragedy King'. According to author and film critic Nikhat Kazmi:

> Dilip Kumar had become more an aggrieved hero, rambling aimlessly, bottle in hand, a dirge on his lips and the shadow of death looming ahead, the invested flesh and blood of the prototype of the Greek tragic hero. Like the Greek tragic king, he believed that the only way to encounter grief was to surrender before it, sometimes meekly and sometimes with masochistic glee. The unrequited, rejected lover of films like *Andaz*, *Deedar*, *Devdas*, firmly believed that happiness was an impossible eventuality in a world riddled with class and caste differences and an interfering hostile providence. The only course left was to give up the pursuit of happiness and settle down for sorrow instead; to forget about union and make a virtue of separation; to frantically weed out optimism and resilience from the virtuously masochistic mindset.[2]

Kazmi further adds that, 'Dilip Kumar made a virtue of sorrow by consciously opting for grief, separation, sacrifice and even suicide in most of his earlier films, where he lent a tragic grandeur to the third angle.' By and large, in films such as S.U. Sunny's *Babul* (1950), Amiya Chakravarty's *Daag* (1952), Mehboob Khan's *Amar* (1954) and Bimal Roy's *Devdas* (1955), he immortalized the angst of the unrequited lover, who must give up his loved one to someone else. In fact, the tone was set up with his very first box-office success, Mehboob Khan's *Andaz* (1949), where he suffered in silent anguish as he stood by and watched the love of his life, Neena (played by Nargis), drift into the arms of her dashing beau, Rajan (played by Raj Kapoor).[3]

In Dilip Kumar's filmic code, positivism had no place since any attempts to ameliorate the existing turmoil would weaken the aura of the tragic hero. His reaction to the quixotic inconsistencies of fate was a totally nihilistic one, which often ended in harming the protagonist himself, instead of providing succour. For example, in Nitin Bose's *Deedar* (1951).

Dilip Kumar's earlier films included *Jwar Bhata* (1944), *Pratima* (1945), *Milan* and *Jugnu* (both 1947), *Anokha Pyar*, *Mela*, *Ghar Ki Izzat* and *Nadiya Ke Paar* (all 1948).

Dilip Kumar with Mridula in *Jwar Bhata* (1944)

By the time Indian cinema entered its classical phase in the late 1940s, Dilip Kumar had completed his self-discovery as an actor to a large extent. The basic features of his hero were earmarked: an introvert who had been wronged, takes it to his heart and generates a complete catharsis of a whole range of emotions. He portrayed the search for an ideal self—one proclaiming true emancipation through love but desires it to be materialized only in a just society; and as that is not possible in actual reality, the self has to perish to validate this idealized conviction. The actor, in fact, represented the popular novelist Sarat Chandra Chattopadhyay's model of a vulnerable, self-destructing hero in Bengali literature.

Several of his films depicted Dilip Kumar as an unrequited lover seeking a kind of liberation from the unjust world through a prolonged internalized suffering (often ending in death) as seen in S.U. Sunny's *Mela*, S.K. Ojha's *Hulchul* (1951), Nitin Bose's *Deedar* and *Gunga Jumna* (1961), Ram Daryani's *Tarana* (1951), Bimal Roy's *Devdas*, S.U. Sunny's

Dilip Kumar and Nargis in *Hulchul* (1951)

Uran Khatola (1955), Hrishikesh Mukherjee's *Musafir* (1957) and K. Asif's *Mughal-e-Azam* (1960). In contrast, he, during this phase, was also seen in somewhat morbid anti-hero characters such as in Shaheed Latif's *Arzoo* (1950), S.U. Sunny's *Babul*, Mehboob Khan's *Andaz* and *Amar*, and R.C. Talwar's *Sangdil* (1952).

Explaining the roles Dilip Kumar played in most of his films right through the 1950s, Nikhat Kazmi says:

[He] always opted for internal emigration as a course of action. This was a great escape. A voyage into the unknown, which is undertaken not because one is enticed, but because one is disgusted by something. In his iconoclasm, he represented a rebellion that was akin to that of the Bohemians of Baudelaire's age. He was like the group of desperadoes who tried to break away from the nice and easy positivism of bourgeois society. Charles Baudelaire, Verlaine, Arthur Rimbaud, Paul Gauguin, Van Gogh were the tramps, the heavy drinkers and the unrivalled artists who chose to destroy everything in themselves that may be of no use to society, who raged against themselves too. For them and for the hero as immortalized by Dilip Kumar, happiness itself was something that is banal and vulgar. In a letter of 1845, addressed to a friend, Baudelaire writes: 'You are a happy man, I feel sorry for you, Sir, for being happy so easily. A man must have sunk low to consider himself happy.' However, Dilip Kumar never wanted to sink so low. On the contrary, he doggedly sought nobility in sorrow and imbued it with a romanticism that lingers even today.[4]

Remember his famous dialogue from *Devdas*:

Kaun kambakat hai jo bardasht karne ke liye peeta hai, main to peeta hun ki bas saans ley sakun
(Which wretched person drinks to tolerate, I drink so that I can at least take a breath.)

No wonder, the world of acting often ushers performers into the limelight, where performance anxiety can run high. The stakes are elevated, and heart rate may surge. Surprisingly, sometimes this stress can become a catalyst for improved performance, embracing the concept of positive stress in challenging situations.

However, a more complex challenge arises when method actors choose to inhabit their characters beyond the stage or camera's lens. As they tap into past emotional experiences, whether joyful or traumatic, unresolved emotions can linger. This emotional baggage may manifest as heightened emotional instability, intensified anxiety, fear or even a sense of falsehood, accompanied by bouts of acute sleep deprivation. Such emotional turbulence can pave the way for psychological distress, leading to emotional fatigue.

Dilip Kumar and Meena Kumari in *Azaad* (1955)

According to experts, this emotional fatigue often arises when actors create dissonance between their actions and authentic feelings. Research indicates that when method acting is employed judiciously and with proper emotional regulation, it need not lead to excessive fatigue. The key lies in striking a balance between immersion in the character and the ability to resurface, ensuring a harmonious coexistence of art and emotional well-being.

Dilip Kumar's profound commitment to his roles and his deep involvement with the character he portrayed, in film after film, at that stage of his career, led to serious psychological issues, so much so that he had to consult a psychiatrist in England. The advice given was simple: switch to comic roles, which he did with aplomb and poise! His consummate performances in S.M.S. Naidu's *Azaad* (1959) and S.U. Sunny's *Kohinoor* (1960) in a carefree, jovial and jaunty manner revealed how he could move from one genre to another with remarkable ease and finesse. However, later in A. Bhim Singh's *Gopi* (1970) and Tapan Sinha's Bengali film *Sagina Mahato* (1970), *Sagina* in Hindi (1974) and Asit Sen's *Bairaag* (1976), Dilip Kumar attempted to introduce some new elements in his acting style, though not always with much success. He designed his comedy through an over-talkative, one-track mind and as an obsessed simpleton who was a victim of the circumstances, but unlike his earlier roles, he did not internalize his suffering; he responded to it with a sense of simplicity, quite the same way Raj Kapoor did in film after film. He also improvised his mannerisms spontaneously to depict the character he was portraying on the screen such as repeatedly jerking his head and clinking his eyes. However, the audience did not take to it. Dilip Kumar lost the space he occupied in Hindi cinema.

After a self-imposed five-year wait in the wings to rediscover that 'lost space', Dilip Kumar's second innings began with the 1981 multi-starrer *Kranti* by Manoj Kumar followed by Ramesh Sippy's *Shakti*. Eight films followed through the 1980s and another three in the 1990s, in which Dilip Kumar made his presence felt with his individualistic stamp and authority. These films included Subhash Ghai's *Vidhaata* (1982), *Karma* (1986) and *Saudagar* (1991), Ravi Chopra's *Mazdoor* (1983), and Yash Chopra's *Mashaal* (1984), not of course counting the 1998 *Qila* by Umesh Mehra, which was a complete dud—a film that Dilip Kumar ought not to have done.

After carving out a niche for himself as a front-rank artiste in Indian cinema by the early 1950s, Dilip Kumar sought to attain perfection not only in acting but also in other departments of film-making, such as direction. From a purely *creative* perspective, he would delve deep into the intricacies of the script and the interplay of characters. He invariably came up with his own ideas, concepts and views on the finer points of various aspects related to the making of a particular film, including music. He would go into the 'minutest details of make-up, costumes, characterizations, mannerisms. In short, literally everything'.⁵ For example in his home production of *Gunga Jumna*, or *Dil Diya Dard Liya*, or *Ram Aur Shyam* to name a few. His main objective was to achieve excellence to the extent possible, keeping in view the diverse features associated with the enchanting celluloid experiences for the viewers.

As far as music was concerned, Dilip Kumar had the good fortune to lip-sync on screen a wide variety of superb and captivating songs, composed by some of the most distinguished and respected virtuosos. And of course, it goes without saying that the poet–songwriters and singers of that era too were immensely accomplished in their respective spheres.

Though it was music directors such as Anil Biswas and C. Ramchandra who were the favoured ones in the earlier years, providing music to four films each, S.D. Burman and Shankar–Jaikishan had between them three films each. However, when it came to *Madhumati* (1958), Bimal Roy signed Salil Chowdhury. And what a musical score he gave! Yes, there were the stalwarts of the Hindi film music world, such as Ghulam Haider, Khayyam and Sajjad Hussain too, who made their presence felt, but it was Naushad Ali who soon became the actor's favourite. He scored the music for fifteen of Dilip Kumar starrers, right through S.U. Sunny's *Mela* in 1948 to H.S. Rawail's *Sunghursh* in 1968, with Naushad's cherished poet–lyricist Shakeel Badayuni writing the songs. Dilip Kumar enjoyed a wonderful rapport with both.

In the 1940s and the early 1950s, it was mainly Talat Mahmood and Mukesh who used to 'playback' for Dilip Kumar. However, as time rolled by, it was Mohammed Rafi who came to be widely accepted as the 'voice of Dilip Kumar', and there was no looking back after that!

Dilip Kumar with Mohammad Rafi

Rafi's range was incredible. From the lowest notes to the highest ones, his vocals could cover the entire spectrum with mellifluous ease. From *Jugnu* to *Deedar*, from *Kohinoor* to *Sunghursh* and *Kranti*, Rafi sang his heart out and Dilip Kumar did full justice on the screen to the former's extraordinary renditions—whether they were romantic, melancholic, rollicking, patriotic or inspirational.

The other notable singers who sang for Dilip Kumar in the later years were Mahendra Kapoor, Kishore Kumar, Anwar Hussain and Mohammed Aziz. Although these artistes sang to the best of their ability, they somehow could not create the spellbinding magic of Rafi's vocals, nor the velvety and silky voice of Talat Mahmood. In fine, there was one and only one Mohammad Rafi on Dilip Kumar.

2

UNLOCKING THE CRAFT

IN THE WORLD OF CINEMATIC ARTISTRY, THERE EXISTS A profound legacy known as the Indian School of Method Acting, pioneered by none other than the legendary actor Dilip Kumar. Hailed as the 'ultimate method actor' by the much-celebrated film-maker Satyajit Ray, Dilip Kumar's contributions to the craft of acting are nothing short of remarkable. His school of method acting stands as a trail-blazing institution in cinematic acting, a one-of-a-kind contribution to the world of cinema. While it may not be formalized as a textbook or academically recognized, it represents the journey of an 'acting teacher' who developed his theory through practical demonstrations in his films. Even today, it remains the cornerstone of cinematic acting in Indian cinema. Its influence is so enduring that no newcomer in film acting, or even the stalwarts, can thrive without studying the principles of this school and incorporating elements from the master's vast inspirational repertoire.

According to Saira Banu: 'Dilip Sahab has, in his illustrious career, refined acting to an art form of exalted brilliance. Down the decades every actor of calibre has held him in high respect as the reference point in acting. He went to no school of acting but created his own method of emoting long before "Method Acting" came to be known in India or abroad.'[1]

Actor Anupam Kher recalls: 'One day he asked me: "Anup (as Dilip Kumar always referred to Anupam), can you tell me what method acting is? *Log mujhe bolte hain ki main method acting actor hoon* (People tell me that I am a method acting actor). But I have no idea what it is." "I know that you are pulling my leg. There is a method in acting and there is no method in acting. That's all. You have become an actor now," I replied.

"No, no," he laughed and said, "No, I am always aware of the fact that I am Dilip Kumar".'[2]

However, producer–director Yash Chopra, who made many a film with Dilip Kumar, differs. According to him:

> Dilip Kumar is *not* a Method actor as many cineastes think. He is a spontaneous actor who draws from his emotional reserves when he performs those marvellous dramatic scenes. I am saying this after watching him for fifty years or more. This alone was the reason why he had to seek the help of a psychiatrist to purge himself of the melancholy that had set in after all the tragic films he did in a row at the start of his stardom. In his personal life, he was a loner till he married Saira . . . He spent a lot of time reading and writing and working on the interpretation of the roles and screenplays that he selected.[3]

Dilip Kumar himself did not know how he came to be known as a method actor. He said:

> Marlon Brando [the acclaimed Hollywood actor] was called a Method actor . . . The epithet was used to describe me much before it was used for Brando. [Brando started work much later—first in theatre with Elia Kazan's Broadway hit *A Streetcar Named Desire* in 1946 and his debut film was *The Men* in 1950]. The truth is that I am an actor who evolved a method, which stood me in good stead. I learned the importance of studying the script and characters deeply and building on my own gut observations and sensations about my own and others' characters. It was always meaningful for me to study

even those characters who would be close to me or opposed to me. I was also lucky to have worked with directors who trusted me and allowed me to work without restraint. They believed as much as I did in the necessity of teamwork. Unlike many other arts and crafts, the art of filmmaking draws its sustenance from teamwork.[4]

Dilip Kumar's method brought about a revolutionary change in the portrayal of the Indian hero, significantly influencing not only Indian cinema but also the art of film acting. He showcased the hero in his finest form, drawing from his vast array of histrionics.

According to actor Kamal Haasan:

It was during a conversation with (film maker) Ramesh Sippy before I started work in his film *Saagar* (1985), which had Rishi Kapoor and Dimple Kapadia with me, that he asked me to 'see *Gunga Jumna* before you start work in *Saagar*. It will help you'. He maintained that every actor should compulsorily watch *Gunga Jumna* and what a revelation it was! I have some of the scenes from the film eternally embedded in my psyche. I am and always will be amazed by the layers of emotions he evoked in the viewer. I must admit that it was after films such as *Gunga Jumna*, *Mughal-e-Azam*, *Devdas*, *Kohinoor* and many other unforgettable classics of his that I began to understand the meaning of subtlety. I was able to appreciate the Western actors and the refinement of their acting also. It began to crystallize in my understanding of the eloquence of the medium that a mere look or sheer silence can convey so much so powerfully.

I am amazed at the layers of emotions he evoked in the viewer when he, as Prince Salim (in *Mughal-e-Azam*) simply sat in the royal darbar, saying nothing and doing nothing as Anarkali (Madhubala) performed the provocative *Jab pyar kiya toh darna kya* number. As an actor, I know how difficult it is to create an impact in a sequence like that where you have nothing to do and still maintain the composure of the character of Prince Salim. I can go on like this about umpteen sequences, in other films of his . . . From Dilip Kumar one learnt that there can be immense power in stillness . . . that still waters truly run deep.

I agree that it is not easy for every actor to achieve the brilliance he achieved with such seemingly effortless gestures, but it is what every actor should try to emulate. My performances would not have been what they are if I had not studied Dilip Sahab's works. He changed much in the way actors performed in his time, and he also changed a lot many actors' lives in later times, and I must confess that I am one of them.[5]

Narrating her experiences, Vyjayanthimala Bali, who worked with Dilip Kumar on a variety of subjects in the seven films they did together, says: 'He was a very helpful co-star who never tired of rehearsals and gave his co-artistes as much time to work up an emotion as was needed in critical situations.'[6]

Amitabh Bachchan explains that 'no art in the entire universe can ever exist, flourish, or even take birth without an "unconscious assimilation" of influence that eventually propels it to its creation. Writers, poets, painters, artists of any category need stimulation from what they may have encountered during the process of their creativity. If you attribute my source of influence to be Mr Dilip Kumar, then that would be the biggest compliment you could pay me, because I believe that he is, what was and is correct, right and the best'.[7]

Rishi Kapoor described a scene at the iconic R.K. Studios where he was shooting for Raj Kapoor's *Prem Rog* (1982):

> I had to bring the intense expression of a despondent lover, and as hard as I tried, Raj Kapoor the director was not getting the look he wanted, which was irritating him. Then he shouted at me in the presence of the entire unit, '*Mujhe Yousaf chahiye* [I want Yousaf]. I want you to give the look Yousaf would have given in this situation. I want that look when his eyes express love, his intensity, his realism.' The unit was silent. Nobody could believe that he was talking about his professional rival Dilip Kumar. I think it was the ultimate acknowledgement of the actor–director Raj Kapoor for Yousuf uncle's unmatched ability to portray love with all its agony and ecstasy. It was possible only because they had that kind of genuine respect and love for each other. Will you hear Shah Rukh [Khan] say that about Salman [Khan] or vice versa?[8]

The fact is that Dilip Kumar's method of acting was a school, an institution in itself for acquiring cinematic excellence. Dilip Kumar the actor occupying a central position in cinematic discourse, profoundly shapes the sociocultural and political underpinnings of Indian film melodrama. It articulates the aspirations, dreams, historical ties and inner conflicts of the people in an indigenous language, evoking a surge of mass empathy and adoration. Thus, the evolution, development and mass acceptance of his acting becomes intertwined with the history of cinema itself. Moreover, the hero sets unparalleled standards for portraying a diverse range of characters, creating a new paradigm in film acting.

Naseeruddin Shah, the acclaimed film and stage actor who shared the screen with Dilip Kumar in Subhash Ghai's *Karma* (1986), once sparked a debate in a candid and critical assessment of Dilip Kumar's legacy. In an article he wrote in the *Indian Express* dated 10 July 2021, about Kumar's enduring influence on Hindi cinema, he recalled an incident where Kumar had advised him to abandon his film aspirations, stating, 'People from decent families don't join the film business.' Yet, years later, Shah provocatively questioned whether Kumar's example as a star was truly worth emulating. He raised the point whether Dilip Kumar genuinely pushed the boundaries of artistic progress or, instead, contributed to the industry's decline into a culture of star-centric mediocrity— one where celebrity-eclipsed craft and stardom frequently took precedence over substance.

Shah's observations offer a revealing glimpse into his complex and sometimes conflicted regard for Dilip Kumar. He admitted that there is no disputing that until *Gunga Jumna* (1961), Kumar's performances were a masterclass in restraint and authenticity. His nuanced portrayals, dignified screen presence, mellifluous dialogue delivery and controlled yet powerful emotional expression redefined acting in Indian cinema. At a time when actors often resorted to theatrical

Dilip Kumar and Naseeruddin Shah in *Karma* (1986)

gestures—waving their arms, clenching their jaws and arching their eyebrows—Dilip Kumar's stillness and quiet intensity were revolutionary. His minimal yet impactful movements were often misunderstood or poorly imitated by many of his peers and numerous successors.

Yet, Shah pointed out that despite his iconic status, Dilip Kumar was not a prolific actor by Bollywood standards. With a relatively modest 'filmography of around fifty films, his output was small'. While some of these works continue to stand the test of time, his broader contribution to cinema appears limited. Considering the position he held, it is striking that he did little beyond acting and supporting select social causes. He produced only one film, never officially directed any and left behind no substantial legacy of mentorship. He made no formal effort to pass on his wisdom to future generations, and his autobiography, while charming, offered hardly any technical insights or revelations about his craft. It remains perplexing that someone so acutely aware of his historical significance refrained from documenting his experiences with some of the greatest film-makers of his era or offering deeper reflections on his own creative process.

Naseeruddin Shah further observed that what Dilip Kumar did master, however, was the art of self-mystification. His rare appearances—starring in one film every few years while his contemporaries worked on several annually—were strategic. Each carefully curated performance was designed to heighten his allure, fostering an image of artistic selectivity and intellectual sophistication. His deliberate pacing created an aura of exclusivity that distinguished him from the industry's more prolific stars.

However, its Dilip Kumar's later career choices that remain a subject of speculation for Naseeruddin Shah. His transition from meaningful cinema—defined by collaborations with directors such as Bimal Roy, Mehboob Khan, K. Asif and

B.R. Chopra—to more commercially driven projects is often attributed to personal motivations. Some speculate that a psychoanalyst advised him to take on lighter, mainstream roles, while others believe it was a calculated effort to broaden his range or sustain public adoration. Whatever the reason, the shift marked a departure from his earlier artistic commitment. It often appeared as though he was attempting to outdo his own towering performance in *Gunga Jumna*—a feat even he could not replicate.

In an industry as fickle and ephemeral as Bollywood, Dilip Kumar's decision to play it safe is a lingering enigma for Naseeruddin Shah, who feels that here was an actor whose mere nod could greenlight any project, who was revered as the finest in the country and who was financially secure for generations. Yet, despite his stature, Dilip Kumar seldom used his influence to promote experimental cinema or scripts that reflected social realities. Instead of championing films that could have reshaped the perception of an actor's role, he opted for a string of formulaic, sometimes clumsy, crowd-pleasers. Though many of these were box-office hits, they also disillusioned some of his most ardent admirers, forcing them to reevaluate their once-unquestioned reverence for him. For Shah, the paradox of acting is perhaps best exemplified by Kumar's career: an art that demands both detachment and immersion, where the moment actors begin to believe in their own greatness, they risk losing it.

Yet, despite the contradictions and frustrations surrounding his later years, Dilip Kumar's magic on screen remains undeniable—a legacy that continues to enchant countless millions.

Method acting as a formal discipline owes its origin to Konstantin Stanislavsky, a Russian visionary, often heralded as the world's foremost theoretician of dramatic arts. Stanislavsky's school of method acting strove to bring characters to life by connecting with the essence of the human spirit on stage. Rejecting stylized theatrical conventions and instinctual acting, his approach demanded more. It argued that merely mimicking gestures and intonations wouldn't suffice in portraying a character's inner world. Instead, method acting focused on the 'art of experiencing', enabling actors to acquire their character's essence and translate it into a convincing external expression. This bridged the gap between the actor's subjective psychological states and their external manifestation, creating a preferred connection with the audience.

According to the famous Indian stage and film actor who has worked in Hollywood too, Amrish Puri:

> Every actor has his own brand of projection. Amitabh Bachchan is a natural and intuitive actor, while Rajesh Khanna was a stylized actor. Many a treatise has been written on acting, but the Russian born Stanislavsky is considered the greatest teacher, who in the nineteenth century, had a more profound effect on the process of acting than anyone else in the following millennium. His method of acting is vastly taught and followed by many an actor the world over . . .
>
> The Stanislavsky system, or the method, as it has become better known, held that an actor's main responsibility is to be believed, rather than recognized or understood. And to reach this 'believable truth', he first employed methods such as 'emotional memory'. Say, for instance, to prepare for a role that involves fear, the actor must remember something frightening and attempt to act the part in the emotional space of that fear they once felt. He strongly believed that an actor needed to take his or her personality onto the stage when they began to play

a character. This was a clear break from previous modes of acting that held that the actor's job was to become the character and leave his or her emotions behind. Later Stanislavsky concerned himself with a creation of physical entry into the emotional state, believing that the repetition of certain acts and exercises could bridge the gap between life on and off the stage.[9]

Explaining the hypothesis of 'method acting' and its leading exponents further, Amrish Puri adds:

In his travels throughout the world with the Moscow Art Theater, he earned international acclaim along with his collaborators like the Russian great masters Leo Tolstoy and Anton Chekov. While Stanislavsky's new method of acting supported actors in breaking from the exact lines and actions of the script, it also demanded that they pay closer attention to the important unsaid messages within the writing. This promoted writers like Chekov to make subtler and emotionally alive work. In Hollywood actors like Marlon Brando and Gregory Peck continued to experiment with his ideas.

However, I personally don't believe in Method acting. I think and feel, it is pretentious. As an actor you have to be rich in your references. That is how I make a deliberate effort to not only see life but to observe it, and then assimilate it all into the storehouse of memory. You certainly need clarity of mind to register what is happening around you and then project it back on the screen.[10]

In the annals of Hollywood, the realm of acting underwent a transformation, thanks to the tireless efforts of several disciples of Stanislavsky. Among them four luminaries stand out: Lee Strasberg, founder of the Actor's Studio and the Lee Strasberg Theatre and Film Institute, who presented a nuanced revision of the master's approach, delving deep into the psychological facets of character portrayal. At its core, Strasberg's method emphasizes 'affective memory' as the driving force behind a performance. The second was the American actress and acting teacher Stella Adler, who forged her own path by rejecting the use of emotional memory to evoke emotions, deeming it unhealthy for actors. Instead, her method revolves around the creation of characters through imagination, not memory. Then there was another American actor and acting teacher, Sanford Meisner, whose technique comprised four components: the power of response, progressive exercises, repetition exercise and spontaneous expression. Fourth is the German Broadway luminary and acting professor Uta Hagen, who advocated a balance between internal and external work, emphasizing key elements such as substitution, transference, destinations, performative phenomena and script analysis. Hagen's influential book *Respect for Acting*[11] remains a vital source for acting students and teachers alike.

The legacies of these four masters continue to shape the world of acting, providing a diverse array of methodologies for aspiring actors to explore and master. They all 'helped actors become artists . . . I know for the best of reasons; I have worked with their actors in films . . . As in other human endeavour in the arts, there is a fascinating variety. But despite that, these teachers make the same basic emphasis, which is fundamental: experience [in acting] must be actual, not suggested by external imitation; the actor must be going through what the character he's playing is going through; the emotion must be real, not pretended; it must be happening not indicated', says Elia Kazan, one of the most honoured and influential directors in Hollywood and Broadway.[12]

Within the sprawling realm of Hollywood method acting attracted a constellation of greats, including Marlon Brando, John Garfield, Paul Newman, Gregory Peck, Montgomery Clift, Al Pacino, Robert De Niro, Marilyn Monroe, Jane Fonda, Dustin Hoffman, Jack Nicholson and Paul Muni, to name a few, who shaped their careers through the unwavering dedication to the method. Of all these, the one that impressed Dilip Kumar the most was the American actor, Paul Muni. As Dilip Kumar once told actor Anupam Kher during the shooting of *Saudagar*:

> I would go to watch his movies like *The Last Angry Man, Angel on My Shoulder* and *A Song to Remember* at the Metro Theatre [Bombay]. At one stage he was one of the most prestigious actors. He was a brilliant realistic actor who I learnt would always do intense preparation for each role of his, often immersing himself in the study of the real character's traits and mannerisms. Anupam, you did a 70-year-old man's role at 28, but do you know that Muni played the role of an 80-year-old at the age of just 12. I always wanted to be like Paul Muni. He indeed impressed me a lot. But I can't say he influenced my acting. No, he didn't.[13]

In his autobiography *Songs My Mother Taught Me*, Marlon Brando, often hailed as the quintessential actor of all time, who introduced a new era of realism to Hollywood reflected on the cathartic nature of acting, a channel of emotions too profound for everyday life.[14] His unwavering commitment to authenticity touched hearts and stirred souls. Film director Martin Scorsese encapsulated his influence aptly remarking: 'He is a marker. There's *Before* Brando and *After* Brando', something, as quoted earlier, that was said about Dilip

Kumar by Amitabh Bachchan too. In his award-winning documentary by Steven Riley *Listen to Me Brando*, the actor talking about doing a death scene said: 'That's a tough scene to play. You have to make them believe what it is.'[15]

One can't think of any other hero having died in so many films as Dilip Kumar, who it seems was deeply preoccupied with death, as if the ultimate martyrdom would take him to greater heights of adulation by the audience. Method acting or no, whether, as mentioned above, he was the 'Ultimate Method Actor', as Satyajit Ray said about him, or Saira Banu says: 'He created his own method of emoting long before Method acting came to be known' or disagreeing with them all Yash Chopra, having worked with Dilip Kumar in a number of films, remarked that 'he is not a Method actor but a spontaneous actor'. Whether it was Dilip Kumar's unique Indian Method or Hollywood's iconic method acting, the dedication to his craft continued to captivate audiences, ignorant about any method acting; those were incredible and mesmerizing scenes which are fresh in our minds even today after decades. Scenes where emotions were real, where it seemed to be all happening, where we all sang in depression and sadness as he lip-synced Mohammad Rafi's songs, where we all had moist eyes and silently cried when he lost his love or died. And he did make us all 'believe' in what he did, believe in the celluloid world he lived and performed in.

3

Birth of a New Art, New Craft

Dilip Kumar pioneered the great transformation of classical acting to an indigenous form of cinematic acting that was to have a far-reaching influence on Indian films. He introduced a paradigm of a truly Indian method of acting providing a universal perspective for the new incumbents planning an active career in cinema. Far more purposive in its intent, his method played a pivotal role in liberating Indian film acting from the prevalent theatrical style: overacting, unnecessary stylization, glamour and an overall sense of simplification (just saying lines in front of the camera and nothing beyond). His method postulated a natural kind of acting that was functional without conventions and that could be received as self-evident and universal. He created a unique blend of the melodramatic tradition in Indian drama and the cinematic emphasis on visual imaging and underplay. It was a unique exercise in establishing the basic methodology of acting for an Indian film hero, based on various forms of Indian drama traditions, including the Parsi theatre and Bengal's romantic tradition.

Dilip Kumar developed his method as an antithesis to the widely followed classical acting. Having its origins in the long formal history of stage acting, classical acting was to be simply 'observed' by audiences in a highly formal milieu. It demanded a degree of exactness to drive the meticulously crafted script. For a classical actor, the character they were portraying was a convenience not necessarily a naturalistic or realistic depiction of a person one might encounter in life. Perhaps, Dilip Kumar's indigenous and highly effective method would have made Stanislavsky truly proud.

Dilip Kumar's method was deeply rooted in the very indigenousness of the characters he played. The method as well as the characters he portrayed carried a strong social and cultural bearing. In practising it, he appeared to be reliving the internal suffering of a nation that was undergoing in the aftermath of the Partition of 1947. This suffering was reflected in the deep sense of uprooting and loss as also the growing disillusionment of the people with the grand hope of a happier life after Independence.

The main emotive basis of this reliving was the intense pathos caused by a failed painful love the artist was nurturing by submerging his being in the puritan, sublime desire for his soulmate. The protagonist of this narrative was designed essentially as an introvert, a restless soul in search of his emancipation in love and suffering. Dilip Kumar the artist thus created his own tools to bring the characters he played at par with the prevailing milieu and to make them highly appealing to the masses. Significantly, this melancholy made a big turnaround in the 1970s, when Amitabh Bachchan's Angry Young Man reflected the state of society in the same way as Dilip Kumar's but in a different social setting.

Dilip Kumar's method was primarily focused on developing a methodology for 'experiencing' the role an actor was to play by establishing its purpose internally and preparing a perspective for the role. His method was rooted in a kind of a cultural rediscovery that needed to be carried out by an artist in order to acquire the ability to become an effective observer, one who has insights into the peculiarities of people and the happenings that occur in society. By this technique, he was able to capture the socio-historical significance of the character's behaviour and actions by employing specific performance choices.

In this cultural significance, he saw things with new insights and tied to history, values, beliefs, lifestyles, languages, dialects or heroic/evil deeds of people and the impact of his own spiritual formation and convictions. Equally crucial was the recognition of what appeared to be mundane, seemingly unimportant events. Thus, Dilip Kumar very effectively employed a kind of 'culture memory' for locating a character in a definite sociocultural milieu. This, in turn, required an understanding on the part of the performer to access an emotional experience, and then to bring in the spontaneity of improvisation and the richness of personal response to the requirements of the textual script. Dilip Kumar did this by interpreting and realizing the specific attributes of the character that would support the overall perspectives of the film on hand. He becomes aware that he has emotional resources; that he can awaken, by this self-stimulation, a great number of intense feelings; and that these emotions are the ingredients of his art. This was the (re)experiencing of life by the actor within the fiction of the story as if it were true and happening now.

In this way, Dilip Kumar's hero brought out real, powerful emotions to breathe life into a character. In the creation of this living experience, the actor, therefore, developed the ability to stir his inner life, that is, awaken his initiative in response to the needs of a characterization. For this, he very creatively adopted from the Indian romantic literary tradition in which a protagonist in search of his inner truth finds personal emotions and traumas triggering and fuelling his emotional existence. He employed the natural, the spontaneous and the instinctive as a means to produce the desired effects. It means that the actor's gestures, intent, facial expressions, intonation and other vocal qualities, and rhythm got related to the overall narrative being pursued. The result was that the performances in a true sense became natural and believable and far above what is rhetorical and theatrical.

However, Dilip Kumar's reincarnation of a role was not his complete identification with the character on hand; rather, some part of the actor's personality remained independent of the role to subordinate it to the needs of the film as a whole. Through conscious control, he internalizes the duality in portraying a character: 'It is me; yet, it is not me.' In this way, he created a reality amicable with the character rather than imitating it. A self-induced subjectivity—rather than objectivity—as created by a high involvement and a high level of insight led to introspection and low-profile acting rather than actual physical expression and projection of a character. Thus, for Dilip Kumar, a total identification of an actor with a particular role—as generally believed desirable—is a misnomer and amounts to a purely clinical approach to acting.

Dilip Kumar, the theorist of the acting craft, postulates that natural acting per se is more or less a misnomer. As nobody can be natural in front of the camera, in any role, an actor must study every word he utters with attention and intention, every move he makes, and plans meticulously. The challenge is that the artist ought to be expressive in a situation, just as a real man, through introspection and sensitizing mental and body expressions as per the needs of the character. As he himself once said: 'As an actor and a performer, I am evolving and developing. I don't feel that I have fully grown or emerged. So, I see room for growth all the time . . . with every film . . . that is why I have not done many films.'[1]

In fact, after the debacle of B.R. Chopra's *Dastaan* (1972) and Tapan Sinha's *Sagina* (1974), when Asit Sen's *Bairaag* too failed at the box office in 1976, to become his third consecutive film to do so, thus scoring a hat-trick, Dilip Kumar went on

Dilip Kumar and Saira Banu in *Sagina* (1974)

a hiatus for five years, re-emerging only with Manoj Kumar's *Kranti* in 1981. Such are the uncertainties and incertitudes of the box office, the insecurities and scepticisms of any artiste in the harsh, callous and cruel world of cinema. Dilip Kumar was no different. In a conversation with Anupam Kher when asked if he, 'as an actor ever felt insecure because of a film not doing well . . . or because you were not sure about your role . . . or because the film hadn't turned out the way you had visualized when you had taken it on,' he admitted: 'Yes, I am always insecure. But remember that it is the insecurity that makes you do well. However, it's not that everybody goes through these issues. Negative qualities are not negative until you start thinking about them as negative qualities.'[2]

Anupam Kher with Dilip Kumar in *Karma* (1986)

Dilip Kumar was anguished about this five-year hiatus, and he recorded:

The regret apart, the wound that I have nursed for years, about the five years of self-imposed absence from the screens across the country and elsewhere, which mystified those who have followed my career graph avidly, is that I could not focus attention on the scripts I had written for myself and Saira to act as a lead pair in the films that I wished to launch. The most engrossing of them, *Kashmir Valley*, was written for Saira to co-star with me before we were married. It had a spectacular backdrop and a canvas comparable to that of David Lean's epic creation *Dr Zhivago* (1965). I had thought of producing it after *Bairaag*. The other scripts included *Kali Sarson,* which focussed on a dark-skinned girl's saga and was also written with Saira in mind, apart from *Jala Aadmi* and *Babajan.* The last mentioned had a riveting, suspense plot centring on a schizophrenic banker's diabolic bid to rob a bank. I had several meetings with Jabber Patel, to whom I wished to entrust the direction. I had to shelve all these projects for which financiers were more than willing to loosen their strings.[3]

Dilip Kumar's acting can be further elaborated in terms of his extremely innovative development of what has been referred to as the 'Visual-Verbal Personality Composite'. Through this complex mechanism, he contributed single-handedly to giving film dialogue an entirely new cinematic interpretation. Before his arrival, dialogue delivery was a rudimentary extension of the theatrical style, represented by early actors such as Master Vithal, Sohrab Modi and Prithviraj Kapoor, to name just a few. One genre of particular importance was the discourse between two characters based on dialogues and counter dialogues, used as an essential strategy in the narrative of a film.

Dilip Kumar emerged as the first actor in Indian cinema to carry out a unique integration of dialogue with a presentation. This helped not only in the development of a truly cinematic approach to narration and treatment in commercial cinema but also in liberating Indian films from the perpetual hangover of theatre. And yet, it was not merely the subordination of the 'word' to the 'visual' as per the aesthetics of parallel cinema.

In this complex integration, he introduced a remarkable differentiation between the 'visual personality' and the 'verbal personality' in the cinematic presentation of a character, locating the two in separate spaces, which, in an enactment, overlap in varying degrees as well as move in different planes. In the relative dynamics of these spaces, the verbal personality sometimes gradually gets dissolved into the visual personality and then starts engulfing and overriding it. The result is a vivid manifestation of mutual enrichment of the two through either their relative contraction or expansion. At the same time, their distinctions are kept apart.

In his characteristic blending of underplay and overplay, Dilip Kumar often first gradually brought the visual personality on the desired fulcrum as per the enactment on hand (through initial sustenance of expressions and gestures) and then started building up the verbal personality, albeit reluctantly. But this reluctant speaker either scuttles its formation, making it linger on, or develops it exponentially like a continuous explosion which begins to resound in the whole space.

As he completes this apparent deconstruction of the verbal personality through the lingering effect, the words fumble, lose their meaning and become emotive sounds, as if coming as an echo from a deep reservoir or a distant place. What is being conveyed to the viewer is not the words and their meaning (as when one reads a text), but a strange modulation of the sounds of these words by the emotions being conveyed. Thus, the spoken dialogues appear to be not only internalized by the actor, but they also reverberate in the viewer's consciousness. This innovative treatment provided by Dilip Kumar provided a new dignity to the verbal personality as also a new sense of aesthetics to it, in relation to the visual personality not seen earlier in Indian cinema.

In the romantic scenes, the verbal and the visual personalities are kept at ease with each other, and Dilip Kumar treated his beloved as the beauty and voice of nature, as for example, Vyjayanthimala, seen in Bimal Roy's *Madhumati* or Nitin Bose's *Gunja Jumna*, Madhubala in K. Asif's *Mughal-e-Azam*, or even, nearly a decade later, Waheeda Rehman in A. Bhim Singh's *Aadmi* (1968) in which, with his expressions the actor whispers praise to her, teases her, plays with her and embraces her. In such scenes, he blooms like a flower for which the beloved is the spring and thus he symbolizes nature. The soft and sweet spoken words become the breeze, which seem to give a soul to the flower. As Vyjayanthimala, his co-star in seven films, says: 'In serious dramatic situations and love scenes he went out of his way to create an environment on the sets, which made everybody comfortable. He consciously saw to it that the love scenes were taken beautifully with looks conveying the emotions rather than any explicit depiction of physical closeness.'[4]

The nuances of his blending of acting and dialogue delivery made Dilip Kumar's style an art. The strategy appears to be based on an inane sense of asynchronization in which he revealed the minute preparation of the facial expressions and selective body movements just before a build-up for taking up the dialogue, and during this delivery, began to reveal the expression required.

In this underplay, the basic building block was *silence*. He would play with silence; he would carry and regulate the amount and the timing of what was to be communicated in a few moments. And if the situation demanded, there would be a sudden burst of pent-up high electric surge, being accumulated from the prevailing silence, which would take the form of a dialogue and often accompanied with well-timed swift body movements. But if that was not enough to empower the viewer, there was often a complete collapse in the same scene, where he would fumble and gradually take recluse again in the vast reservoir of his silence.

According to the eminent actress Sharmila Tagore, who acted with the legend in *Dastaan*:

He demonstrated that it was not necessary to raise one's voice to be heard. He showed how natural and nuanced body language, and sometimes, even silence, conveyed far more than a thousand theatrical emotions—sorrow and heartbreak—in films like *Footpath* and Bimal Roy's

Dilip Kumar and Sharmila Tagore in *Dastaan* (1972)

Devdas. He was equally brilliant in bringing comic characters alive in *Azaad*, *Kohinoor* and *Ram Aur Shyam*. He gave film acting a kind of layered edge, which was marked by self-conscious histrionics till that point in time. Many actors have tried to copy his style over the years and rightfully so, as I feel that there is much to learn from his school of acting.[5]

The pauses between the words were as important as the words themselves. Though virtually unexpected, they seemed so expected that the eventual synthesis was easily discernible by the audience. He would also sound incoherent, which itself was employed to depict the intensity of what was churning within the soul of the character but unable to find the full expression. These attributes made Dilip Kumar, the master of the interplay between silence and verbosity in which silence often emerged even more expressive than spoken words. Through an extensive use of body language, he would engage in an extremely well-timed and progressive revealing of emotions and other enactments. Often, he would speak chewing the words in his desperation, as if modulating their meaning with his inner emotional state.

In underplay, in particular, Dilip Kumar started talking to the self, the soul, least aware of the other artistes, the running camera, the director and all the other people on the sets. As he would immerse himself and go into the short spell of trance, the words went beyond his control and the responding soul would begin to get reflected on his face. His whole being would then transcend time and space, connecting the viewer to the subtleties of a highly intimate human experience.

In his method, Dilip Kumar laid the foundation of an extensive emotive and poignant experiment on celluloid aimed at delinking the audience from what they are and facilitating their complete empathization during the course of a film experience. In his meditation with the audience, he became a vehicle for an intensely emotional experience. His method inadvertently exhibited many techniques similar to those articulated by the celebrated Russian filmmaker and theoretician Sergei Eisenstein in his works, including *Film Form: Essays in Film Theory*.[6]

Dilip Kumar can be seen as truly Einsteinian in the manifestation of his romantic/serious scenes. He appeared to be articulating a dream in which the desire, the longing and the pain simply became a deep whisper from within. But soon he consciously would undermine his dream as it would get affected by the outside reality through self-interrogation. Here, the dream and the range of emotions that arrived with it were juxtaposed with a formidable reality. This activated the devise, Einsteinian in nature, a single-point generation of emotions of love, helplessness, despair (whatever the case may be) overtaken further by unforeseen flooding of anger, hatred or spontaneous outbursts which, in turn, led to settling down of the emotional flux already created. Thus, the joy of being in love and other good feelings were consciously guarded, soon to be induced with a sense of vulnerability.

The above state would soon result in the anticipation of suffering, devised (again consciously) by the artist to intensify the very importance of it. But either through a sequence of events or intermittently, he would simply burst like a well-timed blast, releasing a whole spectrum of depressed energies, an unexpected powerful outflow of negative emotions. Dilip Kumar adopted this duality, the conscious splitting of the positive and negative emotional fields, as the basic strategy in articulating the various aspects of his portrayals. Thus, the hallmark of his method was a well-designed structuring of emotions entirely on an unexpected plane, and yet creating systematically in this process, a predetermined impact on each element on the emotional response system of the audience.

Another unique aspect of Dilip Kumar's method was conveying a myriad of emotions through brevity of style. It was largely the facial expressions, which did most of the talking. Equally important was the improvisation by which he connected his expressions and body movements to a gradual revealing of the intended emotional plane to be taken up immediately in a giving situation. Thus, with these techniques devised by him he could impart a similar cinematic clarity in different roles.

In-built into Dilip Kumar's method was yet another mechanism. He operated a two-way 'gestalt switch' for his responses to his environment and their impact on the viewer. Through his subtle transitions even within a scene of a very short duration, he conducted an interrogation of his inner self with the outside reality whereby the viewer would get closer to the reality through a visual interpretation of the inner self. Yet, in another situation, he would choose to reach the reality outwardly but soon would switch over to his inner self, indulging in self-defeating thoughts, and getting possessed with a strange passivity while pushing the reality to the background. Thus, as the viewer viewed the reality in the narrative of the film, they perceived it as their own affected self and went into self-indulgence on the pattern projected by him.

In fine, Dilip Kumar's cinema can be considered as the ultimate epitome of catharsis, which is the effect of a tragedy on the mind of a spectator, which, in turn, leads to an effect on his body. According to drama theorists, catharsis results in a kind of purification/purgation of emotions, particularly pity and fear. This means that the depiction of an extreme emotional change brings forth the renewal and restoration of the spectator's mind due to the purging of excessive passions held in it. Thus, catharsis helps in moderating an individual's passions through watching tragedies which helps him feel the emotions at proper levels.

The affected individuals often use social sharing as a cathartic release of emotions. They talk about such experiences in a cathartic scene to people around them, and through such sharing, there is a reciprocal stimulation of emotions among others, leading to a kind of social integration and strengthening of life's experiences. This helps individuals experience renewed trust in life and an increase in self-confidence. A scene in a film creating a catharsis becomes unforgettable moments and their effects keep on reviving memories of being moved to tears, laughter or reflection.

Similarly, there is a catharsis of the comic emotions as well, where the viewers indulge in sympathetic ridicule of the comic hero.

4

HIS MUSIC MAKERS

SONGS HAVE BEEN AN INTEGRAL AND, AT TIMES, indispensable, part of Hindi cinema right from the release of India's first talkie movie *Alam Ara* in 1931. Dilip Kumar's films were no exception. In fact, some of the most mellifluous numbers in the annals of Hindi cinema have been picturized on him. He always loved music. And poetry. His sensitivity for music, as his love for prose, particularly literary classics, and kinaesthesia for poetry were deeply personal, a catalyst for pent-up emotional moments, the means of evocating nostalgic and sentimental periods of his personal life and emotional experiences. He took great care to understand the nuances of the lyrics and the tunes and comprehend the exact mood of the melody, the way songs were sung synchronizing with the scenes to be filmed on him. Those were the times when most heroes would sit during music practice sessions for days together and during final recordings. And Dilip Kumar was no exception.

Writing about music sessions, film actor Rishi Kapoor mentioned:

I worked at a time when actors took an active interest in music sittings. Dilip Kumar, Raj Kapoor, Shammi Kapoor, Rajendra Kumar, Guru Dutt and Dev Anand all gave as much attention to the song they were going to sing on screen as they did to a scene. They did this because they understood the critical part music played in enhancing

39

Rishi Kapoor with Dilip Kumar and Subhash Ghai

their on-screen appeal and the close interactions between actors and the music team brought out the best in everybody . . . One of the defining traits of Hindi film music was how a singer's voice came to be associated with that of an artist. You could close your eyes and listen to a Mohammad Rafi song and be able to say which actor he was singing it for. Rafi Sahab's voice was totally in sync with stars like Dilip Kumar, Shammi Kapoor and Dharmendra. Mukeshji's voice was, of course, the voice of my dad. For Rajesh Khanna and Amitabh Bachchan, you cannot imagine anyone but Kishore Kumar. Today's singers and musicians don't even know which actor will portray their song in a film. But, in those days actors would inspire the singer to sing in a certain way . . . Even at the peak of his stardom, Rajesh Khanna would always go to all the music sittings. Every song those days was the product of a lot of teamwork.[1]

The Hindi film music historian, Raju Bharatan, once told this author that one could understand Raj Kapoor or Dev Anand or his brother Goldie Anand or Guru Dutt sitting through the music sittings, as they were all producers and directors of a film and their investments were high, but even actors like Dilip Kumar, Shammi Kapoor, Rajendra Kumar and Bharat Bhushan too would make it a point to be present. An exemplary case was of Dilip Kumar, who would go through the lyrics and the tune in detail, investing a lot of time and energy in the recording studios discussing the way a particular song would be sung and later picturized on him. For him, the stakes on a song and it's picturization were always very high.

Adds Bharatan:

I have often wondered about the beauty and diversity of our music in cinema. Picture Raj Kapoor in the recording studio with his music 'take' that was so radically different as to make it ring in your ears as the ultimate in cinematics. Having heard Goldie Vijay Anand talking on making and taking music, I felt that I was getting the essence of it all from the true master's lips. Raj Khosla made no secret about how he learnt all his song-taking from Guru Dutt but absorbed it all so well to invest it with his personal touch. Writer–director Gulzar displays a different outlook altogether, controlling his mode of song-taking through his own screenplay, then bringing his own form and feeling to the composers' tunes with his own facile pen. Subash Ghai is no different. Like Guru Dutt, with rare passion, he holds forth, about cinema and the role of music in enhancing its effect. Each one of them had made music lucidly running in their veins.[2]

About Subhash Ghai, film and stage actor Amrish Puri, who worked with him in a number of his films, comments: 'If

Raj Kapoor was the real showman of yesteryears, today we have Subhash Ghai, the showman with a tremendous sense of music. Apart from the story, his forte has been as to how successful the music of his film would be. Music is the soul of his projection, and he does it subtly . . . he uses his music sense so creatively, extracting the best out of his music directors as much out of his actors.'[3]

Ghai's *Karz* (1980), *Taal* (1999) and *Saudagar* are prefect examples.

Most unfortunately, with the passage of time, many songs—unimaginably cacophonous—have unleashed a jarring assault on the eardrums. It is as if they want the listeners to become tone deaf. For the older generation of music listeners, the songs in today's films do not have the same musical flavour as they did at that time. The eminent lyricist Javed Akhtar, when asked about the quality of film songs that were being written today and their future, once said: 'Let them be written in whichever way they are but let them not be written as they are being written today.'[4] During this author's last meeting with music director Naushad during the release of Bunny Reuben's biography of Dilip Kumar, which I had published for HarperCollins in 2011, at the Crossword Books in Mumbai, making a comparison of then and now, he put it aptly: 'That was music for the soul, now we have music for the heart.' To this I would add that today's film music is just for the lips, albeit alive just for a few moments, if at all. It no longer has a place in our lives, not to talk of a place in history. It does not transport one to another era—to an era when music was the king and melody was the queen.

However, before going further, let's have a closer look at the world of music in Hindi cinema, right from 1931, so as to understand the intricacies involved in its making and how actors of the time, like Dilip Kumar, too, would get involved with it.

The year 1931 stands out as a watershed in Indian cinema. That was the annus mirabilis when films 'broke the sound barrier' and began to 'talk' (and 'sing'), thanks to Ardeshir Irani's pioneering venture, *Alam Ara* (based on Raag Bhairavi; ornament of the universe), which hit the screen in March that year and, to use a standard cliché, created history. Astonishingly (and tragically), not a single print of this landmark movie is available today.

In *Alam Ara*, Wazir Mohammad Khan burst into song with *De de Khuda ke naam pe pyaare taaqat ho agar dene ki* (Give in the name of God my dear one/friend if you have the power to give) and etched his name as the first singer in the annals of Indian movies. After that, there was a virtual tsunami of songs, which showed no sign of abating in the near future! As the singing legend Lata Mangeshkar once aptly remarked: 'In India, cinema is an excuse for songs.'

As the 1930s unfolded, a slew of composers, songwriters, singers, instrumentalists, technicians and others—belonging to different religions and coming from diverse backgrounds—made their presence felt and attained fame and recognition far and wide. In no time, many films went on to gain superhit status solely on the basis of their songs.

Among the composers—some of whom were fairly good singers—the trailblazers included R.C. Boral, Timir Baran (Bhattacharya), Pankaj Mullick, K.C. Dey, Khemchand

Prakash, Govindrao Tembe, Master Krishnarao, Keshavrao Bhole, Pandit Amarnath (Sharma), Ghulam Ahmed Chishti, Anil Biswas, Ghulam Haider, Lal Mohammed, Shyam Sunder, Naushad Ali, the duo of Husnlal Bhagatram (the two were the younger brothers of Pandit Amarnath), Sachin Dev Burman, C. Ramchandra, Vasant Desai, Hansraj Behl, Khayyam (Mohammed Zahur Khayyam Hashmi), Chitragupt (Shrivastava), the melodious Madan Mohan (Kohli), who gave innumerable immortal ghazals, Ravi (Shankar Sharma), Shankar (Raghuvanshi)–Jaikishan (Dayabhai Panchal), O.P. (Omkar Prasad) Nayyar and Roshan (Roshanlal Nagrath), to name just a few.

Among the early songwriters were prominent names such as D.N. Madhok, P.L. Santoshi, Kidar Sharma, Tanveer Naqvi (born Syed Khursheed Ali Khan), Naqshab Jarchavi and Raja Mehdi Ali Khan, apart from superlative poets—who had a respectable standing in the world of Urdu or Hindi literature—such as Shakeel Badayuni, Majrooh Sultanpuri (born Asrar-ul Hasan Khan), Sahir Ludhianvi (born Abul/Abdul Hayee), Kaifi Azmi (born Sayyid Athar Husein Rizvi), Jan Nisar Akhtar, Shailendra, Hasrat Jaipuri (born as Iqbal Husain), Pradeep (born Ramchandra Narayanji Dwivedi), Narendra Sharma and Bharat Vyas. And, of course, there was Anand Bakshi, who wrote over 4000 songs for a record 638 films in a period of six decades. (There was also a multifaceted poet-cum-writer Rajinder Krishan, but more about him later.) Here, I must mention that many Urdu/Hindi poets had, and have, a predilection to take on a *takhallus/upnam* (or pen name). For instance, the real name of the eminent Persian and Urdu poet Ghalib was Mirza Asadullah Baig Khan. The actual name of another esteemed Urdu poet, Firaq Gorakhpuri was Raghupathi Sahay.

Among the early male singers—some of whom were actors as well—who made their mark were Kundan Lal Saigal, Pankaj Mullick, K.C. Dey, Ashok Kumar (born as Kumudlal Ganguly, who went on to become one of India's greatest actors), Karan Diwan, Surendra (Surendranath Sharma), Shyam (Sunder Shyam Chadda) and G.M. Durrani. The next lot of singers went on to elevate film music to new heights, among whom were Manna (Prabodh Chandra) Dey, Mukesh (Chand Mathur), Talat Mahmood, Mohammed Rafi and Chitalkar (who also composed music as C. Ramchandra).

The early female singers' array is no less impressive. The significant voices were Noor Jehan (born as Allah Rakhi Wasai), Khursheed (Bano), Kannan Devi, Parul Ghosh, Amirbai Karnataki, Zohrabai Ambalewali, Sadhana Bose, Rajkumari (Dubey), Surinder Kaur, Shamshad Begum and the singing star Suraiya (Jamal Sheikh) among others. Interestingly, there was an actress–singer called Asha Latha (born Mehr-un Nisa), who was the first wife of composer–singer Anil Biswas; after their divorce, he married singer Meena Kapoor.

In fact, during the early years of Hindi cinema 'while they [singing stars] ruled, they were the monarchs of all they purveyed—even if they were mediocre singers'—they sang on all the same because they looked at the face first, only then heard the voice. For example, if one liked the face of Suraiya (Jamal Sheikh), who first appeared as a child artiste in Jaddan Bai's 1936 film *Madam Fashion,* one fell in love with her voice too 'with its tender tang of *Beech bhanwar mein aan phansa hai* in hoi-polloi Raag Darbari as envisioned by Naushad in A.R. Kardar's *Dard* (1947)' or *Yeh kaisi ajab daastaan ho gayi hai, chupate chupate bayan ho gayi hai,* based on Raag Asavari, in Vishram Bedekar's long in the making, too long in fact, *Rustom Sohrab* (1963), based on the legendary poem 'Rastam and Sohrab in Shahnameh' by the Persian poet Ferdowsi, where she was ill-cast with Prithviraj Kapoor in the lead role. But to be fair to Suraiya, she once admitted: 'You know I never wanted to sing. It was Naushad Saab who compelled me to do so.'[5]

Naushad with Suraiya

The fact remains that Suraiya was a popular singer, who according to composer Khurshid Anwar, 'was like a blotting paper who had the gift of absorbing the *notes* exactly as I gave them to her in spite of the fact that she knew no music at all.' And as Raju Bharatan wrote:

'Yes, Suraiya had the looks, and her voice was far better than the vocals of any other young heroine of her time. Or how could one explain a vocal simpleton like her take over, as a singing-star, from a performer so accomplished as the *Malika-e-Tarannum* (Queen of Melody) Noor Jahan? So much so that she could pass vocal muster opposite even Kundan Lal Saigal in Khurshid Anwar's *Parwana* (1947).'[6]

However, by 1950, when she was at the peak of her career with *Nainon mein preet hai* (There is love in the eyes) based on Raag Bhimpalasi from A.R. Kardar's *Dastaan*, with Raj Kapoor as her leading man, Suraiya sensed that the change was

Naushad with Lata Mangeshkar

imminent, and she was the last of the singing stars (not to count the over-ambitious mediocrities with somewhat 'jarring voices' like Sulakshna Pandit or the likes of Salma Agha, who suddenly appeared on the film scene in the late 1970s and disappeared equally fast). 'I had my first inkling of it when recording the Naushad-composed duet in Kardar's *Diwana* (1952) with Lata Mangeshkar: *Mere chand, mere lall tum jeeo hazaron saal* (based on Raag Shivrangani; My moon, my love, may you live a thousand years). Vocally, I realized that I was nowhere near her.'[7]

Most of these voices were overshadowed by the spectacular rise of a meteoric phenomenon called Lata Mangeshkar in the late 1940s. This period also witnessed the emergence of two exceptionally talented divas: Geeta Roy—later Geeta Dutt, after her marriage in May 1953 to producer-director-actor Guru Dutt (born as Vasanth Kumar Shivshankar Padukone)— and Asha Bhosle (Lata Mangeshkar's younger sister). There were others too like Suman Kalyanpur with an uncannily similar voice as Lata Mangeshkar's, Vani Jairam and Sudha Malhotra. But most were just imitations rather than originals. No wonder they faded away as fast as they came, perhaps because no one wants imitations with originals already dominating the film music world.

Lata Mangeshkar is the 'voice of God—certainly a unique favour of Mother Saraswati' (the goddess of art, music, knowledge, wisdom and learning) and as the tablanawaaz par excellence, Alla Rakha (Qureshi), declared: 'There will not be another Lata for the next one thousand years.'[8] All this praise may seem like hyperbole to the sceptics, but it definitely is *not*. In fact, her voice, like those of Mohammad Rafi, Talat Mahmood, Manna Dey, Asha Bhosle, Geeta Dutt, Shamshad Begum and Mukesh, among others, is part and parcel of the subconscious of several generations, around the world, but particularly so in the Indian subcontinent.

The 'Lata saga' is definitely stranger than fiction. It reveals how a determined, persevering, courageous and strong-willed individual overcame seemingly insurmountable obstacles to attain the summit of fame and success. Losing her father, the noted Hindustani vocalist and a *natya sangeet* (musical dramas) musician, Deenanath Mangeshkar, when she was barely thirteen, the entire burden of supporting her family, comprising her mother and four siblings, fell on her tender shoulders. Thus, she had to, perforce, give up her desire to become a classical vocalist and try her luck in films to make both ends meet. To cut a long story short, she got her break in the 1942 Marathi film *Kiti Hasaal* by Vasant Joglekar under the music direction of Sadashivrao Nevrekar. Her first song in Hindi films was *Pa lagu kar jori re Shyam mose na khelo hori* (I fall at your feet. That is, beg you Shyam [one of the names of Lord Krishna], don't play Holi [the festival of colours] with me) based on Raag Bhairavi in Vasant Joglekar's *Aap Ki Sewa Mein* (1946) under the music direction of Datta Davjekar.

During these years of struggle, several big guns of the film industry disparaged her voice as being 'too thin'. But Lata Mangeshkar was not deterred; she circumvented all obstacles and etched her name in the annals of film music much before terms like 'women power' and 'woman empowerment' were in vogue. After that, there was no stopping the mellifluous and spellbinding voice with an extraordinary range. Her voice seemed to glide gracefully from the lowest to the highest notes and vice versa (the glissando effect, if one may call it that). She soon became a boon for every composer who could rest assured that she would take in her musical stride any complex tune. She sang in a variety of languages and in almost all genres of music for all the composers of the day (old and new) except of course for the legendary O.P. Nayyar, who refused to let her into his musical landscape domain. Why so? That is another story for another day. Entire generations sang with Lata Mangeshkar. Her last song was *Suganah mujhe is mitti ki* (I swear upon this soil), in Raag Yaman, a patriotic song recorded in March 2019, when she was nearing her ninetieth birthday.

Although most, if not all, music directors could play a range of instruments (mainly the once-ubiquitous harmonium, on which they composed the basic tune of a song), let us not forget those associated with specific ones. Among them some individuals have become symbolic. Ustad Bismillah Khan, whose name has become synonymous with the shehnai (a wind instrument resembling the clarinet), played in Vijay Bhatt's 1959 film *Goonj Uthi Shehnai* (The Shehnai Reverberated); the songs of this film were composed by Vasant Desai to the lyrics of Bharat Vyas. Similarly, sitar maestro Pandit Ravi Shankar composed the music for a few Hindi films such as Chetan Anand's *Neecha Nagar* (1946), K.A. Abbas's *Dharti Ke Lal* (also 1946), Hrishikesh Mukherjee's *Anuradha* (1960), Trilok Jetley's *Godaan* (1963) and Gulzar's *Meera* (1979). Ustad Abdul Halim Jaffer Khan, another noted sitar player, enriched quite a few compositions, especially *Madhuban mein Radhika naaache re* (Radhika, a beloved of Lord Krishna, dances in Madhuban), based on Raag Hamir, from S.U. Sunny's 1960 film *Kohinoor*. It had music by Naushad, with lyrics by Shakeel Badayuni and rendered by Mohammed Rafi for Dilip Kumar on the screen.

Initially, Pannalal Ghosh and, later, Hari Prasad Chaurasia played the flute entrancingly for many composers. Santoor wizard Shivkumar Sharma left his mark in many a melody. Hari Prasad Chaurasia and Shivkumar Sharma, as Shiv Hari, have composed the music for a *silsila* (series) of films beginning with the respected producer–director Yash Chopra's 1981 romantic venture *Silsila*.

Anthony Gonsalves was a proficient violinist (as well as an arranger), who was once an important part of Naushad's orchestra. Ghulam Mohammad (Naushad's assistant, but senior in age, and also an independent music director himself) was a top-notch dholak (a two-sided drum) player.

Singer–composer Bhupinder Singh played the guitar skilfully and Van Shipley, the electric guitar. While Manohari Singh (an associate of the trendsetting composer–singer Rahul Dev Burman) was a remarkable saxophonist, Enoch Daniels was an excellent piano accordion player as was Kersi Lord as also Pandit Ram Narayan, the acclaimed specialist of sarangi, a stringed instrument played with a bow like the violin. Ustad Zakir Hussain, the internationally famous tablanawaaz, is known to have played in many a prestigious Hollywood film including *Custody* and *The Mystic Masseur* by Ismail Merchant, Francis Coppola's *Apocalyse Now* and Bernardo Bertolucci's *The Little Buddha*.

Thanks to the deft fingers of Sunny Castelino, the keys of his piano produced magical music in an assortment of songs. Cavas Lord was a well-known bongo player and Dattaram Wadkar (an assistant of Shankar–Jaikishan and a music director in his own right) was an ace 'dafli-ist' (dafli is an instrument similar to the tambourine). Chic Chocolate (born as Antonio Xavier Vaz) was a much-admired trumpeter; he also composed music in a few films. There are numerous other talented instrumentalists, but listing all of them is beyond the scope of this book. Sadly, with the advent of the synthesizer—now almost omnipresent and omnipotent—the era of the individual instrument, at least in the domain of film music, seems to be nearing its end.

As time rolled on, the tide of composers, songwriters, singers, instrumentalists, technicians and others moving towards Bombay began to swell appreciably, some of whom turned out to be brilliant, some mediocre and some downright indifferent. The medley of songs that they brought into existence was at times exceptionally melodious, at other times, passably so.

By and large, the typical Hindi film song consists of a *mukhda* (introductory stanza) and some *antara*s (stanzas), with interlude music in between. In many songs, the mukhda could be repeated after each antara as a refrain. This is the general pattern for a majority of film songs, with the number of stanzas varying.

In the case of ghazals (a genre of Persian/Urdu poetry, written strictly according to metre), there is the opening *sher* (couplet) called the *matla*, followed by three or more shers. The rhyme is called *qafiya* and the common word/s repeated after the qafiya are known as *radeef*. For example, let us take the matla of the following ghazal from the historical drama based on the fifth Mughal Emperor Shah Jahan's daughter *Jahan Ara* (1964), penned by Rajinder Krishan (Duggal), composed by Madan Mohan in Raag Kedar and put across delectably by Mohammed Rafi:

Kisiki yaad mein duniya ko hai bhulaaye hue
Zamana guzra hai apna khaayal aaye hue.

(I have forgotten the world in someone's memory
It's been ages since I have thought about myself.)[9]

Here, the rhyming words *bhulaaye* and *aaye* are called the qafiya and the common repeated word, *hue*, is the radeef.

There are, however, exceptions to the 'set patterns' of film songs. Here are a few examples.

Let us begin with the three-part medley from Raj Kapoor's 1951 film *Awaara*, from the magical pen of Shailendra (Shankardas Kesarilal Shailendra) and composed by the versatile duo of Shankar–Jaikishan. This was probably the first 'dream sequence' in Hindi films featuring Nargis (born Fatima Rashid) and Raj Kapoor. The first part (in slow tempo,

'Dream Sequence' from *Awaara* (1951)

Shankar–Jaikishan

depicting paradise) of the medley starts off in the serene vocals of Lata Mangeshkar and chorus: *Tere bina aag yeh chandni* based on Raag Bhatiyaar (Without you, the moonbeam is like fire). In the second part (depicting hell), enter Manna Dey and chorus in a fast-paced, agitated manner with: *Yeh nahi hai yeh nahi hai yeh nahi hai zindagi* (This is not this is not this is not life). Finally, the medley is rounded off by Lata Mangeshkar and chorus in Raag Bhairavi (again in slow tempo, again depicting paradise) with: *Ghar aaya mera pardesi, pyaas bujhi meri akhiyan ki* (My stranger has come home, the thirst of my eyes has quenched) 'an import of Egyptian diva Umm Kalthoum's repertoire'.

Next in this lot comes yet another medley—penned by the same Shailendra and composed by the same Shankar–Jaikishan—from the 1954 Prakash Arora's children-oriented movie, *Boot Polish* put across by Manna Dey, Asha Bhosle

and chorus. Manna Dey sets the musical ball rolling in
Raag Bhairavi with (at a slow pace): *Raat gayee phir din
aata hai* (The night has gone then the day comes). Then,
Asha Bhosle and others take over (in a lively manner) with:
John Chacha (paternal uncle; played masterfully by character
actor David Abraham Cheulkar) *tum kitne achche tumhen
pyaar karten sab bachche* (John Uncle you are so good
that all children love you). Finally, Manna Dey and chorus
chip in vigorously with (in a marching tune): *Badhta
chal . . . badhta chal . . . tu ek hai pyaare lakhon mein tu
badhta chal* (Go forward . . . go forward . . . you are one in a
lakh dear . . . go forward).

The next song too—in a question-and-answer format,
again penned by the same Shailendra and composed by the
same Shankar–Jaikishan—is from the same *Boot Polish*, this
time rendered by Mohammed Rafi, Asha Bhosle and chorus.
It is a song not strictly based on a raag but composed in a
light catchy tune meant for a broader audience. In later years,
R.D. Burman, too, composed plenty of such numbers. In this
number: *Nanhe munne bachche teri mutthi mein kya hai?*
(Little child, what do you hold in your fist?) 'John Chacha'
asks one question after another, and a bunch of children give
the answers.

After *Boot Polish*, we come to the song from the 1959
movie *Sawan*, penned by Prem Dhawan, also a composer
and choreographer and composed by Hansraj Behl in Raag
Desh and· rendered by Mukesh and Lata Mangeshkar. The
first line is in Mukesh's voice in a low note and at a very
slow pace:

Nain dwaar se man mein woh aake tan mein aag lagaaye.

(Through the doors of my eyes she entered my heart and
set my body on fire.)

The next line is in Lata Mangeshkar's voice in a high pitch and at a fast pace, which slows down towards the end of the line:

Haaye rasiya haaye re . . . koi chhaliya chhal kiye jaaye . . . jiyara liye jaaye . . . chain nahin aaye

(A rakish lover . . . a trickster is cheating me . . . he takes my heart away and also my peace of mind.)

Mukesh then comes in at a low pitch and at a slow pace.

After that, let us move on to a racy medley (in the vocals of Mohammed Rafi and Asha Bhosle) from the 1962 musical venture, Raj Khosla's *Ek Musafir Ek Hasina*, penned by Shams-ul Huda (S.H.) Bihari and tuned by O.P. Nayyar. The medley begins with Rafi belting out: *Teri talaash mujh ko layee kahaan kahaan se?* (Where all has your quest taken me?). Later on, Asha Bhosle enters with a flourish in a totally different tune. The song then alternates between the two singers with a variety of tunes. In this medley, there is a line in Persian: *Zabaan-e-yaar man Turkie wa man Turkie nami daanam* (My darling speaks Turkish, and I do not know that language)— rendered mellifluously by Asha Bhosle. (This line is attributed to the Indo-Persian Sufi singer Amir Khusrau, the iconic figure who lived during the period of the Delhi Sultanate and has many accomplishments in the fields of music, poetry and literature to his credit.)

The next song (in the 'exception category') is in the form of a *nazm* (a form of Urdu poetry usually written on a particular topic which can be in rhyme or in blank verse). For example, one should read or hear Sahir Ludhianvi's thought-provoking nazms 'Taj Mahal' and 'Parchhaiyan'. Or 'Charagar' (healer), penned by the rebel poet from Hyderabad (now the capital of Telangana), Makhdoom Mohiuddin (1908–69)—a leftist who was opposed to the rule there of the nizam. This nazm, included in the 1964 film *Cha Cha Cha*, was set to tune by Iqbal Qureshi and rendered enchantingly by Mohammed Rafi and Asha Bhosle. Beginning with *Ek chameli ke mandve tale, do badan pyaar ki aag mein jal gaye* (Under a jasmine tree's shade, two bodies were burnt in the fire of love), the Raag Asavari nazm flows on and on.

Yet another example is the exquisite melody—*Baad muddat ke yeh ghadi aayee* (This moment has come after a long time; set in Raag Chhayanat)—from the aforementioned *Jahanara* (1964), composed by Madan Mohan, penned by Rajinder Krishan and rendered ethereally by Mohammed Rafi and Suman Kalyanpur. Here, too, the song just goes on and on with very little interlude music.

Two typical 'songs'—in fact, more in the nature of dialogues—are worth recalling. As mentioned above, both have been 'composed' by Rahul Dev Burman in his inimitable style without being based on a raag, but which blend Indian classical music elements with a contemporary style. The first—*Dekhiye sahibon woh koi aur thi* (Look here gentlemen she was somebody else)—has been penned by Majrooh Sultanpuri and put across by Mohammed Rafi and Asha Bhosle in the 1966 Vijay Anand 'musical murder mystery' *Teesri Manzil*. The second (in Asha Bhosle's sensuous vocals)—*Mera naam hai Shabnam* (My name is Shabnam)—has been written by Anand Bakshi in Shakti Samanta's 1971 romantic venture *Kati Patang*.

Next is a dreamy Raag Yaman based Mohammed Rafi–Lata Mangeshkar duet from the 1969 film *Sajan*: *Resham ki dori . . . kahan jaiho nindiya churaake chori chori?* (Silken thread . . . where are you going after surreptitiously snatching away my sleep?). The melody—composed by Laxmikant–Pyarelal and written by Anand Bakshi—just unfolds, stanza after stanza. The exceptional feature of this melody is that the songwriter has chosen certain objects—for example, apart from *resham ki dori*, he has taken *peepal ki chayyain* (the shade of the banyan tree), *ambar pe taaren* (stars in the sky), *parbat pe jharna* (the waterfall on the mountain) and so on—and dexterously built up the verses around such objects.

These were just randomly taken examples to illustrate the 'offbeat' group.

Qawwaalis (a style of devotional music associated with Sufism, but the 'filmi' versions are quite different: with racy rhythms) form a separate genre and vary in structure and length, depending upon the individual music director. Roshan was a master composer in this genre—as amply proven by the Raag Kalawati-based qawwaali, *Na to kaarwaan ki talaash hai na to humsafar ki talaash hai* (The search is neither for the caravan nor for a companion), from P.L. Santoshi's 1960 film *Barsaat Ki Raat*, penned by Sahir Ludhianvi and rendered by a medley of singers, including Manna Dey, S.D. Batish, Mohammed Rafi, Asha Bhosle and Sudha Malhotra.

Folk songs fall into a separate category and do not follow any conformed pattern. Most of them bring alive the beats, rhythms and lingo associated with rural ambience. Here, Naushad was at the forefront as exemplified by his breathtaking compositions in movies such as Mehboob Khan's *Aan* (1952), Nitin Bose's *Gunga Jumna*, followed by the 'most rhythmic and melodious' O.P. Nayyar in B.R. Chopra's *Naya Daur* (1957)—all of which had Dilip Kumar as the hero.

That brings us to the world of trios—the composers, the lyricists and singers—of Hindi cinema who created and gave us musical gems. That was the time when, just by hearing the first few notes a film buff could easily identify the composer and the singer, and at times even the lyricist. Such was the stamp of individuality that one knew that if Madan Mohan was the composer, it would be Lata Mangeshkar as the singer and

Raja Mehdi Ali Khan or Kaifi Azmi as the songwriter. And if Shankar–Jaikishan were composing, it would be the lyrics of Shailendra or Hasrat Jaipuri, which were being sung by Mukesh. From the very foot-tapping prelude of a song one could easily make out that it was O.P. Nayyar's music, with Asha Bhosle singing the words of Shams-ul Huda Bihari or Majrooh Sultanpuri. And, of course, there was that first trio of Hindi cinema—Naushad Ali, Shakeel Badayuni and Mohammed Rafi—who, as a team, gave us musical gems in scores of films and in particular, as many as fifteen of Dilip Kumar films.

There is such a plethora of information available on the trio, and individually on each of them, on Google and YouTube, in books and magazines, as well as in the print and electronic media, that to add any more text would be like gilding the lily. Yet, one is on the quest for hitherto unknown facets of their music which only whets one's appetite for discovering more and more about the three and their incredible repertoire. Their oeuvre covers an assortment of genres, such as romantic melodies, sad songs, patriotic songs, comical capers, zestful songs, rock'n'roll and disco numbers, ghazals, qawwaalis, bhajans (religious songs), shabads (sacred songs associated with Sikhism), naatiya kalaam (poetry in praise of Prophet Muhammad) and much more.

First the mesmerizing Mohammad Rafi, who according to Google, recorded 7405 songs in different languages. His outstanding feature was that he could mould his voice to blend perfectly with that of the character on screen and it appeared as if the actor himself was singing! In fact, many actors owed their careers to Rafi, who sang in a variety of languages with élan, finesse and distinction. His voice is crystal clear and highly resonant, enough to hold one and all spellbound. His range, from the abyss to the peak, was nothing short of phenomenal. He could dip his voice to cover the lowest notes and then let it soar to attain the highest notes, almost effortlessly. Even at the crescendo, his voice sounded extremely mellifluous, not screechy as many other voices do.

According to the famous author–television producer–director Nasreen Munni Kabir, 'If Dilip Kumar moved audiences, it is in part because of the expression Rafi gave to the songs.'[10]

The composer who was 'instrumental' in shaping Rafi's career graph was none other than the legendary Naushad Ali, the Bhisham Pitama (one of the most powerful warriors of his time in the epic Mahabharata) of Hindi film music. He once poignantly stated that Rafi was like a *phaldaar darakht* (a fruit-laden tree), whose branches bent even more as new fruits grew. In other words, the more Rafi sang, the more humble he became.

As in the case of Mohammed Rafi, so also with respect to Naushad (he preferred to use only his first name), there is a plethora of information available on the internet and in books, journals and other sources. Born in Lucknow, Naushad epitomized the once famed *tehzeeb* (culture) and *akhlaaq* (etiquette) of that city. Soft-spoken, eloquent (in chaste Urdu), polished and dignified, he was not only a revered musician—most of his compositions are based on classical raags, which inevitably include *gamaka*s, or ornamentations, which involve complex movements of tune and vocals or instrumental music—he could play a variety of instruments and was also an accomplished Urdu *shayar* (poet). Here is a sher (couplet) from one of his noteworthy ghazals (the reference is to imitating, and borrowing tunes indiscriminately from, the West):

Dar-e-ghair par bheek mango na fan ki
Jab apne hi ghar mein khazaane bahut hain.

(Do not seek alms for art at the door of strangers
When there are many treasuries in the home itself.)

Naushad was very passionate about music from his childhood, but his *waalid* (father) was vehemently opposed to his *farzand*'s (son's) proclivities. It was the era of silent films. Fortuitously, close to his house in Lucknow was a cinema hall, and the music played there (according to the scene on the screen) by the orchestra members, led by one Laddan Khan—usually seated in a kind of huge pit in front of the stage—attracted him like a magnet. He picked up the fundamentals of music from there and later took up a job in a well-known music shop in Lucknow. He soon learnt to play several instruments including the piano, the harmonium, the violin and the sitar. He also learnt Hindustani *shastriya sangeet* (classical music) from *ustad*s (specialized teachers). In his teens, he got a chance to play in Laddan Khan's orchestra.

Naushad's father was furious when he came to know about his son's musical obsession because he felt that one could not make a living by music alone. The waalid severely reprimanded the farzand, who decided to run away from home in 1936. After brief sojourns in many places, the youngster eventually landed in Bombay, the city of dreams. But he had to wait for a while before his dreams could come true, as he was forced to sleep on the footpath opposite the once-thriving Broadway cinema hall in Dadar (a locality in central Bombay). Ironically, it was in the Broadway cinema hall that the musical masterpiece of Naushad, directed by Vijay Bhatt, was released in 1952. Apparently, an emotional Naushad had then stated that it had taken him sixteen years to cross the footpath.

After a period of intense struggle, he managed to bag his first film, M. Bhavnani's *Prem Nagar* (1940), but it did not make any waves. However, after eleven more films, which too did not exactly work wonders for him, came the turning point in 1944, in the form of *Rattan* (directed by M. Sadiq, with the songs penned by D.N. Madhok), which catapulted him to new musical heights. The rest is history. His long musical journey—lasting sixty-five years: his final film was Akbar Khan's *Taj Mahal: An Eternal Love Story* (2005)— is studded with numerous milestones, comprising four diamond jubilees, twelve golden jubilees and thirty-five silver jubilees. Most of the songs from these movies are a music aficionado's delight and a part of the subconscious of generations of music lovers.

In a *signed* article that Lata Mangeshkar wrote on Naushad, she said:

> If Ghulam Haider, Shyam Sunder, Khemchand Prakash, even Anil Biswas and C. Ramchandra, were quick at composition—taking sometimes as little as ten minutes to create a melody—Naushad labours long and hard at his compositions. He builds the music, studies every detail at every stage of composition. He is very particular about the *bol* (words). If one little *bol* is not to his satisfaction, he asks the lyricist to alter the whole line. Thus, it takes him about 15 days to compose the music for a song. He writes the music of a single song over and over again, until he is satisfied with it, and it suits the situation exactly. Over the years, Naushad has changed his style effectively, his music evolving and becoming new with the passage of time. His works in *Sharda* [1942, by A.R. Kardar] to *Rattan* [1944, by M. Sadiq] to *Anmol Ghadi* [1946, by Mehboob Khan] mark his development.
>
> In the *Anmol Ghadi–Anokhi Ada* period [1946–48] he maintained roughly the same style. After *Anokhi Ada* [by Mehboob Khan] his music underwent a subtle change. I was astonished with Naushad's music in *Baiju Bawra* [1952, by Vijay Bhatt]. Its style was completely different from everything he had done before. Every situation had

a raag—Malkauns, Todi, Desi, Purya, Dhanashri, Bhairavi, Bhairav—and the purity of each raag was preserved. Naushad's music is indeed unparalleled in its polish. Even if the melody is not extraordinary, it is fashioned and orchestrated in such perfect arrangement as to thrill and inspire. Naushad has not only an extensive knowledge of music but of allied subjects as well. He studies the story, the situation, the editing, the sound recording, the music recording and the re-recording. He is an accomplished piano player, and he is familiar with Western notations. He knows every instrument in his orchestra and what instrument is best for a certain piece of music. He was the first to present combinations of the flute and the clarinet, of the sitar and the mandolin. He also introduced the accordion, the *been*, the brass instruments, the *daff* and the vibraphone.[11]

After the untimely demise of his favourite shayar, Shakeel Badayuni, with whom he had built up a remarkable relationship over the years, on 20 April 1970, Naushad's career went downhill, and he never again achieved the heights that he had in the 1950s and 1960s. Though he continued to score music for films, TV serials and private albums, the magic was somehow lost.

Before moving on to Shakeel Badayuni, the sublime shayar, one must clarify that in 1947, a composer by the name of Shaukat Dehlavi (born as Shaukat Ali Hashmi) entered the realm of film music with *Dildaar*. A year later, in 1948, he composed the music for a couple of films using the name Shaukat Ali. The same year, he then switched back to Shaukat Dehlavi. After composing for three more films, under that moniker, eventually, in 1953, he took on the name 'Nashad', which muddied the musical waters (so to say) because it was very similar to 'Naushad'! I daresay Naushad Ali, who was then riding high, must not have been exactly amused.

Anyway, after scoring music for a string of films, which at best could be described as average to below average, came, in 1955, *Baaradari*, with lyrics by Khumar Barabankavi (Mohhamed Haider Khan), which was an instant hit with Talat Mahmood's velvety Raag Pahadi-based *Tasveer banaata hoon, tasveer nahin banti* (I try to make your portrait but I cannot) and the peppy Mohammed Rafi–Lata Mangeshkar duet, *Bhula nahin dena ji, bhula nahin dena* (Do not forget me, do not forget me). Film music buffs, to this day think that the songs were composed by Naushad. Strangely, after that, Nashad ran out of work and left for Pakistan in 1964, never to be heard of again.

Shakeel Badayuni symbolized a bygone era when certain film songs could pass muster even by the high standards of Urdu shayiri. Sadly, that era is now merely a distant memory. After completing his studies and making his mark in mushairas (a gathering of poets who recite their works in front of the public), Shakeel, in 1944, decided to try his luck in films and landed up in the lodestone called Bombay. There, he was assigned to pen four songs in *Natak* (1947) with music by Naushad. Next, he wrote all the songs in *Dard* (1947), directed by Abdul (or Abdur) Rashid Kardar (a big name then in the Hindi film industry) again under Naushad's musical baton. Soon, Shakeel and Naushad went on to develop a lifelong relationship till the former's death. They were like peas in a pod.

Dard turned out be a musical marvel, with songs such as the Raag Kafi-based *Afsana likh rahi hoon dil-e-beqraar ka* (I am writing the story of a restless heart; sung by Uma Devi, who later, as an actress, took on the name Tun Tun), *Betaab hai dil dard-e-mohabbat ke asar se* (The heart is impatient due to the effect of love; rendered by Uma Devi and Suraiya) and the Raag Bhairavi-based *Hum dard ka afsana duniya ko suna denge* (I will narrate my tale of woe to the world) in Shamshad Begum's voice), which became very popular.

Post-*Dard*, Shakeel's fortunes soared. He was the songwriter (and a highly creative one at that) for all of Naushad's movies after 1947 except three: Mehboob Khan's *Andaz* (1949) and C.V. Sridhar's *Saathi* (1968), whose lyrics were penned by Majrooh Sultanpuri, and Subodh Mukherji's *Saaz Aur Awaaz* (1966), whose lyrics came from the pen of Khumar Barabankvi.

For *Baiju Bawra*, a classical masterpiece from a musical perspective, the director, Vijay Bhatt, had chosen Naushad as the composer and was keen that a poet with a Hindi—rather than an Urdu—background pen the songs, some of which were bhajans. However, Naushad managed to convince him that Shakeel was quite equal to the task. Shakeel proved to be more than equal! The soulful bhajans he wrote for this film, in combination with Naushad's divine tunes and Rafi's enthralling voice, made a tremendous impact on the public then. Even today, these bhajans hold one enraptured.

Apart from Naushad, for whom Shakeel wrote the maximum number of songs, including bhajans, ghazals and qawwalis, he teamed up with almost all the composers of the day which resulted in many memorable melodies.

Many of Shakeel's non-filmi ghazals have been rendered soulfully by Begum Akhtar (born Akhtari Bai Faizabadi, a respected classical singer) and Talat Mahmood, among others.

Coming back to the trio, there are ever so many outstanding melodies that it would be next to impossible to discuss all of them here. However, outside those that were meant especially for Dilip Kumar films, which have been discussed later while discussing each of the legend's films, one must mention few of the 'choicest' of songs from their treasury.

The selection of course is subjective. Moreover, it is just to give one a flavour of their work.

An all-time favourite gem of the trio *Suhaanee raat dhal chuki* in the popular and little playful Raag Pahadi—picturized on Suresh (born as Naseem Ahmed)—from A.R. Kardar's black-and-white venture *Dulari* (1949), embellished with no less than twelve musical pearls. This venture brought together two highly talented heroines: Madhubala (born as Mumtaz Jahan Begum Dehlavi, as mentioned earlier, on Valentine's Day, 14 February 1933) and Geeta Bali (born as Harkirtan Kaur in 1930)—both of whom tragically departed from this world in their thirties due to serious health problems.

Suhaanee raat dhal chuki, set in Raag Mishr Pahaadi (derived from the word *pahaad*, meaning mountain), which is supposed to transport the listener to hills and dales, consists of the mukhda and two antaras, each in a different tune. This composition poignantly expresses the longing of a forlorn lover for his beloved. The wistfulness of the Naushadian tune, the *lataafat* (elegance or daintiness) of Shakeel's lyrics and Rafi's languorous tones cast their own spell. The mukdha sets the mood for the rest of the song:

Suhaanee raat dhal chuki, na jaane tum kab aaoge
Jahaan ki rut badal chuki, na jaane tum kab aaoge.

(The pleasant night has gone by; one does not know when you will come
The season of the world has changed, one does not know when you will come.)

The first two lines of the first stanza have been set in high notes, scaled effortlessly by Rafi, and the last line has been set in a low note, where the singer subtly dips his voice. But it is the second, which is the last, stanza (set in low notes) that captures the agonized pining of the restless lover:

Tadap rahe hain hum yahaan tumhaare intezaar mein
Khizaan ka rang aa chala hai mausam-e-bahaar mein
Hawa bhi rukh badal chuki, na jaane tum kab aaoge.

(Here I am agonizing while waiting for you
The tinge of autumn has crept into springtime.
Even the wind has changed direction, one does not know when you will come.)

Like many songs of the trio, *Suhaanee raat dhal chuki* too has transcended the barrier of time. The nation sang and sings it even today. It still hums and strums on its mental guitar.

In October, the same year, 1952, came the Rafi–Naushad–Shakeel trinity's masterpiece in the form of the historical, in black-and-white, titled *Baiju Bawra* (with excellent performances by Bharat Bhushan and Meena Kumari in the lead roles). *Baiju Bawra* is considered a musical benchmark even today by connoisseurs. Each one of the thirteen compositions has its own appeal and charm, including the Lata Mangeshkar solo, *Mohe bhool gaye sawariya* (My beloved has forgotten me). The movie provided ample scope for Naushad to compose all the songs based on classical raags plus, in a sequence depicting the hero's *riyaaz* (practise to hone one's art or skill), Rafi's vocals pranced over raags such as Lalit, Puriya, Gaud Malhar and Bageshri. In fact, on the basis of his impeccable reputation as one well versed with the nuances of Hindustani shastriya sangeet, Naushad managed to rope in two renowned classical vocalists. One was the child prodigy, Pandit D.V. Paluskar, who inherited the Gwalior gharana. Second was the self-taught musician who founded the unique style, known as the Indore gharana, which blends the spiritual flavour and grandeur of Dhrupad with the ornate vividness of Khyal, Ustad Amir Khan. The two sing in *Baiju Bawra* for the climax scene which leads to a musical clash between Mian Tansen (circa 1500 to 1586: born as Ramtanu Pandey), one of the navrattans (nine gems) in the darbar of the third Mughal Emperor, Jalal-ud-din Mohammad Akbar and Baijnath (i.e., Baiju).

Of the three Rafi solos in *Baiju Bawra*, one has chosen the Raag Darbari-based bhajan *O duniya ke rakhwaale/Sun dard bhare mere naale* (O protector of this world, listen to my pain-filled lamentations; these two lines form the mukhda). The other two solos—*Hari . . . man tarpat Hari darshan ko aaj* (The heart today yearns for the sight of Hari, another name for Lord Krishna)—a bhajan in Raag Malkauns; towards the end, a chorus joins the main singer) and *Insaan bano* (in Raag Gujari Todi, mentioned earlier)—are also noteworthy. Before the mukhda comes the prelude (in long notes) made up of just one word: *bhagwaan* (God). The mukhda is followed by four antaras, each a superb blend of music, poetry and vocals.

It is important to note here that these bhajans were written by a Muslim, composed by a Muslim and sung by a Muslim—an excellent example of India's religious harmony.

Each of the antaras were scrupulously configured by Naushad, keeping in mind the subtle symmetry of the lyrics, the ambience and its aura. And, to top it all, Rafi's flawless vocals keep the listener enchanted. Apparently, for this classical composition, Naushad's rehearsals for Mohammad Rafi were spread over twenty-one days! No wonder, more than six decades later, the overwhelming impact of the song is very much intact. The second stanza, through vivid poetic imagery, sums up the protagonist's despondent and frustrated frame of mind:

Aag bani saawan ki barkha
Phool bane angaare
Nagan ban gayee raat suhaani,
Patthar ban gaye tare
Sab toot chuke hain sahaare
Jeevan apna wapas lele, jeevan dene waale
O duniya ke rakhwaale . . .

(The monsoon rain has turned into fire
The flowers have turned into embers
The pleasant night has morphed into a serpent   ·
I have lost all support
Take back my life, giver of life.)

The high point of *O duniya ke rakhwaale* is, undoubtedly, Rafi's raising the pitch of his voice, higher and higher, notch by notch, till a crescendo is attained. According to some sources, while scaling the high notes, Rafi's throat started to bleed, but he continued singing till the song was fully recorded.

Baiju Bawra consolidated Rafi's position in the Hindi film industry, as all the composers could now feel free to create the most complex tunes with the assurance that full justice would be done to them. Naushad shaped Rafi into The Great Caruso that he became (title of the 1951 MGM film based on the life of Enrico Caruso, master tenor). The same contention would as well apply to Lata Mangeshkar, who infused the song *Mohe bhool gaye sawariya* (in Raag Bhairav) with a subtle tinge of pathos and anguish.

The next offering from the trio is from yet another musical—M. Sadiq's *Shabab* (mid-1954; in black and white, featuring the same Bharat Bhushan as hero), embellished with a string of eleven songs. It won plaudits from the discerning aficionados.

In *Shabab*, as in *Baiju Bawra*, from the three Rafi numbers, the one selected is *Yahi armaan lekar aaj apne ghar se hum nikle* (based on Raag Mishr Tilang), which comprises the mukhda and two antaras. The other two are *Aaye na baalam vaada karke* (My beloved did not come after making a promise to do so; in Raag Gaud Saarang) and *Mahlon mein rahne waale humhen tere dar se kya* (Those who stay in palaces, what have we to do with you; Rafi and chorus in Raag Shahana).

Shakeel Badayuni wrote this ghazal in the same metre as the eminent Mirza (Beg Asadullah Khan) Ghalib, which begins with the line: *Hazaaron khwaishen aisi ki har khwaish pe dum nikle* (Thousands of desires were such that it was worth dying for each of them). The perceptive reader would have noticed that the radeef of Ghalib's and Shakeel's ghazals is the same: the word *nikle*. These are known as 'humradeef' ghazals.

Naushad's mellifluent notes, Shakeel's absorbing lyrics and Rafi's enticing rendition draw attention to the affliction of a disconsolate lover.

In *Shabab*, Shakeel begins a song in a unique way, with the word *marna*, meaning to die. The mukhda is:

Marna teri gali mein, jeena teri gali mein
Mit jayeegi hamari duniya teri gali mein.

(I shall die in your lane, I shall live in your lane
My world will be destroyed in your lane.)

It is indeed strange to have 'dying' as the first word of a song; one would expect it to come towards the end. That apart, Naushad cast the song in the euphonious Raag Pahadi which like Raag Sohini and Raag Jhinjhoti is a little playful and teaches *gayaki ang* (singing style); Lata Mangeshkar's dulcet tones greatly enhanced the impact of the melody picturized on the heroine Nutan.

Shabab added one more proverbial feather to Naushad's cap! Of the many compositions in this film, Naushad's tune, Shakeel's lyrics and the Mohammed Rafi–Lata Mangeshkar amalgamation created an exceptional rhapsody in the form of *Man ki been matwaari baaje* (The intoxicated *been** of the heart rings out) in Raag Bahar with a touch of Raag Basant.

By this stage, Naushad had established himself as a composer par excellence. And he strove diligently and assiduously to maintain his position in the face of stiff competition from a host of highly talented composers, with Shankar–Jaikishan, C. Ramchandra and O.P. Nayyar in the vanguard.

When one writes about Naushad and Shakeel Badayuni, how can one forget those melodies of the one and only Lata Mangeshkar in and outside of Dilip Kumar films?

As in the cases of Mohammed Rafi and Naushad, there is a surfeit of material available (including a huge pile of minutiae) on Lata Mangeshkar in various sources that one wonders what more can be added!

One could run out of superlatives while writing about Lata Mangeshkar. 'Her voice is the gift of God' lauded Dilip Kumar, who considered Lata as his younger sister. Even the staunch purists of classical music showered immense praise on her. If the music maestro Ustad Allauddin Khan called her '*Aasman se aayi hui pari*' (An angel who has descended from the heavens), the musical genius Bade Ghulam Ali Khan once remarked about her: '*Kambakht kabhi besuri hoti hi nahi*' (The damned girl is never out of tune). The eminent sarod player, Ustad Amjad Ali Khan, eulogized her voice as 'a

---

* The *been* is a wind instrument played by snake charmers in the Indian subcontinent.

unique favour by Mother Saraswati' (the Goddess of art, music, knowledge, wisdom and learning) and the tablanawaaz par excellence, Alla Rakha (Qureshi), declared that 'there will not be another Lata for the next one thousand years'! All this praise may seem like hyperbole to the sceptics, but it is definitely *not*. In fact, her voice and the voices of Asha Bhosle, Geeta Dutt, Mohammed Rafi, Mukesh, Manna Dey and Talat Mahmood, among others, are part of parcel of the subconscious of several generations.

Coming to Dilip Kumar films, nineteen music directors composed music for his fifty-seven films in the nearly six decades of his life in cinema. While eight of them—Arun Kumar, Feroz Nizami, Gobindram, Ghulam Haider, Bulo C. Irani, O.P. Nayyar, Khayyam and Tapan Sinha—were able to work on only one film each, the others ranging from Anil Biswas in the earlier days to C. Ramchandra, and Shankar–Jaikishan to S.D. Burman to Salil Chowdhury had two to four films each. Later, during Dilip Kumar's second innings, music composers ranging from Laxmikant–Pyarelal to Kalyanji–Anandji to R.D. Burman came in with three to five films each. However, the man who provided music to as many as fifteen of his films was none other than the 'Badshah' of the Hindi music world, Naushad. This was right through from S.U. Sunny's film *Mela* (1948) to H.S. Rawail's *Sunghursh* (1968).

In most of these films, it was Shakeel Badayuni who penned the songs and Mohammad Rafi who sang for the thespian. The three formed a sublimely creative trio. After Shakeel Badayuni's untimely demise on 20 April 1970, at a young age of fifty-four, Naushad did go on to score music till 2000 teaming up with noted songwriters including Rajendra Kishen (one of our most underrated lyricists), Majrooh

Sultanpuri (who had written for Naushad earlier also, in Mehboob Khan's *Andaz*), Hasrat Jaipuri, Jan Nisar Akhtar, Anand Bakshi and Hasan Kamaal, but it was never the same again. Naushad's compositions, for whatever reasons, seemed to flounder. Perhaps he could not achieve the same remarkable rapport that he had established with Shakeel.

In the picturization of songs, Dilip Kumar evolved a cinematically mature style of providing dignity to the song and enchanting its appeal. As mentioned earlier, he would study the lyrics in great detail, interpret them as intended by the lyricist through natural expressions and originally conceived movements. For example, in B.R. Chopra's *Naya Daur*, Nitin Bose's *Gunga Jumna* and H.S. Rawail's *Sunghursh*, Dilip Kumar emerged as the pathbreaker in choreography. Borrowing elements from the folk dances of Punjab and Uttar Pradesh, he used his ingenuity to improvise a dance style hardly seen in Indian cinema. A whole sense of *ulhas* (celebrations) was created by an intricate combination of body movements accompanying the rhythm and coupling of the movements with those of the co-dancers. Observe that famous step of his in *Gunga Jumna* while singing *Nain lad jaie jainhe to manavaa mein kasak hoibe kari* or *Ho uden jab jab zulfein teri, kunwari ka dil machley jind meriye* from *Naya Daur*. Once on being asked how he managed to do it, his modest reply was: 'Lale, *mere se dance wance nahi hota tha* (I could not dance). I would just enjoy the rhythm and do whatever I could.'[12] Later, many actors tried to either copy the same or worked on his style, but none could make it as a hallmark of his screen image.

In the years to come, much changed and changed rapidly. Different film-makers brought in different composers, lyricists and singers to provide an alternate combination for the musical notes. For a Dilip Kumar film, the musical notes that two generations of the audience had grown up singing and enjoying; the musical notes that had transformed the emotional domain of the viewer and modulated his behaviour in his day-to-day life replacing his own 'being' with the 'being' on the celluloid; the musical notes which made us all go through the pain and suffering, the joy and happiness, they saw the actor going through. But the trial-and-error method did not work. Try as hard as each composer of the day did, the audience, used to that mesmerizing Dilip Kumar 'feel' and 'touch' for singing in the voice of Mohammad Rafi, was left unenthused. Whether it was Mahendra Kapoor, whom Dilip Kumar had specially brought in, in place of Mohammad Rafi as his music voice, in a number of films starting with A. Bhim Singh's *Gopi*, or Amit Kumar in Umesh Mehra's *Qila*, or Kishore Kumar in Yash Chopra's *Mashaal*, the audience could not resonate. Even Suresh Wadkar and Mohammad Aziz in Subhash Ghai's *Vidhaata* and the Laxmikant–Pyarelal–Anand Bakshi's score *Ilu, ilu* or *Imli ka buta, beri ka ber* from *Saudagar* failed to bring back that 'feel', that 'touch' the listeners were used to humming. Although each of these singers tried his best to blend his voice adeptly with that of Dilip Kumar and sang with his characteristic verve and élan, somehow the Rafi enchantment was totally missing. And the audience missed it immensely. Nostalgia for those old songs gone by reigned high.

With it the Dilip Kumar song–music magic was gone!

5

MANY FACES, MANY HUES, MANY SHADES

THERE IS A FAMILIAR AND AN OFT REPEATED STORY FROM 1944, just three years before the country gained independence, when the Indian film world witnessed a rare incident of talent scouting. Devika Rani, the first 'wonder lady' of Indian cinema, after her studies at the Royal Academy of Dramatic Arts and the Royal Academy of Music in London, returned to India with her equally illustrious husband Himanshu Rai, to finally lay the foundation of Bombay Talkies in Bombay. One day, as she was out shopping in the local market, she noticed a young man with a sensitive face and expressive eyes which she thought to be quite unusual.

The young man was Mohammad Yousuf Khan. After preliminary screen shots, he was selected as an apprentice at Bombay Talkies, where Devika Rani started grooming him as the company's new hero under the screen name Dilip Kumar. As B.N. Sircar, the founder of New Theatres, in the 1930s, sensed the immense cinematic possibilities in K.L. (Kundan Lal) Saigal, she, a decade later, perceived the need for a new kind of acting talent for further enrichment of Indian cinema. This was perhaps because of a growing stagnation in themes and style in films, coupled with lukewarm responses to many of the Bombay Talkies films at the box office during that period.

The entry of Dilip Kumar into the film world was very low key; he was just one among the many faces of the new generation

74

Dilip Kumar and Mridula in *Jwar Bhata* (1944)

being experimented with by the film directors. Devika Rani introduced her discovery in a film titled *Jwar Bhata*, under the direction of the veteran Amiya Chakravarty. The heroine, Mridula, too, was a new find of Bombay Talkies. *Jwar Bhata* had the distinction of having the 'legendary luminaries' of the literary and cultural world associated with it. The doyen music composer of the times, Anil Biswas, was to provide music to the songs written by the famous poet Pandit Narendra Sharma, while the eminent novelist Bhagwati Charan Verma wrote the dialogues and R.D. Mathur provided the cinematography.

Jwar Bhata (1944)

The film cast Dilip Kumar in the role of a *nautanki* (folk theatre) artiste, named Jagdish—a sensitive young man who provides support to a girl in distress. She is one of the two daughters, both of marriageable age, of an old patriarch. The marriage of the heroine Renu (Mridula) is arranged with a rich urban youth Narendra (Agha Jaan), who, during a visit to the family, mistakes the elder sister Rama (Shammi) for Renu, falls in love with her and marries her. After the marriage, Rama becomes suspicious of Renu's evil designs to win back Narendra. As things turn out, Renu is thrown out of the house. She thereafter meets the wandering musician Jagdish and to conceal her identity joins his troupe. The two fall in love. On finding about Renu's background, he persuades her to go back home to her family.

On her return, Renu finds Rama pregnant and very ill, and a choice must be made between saving the foetus or the mother. Renu forgives her sister and invokes the gods to provide a miracle and save the lives of the two.

Anil Biswas composed the music for the nine songs in the film, eight of which were sung by Manna Dey, Amirbai Karnataki, Parul Ghosh and Aroon Kumar. Anil Biswas also sang the popular number *Gao Kabir udao Ahir* (Sing Kabir, pick up Abir).

The film failed at the box office and was declared 'below average'. While the general response was not encouraging, the critics as well as those in the industry felt that the new actor did not have much spark in him and the quality of his voice in particular was bad for an actor, though the heroine had potential to become a good actress. The acid pen of Baburao Patel, the powerful editor of his monthly magazine *Filmindia*, said: 'Dilip Kumar, the new hero of Bombay Talkies is an anemic addition to our film artistes. He needs a lot of vitamins and a prolonged treatment of proteins before another picture can be risked with him. He looks gaunt and famished and strikes one as a long-ill-treated convict who has escaped from a jail. His appearance on the screen creates both laughter and disappointment. His acting effort amounts to nil!'[1]

However, the film critic of the *Times of India* in its edition of 9 December 1944 noted that the film 'had some of the best acting seen on Indian screen for years'.

Film writer and scenarist Inder Raj Anand wrote that 'one didn't think much of Dilip Kumar and didn't see a bright future for him ... One has all hopes pinned on Mridula'.[2]

However, time proved them wrong; none of them indeed had the slightest idea that this 'shaky, unimpressive' new talent would soon become the 'founding father' of cinematic acting, taking his art form far beyond the domain of the legendary artistes ruling the world of films at that time.

For Dilip Kumar, in those formative years, Bombay Talkies was an institution ...

> [T]he like of which, I cannot sight anywhere today. It was said in those days that it had the aura of Shantiniketan [the prestigious institution near West Bengal founded by the Nobel Laurate Rabindranath Tagore]. I can vividly recall the mornings with Mrs. Rai [Devika Rani] tending to the flowering plants in the garden herself. She was so poised and dignified and elegant and very kind. She was a remarkably intelligent woman herself and was a perfectionist in her work. We were in awe of her, too. It was she who gave me the first break in films and I learned a number of useful lessons from her. She noticed that I had potential and talent and certain natural propensities, and she saw my application to my work and so she used to call me sometimes and give me very useful advice ...
>
> The studio employed practically all the established writers of the time. They were not required to write regularly, but as and when their services were required, they were sought and consulted. I must say that Bombay Talkies produced men and women who went on to achieve great fame ... If you take a count of all the men and women who emerged from Bombay Talkies you will find quite a few illustrious names of today. Later, when one went over to other studios in those days itself [sic] was something of an achievement ...[3]

Pratima (1945)

The Dadasaheb Phalke Award winner Paidi Jairaj, known for producing and directing films in Hindi, Marathi, Gujarati and Telegu languages, besides, at times, acting in them too gave Dilip Kumar his next film—*Pratima*. With him in the lead was the famous Swaranalata, who had just starred, a year earlier, in M. Sadiq's *Rattan* with Karan Dewan as her hero and Naushad as the music director. It turned out to be a huge success.

Pratima presented Dilip Kumar (whose name was spelt in the credits as Dileep) as a seeker, who in pursuit of an idolized love, would defy every social convention to reach out to the world of eternal beauty and innocence. Here, Dilip Kumar, (as Rajan) appeared as a persuasive lover entangled in a curious plot. He falls in love with a poor girl Pratima (Swaranalata) brought up by Parvasi (Pithawala), a curio-dealer, who apparently had once been a notorious dacoit. Rajan's family wishes him to marry the rich Lal Saheb's spoilt and pampered daughter.

In the haveli of Lal Saheb, there is a statue of a female in the courtyard, after whom his heroine has been named. It is noticed that the very mention of this statue makes Lal Saheb

shudder with fear, and he instantly starts looking at a picture of his country house hanging on the wall.

The hero Rajan, who by now has turned into a desperate lover, starts worshipping the statue, the Pratima, and decides to restore the shrine in the model village which he has constructed for the poor. However, the shrine is jealously guarded by a demented-looking woman.

The story thus moves on, and it is only at the end that the mystery about the birth of the heroine and the statue is revealed. The mentally unstable woman is the mother of Pratima, the heroine, and the real owner of the entire estate and the riches of Lal Saheb. Apparently, he had usurped it all by killing the old lady's husband in the country house. It was Parvasi who had saved the girl from the evil eye of Lal Saheb and her mother had installed the statue of her long-lost daughter to remind the world about the misdeeds of the villain, Lal Saheb.

The film also had Mukri, cast in his debut role personally by Devika Rani, who is stated to have 'liked his smile and off-screen enthusiasm'. Mukri went on to star in almost all of Dilip Kumar films after that.

The film had music by Arun Kumar Mukherjee to the lyrics of Narendra Sharma.

The film and its music sank without a trace to the point that it was declared a 'flop'. In fact, worse than Dilip Kumar's debut film *Jwar Bhata*. Baburao Patel, the editor of *Filmindia*, who had torn Dilip Kumar to bits in the earlier film, now wrote in his review: 'Dilip Kumar seems to have gone more anaemic since his last picture. He now presents a hollow chest, limp arms, shaky legs, and a woebegone look, suggesting a patient illness of several years. When a man with those looks plays a hero, it must be the end of motion picture glamour. Dilip Kumar does not act at all, and we doubt whether he will ever act in future.'[4]

Milan (1946)

But act again he did. Come 1946 and Nitin Bose signed Dilip Kumar for his new film *Milan* with Meera Mishra, Ranjana, Pahari Sanyal and Moni Chatterjee, all well-established names, in the cast.

Nitin Bose, a cameraman-turned-director, was one of the early founders of the realist genre in Bengali and Hindi cinema. A child prodigy, he learned photography even before his teens. Then he began making home movies, which he developed himself. Soon, he joined the film world as a cinematographer and made his directorial debut with *Chandidas* (1934), which was to make him one of the most important directors at New Theatres, helping even K.L Saigal in realizing his full potential as an actor–singer. Bose also influenced the films of his own student and cameraman Bimal Roy, who like his senior, went on to direct such films as *Devdas* and *Madhumati*.

Dilip Kumar with Meera Mishra in *Milan* (1946)

Milan was based on Rabindranath Tagore's famous novel *Nauka Dubi*, which marked Bose's debut at Bombay Talkies. It was a meaningful commentary on the sanctity of marriage and the role of destiny in separating and reuniting two souls in love.

The film portrayed Dilip Kumar as an upright landed aristocrat, Ramesh, who upholds the dignity of a newly married woman under testing circumstances. He has had to forgo his beloved and marry, under family pressure, another woman, who he loses when the boat in which the marriage party is travelling gets caught in a storm while crossing the river.

Meanwhile, the boat of the bride in another wedding party too gets hit by the same storm in which the young bride loses her husband but starts believing that Ramesh, who has discovered her lying unconscious on the shore, is the one to whom she was married off to. Ramesh takes care of her till her groom, who was believed to have drowned in the storm, is found to be alive.

Milan, like Dilip Kumar's earlier two films, too flopped at the box office. Though praised by some critics for the effective treatment of the theme and for the photography, particularly of the outdoor night scenes, it came in for severe criticism overall. Baburao Patel, editor of the powerful *Filmindia* in its edition of June 1946, tore it apart:

> Tagore's 'Wreck' Wrecked on Screen!
> *Milan* Becomes Lousy, Boring Stuff.

> . . . If you have the nerve to keep awake till the interval, you may probably see the end of *Milan* on the screen. The picture has a terrifically hypnotic value, and it takes all your will power to keep your eyes open . . .

Dilip Kumar is a heart-rending choice for the hero's role. The boy still looks anaemic and though he seems to make an honest attempt to deliver the goods as an artist, he sadly fails to convince. Dilip Kumar has come to the screen with an unfortunate face, and no one is going to imagine a hero's portrait on the screen with that face . . . The way we find Dilip Kumar constantly twitching fingers, as if he is constantly in epileptic convulsions. When the boy has a face on his shoulder one wonders why the fingers were used so often and so clumsily to portray inner emotions.

Yet, the film-makers felt differently. The film greatly helped Dilip Kumar in defining his screen persona. As he mentioned:

My work choices from the very beginning were not governed by the remuneration I was offered. This was something I learned from Nitin Bose and Devika Rani who were my first and most inspirational teachers. While working with Nitinda, during the making of *Milan*, I understood how vital it is for an actor to get so close to the character that the thin line between the actor's own personality and the imagined personality of the character gets ruthlessly rubbed off for the time when you are involved in the shooting. To get that close to the character it is very important to know everything about the character and his mind and emotions . . . Nitinda groomed me. He explained that a good script always helped an actor to perform effectively but there were areas beyond what was given to him in the script that were waiting to be explored by one who wished to rise above the given areas in his performance . . . 'There is no stopping you if you as an actor felt emboldened to discover niches in the actor's emotional make-up that you would like to bring to the fore even if they are not there in the script,' Nitinda explained . . . One very important thing I learned from him was the value of silence—that silence is really golden at certain moments. When combined with a nice balance with words and background music, it can go straight to the viewers' soul.[5]

Dilip Kumar never forgot the debt he owed Nitin Bose, with whom he was to work later in *Deedar* in 1951, which was to become one of his biggest hits of the time. No wonder, for his home production *Gunga Jumna*, which was to become a blockbuster at the box office, he chose Bose as director.

Dilip Kumar also mentioned what Devika Rani advised him: a lesson he bore in mind and applied to his work, sometimes even to the surprise of his directors and co-stars:

A director may be satisfied with the shot that an actor had given, but it is for the actor to discern for himself whether he had really given his best. The actor was within his rights to request for another take if he felt he could do better . . . it is important to rehearse till a level of competence to perform is achieved. In the early years, it was a necessity for me to rehearse, but, even in the later years, her advice stayed with me when I had to match a benchmark, I had mentally set for myself. In fact, I am aware that I am known for the number of rehearsals I do for even what seems to be a simple scene.[6]

Milan had music by Anil Biswas to the lyrics by P. L. Santoshi and Arzu Lakhnavi. Parul Ghosh, the younger sister of Anil Biswas sang five of the eight songs while Geeta Dutt sang two and Shankar Dasgupta one. None of the songs could help save the film. However, destiny had its own role to play and proved that what the critics were writing was just in a superfluous outburst of pessimism. Perhaps none of them had read the Muslim scholar-poet Waheed Akhtar's couplet:

Khushk aankhon se uthi mauj to duniya dubbi
Hum jisse samjhe they sahra woh samundar nikla

(From the dry eyes when a wave rose the world was submerged
What I thought was a desert turned out to be an ocean)

And an ocean of talent was Dilip Kumar.

Jugnu (1947)

A hat-trick of flops at the box office and that too at the start of a career in films is something that would have unnerved not only any film-maker but also any aspiring youngster. Had it been anyone else, he would never have got another chance in the brutal and heartless world of Bollywood to climb that greasy pole to stardom. So many had come and disappeared leaving behind no trace whatsoever, a world where an actor is as good as the last Friday—the day a film is released, and the verdict is announced on the success or flop of a film. And with it the future of the hero too.

However, there was certainly a spark somewhere in Dilip Kumar which one film-maker after another saw. And one of them was Shaukat Hussain Rizvi, a known film director, who was optimistic about him and decided to cast him in his new project *Jugnu* and that too opposite his wife, the iconic singing-star of the time, Noor Jehan, who was later to be labelled Malika-e-Tarannum (Queen of Melody).

Rizvi's *Jugnu* was a scathing attack on the decadent feudal values. It can be considered as the first tragedy film of Dilip Kumar.

Dilip Kumar with Noor Jehan in *Jugnu* (1947)

In this extremely passionate love story set amid a university campus, Dilip Kumar, for the first time, revealed his trademark ability to transform the character from a rib-tickling comedian in the first half of the narrative to a tragedian par excellence in the later half, a trend seen in many of his subsequent films.

Suraj (Dilip Kumar) is a jovial, fun-loving college student from a rich aristocratic family. He and his college mates, which included the singer Mohammad Rafi who appeared in a small role, play a prank or two with a bunch of girl students who have come to enjoy a picnic by the banks of a lake.

Suraj falls in love with Jugnu (Noor Jehan), an orphan. However, she refuses to accept the overtures of this passionate suitor. Consequently, he climbs on to a boulder and threatens to jump into the lake and kill himself if she keeps on rejecting him. Jugnu is swayed by this antic and pleads with him to come down.

As the love affair builds up through a series of comic encounters, Suraj's father, a landed aristocrat gone bankrupt, forces him to marry a girl of his choice. The girl is from a rich family and as promised by her father will bring in a large dowry, which will help him pay off the debts he had incurred to maintain his feudal lifestyle.

When informed of this, Jugnu, heart-broken, falls seriously ill and eventually dies. Unable to bear the anguish of lost love, Suraj too goes into depression and finally jumps into the lake from the same boulder from which he had threatened Jugnu to commit suicide.

As soon as the film was released on 23 May 1947, it came in for much criticism for the way it depicted romance—flirting and dancing on a college campus. The film was even banned for a short duration and re-released only after the censors ordered cuts totalling around twenty-five minutes of the film. The reviews were mostly critical, with Baburao Patel in his film column in *Filmindia* leading the attack:

> *Jugnu* a Dirty, Disgusting, Vulgar Picture!
> Students and Colleges Slandered

> . . . it tells us that college life in India is nothing more than a long sex hunt in which boys chase girls, explore their handbags, rob their tiffin boxes and sing suggestive love ditties while making vulgar gestures; while girls sigh about heavily, seduce boys to tea, pimp for their friends and sing songs to frustrate lovers . . . No decent exhibitor with any pride for his profession or any self-respect should exhibit it in his theatre.

However, no exhibitor took heed, and they all exhibited the film. It was a runaway success and was officially declared a 'big hit' by the film trade. By and large, critics lauded Dilip

Kumar's role as Suraj, except of course for Baburao Patel who wrote: '... Dilip Kumar as Suraj looks the average college boy but a poor hero—indeed very poor. He tries to do his bit, but he doesn't match well with Noor Jehan. Dilip however speaks his dialogues well.'[7]

On the other hand, the *Times of India,* in its edition of 16 October 1948, carried a review of the censored version by its film critic Clare Mendonça and wrote about Dilip Kumar: 'He improves with every picture. He plays his role with an unconscious art which creates an impression of naturalness, that is great acting.'

Writing in the film magazine *Star & Style,* 23 October 1948, film journalist and author Bunny Reuben wrote:

Here was the first indication of the irresistible Dilip Kumar, who went on to develop his individual and distinct style. He spoke dialogues colloquially—naturally, effortlessly and with casual inflexions, the occasional stumblings, the occasional throwaway manner of delivering scenically significant dialogues . . . The cadences were measured and the impact on the audiences was mesmerizing. And watch how the manner of his dialogue delivery matches his facial expression, watch every shadow of a thought, an emotion, a desire left unexpressed, flit across his face.

As mentioned earlier, whatever the critics said, negative or positive, about *Jugnu,* about Dilip Kumar's performance, lady luck had finally smiled on him. As they say nothing succeeds like success and the fact was that one and all knew, Dilip Kumar had 'arrived' to soon become the numero uno.

The music of the film was by Feroz Nizami, who after Partition of 1947 shifted to Pakistan, where he carried on in cinema. Of the lyrics of Tanvir Naqvi and Asghar Sarhadi for eight songs, four were sung solo by Noor Jehan, one by

Mohammad Rafi, and a solo each by Shamshad Begum and Roshanara Begum. Each song, based on Raag Desh and Raag Yaman, respectively, became popular, with the biggest hits being the Tanvir Naqvi lyrics sung by Rafi and Noor Jehan:

Yahan badla wafaa ka bewafai ke siwa kya hai
Mohabbat kar ke bhi dekha, mohabbat mein bhi dhokhaa hai

(Here, the revenge for loyalty is disloyalty
I tried love also but there is deception in it too.)

As also the Asghar Sarhadi written, Noor Jehan solo:

Hamein to sham-e-gham mein katni hai zindagi apni
Jahan woh hain wahin ai chand le jaa chandani apni

(I have to spend my life in the sorrow of the evening wherever he be, ye moon take your light there.)

Anokha Pyar (1948)

1948 was a special year for Dilip Kumar for he had as many as five films releasing during those twelve months. The first of these was M.I. Dharamsey's *Anokha Pyar*. He was now in the top league and in this film, he was pitied against two of Hindi cinema's top actresses of the time: Nargis and Nalini Jaywant.

The story of the film revolves around Ashok (Dilip Kumar), who is an inspiring writer. One day, he comes across a flower seller, Bindiya (Nalini Jaywant), who persuades him to buy just one flower. Since he has just enough money to buy one rose, he feels sorry for her and buys it. A tramp tries to rob the money from Bindiya. While protecting her, Ashok gets hurt and loses his eyesight. Bindiya, who has fallen in love with

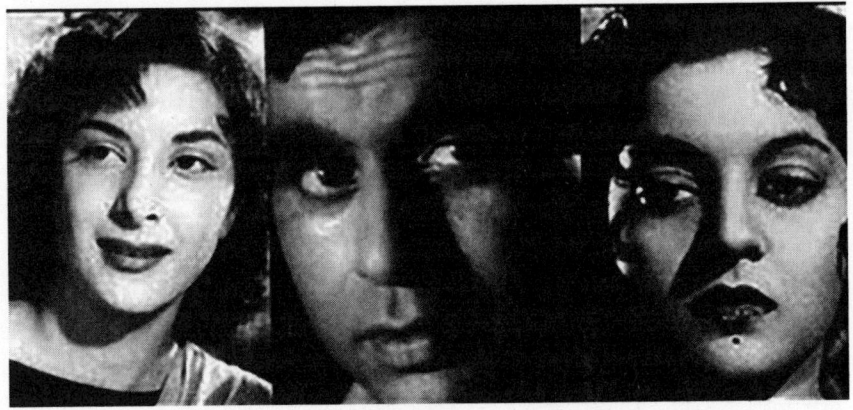

Dilip Kumar with Nargis and Nalini Jaywant in
Anokha Pyar (1948)

Ashok, escorts him to a nearby doctor's clinic for treatment. There, Ashok meets Geeta (Nargis), the doctor's daughter, who takes care of him during his convalescence and falls in love with her.

In a story of twists and turns, Ashok is implicated in a murder case and imprisoned. It is Bindiya, who not only loves him but cares for him immensely, who manages to find a suicide note by Ashok's alleged victim. Ashok is proven to be innocent. Ashok still loves Geeta. After some more melodramatic twists in the story, Bindiya dies. Ashok and Geeta get married. Ashok's book is published and it becomes a bestseller, whereby he becomes popular.

The music for the thirteen songs in the film was composed by Anil Biswas with lyrics by Zia Sarhadi, Gopal Das Nepali, Behzad Lakhnavi and Shams Azimbadi. It was a big hit. Anil Biswas, who had already recognized Lata Mangeshkar's voice, now opened his musical doors for her by giving her six solos, one duet each with Mukesh and Meena Kapoor, who had a duet with Mukesh too.

Biswas tried out a new experiment by repeating most of the songs in different voices. For example, the famous Raag Hamsadhwani number *Yaad rakhna chand taroon iss suhaani raat ko* (Do remember ye moon and stars this night) had two versions: one sung as a duet by Lata Mangeshkar and Mukesh and the other as a solo by Meena Kapoor. Another popular number, based on Raag Bhimpalasi, *Mera jeevan sapna toot gaya, ik musafir aa key dil ki duniya loot gaya* (Life's dream is broken, a traveller came along and robbed me of my emotional world) too had two versions: both sung solos, one by Mukesh and the other by Lata Mangeshkar. Similarly, *Aab yaad na kar bhool ja woh dil ka fasana* (Don't remember me, just forget the tale of the heart), based on Raag Bhairavi, was sung in one version as a duet by Meena Kapoor and Mukesh, and the second version solo by Lata Mangeshkar.

Despite the fact that *Anokha Pyar* had an unmatched star cast, despite the fact that the performances of each of the actors was extraordinary, despite the fact that Dharamsey's direction was brisk and despite the fact that the soundtrack was very hummable, with some of the melodies still being popular, the film ended as 'above average' at the box office.

Clare Mendonça's review in the 25 June 1949 edition of the *Times of India* commented:

> . . . as far as the acting is concerned, I frankly found no attempt, at any rate, on the part of Dilip Kumar and Nargis, both of whom appear to be content to merely amble through their none-too-exciting roles. Dilip can clearly do better but is content to act what he probably is building up for a formula of success for a type of romantic lead for which he is constantly in demand. He is typecasting himself with his dishevelled locks worn the peek-a-boo way, his down-at-heel clothes and lack-lustre air, his staccato speech, and his formless emoting. Into this particular film he has put nothing.

The biggest gain of *Anokha Pyar* was for Lata Mangeshkar. According to authors Trinetra Bajpai and Anshula Bajpai, '. . . it was Lata's voice, which attained unmatched glory. It was Anil Biswas who brought her out of the shadow of Noor Jehan, imparting her fabulous voice its own magnificent identity. Lata sang like a champion . . . a fragrant bunch of blooming melodies par excellence.'[8]

Ghar Ki Izzat (1948)

The only Dilip Kumar film, of the five released in 1948, that flopped at the box office was *Ghar Ki Izzat*, which had Mumtaz Shanti (the then 'Jubilee Girl' of cinema, who had also worked in Gyan Mukherjee's *Kismet* opposite Ashok Kumar, which was the first blockbuster of Indian cinema), Jeevan and Manorma in the cast. It was directed by Ram Daryani, who too was an alumnus of Bombay Talkies.

It was perhaps the first family drama on the conflict between orthodox parents and a noble daughter-in-law, in

Dilip Kumar with Mumtaz Shanti in *Ghar Ki Izzat* (1948)

Hindi cinema. The plot centred on the role of Roopa. Here, Dilip Kumar portrayed a typical upper-class youth, Chander, who wants to be rebellious but is unable to challenge parental authority.

Chander, who lives in a joint family and is an educated man working as a lawyer, falls in love with Roopa, a middle-class girl, and marries her without the consent of his parents. As is to be expected, the parents make Roopa's life miserable by taunting her all the time about her lowly background. Chander, unable to go against the orthodox thinking of his parents, is unable to help his wife by ensuring her dignity and happiness. Unable to take the atmosphere of animosity and hatred against his wife, he eventually leaves home for which too his mother puts the blame on Roopa, who left alone becomes more miserable.

An unhappy and totally helpless Chander takes to drinking and gambling until finally seeing the degradation of their son and the level he has fallen to, good sense prevails over his parents, and that brings Chander back. They all live happily thereafter.

Ghar Ki Izzat, like *Jwar Bhata*, *Pratima* and *Milan*, was a strong heroine-oriented subject, with Dilip Kumar cast as the usual romantic hero, simply filling the need of the character in the overall mood narration. In many ways, it was like Jubilee Kumar, Rajendra Kumar's or ever-dependable Dharmendra's roles in many such films later. For example, Rajendra Kumar in Kedar Kapoor's *Devar Bhabhi*, V.M. Vyas's *Ghar Sansar* (both released in 1958) and Yash Chopra's *Dhool Ka Phool* (1959), and Dharmendra in A. Bhim Singh's *Pooja Ke Phool* (1964) or Mohan Kumar's *Anpadh* (1962).

As mentioned above, *Ghar Ki Izzat* failed at the box office. Neither the audiences liked the film nor the critics with Baburao Patel discerning it in the February 1949 issue of his *Filmindia* as: 'Trash Supreme . . . another of those idiotic stories with reactionary content.' He shredded Dilip Kumar's performance to pieces. However, Clare Mendonça was more accommodating. In her review, she wrote in the 5 February 1949 edition of the *Times of India*: '. . . Dilip who gets better with each performance, acts more naturally as the hero, and is completely convincing.'

Some writers have maintained that for Dilip Kumar, these films constituted a period of apprenticeship. His potential was soon to be recognized, and exploited, by some of the best directors of the period.

Nadiya Ke Paar (1948)

In the same year came two more films which were to change the career of Dilip Kumar for all times to come. Both these films—Kishore Sahu's *Nadiya Ke Paar* and *Mela* by S.U. Sunny, with whom Dilip Kumar was to do the maximum number of four films—were super hits at the box office. These films celebrated the saga of unmerited love in the form of improvised love tale which established not only the dominant

Dilip Kumar and Kamini Kaushal in *Nadiya Ke Paar* (1948)

childhood love theme and the inevitable death syndrome in the cinema of Dilip Kumar but also his persona as a restless seeker of love.

Kishore Sahu was a well-known actor–director in the world of Hindi cinema who acted in twenty-two films and directed twenty films in his nearly four decades' career. Film buffs will recall his roles in films like Vijay Anand's *Guide* (1965), where he played Marco, Rosie's (Waheeda Rehman's) husband and in Dev Anand's *Haré Rama Haré Krishna* (1971) as Mr Jaiswal—father of Janice (Zeenat Aman). Winner of many awards for his directorial ventures who can ever forget his superhit film *Dil Apna Aur Preet Parai* (1960), with Meena Kumari and Raaj Kumar in the lead, and its mesmerizing music by Shankar Jaikishan to this day.

Written, produced and directed by Kishore Sahu, *Nadiya Ke Paar* depicted the immortality of love despite the huge rich–poor divide. In this film, the river is the metaphor, representing not only this divide but also the only path for the emancipation of the lovers.

A curious love affair between the young brother of a zamindar, Kumar Singh (Dilip Kumar), and a fisherwoman, Phoolwa (Kamini Kaushal), takes the lovers through a journey of socially unacceptable love, and in close embrace, they drown in a whirlpool in which their boat gets caught—a scene that was used and shot in many a film later including A. Subba Rao's Sunil Dutt–Nutan blockbuster *Milan*, in 1967.

Nadiya Ke Paar was a big box-office success in which Dilip Kumar made his mark through an eloquent display of emotions—first of joy and hope and then of suffering and despair. It also prepared him for the series of tragedies which he was able to take up after this film. Baburao Patel of *Filmindia* wrote his review in its edition of January 1949: '*Nadiya Ke Paar* is a technically attractive picture with a sparkling performance by Kamini Kaushal . . . Dilip Kumar, who plays the hero, gives his stereotyped performance and becomes boring, being seen in too many pictures recently. The boy has no new tricks left it seems.'

Clare Mendonça reviewed it for the *Times of India* (25 December 1948): '. . . Dilip Kumar as the young zamindar's brother meanders casually through a role which has no meat for an actor of his calibre.'

The music of the film was composed by C. Ramchandra to the lyrics of Moti B.A. It had eight songs, four duets of which one each was sung by Mohammad Rafi and Shamshad Begum and C. Ramchandra, and one by Lata Mangeshkar and C. Ramchandra.

Shabnam (1949)

Filmistan's musical hit *Shabnam* was the second film in which Dilip Kumar was once again paired with Kamini Kaushal. It was directed by Bibhuti Mitra.

The plot once again involves a love triangle. Heroine Shanti (Kamini Kaushal), her aged father and a young man Manoj (Dilip Kumar), are refugees fleeing Rangoon in Burma after the 1942 Japanese bombing. They try to make their way across the border to Bengal. Initially, Shanti disguises herself as a man to avoid being molested. When Manoj discovers her real identity, they fall in love, although he is ensnared by the charms of a gypsy girl (played by Paro).

During the course of their travel, Paro accepts shelter from a rich zamindar (Jeevan), who too falls in love with her. She next encounters the hero when the zamindar hosts a gypsy dance in his mansion. Manoj, too, is a part of the dancing troupe but misunderstands Shanti's presence in the mansion and views it as a betrayal on her part. However, as is to be expected, it all gets sorted out and the two lovers get united in the end.

Shabnam was indeed an 'out and out entertainer' that hit it big on the box office. 'The on-screen chemistry between Dilip Kumar and Kamini Kaushal was easily visible' and as Baburao Patel wrote in the July 1948 issue of *Filmindia*: 'Dilip Kumar is very good in the lighter moments as well as in the romantic scenes. Kamini Kaushal looks charming and gives an excellent performance. Their love scenes give a glimpse of realism and both artistes seemed to enjoy their romantic scenes.'

However, the *Times of India* critic Clare Mendonça differed and in her review of Saturday, 30 July 1948, wrote: '. . . Dilip Kumar who is just good in the first half, sharing honours with Kamini, falls away hopelessly in the latter portion, giving a performance that is tame and as unrecognizable as he is himself in his painted gypsy face and strange attire.'

Labelled as a 'Thrilling Tale of Sighs and Smiles', S.D. Burman, who by now had established himself in Hindi films because of his film *Shikari* (1946, directed by Savak B. Vacha), composed music for the film to the lyrics of Qamar Jalalabadi. It was to become his biggest hit. It had ten melodious duets sung either by Geeta Dutt or Shamshad Begum with Mukesh and five solos by Shamshad Begum and one by Geeta Dutt.

Three beauties—*Tumhare liye hue badnam* (For you I got defamed), based on Raag Darbari Kanada, by Mukesh and Shamshad Begum, their Raag Hamsadhwani-based duet *Tu mahal mein rahne wali* (You living in the palace) and that

Mukesh duet with Geeta Dutt *Qismat mein bichadna tha* (It was destined we would separate) based on Raag Desh—are still fresh in our minds. So is Geeta Dutt's Raag Bhimpalasi-based *Mera dil tadpa kar kahan chala* (Where did you go after torturing my heart). However, it was the multilingual hit song *Yeh duniya roop ki chor bacha le mere babu* (This world is a thief of the face, save me gentleman) by Shamshad Begum that was an immediate rage those days.

Arzoo (1950)

This was the fourth and last film that Kamini Kaushal did with Dilip Kumar. Written by the eminent writer and a pioneer of modern Urdu literature, Ismat Chughtai, it was directed by her husband, Shaheed Latif.

Dilip Kumar with Kamini Kaushal in *Arzoo* (1950)

Inspired by Emily Bronte's 1847 novel *Wuthering Heights*, it recounts a sad tale of childhood love turned sour due to the obsessive attitude of the hero, Badal (Dilip Kumar). Set against a rural backdrop, *Arzoo* attempts to capture the contradictions in the personalities of the hero and the heroine Kammo (Kamini Kaushal). While Badal is a typical rustic rural youth, who does nothing for a living and still wants to possess his woman, demanding her complete attention, Kammo, on the other hand, is far more logically inclined and tends to look at her world rationally. For Badal, nothing exists beyond his heart-throb Kammo, but for her, in spite of being a poor rural girl, life can be beautiful only if one can have a respectable place of one's own.

Thus, this tension-ridden and uneasy relationship between the two is further shaken when a young, city-bred zamindar pays a visit to his ancestral house in the village. Charmed by the affluent lifestyle of the zamindar, Kammo, in her innocence, tells her lover Badal that it would be nice to be rich, as poverty indeed is a curse. Badal is deeply hurt and decides to leave the village and go elsewhere and make enough money so that he can fulfil Kammo's wish to live in luxury.

The night Badal leaves the village, his family house, in which a beggar had taken refuge, catches fire and his charred body is mistaken to be that of Badal—a concept that has been used in many a film, including in Guru Dutta's 1957 masterpiece, *Pyaasa*, with some variations of course. Kammo's parents then convince her to marry the zamindar, who has developed a liking for her.

Time rolls by. On his return to the village as a rich man, Badal learns about Kammo's marriage. He is unable to come to terms with his misfortune and accuses her of betrayal. He seeks revenge and his mission in life becomes to torment her. He befriends Kammo's husband, the zamindar, and his younger sister Kamla (Shashikala) and begins a long-drawn-out process of cornering Kammo by raking up her past to make her confess that she still loves him. When the zamindar realizes that it is Badal who has been tormenting his wife, he shoots at him, but Kammo shields him and gets killed herself. In the end, Badal, the hero-turned-villain is left repenting.

In its offbeat narrative, *Arzoo* attempts to show that childhood love, as representing the static past, cannot be easily upheld in changing times and obsession with such love can lead to much pain and devastation of the body and the soul. Through its second protagonist, the zamindar, the film also underlines the transformation of the traditionally cruel feudal elite into a more humane, pro-poor and modern class in post-Independence India. But the film also glorifies the suffering of women caused by the erosion of their own independent space by male dominance.

Dilip Kumar, as the obsessive lover-turned-tormentor Badal, leaves his viewers spellbound with his rapid switching of emotions. That is the highlight of the film. At one moment, the glow of the turmoil within him is manifest in his eyes and the next moment, he conceals it with a twinkle in his eyes and a benign smile.

Arzoo had ten bewitching melodies which were aesthetically sculpted by Anil Biswas with lyrics by Majrooh Sultanpuri, Prem Dhawan and Jan Nisar Akhtar. It was with *Arzoo* that Anil Biswas introduced a non-film singer from Calcutta to the Hindi cinema—Talat Mahmood, whose velvet-toned voice was to soon become Dilip Kumar's. The melancholy number *Ai dil mujhe aisi* based on Raag Darbari Kanada evokes a sense of sadness and despondency. The setting for this song is appropriately bleak and dystopian. True to form, the 'Tragedy King' imbued the melody with his range of emotions. The mukhda is as follows:

Ai dil mujhe aisi jagah le chal jahaan koi na ho
Apna paraaya mehrbaan na mehrbaan koi na ho.

(O heart take me to such a place where there is nobody
My own folks or strangers, kind or unkind people, no one
should be there.)

Of the two stanzas that follow, the first one poignantly
reflects the despair and agony of the protagonist:

Jaakar kahin kho jaaon main
Neend aaye aur so jaaon main
Duniya mujhe dhoonden magar
Mera nishaan koi na ho.

(I shall go somewhere and lose myself
I should feel sleepy and should doze off
The world would search for me but there should be no sign
of me.)

This Talat Mahmood mesmerizing number apart, there
were the Lata Mangeshkar beauties such as *Kahan tak hum
uthayein gham* (To what point should I bear my sorrows) and
Mera naram karejwa dol gaya (My fragile heart has given up),
both based on Raag Yaman.

Unfortunately, the film failed at the box office. Baburao
Patel wrote in *Filmindia* of March 1950:

> The Latiffs Make a Mess of *Arzoo*
> Distortion of Hindu Married Life

> . . . the main reason for its failure was the distortion of
> the Hindu married life which is primarily a spiritual bond
> with gods as witnesses. Its sanctity is not only felt by the
> parties to the marriage but also by every Hindu in the

whole of India. Defiance of the spiritual sanctity of the Hindu marriage is scoffed at in the narrative and it is this disgusting aspect of *Arzoo* that has made the picture so unpopular and caused it to fail at the box-office . . . The direction of Shaheed Latif is amateurish . . . Dilip Kumar plays Badal very indifferently. He seems miles away from his situations even though Kamini sits so near to him.

Writing in the *Times of India* of Saturday, 11 February 1950, Clare Mendonça, said: 'Dilip Kumar proves an excellent foil rather than a teammate for Kamini, for with all his naturalness, his greatest asset, which he brings to the role, his studied, typed mannerisms rob his performance of all freshness and spontaneity . . . He is getting to dramatize himself too much and he does it too consciously. He is more himself than the hero of this film.'

6

NEGOTIATIONS WITH GRIEF

In Dilip Kumar's cinema, the romantic tragedies feature mourning the death of a noble human being, who is superior to other people in society but weak as far as his social milieu is concerned. His actions of insistence and endurance do not violate any humanistic norms once the postulates of romance have been established. This hero is exceptional in his society but extremely isolated and alienated. He has passions and his ability to express himself is far greater than that of ordinary people, but what he does face is social criticism. He represents a blend of the inevitable and the nonconformity with the social norms which is particular to tragedy in general. Often, it is simply a matter of being a morally strong character in an exposed position.

In literature, cinema, and theatre, the 'Tragic Hero' is concerned with a character's separation from society. And in it, the tragic hero undergoes suffering, sacrifice or death and evokes pathos in a realistic narrative. He is in a strong conflict with a ruthless figure, and he becomes a helpless victim and is often broken by a conflict between his inner and outer worlds. He can be but is not necessarily weaker than the average person; yet, he suffers severe persecution at the hands of a deranged society. He is a perfectly innocent victim excluded from human milieu.

Dilip Kumar's tragedies treated pity through intense pathos and presented him as a helpless man, which appealed

102

immensely to the audience's sympathy. The audience saw his suffering as being utterly against the long-cherished social ideas of basic humanism and justice. Second, the audience found that the happenings in their hero's life were quite similar, in some way or the other, to what it found in its own experience. A viewer felt he is, or was, or could be in the same situation sometime, as the situations are being judged by the norms of greater freedom in the narrative of a film.

In the classical period, as well as later, the highly moving death scenes enacted by Dilip Kumar, as in the climax of his fourteen films, were a singular trademark of his screen persona and the death syndrome was one of the most compelling points of excellence in his inventory of skills.

In these films, the protagonist, after undergoing an unending struggle and suffering to uphold his convictions, meets his death virtually, as if he is on a sacrificial altar, including death as the final culmination of the tragic journey in love and life at large. In fact, many characters played by Dilip Kumar, at least, in the classical period, tended to show that irrespective of whether one is rich or poor, young or old, life is essentially futile; it must be lost on some context or the other. As the character dissolved his identity in suffering and finally in death, it indeed became a complete annihilation of his being.

One is not sure if the death scene in his films of that period was a consciously designed ploy by the legend and his scriptwriters to precipitate the culmination of the pent-up emotional flux built up in the story and to negotiate with the already emotionally charged audience, the catharsis of suffering and sacrifice, foretold in the narrative. This culmination of the morbidity of the theme helped the audience get a sudden release from the intense melancholic experience which otherwise looked perpetual and unending.

Moreover, through death, the actor not only metaphorized a life worth living but also got the sanctity according to the Indian philosophy, held deep in the psyche of the common man, of sacrificing one's life for a cause, an act, which eventually leads to the salvation of the soul. Thus, death becomes a celebration, met through a prolonged ritual of departure, often in the arms of the dear one, and at times even with the community surrounding the dying man. No other artist, except perhaps Meena Kumari, labelled as the 'Tragedy Queen' of Indian cinema, had this ability to transform a dying character into such a complex aura of emotions.

In several films of this period, Dilip Kumar's characterizations were built around the premise of unrequited love, which defined some of the basic traits of the actor's personality on celluloid. His characterizations determined the very texture of these films.

These characters were centred on a woman's love—the compulsive longing, the short-lived victory, and the aftermath of separation, pain and suffering. They seemed to be interpreting the larger society's suffering as a personal grief. This, in essence, represented an agonized, self-pitying and self-indulgent hero who helped the viewers in releasing their own trapped emotions of helplessness and despair.

For the viewers, the inbuilt metaphor of destruction of the self and a perpetual death wish (or the inevitability of overhanging death) had the same appeal as that of the sacrifice of the hero for an intimate or a greater cause. All the situations in a film had the basic objective of creating a pensive and lugubrious character that appeared to be enjoying his pain but at the same time getting sucked into it. Thus, the source and the nature of the pain looked real and yet remained abstract.

The basic tenets of these films were inspired by the innumerable love legends in which the status quo in society was challenged and provoked through the manifestation of socially forbidden love. This love was internalized by the lovers as suffering, and they would often find their salvation only through the meeting of the souls in heaven after death. Thus, the oriental concept of sacrificing one's physical form, the body, for a cause underlined the immortality of the soul.

This unfulfilled love for the beloved in the folk tales was a central theme in the medieval Bhakti movement, whose origins can be traced to the passive response of the masses to the feudal oppression. The ultimate emancipation was portrayed as an unending internal suffering against the oppressors. The suffering was rationalized through a greater vision of life in which seeking the attention of the beloved was presented as the sole purpose of life. It did not matter whether one was in the arms of the beloved or was going through separation and suffering.

In these films, childhood love had central importance, located invariably against the backdrop of aristocracy and common people divide. The innocent and delicate craving between two young souls would always become a victim of the tyranny of family elders and subsequently of social inequalities. As childhood lovers reached adulthood, they would carry with them the intense childhood infatuation and undergo the agony of separation, which often found solace in death.

Dilip Kumar's persona in this period also had another dimension—the one-way love syndrome, which soon was to become a typical feature of Indian cinema. This love was perceived by the sufferer as his only emancipation, virtually the essence of his existence. And it took a different form in different films.

Mela (1948)

After the success of Kishore Sahu's *Nadiya Ke Paar*, came the fourth Dilip Kumar film to be released in 1948—the legendary film-maker, S.U. Sunny's epic musical *Mela*, a film that was to break numerous records at the box office. It brought together the megastars of the times: Nargis in the female lead opposite Dilip Kumar. It also brought together, for the first time, music director Naushad for a Dilip Kumar film, which was to have Shakeel Badayuni as the lyricist and writer Azm Bazidpur, who went on to work in many of Dilip Kumar starrers during the 1950s. Coupled with them were singers Mukesh and Shamshad Begum to complete the musical magic.

A disciple of A.R. Kardar, Sunny started as an assistant at Kardar studios, eventually becoming a director with *Namaste* in 1943. Like his master's films, Sunny's movies too were characterized by the use of conflicting spaces around

Dilip Kumar and Nargis in *Mela* (1948)

characters in an otherwise direct narrative, neo-classical décor, heavy lighting and a haunting effect further extended by the grandeur of the highly successful musical score provided in all his films by Naushad and lyrics by Shakeel Badayuni. Sunny has the credit of directing the highest number of Dilip Kumar films—four: *Mela* (1948), *Babul* (1950), *Uran Khatola* (1955) and *Kohinoor* (1960)—all of which were highly successful at the box office, with *Kohinoor* being a 'blockbuster'.

In *Mela*, the theme once again is of unfulfilled love and separated lovers.

Set against a rural backdrop, two adolescent lovers, Mohan (Dilip Kumar) and Manju (Nargis), serenade each other, unaware of the cruel and harsh world around them. They represent their love in the form of a pair of mud dolls, living happily in a small mud house, and enter into a pact of upholding their love at all costs. But the resourceful villain (Jeevan), presented as a city-returned conman, creates havoc in their innocent lives. When the lovers decide to recast their love into a marriage bond, Mohan goes to the nearby town to buy jewellery for his to-be bride. But on the way, he is robbed and beaten up and is admitted to a hospital with serious injuries. In the village, the panchayat forces Manju to marry an old widower who wants a wife to look after his young children. After getting discharged from the hospital, Mohan makes his way home singing. The song sequence here shows a rural landscape with the anguished hero (Dilip Kumar) riding a bullock cart while the palanquin carrying the heroine Nargis (born Fatima Rashid), married to someone else, passes by in the opposite direction along with her retinue. He is seen singing the famous Shakeel Badayuni-penned and Naushad-tuned number whose opening stanza (mukhda) is:

Dilip Kumar and Nargis in *Mela* (1948)

Gaaye ja geet milan ke tu apni lagan ke
Sajan ghar jaana hai.

(Keeping on singing songs about coming together and
about your dedication [to love]
You have to go to your beloved's house.)

Of the three stanzas (or antaras) that follow, the first one is
really poignant (as the poetry just flows on and on):

Kaahe chalke nainon ki gagri, kaahe barse jal
Tujh bin sooni saajan ki nagri, pardesiya ghar chal
Pyaase hain deep gagan ke tere darshan ke
Sajan ghar jaana hai.

(Why does the pitcher of the eyes overflow, why is water
pouring [from the eyes]

Without you, your beloved's town is deserted, o stranger
please come home
The lamps of the sky are thirsty [eager] to see you.)

He reaches home only to discover the whole edifice of his
love mercilessly broken down. He keeps moaning *Yeh kya ho
gaya? Bachpan ke khel, jawani ke vaade, sab khatam ho gaye!
Manju chali gayi. Iska ghar bhi chala gaya! Yeh kyun reh gaya?
Ise bhi barbad hona hoga*! (What has this happened? The
games of childhood, the promises of adulthood, everything
has been destroyed! Manju has gone. Her house is also gone.
Why has this survived? This too shall be destructed!)

Completely distraught, Mohan breaks the dolls and the
mud house. Yet, he keeps on cherishing the broken *gudiya*
(doll), which he keeps in a basket. However, one day, he loses
the basket while trying to save Manju's husband, who suffers
a heart attack. On realizing his loss, he goes to Manju's house
and inquires, if by any chance he had left it behind: *Us pitari
mein meri poonji thi. Uske kho jaane se mera sab kuch kho
jayega! Bhagwan ke liye batayyen ki woh yahan to nahin
rah gaya?* (My wealth was in that basket. With its loss, I lose
everything I had! For God's sake, tell me I left it behind here?)
And when, from inside the house, Manju sends the basket
containing the broken doll, Mohan is overjoyed and moved
by this gesture: *Aap ne meri khoyi hui zindagi wapas de di.
Unhen kehna, khilonoo se khelnewale ek pagal ne unhen
pranam kaha hai*! (You have returned my lost life. Tell her, a
mad man, who plays with toys, sends his greetings).

However, Mohan misses Manju all the time. This pathos
of lost love is captured in the beauty of a song: *Mera dil
todne wale mere dil ki dua lena* (My blessings to the one who
broke my heart). After Manju loses her husband, Basanti—
his friend—asks Mohan to accept the widowed Manju. He
refuses, as it would bring a bad name to her.

On a stormy night, extremely sad, Mohan sings, imploring Manju to come to him: *Dharti ko akash pukare, aa ja aa ja prem ke dwaare, aana hi hoga* (based on Raag Asavari; The sky is calling the earth, come to the door of love, you have to come). Manju reluctantly starts to walk from her home in the storm, but unfortunately, on the way falls off a cliff and dies. Mohan holds her body in his arms and says to her about the eternal upholding of their love: *Zindagi ki dor tut gayi, par Manju mohabbat ki dor nahi tuti. Tum duniya ke liye mar gayi, par mere liye zinda ho aur hamesha zinda rahogi. Aab tumhe kohi nahin paa sakta hai Manju. Aaj se tum sirf meri ho, hemsha ke liye* (The thread of life has broken, but the thread of love has not broken. You have died for the world, but for me, you are alive, will always remain alive. Nobody can claim you to be his now, Manju. From today onwards, you are just mine, forever).

Mohan is accused of murdering her and is sentenced to twenty years' imprisonment. Two decades later, after release, he goes to the same place where Manju had breathed her last. He sees her spirit, which beckons him to follow her. As he moves towards her, he falls off the same cliff and dies. The lovers thus are seen upholding their pact of love.

Within this simple narrative, the director shows that life is a mere passage of time in which the only meaningful existence is to live for eternal love.

It was a brilliant portrayal by Dilip Kumar. According to authors Trinetra Bajpai and Anshula Bajpai:

The handsomeness of young Dilip Kumar of *Mela* reflected in his facial anatomy, his forehead, his expressions, his magical voice and his whole being. It created a fresh image of the screen hero which at once caught the fancy of the audiences. Thus, out of Mela came a youthful screen image of a hero passionately in love with love, life and tragedy—

all of which Dilip Kumar, then just 25 years old, came to personify. A legend began taking shape. A star was born.[1]

Though the film was a big hit at the box office, Baburao Patel, once again, as all too often earlier too, was not complimentary in his review of November 1948 in *Filmindia*: '*Mela* is a bad rehash of *Rattan* and as such presents a very familiar story which the spectators themselves can complete at any stage of the picture . . . *Mela* is far from being sensible. It is once stupid and reactionary . . . Dilip Kumar plays the hero Mohan and does the job well.'

However, as in the past, Clare Mendonça was more balanced and wrote in the *Times of India*'s edition of 23 October 1948: ' . . . Dilip Kumar puts out a really fine performance, natural as he is permitted to be in a role so greatly misconceived. He should counter the tendency to keep his mouth half-open. With his facial configuration, it gives him an adenoidal look which sits ill on heroes. And, for a word of personal advice, he should resist all directorial blandishment in future and decline to commit suicide for all the tea in China—for some time at any rate.'

Author Lord Meghnad Desai commented, 'A week story was camouflaged by the stunning melodies of Naushad.'[2]

Yes, the music became immensely popular, and it was described as 'Naushad's Golden Jubilee' (completing fifty weeks of a film running at a stretch in a cinema hall). These rhapsodies comprised the immortal Mukesh number: *Gaaye ja geet e milan ke tu apni lagan ke, sajan ghar jaana hai* (Keep singing songs of reunion, of your love, you are going to your beloved's home), based on Raag Bhairavi—a favourite of many music composers, especially Shankar–Jaikishen. Then there are the evergreen beauties in the hypnotic voice of Shamshad Begum, *Mera dil toodne wale* (You broke my heart) and the duets with Mukesh, *Dharti ko akash pukare, aa ja aa ja prem dwaare, aana hi hoga* (The sky is calling the earth, come to the door of love, you have to come), based on Raag Asavari, and *Taqdeer bani ban kar bigdi* (Destiny was made and unmade) in Raag Darbari Kanada. Another favourite is the Raag Darbari Kanada-tuned *Main bhanwara tu hai phool* (I am a bumble-bee, you a flower) in Raag Asavari.

Of the twelve songs in the film, Mohammad Rafi has just one solo—the title song—which was picturized on one Rafiq Arbi, in a typical village fair scene. This song consists of a mukhda and three antaras in the same tune with an interlude tune in-between. The mukhda reads: *Yeh zindagi ke mele, duniya mein kam na honge, afsoos hum na honge* in Raag Yaman (The fairs of life will not lessen, although regrettably, we shall no longer be there). Of the three stanzas, the essence of the song is summed up in the very first one:

Ek din padaega jaana
Kya waqt kya zamana?
Sub kuch yahan rahega
Koi na saath dega
Jaayenga hum akele

(One day, we have to go [that is die]
What of time and what of the world?
Everything will remain here
Nothing will accompany us
We have to go alone)

Here, lyricist Shakeel Badayuni has underscored the transience of life tellingly in just a few lines. Naushad's undulating tune moves in the form of a gentle wave. Rafi's inflexion of voice (especially in the last line of each stanza, when his voice stretches out the last syllable of the last word; probably a deft Naushdian touch) and his superb rendition evoke an admiration even though over seventy-five years have gone by.

There is no doubt about the fact that 'Naushad was among the most free-wheeling of our music composers—one ready to experiment, a trait accounting for his splendidly consistent success, unprecedented in the film industry. Admittedly, his humility in the face of such singular achievement became a more pronounced happening later in his career when his clout was no longer what it used to be . . . The seven letters in his name Naushad are like the seven notes of Hindustani music—his is a stately persona setting him apart as the auteur of cinesangeet. Unmatched in his finesse has been his virtuoso's virtusos.'[3]

Mela was personally also a memorable film for Dilip Kumar, as it was the beginning of an enduring friendship with 'Naushad Miyan', who had soon become a family member in his large household and 'became a close friend of Aghajee (Dilip Kumar's father), who never ceased to admire his good looks and his natural noble bearings. Naushad Miyan was one of the few regular visitors he truly got along with and what made the bonding easy for Aghajee was Naushad Miyan's ability to regale him with impromptu recitations of good meaningful Urdu ghazals and poetry,' recalled Dilip Kumar.[4]

Jogan (1950)

If ever a list of 'Indian Classic Films' that needs to be revisited is drawn up, Kidar Sharma's *Jogan* will certainly be on the top. Considered one of the classics of the times, the film presents a highly intricate debate of the two possibilities of human emancipation: spiritual solace through *bhakti* (devotion) and the realization of a blissful state through suffering in love, both having an eternal quality of their own. In fact, in its spiritual context, the film attempts to juxtapose the two traditions of

Dilip Kumar and Nargis in *Jogan* (1950)

Bhakti and Sufism (mystical Islamic belief and practice to seek the truth of divine love and knowledge through direct personal experience of the Divine).

The heroine, Surabhi (Nargis), is a young poetess waiting for the arrival of her ideal handsome lover, whom she keeps referring to in her poetry. But when her debt-ridden father and alcoholic brother fix her marriage with an old zamindar, she runs away, becomes a *sanyasin* (hermit) and thus seeks to give up her romantic dream about the ideal lover through bhakti. Virtually depicting the sixteenth-century saint-poetess Meerabai incarnate, Surabhi goes in quest of Lord Krishna, but supresses her desire for her real seeker in life.

While visiting his aunt's village, Vijay (Dilip Kumar) hears a captivating voice singing Meerabai's bhajan *Goonghat ke pat khol tohe piya milenge* (Open the veil and you will find your beloved) in the temple. The voice and the singer's beauty instantly bewitch him. Undeterred by her austere demeanour and air of melancholy, he feels compelled to speak to her, eager to understand what led her to renounce the world. What he doesn't realize is that his presence unsettles the delicate peace she has fought to preserve. Despite her protests, he keeps following her to her *kirtan* (devotional singing) assemblies, where she sings the songs penned by Meerabai. Once when the mendicant falls sick, she confines herself to her room in the temple and keeps the door closed, outside which Vijay places a fresh flower, every day. After she partially recovers, she decides to leave, unnerved by the constant seeking by the hero for an intimate interaction. Vijay asks for her notebook in which she writes poetry but she refuses to give it to him.

When she leaves, she prohibits Vijay from crossing the banyan tree at the end of the village. She goes away and takes her final refuge in the ashram of her *guru-mata* (the spiritual mother) where she begins praying and fasting. Because of her unending *tapasya* (penance) for self-purification, she falls seriously sick. Months later, when she is about to die, she tells a fellow colleague: 'After I die, please go in the direction of that village. On reaching the big banyan tree, you will find a man sitting there. Please give this notebook to him.'

The colleague indeed finds Vijay waiting by the tree and hands over the notebook to him. Thus, by presenting her poetry to her seeker before dying, the *jogan* (ascetic) pays tribute to her lover and finally achieves *moksha*, or liberation from physical existence.

Thus, we see that the heroine, Nargis, in her bhakti wants to annihilate herself to be one with the Creator, while the hero, Dilip Kumar, who gives the most powerful portrayal of a one-way love seeker, enjoys the pain of separation from his *beloved* so that the pain becomes his being.

Looking at the theme deeper, film director Kidar Sharma built in this conflict the spiritual transformation of the male seeker, who seeks solace in pursuing the woman he desires not only in cajoling her to accept him but through his own self-realization.

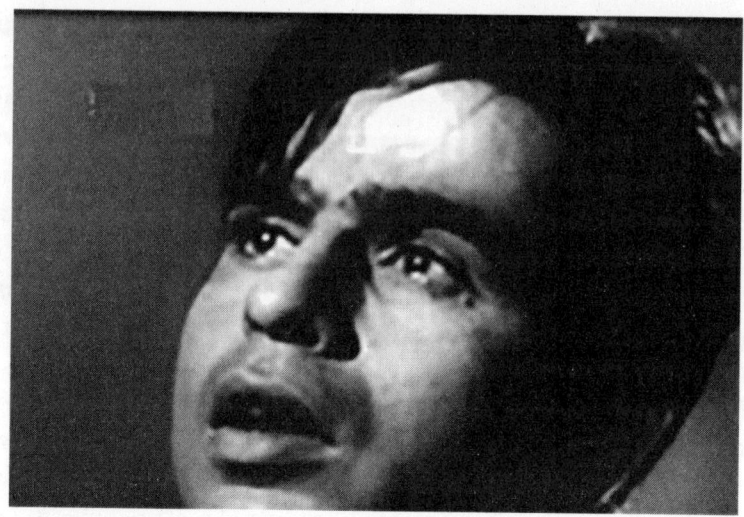

Dilip Kumar in *Jogan* (1950)

The film allegorically shows the man–woman relationship in the context of the spiritual and physical world, in which the separation between the two worlds is represented by the banyan tree as the last boundary of the world—the village. The hero, on the other hand, becomes a saint, so to say, in his own right, as he accepts the pain caused by the separation from his object of adulation, while the heroine pursues eternal peace (Om Shanti) and finds it only in death.

Kidar Sharma, the maker of some offbeat films, was considered a genius par excellence. Working in Calcutta in New Theatres's *Devdas* (1935), as a scenarist, it was he who pioneered a 'de-theatrical' style of dialogue writing. In contrast with the realist school, his cinema largely focused on the spiritual power of eternal love and the possibility of emancipation of souls through separation and suffering. His famous trilogy—*Neel Kamal* (1947), *Bawre Nain* (1950) and *Jogan*—indicates not only a complete break with the formalistic melodrama but also his striking ability to explore complex themes using mystical imagery and an original musical score as also a strong sense of picturization.

In *Jogan*, he employed the convolution of spaces to express his classical romantic idiom. While the heroine has defined her space of autonomy, the hero keeps on moving his space in relation to hers, but her refusals constantly make him feel suffocated and imprisoned. This is indicated by his continually peeping into the temple where she sings bhajans for the people, the way he keeps on offering a flower every day outside the closed door of her room and when the heroine declares the banyan tree as the final point where the space of her seeker ends.

If one were to study the film deeply, what stands out are the portrayals of Dilip Kumar and Nargis. Film buffs may remember the scene where Vijay conducts a discourse with the jogan about love, spirituality and the essentiality and eternality of pain in human life. And, upset by the never-ending pursuit by the lover, the jogan, while leaving the village to go to her ashram, asks Vijay to never cross the banyan tree at the end of the village, which makes the land on the other side a forbidden land for him. Simply outstanding!

Then there is the scene where after the jogan has left the village for good, a desperate Vijay in his restlessness hangs around the temple, and rushes towards the path again and again, which leads to the jogan's ashram, but every time he stops at the banyan tree and sits down, unable to bear the sadness. In one particular scene, at a *kotha* (brothel) where Vijay is with his friend (Rajendra Kumar) to listen to a courtesan, Vijay says: '*Aurat aur mard ke talukat hamesha wohi nahi hote jo tum log sochte ho. Kuch aur baatein bhi aisi hoti hain jin mein kashish hoti hai*' (The relationship between a man and woman is not always what you think it is. There can be other kinds of allures also). Hence, we see that Vijay's fascination with the serene ascetic is spiritual, even though he is not a religious man. And, of course, the scene where Vijay is shocked when he learns about the demise of the jogan.

In *Jogan*, the line between acting and living is indeed thin creating some unforgettable moments which give the viewers, a taste of exhilarating experience of elegance and grace, of sophistication and classicism.

Directed with rare sensitivity, *Jogan* enabled Dilip Kumar to further refine his ability to underplay the character and engage the audience in an enlightening experience far more profound in content and treatment than in his other films of the period.

This was one film which was highly appreciated by the masses as also the media. Reviewing it for the *Times of India*, Clare Mendonça wrote in the edition of 6 May 1950: '. . . Dilip Kumar, who, is also [like Nargis] in a different role than any of his before, acts with a true sympathy and a dignity which lifts the character to a high-level of the heroine and the story.'

This must be the only film ever, in which the credit for writer is given as: '?' Apparently, the owner of Ranjit Studios, also known as Ranjit Movietone, Chandulal Shah, had an idea of a man falling in love with a *sadhvi* (hermit). It was indeed a risky subject for a film, a subject no director perhaps would agree to touch. Kidar Sharma decided to take it up and the result was *Jogan*.

The music by Bulo C. Rani complemented the film with its fifteen songs, including the Meerabi bhajans sung hauntingly by Geeta Roy (later Dutt), which were the best ever composed by Bulo Rani. Even today, they have the same beauty as one hears any of them being played or sung at various religious and spiritual gatherings regularly by all sorts of different voices: *Goonghat ke pat khol tohe piya milenga* (based on Raag Darbari merging into Jaunpuri); *Mat jaa, mat jaa jogi, panv padoon mai tore* (Don't go ascetic, I fall at your feet) in Raag Bhairavi; *Daaro re rang daaro re rasiyaa* (Throw colour on me and colour my beloved) in Raag Tilak Kamod; the Raag Yaman-based *Pyaare darshan deejo aaj tum bin raho naa jaae* (O dear one let me catch sight of you; today I cannot live without you); *Aaeri main toh prem deewani, mera dard na jaane koi* (I am besotted in love; nobody understands my agony) in Raag Jogia; and *Main to Girdhar ke ghar jau Girdhar maharo sacho pritam* (I will go to Giridhar's house; he is my true beloved) in Raag Bhairavi.

They say nothing succeeds like success and 'if all mankind loves a lover', as Ralph Waldo Emerson put it, after the huge success of *Jogan*, Dilip Kumar was on a roll.

A legend had begun taking shape!

Deedar (1951)

Based loosely on Sophocles's famous Greek tragedy *Oedipus Rex*, Nitin Bose's star-studded, melancholic melody *Deedar* was released in 1951. It was an instant hit. It had besides Dilip Kumar, Ashok Kumar, Nargis, Nimmi, Yakub and baby Tabassum as the main players with the by now well-established combination of Naushad as the composer, Shakeel Badayuni as the songwriter and Mohammad Rafi lending his voice to four incredible solos. The film was Dilip Kumar's first with Ashok Kumar, who had predicted about the young actor: '*Usko dekho, khoya, khoya sa rehta hai aur chup rehta hai. Ek din sabse star hoga aur uska naam puri duniya mein phel jayega*'[5] (Look at him. He appears to be lost in thought and remains silent. But a day will come when he will become the biggest star and attain fame and recognition the world over).

'Performers, even mediocre ones respond well to a director who is understanding, sympathetic and can allay their fears. It is worth remembering here that it was under Nitin Bose that

Dilip Kumar and Nargis in *Deedar* (1951)

Dilip Kumar first honed his talent in Bombay Talkies' *Milan* and perfected a style that was to become his hallmark.[6] *Deedar* undoubtedly has one of the best-known tragic performances by Dilip Kumar which formally established his style of acting and film persona. The film evoked the Oedipus legend with blindness signifying for lost innocence as Dilip Kumar plays the role of a visually challenged singer in search of his lost childhood sweetheart.

Drawn again on the rich–poor divide, the film tracks the painful journey of poor Shammu (Dilip Kumar), who is unable to forget his childhood love, Mala (Nargis), the daughter of the landlord in whose house Shammu's mother works as a housemaid. For a riding accident in which Mala escapes being hurt, Shammu is blamed and along with his mother is thrown out of the house. The mother dies in a storm and Shammu loses his eyesight. He is rescued and brought up by Champa (Nimmi) and her canny guardian, Chaudhary (Yakub).

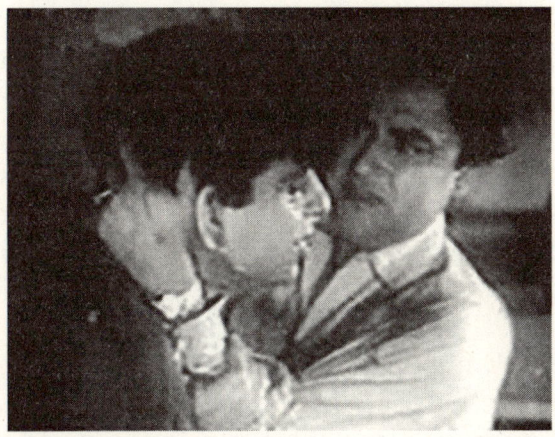

Dilip Kumar with Ashok Kumar in *Deedar* (1951)

As time goes by, Champa falls in love with Shammu, who still cannot forget Mala. He keeps wandering, singing songs in remembrance of his love, modelled loosely on K.L. Saigal's portrayal in Phani Majumdar's *Street Singer* (1938). Dr Kishore (Ashok Kumar), an eye surgeon and Mala's fiancé, is moved by the songs Shammu sings and decides to operate and restore his eyesight.

The vision restored, Shammu realizes that the love of his life, Mala, is betrothed to Dr Kishore. He pierces his eyes immediately after getting a glimpse of her. He thus avenges himself by going back into the dark alleys of his lost love and wants nothing more.

At certain levels, the film seems to be articulating the basic premise of Sufism—at last, one glimpse of the beloved!

The immense cinematic impact of *Deedar* was facilitated by Dilip Kumar's enactment of the obsessed and doomed blind lover. Nitin Bose once commented:

After *Milan*, Dilip and I got together once again for *Deedar* and everyone knows how well the film was received. It was a multi-starrer of those days with Dilip, Nargis, Nimmi, Ashok Kumar, Yakub and others. But they were all chosen because of their suitability for the respective roles. In the four years' gap between *Milan* and *Deedar*, I noticed how Dilip had grown as an artist by leaps and bounds. Dilip was never oversure of himself and could understand my needs with a minimum of explanation. I have never come across any other artist who could absorb everything so well.[7]

'Nitin Bose's impeccable craftsmanship was mixed with a strong romantic-humanistic streak that set his films apart and earned him a special place of his own in the world of cinema.'[8] As mentioned earlier too, when in 1960–61, Dilip Kumar wrote the story of *Gunga Jumna* and decided to make the film, he chose Bose as the director, though later he admitted that much of the film was directed by him.

Dilip Kumar may have played a blind man in the film, but it was one whose eyes were open. To study the blind, on a visit to the blind school, he realized that everyone's eyes were closed which was not what he was looking for. As he himself recounted, 'I was looking for a blind man who has his eyes open . . . for the life of me I couldn't spot one, not even in the school for the blind. I went here, there, all over Bombay, but failed.' Finally, it was Ashok Kumar who advised him to 'go to Mahalaxmi, where at the end of the bridge you will find a blind beggar, whose eyes are open. Observe him carefully'.

He did as he was advised and spent a few days with the beggar 'to get an insight into the world within him. I noticed that he was very pleasant and would laugh at the blindness around him. From him I learned to be cheerful and thus had that beatific smile on my face in *Deedar*', recalled Dilip Kumar.[9]

Look at those gut-wrenching scenes from the film which are perfect acting lessons for anyone—blind Shammu, lost as ever in the remembrance of his childhood love sings agonizingly in the streets *Hue hum jink ke liye barbad* (For whom I was ruined), in Raag Bhairavi, which is as engrossing as the other Mohammad Rafi songs in the film, like for instance the Raag Yaman-based *Naseeb dar pe tere aazmaane aaya hoon* (I have come to try my luck at your door), but more complicated vis-à-vis the tune and the lyrics. Then there is that scene on the horse cart where Shammu, sitting with Dr Kishore and Mala, starts singing with much passion and pain the song he and Mala used to sing in their childhood: *Bachpan ke din bhula na dena, aaj hanse kal rula na dena* (Do not forget the childhood days, today we laugh, don't make me cry tomorrow)—a Raag Kafi song that was recorded separately in the voices of Shamshad Begum and Lata Mangeshkar too. There is also that unforgettable scene where Shammu talks to Mala about his final *deedar* (physical look) of her to fill up his heart forever: *Ji bhar kar dekh to lun* (Let me see you to my heart's content). And then after having a glimpse of his childhood love, Shammu carries out a long introspection of his fate and then destroys his eyes by piercing himself.

However, the most captivating song is *Meri kahani bhulne waale* (Who has forgotten my story), which he sings after he has been operated upon by Dr Kishore and has regained his eyesight—a passionate tribute to his lost love, Mala. The song, based on Raag Tilang, comprises the mukhda and two antaras, each in a different tune. Although it is in the second antara that Rafi's voice mellifluously soars to reach a peak, it is the first antara that imaginatively highlights the protagonist's predicament. The mukhda evocatively declares:

Meri kahani bhulne waale
Tera jahaan aabaad rahe
Teri khushi par main mitt jaoon
Duniya meri barbaad rahe

(The one who has forgotten my story
May your world be prosperous
For your happiness, I shall sacrifice myself
May my world be ruined.)

The first antara runs thus:

Mere geet sune duniya ne magar
Mera dard koi naa jaan saka
Ek tera sahaara tha dil ko
Tu bhi naa mujhe pechaan saka
Bachpan key woh geet purane
Aaj tujhe naa yaad rahe
Meri kahaani . . .

(The world has heard my songs
But no one could understand my pain
Yours was my only support
But even you could not recognize me
Those old ditties of our childhood
You may not remember today.)

Naushad's heart-rending tunes which became timeless, Shakeel's plaintive shayiri and Mohammad Rafi's anguish-filled renditions reflect compellingly the plight of a broken heart.

In all this, one can't forget the Lata beauty *Le jaa meri duyain le ja* (Take my blessings; composed in Raag Desh).

With *Deedar,* Dilip Kumar had now starred in fifteen iconic films, each adding to his repertoire of romantic tragedies that swiftly cemented his status as the quintessential epitome of unrequited love. This portrayal became so deeply ingrained in the public consciousness that millions of hearts resonated with his enduring rejection, separation, betrayal, and more often than not, even in his eventual demise. In the dim ambience of the cinema halls, audiences of all ages were moved to tears by his incredible performances. It is a heart-felt salute to Dilip Kumar's legacy, which allowed the audience to grieve alongside Shammu, thus strengthening the connect between him and the viewers. Award-winning author and poet Vikram Seth captured this phenomenon in his 1993 novel *A Suitable Boy*: 'Spectators watching it burst into tears and the people who couldn't get tickets start a riot.' Dilip Kumar had indeed transcended into a profound and enigmatic cultural icon, his essence deepening and becoming more enigmatic over time.

Hulchul (1951)

Though just about a moderate success, S.K. Ojha's *Hulchul* was another saga of the plight of childhood love and the tragic social prosecution of the hero till his death. The film, like many others of its time, depicted the cruel exploitation of the discontented rural migrants by the urban neo-rich to make quick money and alluring them to join in the big crime syndicates. Besides Dilip Kumar, the film had Nargis in the female lead, with Balraj Sahni and dancer Sitara Devi in the cast.

Kishore (Dilip Kumar) is a poor chap in love with the landlord's daughter, Asha (Nargis), whose family rejects him because of his poverty. He vows to become rich and only then ask for the hand of Asha, whom he loves dearly.

Dilip Kumar in *Hulchul* (1951)

Kishore goes to the city and is forced to take up the job of a 'burning man' in a circus. In every show, he would douse himself with fire and jump from a height into the well below. The owner of the circus, Madame Neelam (dancer Sitara Devi), falls in love with him. In a twist of fate, Kishore is accused of a murder and imprisoned, while Asha is married off to the jailor (Balraj Sahni), who develops sympathy for the young prisoner. When the desperate lover comes to know that he has lost the love of his life, he dies of shock.

Hulchul once again reaffirmed Dilip Kumar's excellence in portraying the obsessed lover who takes the cruelties around him with immense inner strength but finally manifests his obsession into inevitable death. In the tragic climax, the heartbroken hero, after seeing that his beloved is now married, falls and rolls down the staircase. The disgruntled lover slowly gets up and climbs up the stairs to go near the heroine, Asha, in a delirious state and unbearable pain but rolls down again and meets his death.

There were many outstanding scenes in the film including when the landlord humiliates Kishore about his lowly status while he painfully bears it and later when fed up with his constant ill-treatment, he prepares to leave assuring Asha of his love: '*Main tumaare liye hi to jaa raha hoon, Asha*' (I am going for your sake, Asha). And if the death scene at the end was amazing, no less outstanding was the confrontation of the lover with the beloved after her marriage: '*Meri zindagi to usi din tabaah ho gayi thi jis din tum mujh se door ho gayi thi ... mere paas aa, mera dum ghoota ja raha hai*' (My life was destroyed the day you went away from me ... come closer to me, I am feeling suffocated).

The critics were all praise for Dilip Kumar's acting. Clare Mendonça reviewed it for the *Times of India* of 17 February 1951: 'Dilip Kumar, gives a remarkably good performance which is deeply stirring in its expression of pathos, grief, gratitude and despair.'

The fearsome critic Baburao Patel commented in the 1951 March issue of *Filmindia*: 'A touching tale of love told in songs and sighs and wound up in tragedy . . . A classic performance in which he (Dilip Kumar) lives his role from scene to scene and attains frightening realism in the climax.'

Tarana (1951)

By the time Ram Daryani's musical *Tarana* was announced, Dilip Kumar—suave, handsome, serious-minded and actor par excellence, with box-office hits such *Mela*, *Shaheed*, *Babul*, *Deedar* and *Jogan*, among others—was the uncrowned king of Hindi cinema. Having worked under the direction of the top directors of the day like Amiya Chakravarty, Nitin Bose, Syed Shaukat Hussain Rizvi, S.U. Sunny as well as with all the established actresses of the times—Noor Jehan, Nargis,

Dilip Kumar and Madhubala in *Tarana* (1951)

Kamini Kaushal and Nimmi—he was now to co-star with Madhubala, who had skyrocketed to fame the previous year with Kamal Amrohi's psychological supernatural horror film *Mahal* (1949), which had Ashok Kumar in the lead

Devika Rani's discoveries both, this star pair would soon capture the heart of the nation and become legendary for they made a great romantic team and triumphed together. The young Madhubala spoke to her sisters of her new co-star: '. . . there's a luminous magnetism in his eyes like they have been filled with crushed pearls . . . you look at him once and your eyes become rooted; you cannot take your gaze away.'[10] A lyrical description, it was from a girl completely in love!

However, this was not the first film in which Dilip Kumar and Madhubala worked together. Before that, in 1949, there was another picture—Mahesh Kaul's *Haar Singhar*—in which

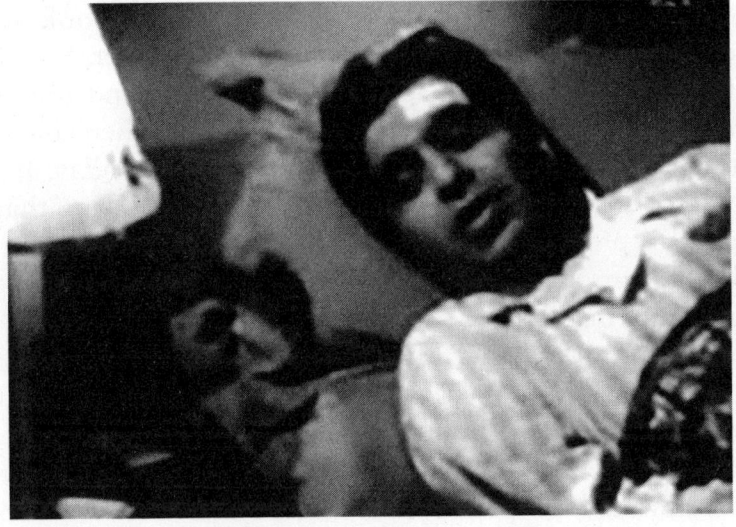

Dilip Kumar in *Tarana* (1951)

Madhubala and Dilip Kumar had shot many scenes together, but the film was soon abandoned.

Tarana was a saga dedicated to the ideals of platonic love set in both the class and urban–rural divides. A young doctor, Motilal (Dilip Kumar), on his return flight from an overseas trip gets stranded in a village as his aircraft develops a technical snag and crash lands. He is provided shelter by a blind old man, Suryadas, and his daughter, a charming village belle, Tarana (Madhubala). During the course of his stay, Moti operates on the old man and helps him regain his eyesight. And as was bound to happen in a Hindi film, Tarana and Moti fall in love.

The villain, Toteram (Gope), a rich villager, driven by his love interest in Tarana, hatches a plot to drive the doctor out of the village and in the process defiles Tarana's character. One day, while out sightseeing, Motilal falls ill and collapses much to Tarana's horror. A heavy thunderstorm ensues, in which Motilal with Tarana's help takes refuge in a village barn. This was the opportunity that Toteram was looking for. He collects the villagers, including Tarana's father, Suryadas, and goes to the barn to find the two inside and comes to the conclusion that Tarana has indeed defiled her character. Motilal is beaten up by the villagers. And Suryadas, feeling humiliated in front of the entire village and believing that his daughter is pregnant—a rumour spread by Toteram to further malign Tarana's character—in a rage burns his entire house with Tarana inside.

The injured lover is taken home by his father, who has promised his son in marriage to Sheela (Shyama), an affluent girl from the city, without Motilal's knowledge. Back home, Motilal keeps hallucinating about the return of his love, Tarana, in his life. He is told that his sweetheart is no more, having died in a fire that engulfed her house. Motilal does go back to the village and seeing the house totally burnt down, returns home in the city in despair. He opts for an arranged marriage. However, on the day of the wedding, he runs away and goes back to the village barn, where he had last been with Tarana. There, he is overjoyed to see Tarana alive.

'It was a simple love story, uncluttered by too many characters or subplots, it had nothing intrusive in the manner of dream sequences or elaborate sets, no fights nor any moral lessons to be learnt. There were no major issues to agitate over. Instead, it is the small grievances and consolations, the quick bursts of temper as quickly pacified, the ordinary flow of life, and the vivid joy of uncomplicated love that were presented so evocatively on the screen that the film continues to delight even today.

'In every scene of theirs [Dilip Kumar and Madhubala] in the film, the world watched pure romance being played out at its heart-searing best,' says Madhubala's sister, Madhur. 'It was a professional association that was waiting to turn the page and become much, much more. They were made for each other. What a pair.'[11]

According to Madhubala's biographer, Khatija Akbar: 'The aura of intimate, unalloyed happiness had never been captured by any film before or since, as it was when with a simple flick of one finger, Dilip Kumar drew Madhubala's stray lock of hair off her face, gazed into her eyes and forgot to look away. All the world loves a lover, and *Tarana*'s enduring magic is its ability to unfailingly leave its viewers with an inner glow of contentment. *Tarana* was truly symbolic of the happy times. It was pure magic. The only time love lent a rainbow to the screen.'[12]

'The substance of the story was thin in *Tarana*,' mentioned Dilip Kumar, 'but the scenes were made interesting. Hence, they stand out. The dialogue was not heavy nor full of deep meaning. It was entirely commonplace and that contributed to the success of the film in a big way. The film was made more on the lines of behavioural scenes and Madhubala stood out in that exercise. However, apart from this, she could also do a film like *Mughal-e-Azam* with its refinement and purity of language and special style of dialogue delivery . . . She could bring a sense of address to the eyes so that when you look at somebody, you *look* at them and the eye doesn't float.'[13]

About Madhubala's acting, Dilip Kumar considered Guru Dutt's *Mr. & Mrs. 55*, Ram Daryani's *Tarana* and K. Asif's *Mughal-e-Azam* the best. According to him: 'She had an obsession about her work. The aptitude and flair [were] there from the beginning. She had a lot of versatility. Had she lived, and had she selected her films with more care, she would have been far superior to her contemporaries . . . Apart from being an excellent artiste and very versatile, she had a very cheerful nature. God had gifted her with so many things.'[14]

Tarana was a huge success. The audiences loved it. The critics lauded it. In his review in the October 1951 issue of *Filmindia*, Baburao Patel, feared for his dour wit and biting sarcasm and not given to any unnecessary praise of a film or its stars, wrote:

> *Tarana*, A Scintallating [sic] Love Story
> Madhubala and Dilip Kumar Triumph Together

> . . . Talking of performances, it is difficult to separate Madhubala and Dilip Kumar. Both have almost lived their roles and their romantic sequences seem to take their hues from the real canvas of life. Madhubala gives the best performance of her screen career in this picture. She seems to have discovered her soul at last in Dilip Kumar's company. She is easily our most talented, most versatile and best-looking artiste.

So true it turned out to be, for it was with this film that the legendary Dilip Kumar–Madhubala romance started. Look at the opening scene with Dilip Kumar's monologue as he drives to the hospital in high speed: '*Musibaten bhaag kar kabhie khatam nahi hotin. Insan ko bas gheren rahti hain* (Troubles don't cease by running away. They just surround a human being), as also the scene where an unhappy and helpless Dilip Kumar as Dr Motilal seeks solace in the presence of Madhubala and says: '*Waqt thahr jaye . . . aur jab maut aaye to main tumhaari godh mein sar rakh kar so jayoon!* (May time stand still . . . and when death comes, I should put my head in your lap and go to sleep).
Coupled with these is the scene when Dilip Kumar prepares for an urgent surgery with another monologue: '*Mere haath kamp rahey they aur meri aankhon ke saamne aandhera sa aa raha tha. Mera mariz mere samne behosh pada tha. Uski*

zindagi aur maut mere haathon mein thi. Lekin ek dubta hua insan kisi dusre ko kya sahaara de sakta hai?' (My hands were trembling and there was darkness in front of my eyes. My patient was lying unconscious in front of me. His life or death was written in my hands. However, how can a sinking man give support to another being?)

The film is full of brilliantly acted and delivered monologues. Relook at the one when the much-grieved Dilip Kumar carries a monologue with himself about his love for Tarana, when his father arranges his marriage with Sheila.

If the film, packed with some passionate scenes between the lead pair which caught the fancy of the audiences, was a big success, credit should also go to Anil Biswas for composing the music to the lyrics of D.N. Madhok and Prem Dhawan. Eyes flushed and sparkling, smiles of pure contentment . . . enchantment in the air and time standing still as Madhubala crooned, perhaps the most evocative and loveliest lullaby ever filmed—the Raag Kafi-based *Beimaan toorey nainwa nindiya na aaye, toki soye jaa ki raat kahin bhaagi na jaaye* (Your eyes are dishonest. I am unable to sleep. Go to sleep quietly so that the night does not run away), sung by Lata Mangeshkar, about whom Anil Biswas tellingly articulated: 'With the advent of Lata, for the first time I, as a composer, could feel free to create. I could mould the tune in any scale I wanted, confident in the knowledge that Lata would take the *murkis* (vocal curves) in her stride.'[15]

There are other timeless beauties in the film too such as the Lata–Talat Mahmood Raag Desh-based duet: *Nain miley nain huey banware, chain kahan mohe sajan saanware* (When the eyes met, eyes became bumblebees, now there is no peace my love), and the Raag Yaman-based Lata–Pankaj Mullick duet: *Ye raaten ye mausam ye hasnaa hasanaa, ye raaten mujhe bhul jana, inhe na bhulana* (This night, this season, this laughter, don't forget them even if you were to forget me). However, the two greatest musical ornamentations of Anil Biswas in the film were the Talat Mehmood solo (penned by D. N. Madhok) which begin with a *sher*:

Jali jo shaakh-e-chaman saath baghbaan bhi jala
Jalake mere nasheman ko aasmaan bhi jala.

(When a branch in a garden burnt, the gardener also burnt
After burning my nest, the sky [also] burnt.)

Followed by the mukhda:

Ek main hoon ek meri bekasi ki shaam hai
Ab to tujh bin zindagi bhi mujh pe ek ilzaam hai.

(I am there and with me is the evening of loneliness
Now without you life is a blemish.)

Of the two stanzas that follow, the second one subtly reveals the agony of the suffering hero:

Aansoon mujhpar hanso mere muqaddar par hanso
Ab kahan woh zindagi jiska mohabbat naam hai.

(O tears laugh at me and laugh at my destiny
Now where is that life which is called love.)

Then there is the intricately crafted Raag Yaman Kalyan-based duet so soulfully rendered by Talat Mahmood and Lata Mangeshkar:

Siney mei sulagtey hain armaan
Aankho mei udasi chhaayi hai
Ye aaj teri duniya se
Hame taqdeer kahan le aayi hai

(In my heart desires burn
My eyes are full of sadness
In your world today
Where has fate brought me.)

Yes, where had fate brought them? With *Tarana*, 'the youthful, bubbly Madhubala had placed herself at a turning from where the road went only in one direction, for when she gave her heart to her co-star, Dilip Kumar, it was for life . . . The path she was so blithely setting out on would end in extreme unhappiness, bitterness, upheavals, trauma and eventually, separation . . . a separation which was difficult to reverse.'[16] As eminent film journalist and author B.K. Karanjia commented: 'The Madhubala–Dilip Kumar romance had all the ingredients of an engrossing drama, complete with the elements of beauty, passion, misunderstandings, court scenes, sickness, and ultimate heartbreak. Only when it reached its catastrophic end, it left its scars on all its protagonists. Most of all on its heroine.'[17]

Insaniyat (1955)

Who can forget the logo comprising 'The Gemini Twins', each blowing a bugle, that appeared on the screen as a prelude to every film produced by Gemini, a household symbol at one time? It was the brainchild of the movie Mogul from south India, the legendary producer–director, S.S. Vasan, who also set up the Gemini Studios in Madras (now Chennai), which became the breeding ground for innumerable artists. Vasan made many successful films in Hindi, Tamil and Telegu. His ambitions were big and his films even bigger. Known as the Cecil B. DeMille of India, to him goes the credit of heralding a new era of the multi-starrer, period spectacles in India with *Chandralekha*, way back in 1948, based on the first chapter

Dilip Kumar and Bina Rai in *Insaniyat* (1955)

of George W.M. Reynold's novel *Robert Macaire: Or, The French Bandit in England*. Vasan showed his immense ability in blending many popular Indian folk tales and legends and projecting them on the screen.

Vasan's spectacles thus involved intricate palace intrigues and counter-intrigues, people's uprising, massive sets, elaborate song-and-dance sequences and terrific battle scenes involving thousands of people. However, beneath these spectacles was hidden Vasan's grand vision of employing cinema for a nationalist mobilization of popular culture, as reflected in his unique and honest manifesto on cinematic populism, *Pageants for our Peasants*.

Gemini's era of grand spectacles came to an end in the late 1950s, when the movie mogul made a sudden shift to the contemporary

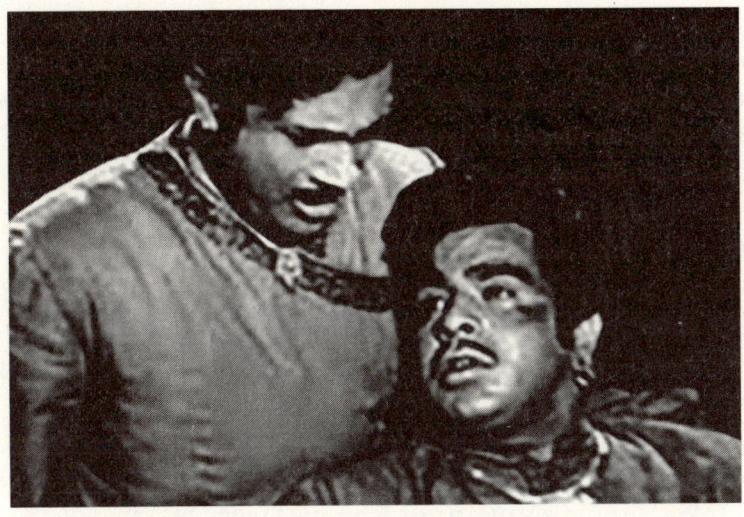

Dilip Kumar and Dev Anand in *Insaniyat* (1955)

milieu, making a series of family melodramas, on the lines of that other big and highly popular south Indian film banner, AVM (Avichi V. Meiyappa) Chetiar. Dilip Kumar's association with Gemini was highly benefitting for the actor. Both *Insaniyat* and later *Paigham* in 1959 offered to him valuable opportunities to further expand and enrich his screen persona in two entirely different domains: first, as a melancholic rural youth and then as a people's leader.

In 1955, Vasan made a remake of his 1950 Telegu film *Palletoori Pilla* in Hindi, *Insaniyat*, which had, for the first and last time, Dilip Kumar and Dev Anand. And Bina Rai as the heroine. It had music by C. Ramchandra and lyrics by Rajendra Kishen.

Dilip Kumar once again appeared as a silent lover, who this time holds the glory of his one-sided love. He not only gives up his obsession for his heart-throb, Bina Rai (who played the role of Durga), which he has been nurturing since childhood, but also transforms it into a sublimated sense of meaninglessness of life, manifesting it further in self-opted death for the well-being of the woman he loves.

The film is the story of a rural uprising against a tyrant ruler Zangura (Jayant). Mangal (Dilip Kumar) is the people's leader who also adores Durga (Bina Rai) since childhood but is unable to express his feelings. Zangura sends his loyalist Bhanu (Dev Anand) to supress the uprising. Once there, Bhanu meets Durga and falls in love with her, whose reciprocation leads to their getting married.

Mangal is shell-shocked but accepts the situation, thus suffering his loss silently. Soon, Bhanu too becomes a rebel and takes up command of the villagers in their struggle against the tyrant Zangura. Thereafter, he faces many challenges. In order to take revenge, Zangura attacks the village but is defeated. He attacks the second time and is able to capture Bhanu this time. Durga accuses Mangal of betraying her, as he has failed in saving her husband. Highly pained, Mangal reaches Zangura's fort, succeeds in freeing Bhanu but in the process of this daredevil mission loses his own life.

Insaniyat performed a significant function for Dilip Kumar, as it provided him with the basic parameters for the role of a typical rustic Indian youth—strong, upright, sensitive and a victim of circumstances. He was to later employ this model to his advantage in films such as *Naya Daur* and *Gunga Jumna*.

Reminiscent of a tribal past, the film tries to establish the transcendental nature of the man–woman relationship. This relationship is seen omnipotent as the inflicted souls move far beyond the limits of the civilizations manifesting either in death for the fortunate ones or in a life-long waiting for the beloved to be joined finally in death. Incidentally, the role of Kamal Haasan in Ramesh Sippy's *Saagar* (1985) was modelled on Dilip Kumar's role in *Insaniyat*.

The film had some outstanding scenes. Revisit that scene where Mangal becomes heart-broken when Durga tells him that she loves Bhanu. Thereafter, it is Mangal who stops Bhanu from leaving the village, as he always wanted Durga's happiness. And then there is a masterpiece of a scene in which a heart-broken Mangal makes the offering of the jewellery he had been collecting for Durga in the temple and seeks solace in his connect with God in the Mohammad Rafi sung song: *Apni chaaya mein ley mujhe* (Take me in your shadow). And who can forget that scene where Durga accuses Mangal of betraying her and her husband Bhanu?

And the last, immensely touching scene, where a seriously injured Mangal brings back Durga's son at the cost of his own life. This powerful death scene was later taken by writers Salim Javed for Yash Chopra's *Deewar* (1975), where Vijay (Amitabh Bachchan) lies breathing his last in the lap of his mother Sumitra (Nirupa Roy). Even the dialogue was the same: '*Maa, mujhe neend aa rahi hai*' (Mother, I am feeling sleepy).

The film was a blockbuster at the box office and the critics too lauded it. The film critic of the *Hindustan Times* wrote in its edition of 16 October 1955:

Gemini films have all that an extrovert would want but I go a step further to assert that this film has at least one good character role assigned to Dilip Kumar. This very popular and at the same time intelligent actor is not just a good looker as he appears in the film but plays the role of a rugged yokel with a heart of gold exceptionally well. Dilip Kumar is made to dance in village lanes and sing for all his worth and of course does a good bit of fencing. All the same, his character is that of an intensely sincere and selfless man which he reveals in a few characteristic words and gestures.

Baburao Patel commenting on the film in the December 1955 issue of *Filmindia* wrote:

A Mighty Entertainer

. . . From the players, no one comes within a mile of Dilip Kumar. In the rustic and sympathetic role of Mangal, this great artist gives one of his best portrayals on the screen. Living the rustic role from head to foot of this fast action drama, Dilip Kumar is paid a tribute of tears from the audience as he lies dying in the lap of his mother. The intense sincerity with which he has portrayed Mangal's role deserved better support from his co-artists. But this support never comes even once and at several places the wound of fury of Mangal's characterization adds only to the artist's individual stature.

Uran Khatola (1955)

An adaptation of Frank Capra's *Lost Horizon* (1937), *Uran Khatola* is the story of a pilot Kashi (Dilip Kumar), who travels by an ill-fated single-seater aircraft, which crashes on the outskirts of an isolated kingdom ruled by a young queen Raj Rani (Suryakumari). Her people worship a local god called Sangha. Kashi is saved by Soni (Nimmi), the daughter of the Peshwa, the minister of the kingdom. As is to be expected in the plot of a Hindi film, Kashi and Soni fall in love, which angers her fiancé Sanghu (Jeevan).

When Kashi goes to Raj Rani to necessarily seek her permission to settle in the kingdom, she finds him handsome and feels attracted to him and soon falls in love with him. She

Dilip Kumar and Nimmi in *Uran Khatola* (1955)

invites him to stay with her in the royal palace and sings for
him. This necessitates for Kashi and Soni to meet each other
secretly, with Soni disguised as a man, Shibhu. Thereafter, it
is one big tussle for both Soni and Raj Rani to make Kashi
her own.

On discovering the truth, Sanghu and Raj Rani conspire
to make Soni sacrifice her life so as to cool down the anger
of the storming sea which has threatened life on the island
kingdom. Kashi even pleads before the priest of the clan to
let him sacrifice his life instead of Soni. But to no avail. After
Soni's death, for years, Kashi keeps waiting for his beloved in
the belief that she will come one day as per her promise. In
this unbearable separation, the lover Kashi becomes a hermit,
grows old and finally one day, his beloved Soni comes happily
on a chariot to take him with her. He follows her in death.
Thus, the two souls finally are together.

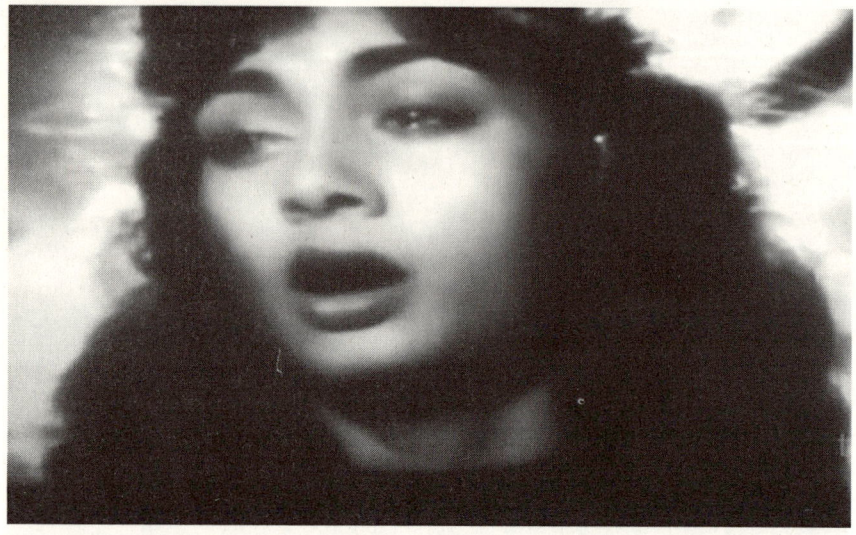

Nimmi in *Uran Khatola* (1955)

Uran Khatola, richly mounted and with an unusual backdrop and setting coupled with an exotic ambience, was a big hit at the box office. This, despite the fact that it was an out and out fantasy. 'The narrative of the film was accentuated by the lead star-cast's superlative performances and the audiences surrendered to the whole make-believe fantasy which consumed them.'

Once again, it was Naushad's musical score that adorned the film and helped it attain the level of popularity it finally did. There was an alluring array of nine songs—three Mohammad Rafi solos and six by Lata Mangeshkar, some with a chorus. Of the three Rafi solos, *Na toofan se khelo na sahil se khelo, mere paas aayo mere dil se khelo* in Raag Bhairavi (Do not play with either the coast or the shore, come near me and play with my heart) and the Raag Jaijaiwanti number *Mohabbat ki rahoon mein chalna sambhal ke, yahan jo bhi aaya gaya haath mal ke* (Tread carefully on the path of love, for whoever came here returned rubbing his hands).

However, it is the Rafi number in Raag Pahadi mixed into Raag Durga: O *door ke musafir humko bhi saath le le, hum reh gaye akele* (Oh distant traveller, do take me along with you, I am left alone) that is an unbeatable number even today because of its mystical aura and entrancing tune.

The song has been picturized by the cinematographer par excellence Jal Mistry in an almost surrealistic manner wherein the scene shows the heroine, Nimmi, walking up a bridge-like ramp, below which rages the stormy sea. As the song—lip-synched by Dilip Kumar, standing on the side of the bridge, expresses the agony of the separation as he sings the departing song for his beloved Soni, on her way to sacrifice her life to calm the roaring sea—reaches its climax, Soni reaches the edge of the bridge and jumps into the churn. It is a song every film music listener enjoys even today.

Naushad once said:

I don't think of the listener when I compose music for a film but only of the character. For example, when I was working on the music of *Uran Khatola*, to me it did not matter, yet it does matter, whether the viewer recognizes Mohammad Rafi to be performing in Raag Jaijaiwanti when his vocals sit so pat on Dilip Kumar as *Mohabbat ki rahoon mein chalna sambhal ke* or *Na toofan se khelo na sahil se kehlo, mere pass aayo mere dil se khelo* in Raag Bhairavi. As a composer you have necessarily to draw upon our classical tradition. But you have, at all times, to do so thinking of the sequence, of its place in the matrix of the theme, of the mood in which the character has to be captured.[18]

This number in Raag Pahadi has an introductory sher, as a prelude:

Chale aaj tum jahan se, huee zindagi parayee
Tumhe mil gaya thidkaana, humein maut bhi na aaye

(You are leaving the world and life has become alien
You have reached your destination, even death has not come to me.)

Naushad, the 'King of Couplets', lived as much for poetry as for music. According to him, the above song was recorded to go on Dilip Kumar, in Raag Bageshree, but the original tune was quite different. 'The situation in which the song occurred in the film was such that, unless we managed to create the optical illusion upon the screen, the whole scene would have fallen flat. Everyone was happy, even the fastidious Dilip Kumar and director S.U. Sunny. But I was not. I felt that in the tune on which the film's theme was going to stand or collapse, there was something missing.'[19]

As was his habit, Naushad thought about it day and night and finally hit upon a ghazal idea to go with the tune of the film's climax. He amended it into a geet. The lyricist Shakeel Badayuni reworked on the words. 'I rarely order a re-recording of any song of mine. But this was an exceptional case. Mohammad Rafi made *Chale aaj tum jahan sey hui zindagi pariye* happen it the end, in terms of that keynote toning with which he also invested the Raag Durga shadings in the song,' explained Naushad.[20]

No wonder Naushad swayed away first from Mukesh and then from Talat Mahmood to turn full time to Rafi.

Coming back to the songs of *Uran Khatola*, we had some mesmerizing numbers from Lata Mangeshkar too comprising: *Hamare dil se na jaana* in Raag Bihag (Don't go away from

my heart), *Na ro aye dil kahin rone se taqdeerein badalti hain*
(Don't cry o heart, do destinies change with crying?) in Raag
Bhimpalasi and *Mera salaam leja* (Take my greetings) in Raag
Desh. And the best of them all—the boatman's song, composed
by Naushad in Raag Pilu and picturized on Nimmi—*More
saiyyanji uthrehnge paar ho, nadiya dheere baho* (My beloved
will alight at the other end, river flow slowly). Shakeel
Badayuni's apposite lyrics and that lilting voice of Lata along
with Naushad's wavy notes (in tune with the situation) create
an over-worldly ambience. The unique feature of this beauty
of a song is that no orchestra was in place; only the humming
of a chorus was used. Lata's *Mera salaam le ja pardes jaane
wale* in Raag Pilu, which topped Amin Sayani's 'Binaca Geet
Mala' that year, also had Shamshad Begum in it but only to
sing *Ahahahaha*.

Do listen to it and you will understand why it is a rare
beauty!

Devdas (1955)

> *Kaun kambakht hai jo bardast karne ke liye peeta hai,*
> *Main to peeta hoon ki bas saans le sakoon*
> *Aur, aisi jagah se ud kar jaane ki takat nahin hai na*
> *Tabhi to yahan pada rehta hun*
> *Bas dekhta rehta hun tumhare moo ki taraf*

> (Which wretch drinks to tolerate
> I drink so as to be able to take a breath
> And, since I have no strength to get up and go away from
> this place
> That's why I keep on lying here
> Just looking at your face.)

Dilip Kumar and Suchitra Sen in *Devdas* (1955)

Would anyone need to be told as to which film this dialogue is from and acted and delivered by whom? Right, it is from Bimal Roy's *Devdas*, a film that marked the crowning of Dilip Kumar as the 'Tragedy King' in Indian cinema. And also, a formal recognition of his school of acting. In its essence, it mourns the inevitable destruction of a man in conflict with the prevailing feudal order, where his aimlessness and alcoholism are symbolic of an individual under the process of decay and degradation, both morally and physically.

The theme appears to be underlining the self-implicated sacrifice of a man at the altar of a woman's love and yet it is far from complex than the traditional view of puritan love and separation. Devdas (Dilip Kumar), a victim of feudal society, cannot marry his childhood love, Paro (Suchitra Sen). He rebels meekly and leaves his village and moves to Calcutta (now Kolkata) to seek solace in the urban life, wherein he takes to alcohol and meets the courtesan Chandramukhi (Vyjayanthimala), who falls in love with him.

In the end, this uncurable restlessness compels him to take recluse in a train compartment and embark on an unending journey to get rid of the hangover of his alienation and to reach someplace where he can just rest peacefully. He fails with his deteriorating health and ultimately decides to go back to his native village. However, as he is about to finally end his journey, his unfulfilled desire overtakes him; he cuts short his train journey and in a poor state of health takes a bullock cart to keep an old promise with his childhood lost love, Paro, who by now is married. But his decaying body caused by his long love for alcohol and prolonged suffering is now complete and he finds his salvation from his life-long agony only in death in Paro's village, just outside her house.

Nearly ninety works of the Bengali novelist and short-story writer Sarat Chandra Chattopadhyay have been made or adapted into motion pictures by various film-makers over the years. Celebrated as one of the most widely translated and adapted Indian authors, his writings focused on capturing the essence of Bengali life and society. Yet, his sharp observation, deep compassion, insightful grasp of human psychology, fluid writing style, and unbiased perspective made his work universally relatable, striking a chord with readers across the Indian subcontinent.

Though no comparisons are intended, Sarat Chandra is in good company of the Russian grand master Fyodor Dostoevsky, who wrote about the disgraced and deceived and was dubbed as 'a sick and cruel talent' in his lifetime.

Sarat Chandra's *Devdas*, which he wrote at the age of seventeen, has been the most favourite with film-makers and television serial producers. More than twenty films and serials have been made on this novel in India, Pakistan and Bangladesh in eight regional languages—Hindi, Urdu, Assamese, Bengali, Malayalam, Odia, Tamil and Telegu. The first version came out in 1928, as a silent film with

Phani Burma in the title role. Then in 1936, P.C. (Pramotesh Chandra) Barua made it for New Theatres, both in Hindi and Bengali, where he played the hero in the Bengali version with the singing-star Kundan Lal Saigal in the title role in the Hindi edition. It turned him and Saigal into cult figures. Bimal Roy was the cinematographer.

Then in 1955, Bimal Roy, known for his romantic-realist melodramas that took on important social issues and had already made award-winning films like *Parineeta* (1953), *Do Bigha Zamin* (1953) and *Biraj Bahu* (1954), was keen to make *Devdas*, fully aware that critics and film buffs would evoke immediate comparison with the earlier, highly acclaimed film which he had photographed. In fact, when the film was still under production, the *Hindustan Times* in its edition of Sunday, 19 June 1955, reported:

Dilip Kumar Repeating K.L. Saigal's Role

In playing the role of Devdas in the film of that name, now being made by Bimal Roy, Dilip Kumar has realized a long-cherished ambition. It was an education to watch him do the famous scenes of the film at Mohan Studios . . . Dilip must remember that in every scene of the film, he will be compared to Saigal and he must therefore be more than normally careful in doing this role . . .

Put the two productions side by side and you have two examples of the film technique—as it was twenty years ago and as it stands today. The large number of Dilip Kumar fans would, of course, be happy to see him in a favourite role.

According to author B.D. Garga,

Those who thought that Bimal Roy would follow with another non-realistic 'everyday reality' film were in for a surprise. He felt that in this 25-year-gap that separated the

Dilip Kumar and Motilal in *Devdas* (1955)

two films, film technique and acting styles had undergone
a sea change. With vastly improved technical facilities and
a highly talented group of artistes like Dilip Kumar for
the title role, Suchitra Sen as his love life Parvati (Paro),
Vyjanthimala as the courtesan Chandramukhi, coupled
with Motilal as Chunni Babu and Nazir Hussain as
Dharamdas, Bimal Roy fashioned the story of a man's self-
destroying love for his childhood playmate into a superbly
crafted film. Its meditative pace, interspersed with long
silent passages, Devdas' complex character, calm outside
and fire within; the emotional intensity of Parvati; and the
final tragic end, gave the film a unique ever-lasting quality.
Much as it evoked an era not without some nostalgia, it
also showed up an untenable social attitude.[21]

Bimal Roy's Devdas is a narcissist, whose self-absorbed
romanticism destroys those very things he loves, including

himself. In his struggle with reality, he emerges as a reluctant rebel—one who, in the end, surrenders his life to uphold the very system he resists.

The cirrhosis of the liver was essentially caused by the pains of a lost past and the inability of the individual to prepare oneself for a brighter future. His rejection of the love of the courtesan, Chandramukhi, was an unconscious desire to get rid of his feudal past. The character thus becomes the archetype of a disillusioned man who seeks his identity through self-inflicting suffering. He could see no other option except to go for the inevitable self-destruction in the face of an oppressive social milieu in which true happiness cannot materialize in the physical unity of the lovers.

As already mentioned above, the character of Devdas had a great universal appeal for the Indian subcontinent mindset because the theme also represented escapism, and indecisiveness, whereby the failures are attributed to the external social factors. It was certainly a Dilip Kumar film all the way and he put in everything that he had in him into playing the role.

In a conversation with the author–television director, Nasreen Munni Kabir, Dilip Kumar said:

> Devdas was all bound in tradition, he does not have the courage to rebel. He loves Parvati tremendously, yet he punished her and punished himself. He couldn't assert himself and do what would be regarded as quite simple by prevailing standards. His crisis was made more acute because that was a time when a man or woman could not think of going against the authority of the elders . . .
>
> Bimal Roy had great sensitivity—it wasn't in the spoken words, but in the quiet interludes. He disliked speech and he would cut as much verbiage as possible. For example, take the scene where Devdas returns from

Dilip Kumar and Vyjanthimala in *Devdas* (1955)

Calcutta as a grown-up man and goes to see Paro. The night is falling, she hears his footsteps and shyly retreats into the courtyard and runs up the stairs to her room. Now, this is the director's ingenuity: he has Paro light a diya (lamp) and as she lights it, light falls on her face, and the camera slowly tilts up to reveal the face of Devdas, who has followed her to her room. Light falls on their faces, they see each other for the first time as grown adults, and there is silence. In the film Devdas speaks little and Paro even less. As an actor, the question in *Devdas* was of trying not to do, rather than doing.[22]

There are numerous similar scenes in *Devdas*. For example, when in his hostel room, Devdas writes a letter to Paro, saying that he is not sure of his relationship with her, and he is not even certain whether he loves her. He gives it to the attendant to post it. But soon his conscious starts pricking him about his untruthfulness. Petrified, he shouts to call the attendant who informs him that the letter has already been posted. Then there is that scene showing the egoistic showdown between Devdas and Paro followed a little later by Devdas at Chandramukhi's *kotha* (brothel) where he sees through the window a marriage ceremony taking place with the shehnai playing. In a spur of a moment, he moves away from the window and starts drinking.

In their last meeting, Paro now married, on learning that Devdas is on a home visit, comes to meet him. She asks him to leave the path of self-destruction and promise to give up drinking. Devdas, now beyond redemption, tells her how she misunderstood him. But he promises to visit her if that would make her happy.

And those scenes where, while living under the love and care of Chandramukhi he tells her: *Sab khatam ho gaya. Woh shaadi ke raaste pe chali gayi aur main barbadi ke. Aab ek naa khatam hone wala natak shuro ho gaya hai* (Everything is over. She has gone on the path of marriage and I on destruction. Now, an endless drama has started). And when his condition worsens, one evening he just leaves her home. Chandramukhi goes all over desperately searching for him and finally finds him in a drain singing *Kis ko khabar thi ke aise bhi din aayenge*, (Who knew such days would also come) based on Tilak Kamod—a raag 'for the second watch of the night, similar to the Raag Sauratha which expresses the pain of the night that is passing, and the ache of lost moments and dread of the coming morning, when the candles will be extinguished, when the flames of the torches will be decapitated'. Chandramukhi brings him to her home, where Devdas, in a drunken state, talks to her about the shallowness in human relations.

Writing in his autobiography, Dilip Kumar said:

I think Bimalda knew from his own sources that I was a stickler for making the writing base strong. So, he made it comfortable for me to participate in the writing work along with his formidable team comprising Nabendu Ghosh and Rajinder Singh Bedi, among others. The lines from *Devdas*, are some of the most responsible and sensitive ever written for a Hindi film hero. In fact, the dialogues of *Devdas* are replete with a haunting sensitivity, spontaneity and meaning. They come from the pen of Rajinder Singh Bedi, one of those writers whose syntax was so perfect that the simple lines he wrote inspired actors to build up emotions in their rendering. Being myself not given to superfluous speech, I appreciated the precision and brevity of the lines he wrote for *Devdas*. They were lines of profound meaning at times, but they were so simply and sensitively worded that generations of viewers have found pleasure in repeating them lovingly.[23]

Dilip Kumar recalled working with Bimal Roy 'a pious man who, during the last years of his life, became increasingly spiritual'; who had won eleven Filmfare awards—the highest number given to any film director. 'I place him head and shoulders above his contemporaries because to this day, I have not worked with any man with such all-round talent . . . Working with Bimal Roy was sheer education. In my formative years it was important to work with a director who [could] lead you gently under the skin of the character.'[24]

For Vyjayanthimala, acting with Dilip Kumar in her first film with him, was a lifetime learning experience. 'I had seen his films earlier with Nargis and Madhubala. By now he was such an established name and simply fantastic. Only he could have portrayed Devdas the way he did. He was a true-blue artiste and really worked on his role. It was the first time that I saw someone working towards such perfection.'[25]

Describing the first day's shooting of her first scene with Dilip Kumar that she enacted as Chandramukhi, she notes:

I was all ready for the scene which had a simple dialogue for me to speak: *Aur mat piyo, Devdas* (Don't drink any more, Devdas) as he stammers and staggers in a completely inebriated state, holds on to something, groans and falls on my shoulder. I had to speak that line with an expression of anguish and helplessness. Being a dancer, expression came naturally to me; so, I thought it would be easy and I would manage it beautifully. As the technicians announced their readiness to shoot, I realized that Dilip Saab was not on the sets. Where is he, I asked an assistant, who whispered that Dilip Saab was taking brisk rounds of the studio to get that tired, weary look and had instructed the cameraman to be ready when he would stagger in with beads of real sweat on his brow and a look of exhaustion. I began to panic internally. Here was an actor who took so much trouble to endow realism to an act and here was me who had not done any preparation and was all set to face the camera with such a tremendous actor. When the camera started and I saw the incredible perfection of his performance, all I could do was speak my dialogue helplessly. Actually, that helpless look on my face was what Bimalda wanted, and it came naturally.

Speaking about this particular scene, Vyjayanthimala further explains :

Though the shot was okayed but deep within me I knew that I had to work hard to raise my acting and not leave any loose ends. It was an education for me. I found him working so hard to bring one particular *ras* (mood) to a character he performed with such dedication. I learned from him the big lesson that the attitude and approach he adopted made all the difference . . . Here was an actor who was the best in his craft, and yet he wanted to better the best. And still, he would ask for more takes ... For one of the scenes, Dilip Saab had thirty retakes but still could not get the expression he desired. I saw such brilliant facets of an actor—the likes of whom have become extinct—the way he sought flawless precision and remained open to constructive criticism. Simply stunned by his approach to work, I picked up all the precious tips than getting flustered. That's why, perhaps, our scenes together in *Devdas* went off so well and the film took us a long way as a lead pair. We did eight films together and all were great hits, some even blockbusters.

Today, the biggest stars try to replicate his scenes enacting the drunkard. Dilip Saab projected it so realistically to bring that feel and the drunkard look. He was phenomenal, a natural ... The authentic version of *Devdas* was in black and white, just wearing those plain bordered sarees, with not a piece of ornament and not the slightest ostentation. The thrust was on emoting and that realism was, what really touched you. Whether life imitates art or art imitates life, today either way you look at it there's a certain feel of falsity. All that glamour and gloss do not reflect life, unless you really identify with the characters. Dilip Kumar as Devdas is a study of how real spontaneity can leave a lasting mark.[26]

The music of *Devdas* was composed by S.D. Burman, with lyrics by Sahir Ludhianvi. Reflected Dilip Kumar: 'Initially, Bimal Roy felt that songs would be a distraction in this tragedy ... except songs in Chandramukhi's *kotha* (brothel) portions like W*oh na aayenge platkar, unhe lakh hum bulayen* (He won't come back even if I call thousands of times) based on Raag Kamaj or *Aab aage teri marzi* (Now it's your

choice) based on Raag Yaman Kalyan. This was discussed in
the story conferences that were regular features of working
in his productions. At the discussions, the songs became a
controversial issue.'[27]

Quickly, as a test, the melancholic song *Mithua lagi re yeh
kaisi* (penned by Sahir) was recorded in the voice of Talat
Mahmood based on Raag Kafi. It had the same melancholy
mood and finally it was decided to retain the song in the
film. The film is studded with several musical gems most of
which were inspired by the *Baul*—group of mystic minstrels of
mixed elements of Sufism, Vaishnavism and Tantra. To create
an atmosphere of Chandramukhi's kotha, Burman brought
in some thumris to demonstrate the culture of *tawaifs*, who
excelled in and contributed much to music and dance and were
considered an authority on etiquette. For example, the Lata
sung: *Jise tu qubool kar le woh adaa kahaan se laaun* (What
you will accept, where should I bring that fulfilment from).
However, it is the melancholic solo filmed on Dilip Kumar
in the vocals of Talat Mehmood that is heart-wrenching. The
mukhda is as follows:

Mitwaa . . . laagee re yeh kaise unbujh aag.

(Companion . . . . I am gripped by this unextinguishable
fire.)

Here is the stanza that follows:

Vyaakul jiyara vyaakul naina
Ek ek chhup mein sau sau baina
Reh gaye aansoo lut gaye raag.

(The heart is restless, the eyes are restless
In silence there are many voices
Tears remain, the song is lost.)

Media reviews were unanimous in their praise both for the film and Dilip Kumar. According to the *New York Times*:

Dilip Kumar plays only one role in *Devdas*, but the title character's spiritual struggle makes it feel as if there are two entities at war. The title role is a calling card akin to Hamlet and a chance for actors to spiral into an abyss of drunken sorrow. Many great performers have hammed it up along the way (see Shah Rukh Khan in the exotic 2002 version), but [Dilip] Kumar's take in Bimal Roy's adaptation is a painfully realistic portrait of a man wrestling with the ugliest parts of his nature.

When Devdas reunites with his childhood sweetheart, Paro (Suchitra Sen), all we hear is Kumar's gentle voice whispering from offscreen. When he finally shifts out of the shadows, his eyes are enraptured and enamoured, delivering one of the most impactful entrances in Indian cinema. It's hard not to fall in love with Devdas—which makes it all the more agonizing when his demons and insecurities turn him violently abrasive. Caught between his love for Paro, the courtesan Chandramukhi and the bottom of his glass, he becomes consumed by his mistakes. The more he drinks, the more ill he becomes, and Kumar's masterstroke is the way he turns a physical ailment into an emotional one, blending together his agony and self-loathing until all that's left is an inescapable haze of regret. Few performances feel as if they have run the entire gamut of human emotion.[28]

The *Hindustan Times*, in its edition of Sunday, 22 January 1956, wrote: ' . . . Anyone who goes to see Bimal Roy's *Devdas* will turn nostalgic for Saigal's voice but what the production loses by way of music and songs it gains in character development and perhaps in acting. Bimal Roy's idea of

Devdas is not merely a story of frustration but that of conflict. That is where Dilip Kumar's acting ability comes in. He makes a fairly facile Devdas.'

Baburao Patel's *Filmindia* hailed the film under the headline: 'A picture of artistic grace and great appeal . . . Dilip Kumar plays the coveted but complex role of Devdas and he fits the role very well. This is the first time that Dilip has made an almost perfect attempt to merge himself into the role and at places, it is extremely difficult to separate the two.'

The author of *Devdas*, Sarat Chandra Chattopadhyay, is said to have once commented that 'Dilip Kumar exactly matched the vision of his character Devdas'.

Musafir (1957)

Dilip Kumar's role in *Musafir*, the directorial debut of Hrishikesh Mukherjee, was an obvious shadow image of Bimal Roy's *Devdas*. A star-studded venture, it was an innovative package of three stories about the lives of families who happen to reside as tenants of the same house in a metropolis, one after another. The film invokes a cyclic sequence of marriage, birth, death and rebirth. Apart from the house, another common backdrop of the stories is the figure of a neighbourhood destitute sick 'madman', Raja (Dilip Kumar), who hangs around on the street, often playing the violin.

The three stories are about desperation and hope in life. The first narration is about an orphaned young woman, Shakuntla (Suchitra Sen), who desperately wants her husband, Ajay (Shekhar) to make up with his estranged parents so that she can be accepted by his family. After she leaves, the house is occupied by a family whose elder son had died and the second son, a wayward young man, Bhanu (Kishore Kumar), is desperate to find a job to support his

Suchitra Sen and Shekhar in *Musafir* (1957)

aged father (Nazir Hussain) and the widowed sister-in-law (Nirupa Roy).

The third narration is about a single mother, Uma (Usha Kiran), who rents this house and soon finds that the madman was her ex-lover. Earlier, when they were to get married, she had disappeared just before the wedding day. The sudden meeting of Raja and Uma at her doorstep brings back old, but never forgotten, memories, though Uma objects to his coming to her area of the house and closes the door on him. However, in this narration, Raja becomes friendly with Uma's highly talkative paralytic child (Daisy Irani) and this relationship rekindles in him some sense of belonging and affection. Dilip Kumar, through his prolonged conversation with the child, expresses his agony about his lost love and the eventual futility of life, communicated through the sad rendering of his violin. Yet, in

Dilip Kumar in *Musafir* (1957)

the end, the madman's death and the miraculous recovery of
Uma's paralysed son coincide, indicating the continuity of life.

Although Mukherjee's film presented Dilip Kumar as
Devdas-incarnated, there was a difference. The lover-sufferer,
in this case, is not restless. Instead, he is in a state of chronic
depression, which finds expression not in self-indulgence
but in resigned sadness. He keeps on playing his violin as if
announcing his inevitable death at any moment.

Musafir, despite its average success at the box office, is one
of Dilip Kumar's most underrated films. It fulfilled Hrishikesh
Mukherjee's cherished desire of doing a film with Dilip
Kumar who, in fact, had encouraged Mukherjee to take up
film direction. On the other hand, it fulfilled Dilip Kumar's
desire to sing in a film. He had always asserted that if he ever
sang, it would have to be a duet with the one and only, Lata
Mangeshkar, whom he would publicly hail as his *chotti bahen*

(younger sister). The dreams of both Hrishikesh Mukherjee and Dilip Kumar were achieved with *Musafir*. The song was *Laage nahin chhoote Rama chaaye jiya jaaye* (Let not the bond break Lord Rama even if I lose my heart) based on the well-known thumri in Raag Pilu—a raag, sung at any time of the day, using twelve notes.

Music director Salil Chowdhury explains:

Musafir was a trilogy in which Dilip Kumar had a tragic role by the name of *Pagla Chacha* (mad uncle) alias 'Raja'. He also played the violin in the film. It occurred instantly to me to try Yousuf (Dilip Kumar) for a song in the film. I told this to Hrishida, who also liked the idea. However, Dilip Kumar was flabbergasted and gracefully refused saying, 'Humming a tune is different but rendering it as a singer requires aptitude and skill.' I told him that it was my responsibility as a music director to finalize the tune which would have the final okay by Hrishida as the producer–director and that until he (Dilip Kumar) was not satisfied, the tune would not be used. With great hesitation he agreed. I told him that he should sing the tune with an open voice, but Dilip Kumar felt very shy. With me on the harmonium, he opened up with the note *shadj* (which is the first note of the musical scale in Hindustani music, like the so in the western *sol-fa*) and slowly started singing with his eyes closed, a tune based on Raag Pilu. We liked his style of singing.

The song was originally planned as a solo, but Dilip felt that his actual singing should be restricted to the bare minimum, that is, he would render only a few lines of the song and there should be either more orchestration, or chorus, or an inclusion of another voice who could also sing a few lines with him. So, poet Shailendra shortened the song, and we brought in the inimitable Lata Mangeshkar.

Purposely, I did not set any complicated tunes for him but only a few *murkis* (notes to embellish the score). The *alaaps* (sustaining notes used in the exposition of the raag) were set for Lata. Hence, Dilip Kumar recorded his first song with Lata Mangeshkar. While leaving the studio, when Dilip Kumar came to shake hands, the inimitable actor could not hide his emotions. I too felt very happy.[29]

Lata Mangeshkar recollects the recording vividly:

. . . whenever there was a recording of a song at Mehboob Studio and Yousuf bhai, to whom I had been introduced by music director Anil Biswas, was shooting there, I never missed the opportunity to call on him. He was a superstar, and I was rising on the horizon as a playback singer; but when we met, he held me close to his heart like an elder brother and gave me the love and respect that only someone as pure as he could.

Another talented music composer, Salil Chowdhury, gave me the opportunity to sing a duet with Yousuf bhai for *Musafir* and it was a memorable experience to observe the pains he took to sing faultlessly . . .

He had the same measure of affection for me as he had for his sisters . . . I remember the evening before my concert at the Royal Albert Hall in London, in March 1974. Yousuf bhai asked me to give him the list of songs I had selected. I had done so carefully since it was my first concert outside India. The first song on the list was *Inhi logoon ne le leena dupatta mera* (It is these people who have taken away my dupatta [the garment used to cover a woman's head and chest, which is considered a symbol of woman's modesty]). I noticed that there were lines on his forehead as he asked: 'Why do you want to sing this song?' referring to the *Pakeezah* number. I told him that it

Introducing Lata Mangeshkar at a stage show

was a very popular number, and the Asian audience would love to hear it live. He was silent for a minute, and I could sense his objection to my singing the song because the lyrics alluded to something he did not want to hear from his sister . . .

His speech at the Albert Hall was a masterpiece. Many speakers have since tried to repeat the same words and phrases in their speeches, but no one could match his eloquence and charisma and the dignity he exuded that evening. He graciously introduced me as his Chhoti Bahen (younger sister) and, as is his won't, every word he chose was carefully chosen:

Khawateen aur hazrat . . .

. . . jis tarah ki phool ki khushboo ya mehak ka koi rang nahin hota, woh mehaz khushboo hoti hai; jis tarah ki

behte hue paani ke jharne, yah thandi hawaoon ka koi maskan, yah koi ghar, gaon, watan, yah desh nahin hota; jis tarah ki ek ubarte hue sooraj ki kirnon ka, yah kisi masoom bachche ki muskurahat ka koi mazhab, yan koi bhedh, bhav nahin hota, waise hi Lata Mangeshkar ki awaz kudrat ki takhiiq ka ek karishma hain. Main, apne tain is liye yahan hazir hua hoon, ke haalanki yeh meri chhoti-si behan hai, badi mukhtsar hai, Lata Mangeshkar, lekin main is ka ehsaanmand hoon, ki main apna izhaar-e-aqeedat aur ehsaan ka ek mamooli iwas dene ke liye yahan aaya hoon, aur is waqt unko madhu karta hoon, daawat deta hoon, ki woh aapke samne tashrif laayen aur aapse darkasht karta hoon ki unka aisa istiqbal ho, aisa khairmaqdam ho, ki yeh hall aapki taaliyon se goonj uthe us khair maqdam se.

Lata ji aap aayiga . . .

(Ladies and Gentlemen,

. . . just as the fragrance of a flower does not have any colour, it is only the fragrance; just as flowing water from a waterfall or chilly winds do not have any abode or house or village or homeland or country; [or] just as the rays of the rising sun or the smile of an innocent child do not have any religion or discrimination between religions, similarly, Lata Mangeshkar's voice is a miracle of nature's creation. I am present here because, although she is my younger sister, I am obliged to her. I am here to express my homage and to give a small reward for her favours. I invite her to come before you and I request all of you to welcome and greet her in such a manner that this hall reverberates with the echo of your applause.

Lataji please come!)[30]

As one watched Dilip Kumar live that evening, one instinctively understood what precisely the singing-star Suraiya had meant when, going by her experience opposite our thespian on the sets of K. Asif's *Janwar*, she had observed: 'The problem with Yusouf is that he continues to act even when the director says cut cut.'[31]

Madhumati (1958)

This memorable film directed by Bimal Roy, perhaps inspired by Nobel Prize winner Rabindranath Tagore's *Hungry Stones* (*Ksudito Pashan*) or Kamal Amrohi's blockbuster *Mahal* (1949), is one of the most beautiful films ever made in Hindi cinema. It was a highly moving story with a reincarnation concept and immortal love. It had Anand (Dilip Kumar) in search of his soulmate amidst a social domain of suffering and helplessness.

Deploying the whole range of his naturalistic style, the actor covered a vast track in terms of acting abilities. He is seen in full bloom in his love for Madhumati (Vyjayanthimala, in a triple role) who metaphorizes nature in all its beauty and innocence. He transcends his present life and from deep down in his subconscious, discovers the pain of injustice to his love in his previous birth.

This classic, which was in an entirely different genre, mood and style—an incarnation-cum-crime drama—was an unusual material. Bimal Roy, 'a romantic humanist' and the

Dilip Kumar and Vyjayanthimala in *Madhumati* (1958)

writer, Ritwik Ghatak, 'an avowed Marxist', analysed social justice through a surrealistic plot in which the age-old feudal oppression is avenged through transmigration of the souls.

Devendra (Dilip Kumar in a double role) takes shelter from a storm in a deserted haveli and believes he hears a woman crying. Exploring the haveli, he finds a painting of its former owner Raja Ugra Narain (Pran). Davendra feels that he must have painted the portrait in a previous life, when he was Anand. This leads to a flashback of Anand's life when he worked as the estate manager on a plantation and loved Madhumati (Vyjayanthimala), a young tribal girl from a neighbouring village. There is a long sequence at the beginning in which he listens to the sound of the anklets and the sobbing of a woman. Then as he stands there, and the curtains sway in the strong wind, he gradually begins to remember his past life: '*Mujhe yaad aa raha hai . . . sab yaad aa raha hai*' (I can remember . . . everything I can remember).

The girl dies escaping from the libidinous Raja Ugra Narain. The hero then lays a trap for the raja employing another woman, Madhvi, (also played by Vyjayanthimala, who had a triple role in the film) who looks like the dead Madhumati. However, it is the original Madhumati's ghost/soul which returns to take her revenge.

In its quality, *Madhumati* looks like a poem on celluloid, in which the photography by cinematographer Dilip Gupta has its own charm as it created the magic of images simply flowing one after another. According to author B.D. Garga, 'Unlike most ghost stories Bimal Roy shot his film largely outdoors, giving it a misty, magical quality. While the interiors, with a cunning play of light and shade, had a rich velvety texture, the exteriors, with rolling mists on the terraced landscape of Gharakhal, Ranikhet and Nainital, had a dream-like quality. Bimal Roy told the story with consummate skill, cleverly blurring the line between the real and the unreal to keep the viewers interest alive to the very end.'[32]

Salil Chowdhury's background score and Hrishikesh Mukherjee's editing beautifully enhanced the eerily romantic

Dilip Kumar and Pran in *Madhumati* (1958)

Dilip Kumar and Vyjayanthimala in the climax scene of
Madhumati (1958)

atmosphere. It's imagery, at times, evoked Ritwik Ghatak's
Ajantrik (1957), linking the beautiful Madhumati with nature
and tribal cultures beyond the grasp of capitalist appropriation
awakening against the feudal order.

According to Dilip Kumar:

Bimalda had a silhouette of *Madhumati* in his mind when
we were concluding our work on *Devdas* and he had
vaguely mentioned it to me. Later when he gave his first
narration, I could sense his unflinching confidence in the
subject . . . Personally, I felt *Madhumati* was a clever and
ingenious script. In the very first draft itself, I could see
the possibilities the script offered. It was never the role
that was of paramount importance when I agreed to do a
film; there were other factors. In *Madhumati*, the incentive
was the construction of the narrative and the layers of
unpredictability in it. It appeared rather tricky for me to be
the pivot of a suspenseful narrative that alternated between
the past and present and threw up gripping situations for
the audience. None of my previous characters had to get

connected to a life that was lived in a previous birth. That was tricky for me . . . I have always enjoyed outdoor work. In *Madhumati*, the outdoor work was to become the core of the film that alone filled me with the excitement of a child who is promised a long vacation at a destination of his choice. To us—Pran (Sikand), Johnny Walker (Badruddin Qazi), Bimalda, Harishda and me—the time after pack-up was really interesting. We got over the pressure of the day's work by spending the evenings in cheerful conversation and poetic exchanges.[33]

It was with *Madhumati* that the on-screen rivalry between Dilip Kumar and Pran started and came through strongly in many a latter-day film.

Vyjayanthimala recalls working with Bimal Roy in *Madhumati*:

Soon after finishing *Devdas*, I was rewarded with an author-backed role . . . It is one film that has remained close to my heart in many ways. First, it gave me the opportunity to work again with one of the greatest directors, who could bring out the best in me—bubbly, impish, childlike innocence and even the endearing ghost. With Bimalda, the whole atmosphere, the set-up was serene and lovely. There was no unnecessary hype; it was always underplayed. Nothing was overdone—a look, a movement, a nod, a gesture—it was all so simple, and yet so natural.[34]

It is said that the real 'hero' of *Madhumati* was the camera, and that it was a race between Bimal Roy the director and Bimal Roy the producer, playing hide-and-seek in the manner of the lovers on the screen! Exploiting the natural scenery of Almora, there was art in every frame of the film. It displayed a wealth of technical excellence.

In the midst of nature and unspoiled folk tradition, the heart-rending melody *Aaja re pardesi* (Come stranger) projected earthy and ethereal permutations of the title. The unaffected enthusiasm and *joie de vivre* of this tribal belle made me live this role. There was this whimsical shot, with fog and mist, when she comes face to face with the protagonist after the fog clears and he asks her: '*Kaun ho tum? Naam kya hai?*' (Who are you? What's your name?) And the way she replies 'Madhumati' in all innocence, addressing him as '*Aye babuji*', her simplicity comes through.

Similarly, that particular shot in the last scene when Dilip Saab doesn't know that it is Madhumati's ghost when she calls him while going up the stairs, and he follows her, was simply awesome. Dilip Saab, as expected, was impeccable, imparting to the role the sensitivity of a painstaking artiste. The concept of Bimalda was amazing. He had the finesse of filmic art—that he could bring almost all the strokes of imagination within the reach of realism. And, since the gospel of birth and rebirth might have created its own confusion, the climatic scenes left the final conclusion to the imagination of the audience. This seemingly interminable story of unrequited love dangled precariously between two worlds, where the past lives of the characters in an eerie mansion were seen through flashbacks within the flashback. The plot, punctuated by plenty of dark cloudbursts, sustained its suspense. Some critics traced its mysterious affinity with the English film director Alfred Hitchcock's *Rebecca* and *Vertigo*.

All in all, Madhumati was a magical film, where everything synchronized, and it became an evergreen classic. It's intrinsic lyrical quality and the scenic beauty of the Himalayan foothills, captured in such an aesthetic manner, made it one the most artistic 'ghost stories' ever presented on the Indian screen.

Vyjayanthimala dancing for the song
Chad gaya papi bichua in *Madhumati* (1958)

The haunting melodies of *Madhumati*, composed superbly by Salil Chowdhury who won the Filmfare award for the best music director that year, with remarkable lyrics by Shailendra, comprised eleven songs—each one better than the other, each one becoming a chartbuster, each one popular to this day. According to music critic Kishore Chatterjee, 'The outstanding orchestration, its musical movements from andante to allegro, the intensely poignant passages, could have been scored by Wolfgang Amadeus Mozart. For the folksy composition *Chad gaya papi bichua* (Raag Sarang with the choral version in the latter part in Drut Khayal or Drut Teental), I am pretty certain that Salil did indeed, cleverly and creatively mingle folk melodies with the Mozartian sense of perpetual movement, which can be termed a divine momentum. Salil must have studied Mozart allegros carefully before composing the song . . . Salil romanticized Mozart.'

Salil's music in *Madhumati* offers an insight into his immense grasp over his art. In fact, in some of his compositions, East and West meet in perfect harmony—a musical marriage.

This also shows how with each film, the method of creation of a music composer is different. It is his or her ability to capture the mood of the song, and the lyrics written that determine a music director's capability. Only when the mood is captured can the song blend arrestingly with the visuals that one sees on the screen. For example, when one finds a whiff of Raag Pahadi in Mohammad Rafi's ever-green beauty *Suhanee raat dhal chuki, na jaane tum kab aaogey* (From A.R. Kardar's *Dulari*, 1949), or Roshan's Raag Darbari Kanada in Mukesh's *Teri duniya mein dil lagta nahin* (from Kidar Sharma's *Bawre Nain*, 1950), or S.D. Burman's Raag Sindhura in Talat Mahmood's *Jalte hain jis ke liye* (from Bimal Roy's *Sujata*, 1959), the mood certainly came first with the composer, the raag later. Salil Chowdhury was very different, with a more modern touch to his music as he studiously tried to avoid employing any distinct emphasis on any raag while scoring music for a film. He was of the strong opinion that his function was to reflect the mood of the moment. Background music, he emphasized, always has to be unobtrusive, merely accenting something that one is already viewing on the screen. If therefore, 'I employ a different raag to communicate that mood of the moment, it can take the viewers' mind away from what he is seeing on the screen. This certainly is not the function of background music.'[35]

In *Madhumati*, Salil Chowdhury used several singers: Mukesh, Lata Mangeshkar, Mohammad Rafi, Manna Dey, Mubarak Begum, Asha Bhosle, Sabita Chowdhury, Ghulam Mohammad and Dwijen Mukhopadhyay. For the soundtrack, he used folk music sung in the tea gardens of Assam and that Mukesh beauty *Dil tadap tadap ke keh raha aa bhi ja, tu ham se aankh na chura, tujhe kasam hai aa bhi ja* (The heart is yearning and saying do come, don't take your eyes away from me, promise to come) was adapted from the eighteenth-century Silesian song *Szla dzieweczka do gajexzka*. The Lata

Mangeshkar number *Aaja re pardesi, main to kab se khadi is paar, yeh aankhiyan thak gayeen panth nihar* (Do come stranger, I have been waiting across since long, and even the eyes are tired waiting for you) in Raag Bageshree Kharra Taal was adapted from the background score of Raj Kapoor's film *Jagte Raho* (1956, directed by Sombhu Mitra and Amit Maitra), for which Salil had composed music. Then there are the arrestable numbers: *Suhana safar aur yeh mausam haseen, humein darr hai hum kho na jayeen kahain* (The journey is wonderous and the season divine, I am scared that I might be lost somewhere) by Mukesh in Raag Bageshree and *Tote hue khwaabon ne humhako yeh sikhaya hai, dil ne jisse paya tha aankhon ne gawaya hai* (Shattered dreams have taught me this, what the heart had won, the eyes have lost) in Raag Darbari Kanada merged with Raag Jaunpuri by Mohammad Rafi. The setting here is a bleak landscape. Dilip Kumar's expressions and body language provide a visual treat. After the above mukhda there are two stanzas in the song of which the second one reveals the despair of the protagonist:

Laut aayee sada meri takraake sitaaron se
Ujdi hui duniya ke sunsaan kinaaron se
Par ab yeh tadapna bhi kucchh kaam na aaya hai

(My voice has returned after clashing with the stars
And with the borders of a devastated world
And yet this suffering has not been of any use.)

'In *Madhumati*,' says film-maker Nasreen Munni Kabir, 'the hero Anand listens out for the cry of the tiniest bird as he walks on the winding roads of a remote hill station— all of nature speaks to him before he sings that *Suhana safar* . . . The film is beautiful and mysterious and made doubly atmospheric by Bimal Roy's clever use of sound in the concluding scene.'[36]

All in all, *Madhumati*—arguably the greatest Hindi film ever made—is top-notch in every respect.

> It cemented the now famous 'reincarnation revenge' saga eventually aped by Bollywood hits like (Subhash Ghai's) *Karz* (1980), (Rakesh Roshan's) *Karan Arjun* (1995) and (Farah Khan's) *Om Shanti Om* (2007). As Anand, [Dilip] Kumar has an unburdened grace and simplicity; he's subtly mischievous in Madhumati's presence and visibly distracted by an unspoken romantic high whenever they are apart. As Devinder, however Kumar pulls off the Herculean feat of turning déjà vu—a fleeting sensation— into an ever-present emotional fabric, as he begins to recall and reckon with an impossible kind of grief, though he cannot yet fathom its origin.[37]

Madhumati was a blockbuster at the box office and the most successful film of Bimal Roy!

Yahudi (1958)

After *Devdas* and *Madhumati*, *Yahudi*—an epic romantic historical drama—was the third film Dilip Kumar did with Bimal Roy in a span of just three years. However, instead of Vyjayanthimala, it was Meena Kumari who was his leading lady this time—'The Tragedy King' with 'The Tragedy Queen'.

Reminisced Dilip Kumar years later:

> All the three films that I did under Bimal Roy's direction gave me pleasure of knowing a man who believed in perfection and hard work, as much as I did. He appreciated my style of working and the pains I took to endow life to the characters. The wonderful trait in Bimalda was his serenity and his refusal to get excited about anything. His

Dilip Kumar in *Yahudi* (1958)

exemplary virtue was his willingness to help his artistes if they failed to understand his vision. He once told me in his own gentle manner that the pain he had endured in his personal life when he was thrown to the wolves as a youth and he had to fend for himself and his mother, had been an experience that taught him not to ever inflict pain on others . . . He was one director who never expressed his delight or approval vocally or through facial expression. If he liked the shot, he just moved on to the next shot, implicitly conveying to us that he had got what he had visualized.[38]

In *Yahudi*, Bimal Roy, the distinguished alumni of New Theatres, reworked Premunkar Atorthy's *Yahudhi Ki Ladki* (1933), which had K.L. Saigal, Pahari Sanyal and Rattan

Dilip Kumar and Meena Kumari in *Yahudi* (1958)

Bai in the cast. In a highly subdued role punctuated with inner conversations with the self, Dilip Kumar as Shehzada Marcus, enlivened the drama of a prince trying to transcend the historical conflict between two communities—Jews and the Romans.

The film, an adaptation of the play *Yahudhi Ki Ladki* by the well-known poet, playwright and dramatist, Agha Hashar Kashmiri, was a classic in the Parsi-Urdu theatre. A costume drama, it depicts the prosecution of the Jews in the Roman Empire over 2000 years ago. The son of Ezra Johari (Sohrab Modi), a Jew, is put to death because a stone of the balcony wall from where the boy was watching the passing parade of Brutus (Nazir Hussain), the Governor of Rome, slips and hits the governor—a scene that reminds one of William Wyler's magnum opus *Ben-Hur* (1959). In revenge, Ezra gets the motherless daughter of Brutus kidnapped and adopts her as Hannah (Meena Kumari).

Prince Marcus of Rome, disguised as a Jew, saves Hannah from a lusty Roman soldier. Thereafter, both fall in love, but

Dilip Kumar in *Yahudi* (1958)

Hannah soon finds that her lover is not a Jew and throws him out of her life. Meanwhile, the Emperor of Rome arrives for the marriage of Prince Marcus with the niece of Brutus, Princess Octavia (Nigar Sultana). On the day of the wedding, Hannah announces that she had been cheated by Prince Marcus. When Princess Octavia begs Hannah to save her marriage, Hannah tells the emperor that the man who had cheated her was not the prince but a lookalike. Brutus sentences Hannah and Ezra to death for telling lies. Unable to bear this atrocity, Prince Marcus blinds himself. Ezra now tells the repentant Brutus that Hannah is his daughter. In the end, Hannah joins the blind prince and together they go away from the cruel world into the distance.

The film has some powerful scenes. For example, the scene where Marcus defends his love for Hannah, when she finds that he is not a Jew by saying that it is beyond worldly conventions; and then in the gloomy darkness and the loneliness, in a bleak setting depicting huge Roman style pillars and some sort of an amphitheatre with Dilip Kumar as Marcus, wearing a roman costume, makes a desperate call to Hannah, singing that gem with a couplet as a prelude in the voice of Mukesh, written by Shailendra and composed by Shankar Jaikishen:

Dil se tujko bedili hai, mujhko hai dil ka guroor
Tu yeh maane ya na mane, log mane ge zaroor.

(You seem to be heartless, but I am proud of the heart, Whether you accept it or not, people will do so.)

Then comes the mukhda

Yeh mera deewanapan hai ya mohabbat ka suroor?
Tu na pehchaane to hai yeh teri nazron ka kasoor.

(Is this my madness or the joy of love?
If you cannot recognize it then it is the fault of your eyes.)

It is the second of the two stanzas that stands out:

Aise veeraane mein ek din, ghutke mar jaayenge hum
Jitna jee chaahe pukaaro, phir nahin aayenge hum.

(In such a desolate place, I shall suffocate to death You can call me as much as you want, I will not come back.)

One of the best melodramatic scenes in Hindi cinema is the one in which both Prince Marcus and Hanna's father, Ezra, express their despair on the indispensability of Hannah in their lives; and of course the scene where after that long introspection about his failed destiny, the prince, unable to bear the separation from his beloved, who has been sentenced to death by the royal court, blinds himself.

Dilip Kumar and Anwar Hussain in *Yahudi* (1958)

Yahudhi was a big success at the box office (the third with Dilip Kumar in it), even though it was an alien theme. But the public appreciated the powerful performances of Dilip Kumar, Meena Kumari, Sohrab Modi and the rest of the cast, the music and the way the film had been guided by Bimal Roy. As Nasreen Munni Kabir says: 'Bimal Roy made extraordinary and compassionate films; he told his stories through dialogue but depended equally on visual imagery to provide a clear and simple narrative thread . . . [and] the most unusual aspect of his work was his use of sound, and he was one of the few film-makers to really use it to create atmosphere.'[39]

For the music component in *Yahudi*, though Bimal Roy stuck to his favourite poet–lyricist Shailendra, with one song by Hasrat Jaipuri, he switched to Shankar–Jaikishan as the composers, who had earlier given music for two of Dilip Kumar films: Amiya Chakravarty's *Daag* and Ramesh Saigal's *Shikast* (1953).

Yahudi also showed the difference between the music of S.D. Burman (*Devdas*) and Salil Chowdhury (*Madhumati*). Unlike Chowdhury or Naushad, Shankar always maintained that:

> . . . a knowledgeable musician always plays in *sur* (note). It is only after that, that the tune he is trying to evoke, to match the mood of the scene, could go into a raag. Take my *Tu pyaar ka sagar hai, teri ik boond ke pyaase hum* (You are an ocean of love, and we are thirsty for every drop of yours), in Amiya Chakravarty's *Seema* (1955). The mood of this bhajan (devotional song) as mirrored by Balraj Sahni, was to determine the focus of the theme. I was essentially concentrating upon creating the mood. In the process, it just so happened that the lyrics by Shailendra went into Raag Todi. Similarly, it was the tone and temper of Bharat Bhushan in Raja Nawathe's *Basant Bahar* (1956), that I was concentrating on to reflect when I composed *Duniya na bhaaye mohe, ab toh bulaa le* (This world doesn't suit me, please call me back). Only after composing it did I realize that I had set it in Raag Todi; that Mohammad Rafi would suit the song better than Manna Dey. Hence, the case of *Yahudi* was no different. *Yeh mera deewanapan hai* was composed to suit the mood on the screen and what the hero Dilip Kumar was going through, that Mukesh's voice would suit better than that of Mohammad Rafi. It just happened to have developed traces of Raag Yaman.[40]

Mughal-e-Azam (1960)

This is one film that is as big as it could get at the time it was made, a film that is popular even today as it was sixty-five years back when released, a film that is still screened regularly in cinema halls and telecast on various channels across the country and overseas, a film that does not belong to one person but to an entire galaxy of artistes led by its director, K. Asif, his

Dilip Kumar and Madhubala in *Mughal-e-Azam* (1960)

star-cast, his music composer, lyricist, story writers, sets and costume designers and several others who were involved, in various departments, in the making of this epic.

As Dilip Kumar pointed out:

> The driving force, the central force of energy of the vast enterprise, was the remarkable K. Asif, but the success of the film was not because of any one person. A host of incredibly talented people, each at the pinnacle of his or her chosen field, contributed their best to the film . . . Each diverse unit had supplemented the other and blended in such complete harmony that it becomes difficult to mark the work of any one in absolute isolation from the whole. *Mughal-e-Azam* was crafted by its master jeweller like a necklace that is so lovingly studded with precious stones, in such a way that had the lustre of even one been any the less, the brilliance of the whole would suffer.[41]

Mughal-e-Azam is undoubtedly one film that will never be forgotten, for it has gained a cult status. An intricate family drama with an epic storyline, it is a true classic in the annals of Indian cinema.

This epitome of historical spectacles in cinema, hailed as an authentic document of India's composite culture, provided Dilip Kumar with a rare opportunity to show his immense talents. As Prince Salim, the master–actor undertook one of the more challenging roles of his career and reaffirmed his status as numero uno of Indian cinema.

Based on the popular legend of Anarkali, a 1922 play by the same name by Imtiaz Ali Taj, narrates the story of the third Mughal emperor, Abu'l-Fath Jalal-ud-din Muhammad Akbar, popularly known in history as Akbar the Great (Prithviraj Kapoor), and his Rajput wife, Maharani Jodha Bai (Durga Khote), who finally manages to have a son—the heir to the throne of Hindustan. Salim starts to grow up as a spoilt, self-indulgent, weak and a pleasure-loving youngster. To teach him to grow up with courage and discipline, the emperor sends him to the rugged battlefields. Prince Salim's deep alienation is vividly captured in a scene from the battleground where he is seen sitting on a horseback directing his troops' movement with the swaying of his sword but looking with forlorn eyes at the far horizon. A little later we see Salim, after the day's battle engagement, in his army camp, writing poetry on his sword using the blood oozing from his wounds as ink. When his commander Durjan Singh (Ajit) inquires about this strange act, he smilingly recites a couplet on the importance of the sword's companionship in the life of a lover–soldier. It seems as if his restless being is in search of real solace. The entire film is replete with such epic scenes.

Having proved himself in battles, he is asked to return to the royal capital, after fourteen years as a distinguished soldier, much to the emperor's pride. Back in the royal palace, he comes across a court dancer, Nadira—a beautiful girl whom the emperor has renamed Anarkali, meaning pomegranate blossom. Salim's real solace materializes in the form of his love for Anarkali, which is shown in that incredible scene where he says to her:

Salim: *Tum tamasha dekhti rahi aur ishq apne kadmon ke saahare apni had se aage bad gaya!* (You were watching the spectacle and love, supported by its own feet, went beyond its limit.)

Anarkali: *Saheb-e-aalam, aftab ki roshni duniya ke har goshe ko roshan karti hai. Khud aapne kyon takleef ki?* (Master of the universe [a title given to Salim], the light of the sun illuminates all corners of the world. Why did you take the trouble [of coming to see me]?)

Salim: *Taaki is mahtaab mein zabha ho jaye* (So that it [the sun] would merge with the moon).

Anarkali: *Khuda ke liye Saheba-e-aalam, shahzaade ko rusva na kiyije. Aap aka hain aur main ek kaneez.* (For God's sake, master of the universe, do not disgrace the prince [Salim]. You are the lord, and I am a slave.)

Salim: *Main aaj is bulandi ki deewar ko gira dena chahta hoon . . . Bhool jao ki tum ek kaneez ho aur mujhe woh dekh lene do jo tumhari zubaan kehte hue darti hai.* (Today I want to break the high wall . . . Forget that you are a slave and let me see what your tongue fears to speak.)

Anarkali: *Mere aaka, mujse mere khawab na chinnye, main mar jaungi* (My lord, do not snatch my dreams from me. I will die.)

Salim: *Anarkali, main in khawabon ko haqeeqat mein badal doonga.* (Anarkali, I will turn these dreams into reality.)

And this is followed by that most romantic and celebrated love scene, where, that night, when Anarkali visits Salim in a secluded terrace of the royal palace, he caresses very tenderly, a white feather on her impassioned face evoking her beauty, and with love-filled eyes keeps on looking at her with immense adoration. She too looks at him in an intense emotive involvement, just for a moment before shyly turning her face away and closing her eyes. Shot in extreme close-ups of just the two faces, the whole ambience is most sensual as the strains of a song of Mian Tansen: *Prem jogan ban ke sundar piya aur challi* (Becoming an ascetic I shall go towards my beloved) in Raag Sohni in the Marwa *thaat* (a parent note in Hindustani music) wafts in the still air, as if travelling through her long tresses. A poet's version of sensuality, it is undoubtedly one of the most sensitively portrayed erotic scenes in Indian cinema. This *aalap* (a melodic improvisation that develops a raag) of

Dilip Kumar and Madhubala in *Mughal-e-Azam* (1960)

Tansen was in the voice of the music maestro, Ustad Bade Ghulam Ali Khan. For those, particularly of the younger generation, unapprised with Mian Tansen, he was one of the nine gems (*navratan*) of Emperor Akbar's court, who invented the night Raag Darbari Kanada, the morning Raag Miyan Ki Todi, the afternoon Raag Miyan Ki Sarang and that seasonal Raag Miyan Ki Malhar.

The relationship is discovered by Bahar (Nigar Sultana), a dancer of a higher rank in the court who wants Salim to love her instead of Anarkali so that she can be the future queen of the Mughal Empire. Unsuccessful in winning Salim's love, she cleverly exposes his forbidden relationship to the emperor, who then pressurises Anarkali to give up Salim, humiliating and imprisoning her but to no avail.

On the other side, Salim remains devoted to Anarkali and disobeys his father to the point of rebelling against him. He goes to the inner royal chambers, where he meets his mother, Maharani Jodha Bai, and begs her to give Anarkali to him as alms in place of his royal inheritance:

Dilip Kumar and Durga Khote in *Mughal-e-Azam* (1960)

Jodha Bai: *Salim, Mahabali ka samna ek laundi ke liye?* (Salim, a confrontation with Mahabali [One having immense strength; referring to Emperor Akbar] for a slave girl?)

Salim: *Nahin, uske liye jo mere ru-baru Hindustan ki aabru aur Mughaloon ke maalikaa bane gi.* (No. For her who in front of me will become the honour of Hindoostan and a Mughal queen.)

Jodha Bai: *Hargiz nahin. Khuddar Mughaloon ki aabru itni halki nahin jo ek nacheez laundi ke barabar toli jaye. Aur hamara Hindustan koi tumhara dil nahin ek laundi jis ki maalikaa bane.* (Never. The honour of the self-respecting Mughals is not so light that it can be weighed against a slave girl and our Hindoostan is not your heart of which a slave girl can become the queen.)

Salim: *Mera dil bhi aapka koi Hindustan nahin jis par aap hukumat karein.* (Even my heart is not your Hindoostan over which you can rule.)

Dilip Kumar and Prithviraj Kapoor in *Mughal-e-Azam* (1960)

The situation finally leads to Anarkali being prisoned with Salim declaring war against his father, Emperor Akbar. Though Salim's commander, Durjan Singh, is able to free Anarkali from the prison, the showdown between the father and son is unavoidable. The emperor visits Salim in his army camp to avert war—another very powerful and emotional scene.

Salim loses the war and is captured. Brought to the royal court in chains, he defends his love for Anarkali and refuses to hand her over to the emperor: '*Aaj Shahenshah insaf ke parde mein apni shikast ka inteqam hi lena chahta hai, use Anarkali nahi mileygi. Use apne bete ki jaan leni hogi.*' (Today the emperor, in disguise of his defeat, wants to take revenge, but he won't get Anarkali. He will have to take his son's life.) He is sentenced to death. Before he can be executed, Anarkali comes out of her hiding and is allowed to sacrifice her life to

save Salim. However, contrary to the legend in which Anarkali
is walled alive, Akbar spares her and secretly exiles her from
his kingdom, while Salim is made to believe forever that she
has been put to death.

Dilip Kumar, cast as it were in a Shakespearean mould, uses
his immense talent to portray the agony of a prince caught
between the wedge of a royalty–commoner divide. Helpless as
he is against the adamant mighty state power, which refuses
gratification of his love, he frets, keeps on shouting out his
frustrations in the corridors of the palace, and even falls on
his knees in the presence of his mother, imploring her to give
Anarkali in charity to him in lieu of all the royal decorations
bestowed on him. Unlike *Devdas*, the self-indulgent lover this
time finally takes the charge and challenges the status quo. He
makes his love for the court dancer, Anarkali, an issue of social
justice and freedom of individual choice.

In this complex role, Dilip Kumar's histrionics, in
counterpoint to Prithviraj Kapoor, were at their best. It was
a unique blending of underplay with the passion of obsessed
love floating in his eyes, interrupted intermittently with
an explosive overplay with rapid body movements. It all
indicated that Salim's restless soul is expanding its space to
engulf the whole royal milieu to attain freedom from his royal
imprisonment. Despite such a memorable performance, Dilip
Kumar's role in *Mughal-e-Azam* has not been given its rightful
due in the evaluations of the film, overshadowed perhaps by
the powerful portrayals of Prithviraj Kapoor as Emperor
Akbar, Madhubala as Anarkali, along with Ajit (born as
Hamid Ali Khan) as Durjan Singh in an elegant and poised
performance with panache and poise, coupled with the overall
ambience of the entire film comprising gorgeous settings,

breathtaking battle scenes, the might of the Mughal court and some of the most seductive song and dance ensembles ever filmed. According to Madhubala's biographer Khatija Akbar, '*Mughal-e-Azam* was the apogee of Madhubala's career. It was the film in which she funnelled all the intensity of her affair with Dilip Kumar—the love and the hate, the rupture and the despair. Giving an intricately layered performance, she achieved her ambition—to be the best Anarkali on the Indian screen ever.'[42]

There are also the gripping dialogues that created a huge impact as also the roles of a plethora of the actors and actresses, each of whom was perfect for his or her role.

And, of course, there was the hypnotic music with stunning visuals whose impact was, and still is, very striking.

In 1953, C. Ramchandra, who was then vying with Naushad for top musical honours in the Hindi film world, had come up with an exceptional score in Nandlal Jaswantlal's *Anarkali*, with the winsome Bina Rai (born as Krishna Sarin) in the title role, with Pradeep Kumar as Salim and Mubarak as Emperor Akbar. Consequently, Naushad had to match, if not surpass, his rival. Naushad put his heart and soul into each of the twelve songs in the film. Each composition has been honed to perfection so that Shakeel Badayuni's remarkable shayiri blends seamlessly with Naushad's *mausiqqi* (music).

Just as in Mehboob Khan's *Amar* (1954), when Dilip Kumar went songless, so too in *Mughal-e-Azam*. Though it had one Mohammad Rafi number but that too was not on Dilip Kumar. Of the other, it was Lata Mangeshkar who bagged nine of them, comprising eight solos and one—a qawwali—along with Shamshad Begum. The remaining two—*Shubh din aayo* (The good day has come) in Raag Rageshari and *Prem jogan ban ke* (Becoming an ascetic) in Raag Sohni—were by the eminent vocalist Ustad Bade Ghulam Ali Khan.

For many music buffs, the song to die for from the film is Lata Mangeshkar's divine melody, where she malleably moves in that raagon ka raja (king of raags) Raag Kalyan Thaat to explore Raag Kedar in all its delicacy to render this naat in the form of a supplication to Prophet Muhammad: *Bekas pe karam kijiye Sarkar-e-Madina gardish mein hai taqdir bhanvar mein hai safina* (Lord of Medina, be merciful upon the forsaken, my destiny is vicissitude and my ship in a storm) lip-synched by that 'Venus in White', Madhubala. The other two numbers that top one's list are the Raag Bihag based:

Aye ishq ye sab duniya wale bekaar ki baaten karte hain
Payal ke ghamon ka ilm nahin, jhankaar ki baaten karte hain

(The world talks uselessly about love
They know not the pain of the anklets, and they talk about chimes.)

And

Hamen kash tum se mohabbat na hoti
Kahani hamari haqeeqat na hoti

(Wish I was not in love with you
My story would not have been for real.)

What tenderly poetic stream of romantic perceptivity! The Raag Bihag and Raag Yaman numbers, respectively, enraptured and bewitched millions. Next, Lata just seems to whisper, in soft tones the mellifluous composition, based once again in Raag Yaman: *Khudaa nigehbaan hon tumhara* (Let God be your protector), and of course, that most popular number of the film, rendered by Lata and chorus, is the song-and-dance number in colour in the original black-and-white film: *Jab*

Madhubala performing on the most popular song *Jab pyaar kiya toh darna kya?* in *Mughal-e-Azam* (1960)

pyaar kiya toh darna kya? Pyaar kiya koi chori nahi ki (Why be scared if in love? Have loved and not committed any theft). Based on the eastern UP Poorbi line of native thought—*Prem kiya ka choori kari*—it became the benchmark of the film. Except, for the prelude (*Insaan kisi se duniya mein ik bar mohabbat karta hai, is dard ko le kar jeeta hai, is dard ko lekar marta hai* [In this world, one loves someone only once, and lives with that pain, dies with that pain]), the song is based on Raag Megh.

The one Mohammad Rafi number *Zindabad, zindabad eh mohabbat zindabad* (Long live, long live, long live love), in Raag Kirwani, apart from a prelude in the form of a *sher* (couplet):

Wafa ki raha mein, aashiq ki eid hoti hai
Khushi manaao, mohabbat shaheed hoti hai

(In the path of loyalty, a lover celebrates Eid
Celebrate joyfully as love has becomes a martyr.)

It comprises the mukhda and four antaras. Shakeel Badayuni's stirring lyrics extol the glory and greatness of love as opposed to riches, opulence and power. The mukhda reads:

Zindabad, zindabad eh mohabbat zindabad
Daulat ki zanjeeroon mein tu rahti hai azaad

(Long live, long live, long live love
You remain free from the fetters of wealth.)

The four antaras selected here try to show—albeit in a somewhat dramatic manner (but such was the situation)—that the arrogance of power (here, alluring to the emperor and his heartlessness) would not last long:

Taj hukumat jis ka mazhab phir uska imaan kahan?
Jiske dil mein pyaar na ho woh pathar hai insaan kahan
Pyaar ke dushman, hosh mein aa, ho jayaga barbad
Zindabad, zindabad eh mohabbat zindabad

(Whose religion is symbolized by the crown and authority, where does he have faith?
In whose heart there is no love, that person is a stone, not a human being
An enemy of love, come to your senses [otherwise] you will be destroyed.)

This spectacular scene—as captured on camera by the ace cinematographer R.D. Mathur, whose work was phenomenal in this film—depicts a large fort within which is a pyramid-like structure having a long flight of steps (quite steep) leading up to the top, where the prince is tied to a flag post. He is to be hit by a cannon ball to be fired from below. A sizeable crowd has gathered to witness the spectacle. As Salim climbs the steps, the *santarash* (sculptor) emerges from the crowd, follows him and begins to sing. As the song unwinds, the throng of people also follows the prince to express their support for him.

As the song reaches its climax, in a distinctly resonant manner, Rafi's voice just rises way above the roar of the multitudes that keeps on shouting *zinadabad, zindabad, ae mohabbat zindabad*. This was the high point of the song that once again brought out Rafi's vocal prowess and range.

It's difficult to choose any number as a 'favourite one'. There is the Raag Jaijaiwanti-based Lata Mangeshkar breath-holder *Yeh dil ki laggi kam kya hogi, yeh husn ka alaam kya hoga, jab raat hai aisi matwali to subha ka alaam kya hoga.* (How will this infatuation be reduced; how will this love be lessened? When the night is so intoxicating; what will the condition be in the morning?) And the divine beauty that is cast in the genre of Hindustani classical music as the thumri ang adapted from the gharana of Kalka Binda Din, dancer in the court of the fifth ruler of Oudh (now in Uttar Pradesh) to merge with Raag Gaara: *Mohe pangat pe Nanadalal chhed gayo re* (Nandlal has teased me at the village well) in the voice of Lata, with her sisters Usha and Meena accompanying her as also Pannalal Ghosh with his seraphic flute.

According to Madhubala's biographer Khatija Akbar:

> Few will remember that *Mughal-e-Azam* was shot in three languages. Its English version, *The Great Mughal*, never saw the light of day. The Tamil version, *Akbar*, was released but created no waves. Close-ups, long shots, songs, everything—each shot was taken three times. Dialogues had to be [written] thrice, contributing to the long duration of its filming and the amount of footage. Sets could not be dismantled until the three shots could be okayed. The quest for perfection resulted in 80,000 feet of negative, of which only a fraction was used. According to one estimate, at least four more *Mughal-e-Azam*s could

have been made . . . Though *Mughal-e-Azam* is not amongst Dilip Kumar's best, his love scenes with Madhubala were the most memorable ever. Enacted by both artistes with great delicacy and sensitivity and an undercurrent of deep passion, they evoked a host of powerful emotions and left a lasting impression on the audiences. Their place is amongst the most unforgettable scenes of cinematic history.[43]

Author Shobhaa De commented in her columns in *Times of India* of Sunday, 14 November 2004: 'Very aesthetic romance but no sex, great war scenes but no violence, beautiful dances but no item numbers, which is why everyone loves *Mughal-e-Azam* . . . There are no words to describe the luminous, ethereal, glorious beauty of the legendary Madhubala; Prince Salim's feather strokes across the cupid bow mouth and lightly shut eyes created an erotic fusion that no amount of Beyoncé's booty-shaking can match.'

Yes, the unmatchable war scenes, all real with thousands of men, horses, elephants and cannons in the battlefields, created in the deserts of Rajasthan, shot over days, was most unlike today. Everything these days is created for war scenes, as it was done, for example, for Rajmouli's blockbusters *Bahubali: The Beginning* and *Bahubali: The Conclusion* through VEX (visual effects) or digitally or computer-generated images with 3D technology, coupled with carbon fibre weaponry and flexi foam lightweight armour with the look of leather. Those days everything was genuine. As Dilip Kumar recalled:

> I had to endure the scorching heat of the desert with all the heavy armour that I was given to wear. The make-up material available was limited in those days and it was quite a test for my personal make-up artiste to camouflage the suntan, and the reddish patches I used to develop due to the heavy metal armour covering my body in the war scenes on desert locations.[44]

On Thursday, 11 November 2004, a colour version of the film was released amid much fanfare. Though it remains a moot point whether the colourization of a classic black-and-white film (with just a song in colour) was a good idea or not, the relevant point is that K. Asif's film worked its spell once again in cinema halls and on television screens, both in India and abroad. It drew in a younger generation to discover what a 'magnum opus' in cinematic terms really meant. A generation that was used to an entirely different format, technique, substance and pace of film-making filled the theatres or sat glued to their television sets along with nostalgic elders. Both sat rapt and lost for three-and-a-half hours.

For the younger generation, it was heartening, as also perhaps surprising, to see each frame celebrate the composite culture that is the hallmark of independent India. Imagine a Muslim emperor, his Hindu wife Jodha Bai and a Rajput commander-in-chief of the Mughal Army, Maan Singh; Akbar's prayers at the shrine of a Sufi saint, his accepting *prasad* (food offerings) after the puja at Janmashtami (the birthday of Lord Krishna). In one of the scenes in the latter half of the film, we see Anarkali offering a special namaz (contact prayer of the Muslims) for the life of Durjan Singh. And there were the preparations for battle which involved a *maulvi* (learned teacher of Islamic law) tying a *taweez* (an amulet) and a pundit applying a saffron mark on the forehead of an egalitarian emperor—pluralism at its best.

Hence, the colour version of *Mughal-e-Azam*, forty-four years after its first release on 5 August 1960, competed with new releases such as Yash Chopra's star-studded *Veer Zaara* and yet holding on its own and running for weeks to full houses. It completed 100 days in scores of theatres across the country thus creating a record for any re-release anywhere in the world! And, of course, Shah Rukh Khan's chemistry with Preity Zinta in *Veer Zaara* was just a pale imitation of any other Indian film—most forgettable. In comparison, Dilip Kumar's acting, his chemistry with Madhubala in *Mughal-e-Azam*, is most seductive, most hypnotic, and most unforgettable!

Bairaag (1976)

Though Hindi cinema has seen twenty-four films with triple roles by actors and two by actresses, only nine heroes have done those with the rest being by accompanying artistes like Mehmood in T. Ramanna's *Humjoli* and I.S. Johar in Vijay Anand's *Johny Mera Naam* (both 1970). While the two heroines were Madhubala in Bibhuti Mitra's *Phagun* and Vyjayanthimala in Bimal Roy's *Madhumati* (both in 1958), the

Dilip Kumar and Saira Banu in *Bairaag* (1976)

Dilip Kumar as a blind man in *Bairaag* (1976)

nine heroes included Dharmendra, Rajinikanth, Shatrughan Sinha, Kamal Haasan, Shah Rukh Khan, John Abraham and Mithun Chakraborty. Along with them was Dilip Kumar, who did the first triple role of his career in 1976, in Asit Sen's *Bairaag* with Saira Banu and Leena Chandavarkar as his co-stars. Seven years later, in 1983, he was followed by Amitabh Bachchan in S.R. Ramanathan's *Mahaan,* which had Waheeda Rehman, Parveen Babi and Zeenat Aman as his love interests. Both films were disasters at the box office.

Bairaag, the one film which more than any other in his career, had vexed him during its making and which, after seeing its first rough cut, worried Dilip Kumar even more. It bombed at the box office.

Bairaag presented Dilip Kumar as a father and two sons, separated in childhood. Located again in the affluent old times, it had all the melodrama given the presence of three Dilip Kumars—the suffering father belonging to an aristocrat

Dilip Kumar and Leena Chandavarkar in *Bairaag* (1976)

class, the playboy extravagant son whiling away his time in the luxuries of life, and the separated one, blind by birth and living a menial existence in a village temple.

Dilip Kumar in his portrayals did a juxtaposing of the three characters designed simply to demonstrate the excellence in three entirely different planes of acting.

Bairaag was Dilip Kumar's last film as a young hero! The story revolves around Kailash (Dilip Kumar), who loses his eyesight in a car accident. After he becomes a father of male twins, one of them being born blind, he decides not to keep the blind infant because he does not want his son to live his life in utter darkness. He persuades his doctor friend (Nasir Khan) to abandon the child. The boy (Dilip Kumar) is left in a temple, where he is discovered by the priest (Nasir Hussain), who raises him as Bholenath.

Bholenath grows up to become a strong worshipper of Lord Shiva. The highlight of the film is the performance of

Kailash when he feels guilty about disowning his blind child and confesses the same to his wife several years later. She dies of the shock.

As the story moves, we see that Tara (Saira Banu), a village damsel, falls in love with this simple-hearted and honest man.

Kailash raises his other son, Sanjay (Dilip Kumar), but he grows up to be a spoilt brat, with no respect even for his blind father. Although he is engaged to Sonia (Leena Chandavarkar), he is involved with a high socialite Lucy (Helen), who has a rich villainous lover Grasco (Madan Puri).

On the other side, Sonia's greedy brother Kunwar Pratap Singh (Prem Chopra) agrees to marry Tara but for a substantial dowry of Rs 3 lakh, which is beyond the means of her family. On learning this, Bholenath plans to steal the money from the temple to help Tara marry the rich Kunwar. However, while committing the robbery, his pet snake in the temple bites Bholenath, but a bit late as the Kunwar takes away the loot. However, a miracle takes place. The snake bite restores Bholenath's eyesight. He promises the temple priest and Tara that he will get the money back from the Kunwar, who has by now left for the city.

In the city, people mistake him for Sanjay, who is in hiding with Lucy after she leaves Garsco, robbing him of a large chunk of his wealth. However, she is found dead with the wealth missing. Bholenath is arrested for committing the murder. As was to be expected, in the end, the real culprit is caught, and the two brothers unite with their father and marry their respective sweethearts.

Though the film failed miserably at the box office, critics did appreciate Dilip Kumar for his triple role, for which he was nominated for the Best Actor by *Filmfare* in 1977 at the 24th Filmfare Awards. It was Dilip Kumar's third flop in a row. The previous two being *Dastaan* and *Sagina*. More about those later.

The movie, dismissed by the audience, was lampooned by the critics. Film critic Bunny Reuben wrote in the 22 October 1976 issue *Star & Style*:

RAM AUR SHYAM GET A FATHER

. . . *Bairaag* was a low light in the actor's career reminding some that portions of it bore a striking resemblance to certain scenes from various of the actor's earlier films, including *Deedar*, *Ram Aur Shyam*, *Andaz* and *Gopi*.

Three box-office debacles in a row must have been alarming for Dilip Kumar. Caught up in the web of his own histrionics, he had failed to uplift the films as a result of his preoccupation with his screen image. The once formidable thespian seemed to have lost his grip and magnetism and was ready to go into oblivion.

It couldn't have gone worse than this!

Bairaag was the first film since the late 1960s, in which Mohammad Rafi—when Dilip Kumar and he, after much hiatus (see Raju Bharatan's, Hindi film music historian, quote below), had let bygones be bygones—sang again three duets penned by Anand Bakshi, for Dilip Kumar in his lively and peppy style, featuring in a chorus with Lata Mangeshkar. These were: *Main bairaagi naachoon gaaon* (Detached from the worldly desires I dance and sing) in Raag Bhimpalasi, coupled with two duets with Asha Bhosle, including the Raag Desh-based *Saare shehar mein aap sa koi nahin* (No one in the city is like you).

The film had some lighter moments of fun and frolic. For example, when Dilip Kumar brings forth the persona of the simple-hearted youth obsessed with himself and that wonderful display of extremely comic gestures by him, as Sanjay, in the Raag Kafi-based duet *Peete peete kabhie kabhie jam badal jaate hain* (At times while drinking the drinks get interchanged), and his comical nodding when Sonia joins him in the singing and dancing.

Explains Raju Bharatan:

That in the late 1960s, the mild-mannered Mohammad Rafi began to get the feeling that after all the years of their association, Dilip Kumar was taking the disciplined performer's playback presence, on him, for granted. Rafi felt further diminished when one evening Dilip Kumar invited only Naushad, not him, to travel, in his car, to a function where Rafi was due to perform, and Dilip Kumar set to preside. Naushad politely refused Dilip Kumar's offer, cleverly staying back, only to behold Rafi, still looking incensed. To Naushad, Rafi stressed on the fact that never before had he felt so slighted. Hence, never again would he sing for Dilip Kumar.[45]

He did not. Till, of course *Bairaag* saw the light of day after a long delay in its making. But that was another story, left to be told later.

7

THE KING OF COMEDY

Method ACTING IS, ABOVE ALL, NOT EASY. IT IS TOUGH, complex and very taxing. It takes its toll on the actors, both physically and emotionally. For Dilip Kumar, doing a series of tragedies in quick succession and a kind of melancholy being caused by them on his mental state, during the initial part of his professional career, seemed to have created a kind of clinical nemesis in him. The problem seemed to have become so acute that he had to seek treatment from an eminent British psychotherapist, Dr W. D. Nicholas in the UK, who was introduced to him by the eminent stage and film actors, Dame Margaret Rutherford and Dame Sybil Thorndike. Dr Nicholas, who had handled such situations earlier too because many of his patients from the acting profession would often consult him with the same fears, proposed one single solution: switch over to romantic/comedy roles.

This advice of Dr Nicholas rekindled a sudden awakening of immense hidden talent for comedy in Dilip Kumar, initiating a complete transformation in his screen persona and his metamorphosis as a complete actor. On his return to India, he discussed the issue, and the advice rendered with Mehboob Khan and Naushad miyan, but they just could not appreciate Dilip Kumar's dilemma. Then, he talked about it with the famous film-makers S. Mukherjee and K. Asif, who had no second thoughts about it: 'Go ahead and do it,' said Mukherjee as Asif too endorsed the view. 'An actor's business is acting, and it should not matter to him whether he is doing tragedy or comedy. What counts is the actor's ability and enterprise.'

The outcome of the advice was more than fantastic in two ways. First, the arrival of some high comedy films in which the protagonist is a dynamic upbeat person who refuses to undergo unending internal suffering but takes action to recover all that is his rightfully and his love as well. The hero now appeared to be not only deriving strength from the suffering but was also addressing wider social concerns to some extent, moving cautiously away from the narrow preoccupations with the woman's love. The outcome is represented with films such as S.M.S. Naidu's *Azaad*, S.U. Sunny's *Kohinoor*, Ram Mukherjee's *Leader* (1964), Tapi Chanakya's *Ram Aur Shyam* (1967) and A. Bhim Singh's *Gopi* (1970).

The second outcome was the inclusion of very heartening romantic/comic scenes in films which were to become tragic/sorrowful towards the end. The roles in these films brought a character's experience to life showing that sometimes the best comedic moments come from real unfiltered reactions. These indeed are a testament to Dilip Kumar's commitment to his art and craft, to his ability to turn any moment into a comedic triumph.

Thus, Dilip Kumar's cinema witnessed his liberation from the stereotyped image of a tragedian. This not only led to an enrichment of his film personality but also resulted in the revision of his syllabus for film acting. The switching over also led to a de-stylization of acting and inculcated a greater sense of spontaneity in the actor's performances. He was an intensely romantic and flamboyant hero, as the singer–lover promised a beautiful interpretation to the songs filmed on him and created an aura of romance rarely witnessed on the Indian screen.

According to Madhubala's biographer Khatija Akbar:

> He was sitting alone at his table. There was a quietness
> about him, but his very presence filled the room. Looking
> at him I found myself struck by the most mesmerizing
> pair of eyes . . . Listening to Dilip Kumar talk on
> Madhubala, a bit on Nargis and Meena Kumari,
> something of Bimal Roy's *Devdas* (1955) and Guru
> Dutt's *Pyaasa* (1957), was an incomparable experience,
> for he spoke with a degree of seriousness which gives
> weight to what he says. He made us feel comfortable, he
> was courteous and patient. When we got up to leave, I
> asked him who was his favourite actress? He could have
> given a vague answer, but he considered the question . . .
> there was a pause, then he replied, 'Meena [Kumari] and
> Madhu [Madhubala]'.[1]

Dilip Kumar thus entered the very domain of well-established
entertainers, including Raj Kapoor and Dev Anand and the
whole set of comedians whom he outsmarted in many ways.
The blending of tragedy with comedy by the actor reflected the
emerging split personality in most characterizations. An actor
now had to balance these two aspects in their roles, with the
outstanding exception of Meena Kumari, who despite *Azaad*
and *Kohinoor,* both with Dilip Kumar, remained largely tied to
her image of a 'Tragedy Queen'.

This chapter presents the comic-romantic films from Dilip
Kumar's filmography which brought forth a great romantic,
immensely lively, jubilant and fun-loving character who
provided to the audiences a whole package of his histrionics
coupled with songs, music and dances.

Azaad (1955)

In July 1954, the well-known Madras-based producer–director S.M. Sriramulu Naidu made an action-comedy film in Tamil, *Malaikallan*, featuring M.G. Ramachandran (aka MGR), who after a phenomenally successful career in films, went on to become the chief minister of Tamil Nadu in 1977. It was a super hit at the box office. The film was later remade in seven regional Indian languages, including Hindi, in which Dilip Kumar was cast along with Meena Kumari in the lead. It was titled *Azaad*. 'It would have meant a complete change of screen image for me,' recollected Dilip Kumar, adding: 'I knew that comedy required a broad base and an exceptional

Dilip Kumar in *Azaad* (1955)

Dilip Kumar and Meena Kumari in *Azaad* (1955)

sense of timing, which was a carefully honed skill, more than just a gift or flair. Initially, my fear was whether I possessed that skill. Now it was a challenge, a necessity that cried out for some daring on my part.'[2]

And what a success story it was! If it broke box-office records, for Dilip Kumar, as also for Meena Kumari, *Azaad* also broke the shackles of tragedy and provided wholesome entertainment. It was about a rich young man's heroic efforts in organizing the poor against the piercing feudal order and creating a true model of a self-governed society, far away from the shadow of the state. Representing liberation metaphorically, the protagonist, la Robinhood, is a dispenser of justice who reallocates wealth looted from the rich among the poor.

Azaad was the first film Dilip Kumar did in the south Indian film industry. He appeared in twin roles of Khan Saheb, who is an urbane businessman by day but becomes the urbane

Dilip Kumar as Khan Saheb with Prakash Mehra in
Azaad (1955)

vigilante Azaad by night. (It is instructive to note that at that
time not even Hollywood or even the famous Amercian comics
had the temerity to cast businessmen as vengeful superheroes.)

The heroine Shobha (Meena Kumari) is kidnapped by
villains Sunder (Pran), Jagirdar (Murad) and Chunder (Nazir).
Azaad rescues her and soon she falls in love with him. Various
efforts by the three villains to kidnap her again are foiled by
Azaad, as are their other crimes, while Khan Saheb takes the
investigating cops (Om Prakash and Prakash Mehra) on a ride
before his identity is revealed.

The light-hearted and frolicsome *Azaad* was one of the
earlier films which laid the foundation for double roles by the
same character through a change of appearance and style. Dilip
Kumar, in his first-ever twin role, mesmerized the audience
with his acumen in depicting two highly diverse characters—
Khan Saheb, the elderly Muslim aristocrat, who talks in chaste
Urdu, has a great sense of humour and is fond of music and
Azaad, the flamboyant dashing young crusader.

Dilip Kumar had done a number of light-hearted romantic scenes in some of his earlier films too, but *Azaad* 'in many ways, was the first film that gave me the much-needed confidence to forge ahead with a feeling of emancipation and sense of achievement,' recounted Dilip Kumar, who on the opening day had deliberately left for Mahabaleshwar (a small hill station in Maharashtra) to stay away from home and friends.[3] It is here that he got the news that the film had turned out to be a super hit. 'I felt ever so happy for Sriramulu Naidu because he had such confidence in me that he gave me absolute freedom to incorporate whatever ideas occurred to me to make the script and screenplay entertaining. It was also a pleasant experience working with Meena Kumari (born Mahajabeen Bano) for whom too the film offered a welcome switchover to light-hearted acting from the serious acting she came to be known for with [Vijay Bhatt's] *Baiju Bawra* and [Bimal Roy's] *Parineeta* (filmed on Sarat Chandra Chattopadhyay's Bangla novella of the same name).'

One has to watch and rewatch some of the scenes from the film to understand the timings for comedy of Dilip Kumar. He certainly had invested a great deal in his role in the film. Some film buffs, even today, will remember the scene in which he, in the disguise of a tribal man, rescues Shobha from her kidnapper Sunder (Pran), and the other one in which he, as Khan Saheb, enjoys the Raag Darbari Kanada-based qawwali *Marna bhi mohabbat mein kisi kaam na aaya* (Even death in love did not help anyone), sung by Raghunath Jadhav and party in the film, enacting comic gestures of appreciation in-between.

Dilip Kumar, along with Meena Kumari, was at his romantic best, when after rescuing her, he takes her back home, riding through a beautiful hilly landscape singing the duet *Kitna haseen hai mausam, kitna haseen safar hai* (How wonderful is the weather, how wonderful is the journey) in Raag Darbari Kanada, as also the scene when he enters Shobha's room at night and as she objects, there is a lovely *nok-jhok* (squabble) between the two lovers, to much applause from the audience in the cinema halls.

⚘

The peppy and chart-topping musical score for the film was the creation of C. Ramchandra to the lyrics of Rajendra Kishan, who as Chitkalkar also lent his voice to Dilip Kumar. Writes film music historian Raju Bharatan:

> 'Naidu requested Naushad to compose ten tunes within 30 days, for which he would get his "due payment". To this Naushad replied: "*Naidu Saheb, yeh koi baniya ki dukaan samjhi hai aapne? Ek gana bhi nahin milega aapko tees din mein*" (Mr Naidu, do you think this is a grocery store? You won't even get one tune in thirty days). What Naushad couldn't do, his main rival at that time, C. Ramchandra, a dam bursting with talent which he had so proved in film after film, did in a quick-fire twenty-three days.'[4] And what music he created!

C. Ramchandra was indeed a trendsetter for all seasons. His *Radha na boley, na boley* (Radha does not speak, does not speak) by Lata Mangeshkar in Raag Bageshree, *Jaa ri jaa ri ooh kaari badariya* (Go away, go away dark clouds) in Raag Bhairavi, *Dekho ji nahar aayi baagon mein khili kaliyan* (See, spring has come, buds have sprouted in the gardens) in Raag Hamsadhwani, and of course the evergreen duet *Kitna haseen hai mausam, kitna haseen safar hai* in Raag Darbari Kanada by Lata Mangeshkar and C. Ramchandra picturized on Meena Kumari and Dilip Kumar, respectively

Azaad was a big hit at the box office and Dilip Kumar won his second Filmfare Best Actor Award. With it the 'Tragedy King' had turned the tables to become the King of Comedy.

Kohinoor (1960)

Having worked with S.U. Sunny in three box-office successes: *Mela*, *Babul* and *Uran Khatola*, Dilip Kumar was seen, five years later in 1960, in the director's full-length fantasy-comedy in the black-and-white *Kohinoor*. Once again, it had Meena Kumari in the female lead. It seems this novel 'reversal of roles' had caught the public's imagination once again. The storyline was nothing to write home about, but the hilarious sequences, including the mirror scene featuring the hero and the villain (Jeevan), coupled with the music, made the film a huge success.

Kohinoor was among the final tributes of our indigenous hero to the classical film era, and he indeed was in his finest elements. The film, more of a musical, in fact, represents a case

Dilip Kumar and Meena Kumari in *Kohinoor* (1960)

study in film-making, with each department perfectly in tune with the overall tenor of the film.

Sunny devised a clever interweaving of diverse components: classical music and dance; the prevailing culture of the princely India with the palace life, the impending intrigues and counter intrigues and an extended celebration of comedy, curtailed intermittently by the designs of the villain. The climax is the underwater fight sequence in which the patrons of love, music and dance ultimately emerge triumphant.

Kohinoor, a landmark in entertainment, was an authentic depiction of the Indian cultural ethos in which Indian music and dance flourished under the patronage of kingdoms during the medieval and later the colonial era. Presenting Dilip Kumar as an exponent of classical music, the film builds up on the music itself and becomes a beautiful tribute of commercial cinema to the Indian classical music and dance traditions. In fact, after Vijay Bhatt's *Baiju Bawra* in 1952, with Bharat Bhushan and Meena Kumari in the lead, and M. Sadiq's *Shabab* (1954), with Bharat Bhushan and Nutan, it was *Kohinoor* which marked the unique contribution of composer Naushad in continuing the trend of classical music in Hindi cinema.

In *Kohinoor*, Dilip Kumar plays an unusual character: a young prince, vagabond-ish, carefree and unconventional, pursuing music and love in great earnest. As the plot develops, the prince enacts the role of Kohinoor Baba, the spiritual healer who mends broken hearts with his soul-stirring music. He also uses his singing prowess to save his fiancée, the Rajkumari (princess), played by Meena Kumari, from the clutches of the villain (Jeevan).

In his role, Dilip Kumar seemed to be attempting a complete amalgamation of some of the elements of his earlier characters: the flamboyant, suave, sword-wielding chieftain of *Aan* (1952), excelling in rapid-fire dialogue delivery; the comical nawab of *Azaad*; and the romantic singer of *Uran Khatola*.

Dilip Kumar with Jeevan and Mukri in *Kohinoor* (1960)

The liberation from his tragic image and the tremendous ease with which he performed comedy, as witnessed in *Kohinoor*, also influenced his screen persona in the coming decade, particularly in *Leader* and *Ram Aur Shyam*.

It is interesting to note that 1960 was a somewhat peculiar year for Dilip Kumar, wherein he enacted two diametrically opposite roles in *Kohinoor* and *Mughal-e-Azam*.

The story of *Kohinoor* is set in the kingdom of Kailash Nagar whose ruler, Maharaj Dhiraj Rana Chandrabhan, passes away and his son, Rajkumar Dhivendra Pratap Bahadur Chandrabhan, is crowned as the new king by the royal Senapati Veer Singh. The new king, however, is more interested in petting a mongoose than looking after the royal duties. Veer Singh's wife (Leela Chitnis), who has brought up Dhivendra like her own son, Surinder, wishes to get the new king married to Rajkumari Chandramukhi (Meena Kumari) of the kingdom of Raj Nagar, whose ruler readily gives his permission and asks his daughter to go to Kailash Nagar. During the journey, she is abducted by her own Senapati (Jeevan), who wants to marry her and take over the kingdom of her father and hold her captive until she agrees to marry him.

Dilip Kumar and Jeevan in *Kohinoor* (1960)

It is Dhivendra who rescues her and the two fall in love. However, both are captured by the forces of the Senapati, but Dhivendra, though seriously injured, manages to escape and is rescued and looked after by the royal *nartaki* (dancer) of Rajgarh, Rajlaxmi (played by Kumkum). Soon, she too falls in love with him.

On recovering, Dhivendra sets off for Senapati's palace in disguise as Kohinoor Baba, a musician and spiritual guru, where his beloved Chandramukhi is kept a prisoner. He is successful in reaching the palace and establishes a trustful relationship with the Senapati. After some twists and turns in the story, during which Chandramukhi is given two choices—either marry the Senapati or witness the execution of Dhivendra—she is freed, and the couple unite to live happily thereafter.

Right from the start of the film, Dilip Kumar plays his part effortlessly and Meena Kumari gives some rare comical scenes. One has to see the scene where Rajkumar Dhivendra enters the royal *durbar* (court) carrying his pet mongoose on his shoulder to much annoyance of the deceitful Diwan, to whom he says: '*Janwaar aadmi se jiyaada wafadaar hote hain, Diwan Saheb*' (Animals are more loyal than human beings, Diwan Saheb); and that comic showdown between Rajkumar Dhivendra and the royal nartaki, about his understanding of classical music: '*Baaji, sur taal samjti ho Baaji? Darbari Kanada aur Maaru-Bihaar mein Jaijaivanti ki jhalak dekhi hai? Dhumar-dhumar mein shuru huyae to dhaar nahin pakad payogi*' (Sister, do you understand musical notes and the beat of music? Have you seen the reflection of Jaijaivanti in Darbari Kaanada). And then he displays the distinctive gestures in one of the best picturized songs in Hindi cinema: *Madhuban mein Radhika nacche re* (Radhika dances in Madhuban) in Raag Hamsadhwani which soon merges with Raag Hamir.

His keen eye for authenticity, his desire to get things right always added credibility to his performance. Apparently, to play the sitar in this scene instead of taking it through a double, as many an actor in his place would have done, he took training from Ustad Abdul Halim Jaffer Khan to get the movement of his fingers correct on the instrument so as to ensure authenticity and realism. It was to become a defining moment in his career.

While Dilip Kumar was at his romantic best in the scene where he tells the court dancer Rajlakshmi: '*Main kho chuka hoon aisi duniya mein jahan prem ki barkha kabhi nahin rukti, jahan prem ke raag ek bar chhid kar kabhi nahin rukte*' (I have got lost in a world where the rain of love never stops, where once the music starts, it never stops), his comic scenes were a sheer delight. Rajkumar Dhivendra as Kohinoor Baba makes a very humorous entry into the palace of the Senapati singing *Zara man ki kivadiya khol, sayian tere dware khadey* (based on Raag Bhairavi; Open the window of your heart, your love is standing at your doorstep), with a jerk of his shoulder, which sparks sudden laughter in the audience, as

also the scene where Kohinoor Baba impresses the Senapati
with a long comic verbose about the spiritual powers of his
music in healing dried-up and unloving minds.

There is also the famous somewhat wacky comedy scene,
where the Senapati, in a drunken state, enters the room
where the Rajkumar and Rajkumari are together. The former
conceals himself in a mirror frame. The Senapati reaches the
frame and takes Rajkumar as his image in the mirror copying
the Senapati's gestures to confuse him. He keeps overreacting
to the villain's reactions with harsh sounds and squeaks as
though he was the Senapati's mirror image.

The very first scene to be shot after the film's mahurat shot
was the song *Madhuban mein Radhika nachhe rey* on Dilip
Kumar where he also had to play the sitar. Naushad suggested
that they would use a duplicate to show the fingers moving
on the strings of the sitar. Dilip Kumar spoke to the director
S.U. Sunny and suggested that the song be picturized after the
entire shoot of the film had been completed in about a year's
time by which time he would have learnt to play the sitar
and also rehearsed to lip-sync the classical notes of the song
correctly. Says Dilip Kumar:

Kohinoor will remain etched in my mind for the efforts I
made to learn to play the sitar. Also, it was another chance
for me to test my flair for the comedy genre in acting. I was
very confident after *Azaad*'s success and I had a fine rapport
with S.U. Sunny, who understood me and my tenacity to
get as close to perfection as is possible in everything I did.
He gave me ample freedom and time to take lessons before
I did a scene. I enjoyed the making of *Kohinoor* also for
the camaraderie that grew between me and Meena Kumari
after *Azaad* as we, who were known for our forte with
emotional drama and tragedy, came together for another
light-hearted film.[5]

Kohinoor, released the same year as *Mughal-e-Azam*, in fact within a gap of just fourteen weeks, was a musical delight and proved an all-songs hit film. Music director Naushad and lyricist Shakeel Badayuni were in full form with the ten numbers that unwound as two Lata Mangeshkar solos, one by Asha Bhosle, three by Mohammad Rafi and four Rafi– Lata duets. Of these, the conspicuously famous song is the Raag Hamir-based *Madhuban mein Radhika naacche re* by Mohammad Rafi, picturized on Dilip Kumar, which has ever so elegant variations of tune and tone. In other words, a masterpiece by any yardstick. Raag Hamir is a difficult raag to play. In fact, in a 1972 radio programme, the veteran composer S.D. Burman stated that while it was very easy to make a simple raag complex, it is very difficult to make a complex raag simple and then present it to the public. He then complimented Naushad for the easy-to-grasp manner in which he had presented the complex Raag Hamir in *Kohinoor*. Those were the days when composers respected and admired each other, despite being rivals.

The visuals too were equally impressive, with dancer Kumkum (born Zaib-un-Nise) exhibiting her skills most appealingly. Some film music critics, perhaps in an outburst of optimism, maintain that there is nothing left to hear after Mohammad Rafi and Ustad Amir Khan's singing *Madhuban mein Radhika naacche re* with Ustad Abdul Halim Jaffer Khan matching them on his sitar. The song, even today, stands out as a real beauty, something out of the world—well composed, well-acted and well picturized.

From the other numbers, the one which is less heard is the Rafi solo, going on Dilip Kumar, the Raag Jaijaiwanti-based dissolving into Raag Khamaj, which has a mukhda and two antaras: *Dhal chuki shaam-e-gham, muskurale sanam* (The evening of sorrow has gone by, smile my love). It endears new hope and joy. Shakeel's poetry flows smoothly as does

Naushad's tune. To top it all, Rafi's rendition provides a magnetic attraction. In this song too Dilip Kumar is shown playing the sitar as Kumkum dances in a sprightly manner. Thus goes the mukhda:

Dhal chuki shaam-e-gham, muskurale sanam
Ek nayi subha duniya mein aane ko hai
Pyaar sajne laga saaz bajne laga
Zindagi dil ke taroon pe gaane ko hai.

(The evening of sorrow has gone by, smile my love
A new dawn is about to come in this world,
Love is being adorned and the instrument [sitar] is being played
Life is about to sing the strings of the heart.)

From the antaras, it is the first one that stands out for its exquisite poetry, which, in itself, is like undulating music:

Aaj payal bhi hai naghma-e-dil bhi hai
Rang-e-ulfat bahaaron me shaamil bhi hai
Aa gayee hai milan ki suhani ghadi
Waqt ki taal pe nachti hai khushi
Ghunghuruon ki sada rang lane ko hai

(Today, there is the anklet as also the song of the heart
The hue of love has mingled with the spring time
The pleasant time of union has come
Happiness dances according to the rhythm of time
The sound of the anklets is about to show its effect.)

Of the four riveting duets of *Kohinoor*, rather than the most popular one—*Do sitaroon ka zameen par hai milan aaj ki raat* (Two stars have a tryst on earth tonight; based on Raag Pahadi)—one has chosen the less heard one again based on

Raag Bihag: *Chalenge teer jab dil par to armaanon ka kya hoga?* (When arrows are shot at the heart, what will happen to its desires?). The duet starts off with a four-line prelude and then comes the mukhda followed by four antaras with a lot of variation in tune and rhythm along with befitting interlude music. It is Mohammad Rafi, once again, who excels here, especially when it comes to scaling the high notes; and Lata Mangeshkar too is in her element in counterpoint to Rafi.

Kohinoor once again confirmed that the trio of Naushad, Rafi and Shakeel Badayuni could come up with irresistible and unforgotten creations.

Kohinoor was a big box-office hit, and the media too was unanimous in its reviews. In its edition of Sunday, 20 November 1960, the *Times of India* wrote:

Kohinoor: A Brew of Rare Vintage

. . . The real highlights of the film are the eye-filling dance ensembles led by vivacious Kumkum, skilfully choreographed by Hiralal, Sitara Devi, Satya Narayan and Chiman Seth. Wajahat Mirza's pithy dialogues enliven the picture, photographed by Faredoon Irani.

Dilip Kumar, matinee idol of the Indian screen, sheds the mask of tragedy to play a flamboyant and out-and-out comedy role. He displays a great flair for comedy and brings the roof down with his utterly delightful characterization . . . Meena Kumari, the supreme tragedienne, joins hands with Dilip Kumar in the merry proceedings and even fights the villains single-handed.

Leader (1964)

After three huge back-to-back successes at the box office—
Kohinoor, *Mughal-e-Azam* and *Gunga Jumna*, which he
himself wrote and produced under his banner Citizen Films—
Dilip Kumar, it is said, decided to make another film, *Leader*,
whose story he had finished writing. However, somewhere
along the line, for whatever reason, he decided not to produce
or direct it. Hence, he gave the story to the eminent film-maker
Sashadhar Mukherjee, who handed over the baton of direction
to his nephew, Ram Mukherjee.

Leader moved our quintessential romantic tragedian from
an agonized existence, often located in a feudal or rural setting,
to his flamboyance and dynamism into a cosmopolitan milieu
and infused in him new self-confidence and courage. Although
Dilip Kumar in this role was articulating his newly found
idealism and anti-establishment stance through an entirely new
technique, the basic moral attributes of the character were the
same as in the classical era: the unshakeable uprightness, a deep
sense of social consciousness and a complete dedication to the
woman he loves. However, at the same time, in the new avatar,

Dilip Kumar in *Leader* (1964)

Dilip Kumar and Vyjayanthimala in *Leader* (1964)

he was sometimes seen even indulging in self-gratification at the expense of others. Hence, Ram Mukherjee's film, in fact, defined the deviant hero in a new setting.

It is the story of a mischievous and rebellious law graduate Vijay Khanna, who loves Princess Sunita (Vyjayanthimala). As the publisher of a tabloid titled *Leader,* he boldly criticizes the political class in general and the government in particular. As the story moves forward, he is accused of murder of Acharyaji (Motilal), the country's leading upright political leader. Gradually, the couple tries to expose a criminal–politician nexus. He masquerades as the son of an industrialist and exposes the real murderers.

For Dilip Kumar, *Leader* performed two important functions. First, it helped him to express his deep admiration for the first prime minister of India, Jawaharlal Nehru, and the Congress ideology. The character of Acharyaji, the typical Congress leader of old times, so ably played by the veteran Motilal, was structured on the Nehruvian model. Second, the film helped him consolidate the gains made by him in his earlier films, adding the elements of glamour as well as humour to his screen image. A comparison with *Kohinoor* would show that Vijay in *Leader* was essentially the same fun-loving and easy-going Rajkumar Dhivendra Pratap Bahadur Chandrabhan, now living in modern times.

For the Hindi cinema too, *Leader*, inadvertently, contributed in two significant ways. First, it anticipated one of the forthcoming genres: the political film. This genre focused on the growing decadence in the country's political culture and its value systems and their repercussions for the individuals in particular and society in general. The film also, perhaps for the first time, depicted political corruption and the nexus among the various corrupt elements for seizing political power.

The second contribution was its shaping the image of a new generation hero, Rajesh Khanna, who was waiting in the wings, so to say. For this superstar in the making, *Leader* seemed to have provided the basic material for developing his cinematic image; in fact, it appeared as if Dilip Kumar had prepared the ground for his arrival, both at the physical and the psychological level. The typical attire was a kurta and trousers. The attitude was one of a go-getter in the romantic sphere and in the political–social arena as well. The emerging manifestation of this superstar, however, largely rejected the previous attributes of simplicity and naturalness of the Indian film hero, and the result was a more glamourous, self-assured, stylized and dashing protagonist who, at times, indulged in narcissism and make-believe.

Leader, however, suffered from one fundamental drawback with respect to the image of Dilip Kumar. It projected him in a role that looked far less dignified and much more emotionally deficient than his earlier portrayals. Moreover, perhaps the timing too was not correct. After four back-to-back films like *Paigham, Kohinoor, Mughal-e-Azam* and *Gunga Jumna*, the audience was not ready to see him in his new avatar. Thus, although he used this film, or wanted to use it, for further

Dilip Kumar with Jayant and Nazir Hussain in *Leader* (1964)

enlarging his screen image, the liberating of the actor from his earlier image did not find much favour with his traditional fan clubs and the film failed at the box office. The audience was not prepared to accept their idol in the role of a leader who indulged in breaking the traditional conventions and bending the rules. For example, we saw him organizing an escapade with his adolescent friends and in a football match, in which his young admirers play against another team; Dilip Kumar, as the referee, takes the side of his 'disciples' and even scores a goal for them. And then, look at that scene where Vijay, in an election meeting of the opposition party, grabs the mike and makes fun of its political agenda. Or when an arranged marriage is forced on Vijay by his family, he delivers a speech on the irrelevance of such marriages in modern times. In fine, Dilip Kumar in *Leader* was something the audience could not understand nor accept.

Leader had become an ambitious project for Dilip Kumar. He wanted to have a new stream of music and lyrics in tune with the changing times. He, disturbingly for Naushad, was endeavouring to foist upon him, that super poet Sahir Ludhianvi as his new lyricist in place of Shakeel Badayuni. It shook Naushad, who was never the same again, nor was his equation with Dilip Kumar after the Sahir interlude.

The Left-oriented Sahir came up with his song lyrics to go on Dilip Kumar and his heroine Vyjayanthimala, in that classically dueting Taj Mahal scene in *Leader* arguing that it was a theme cantering upon landlord versus labourer:

Ek shahenshah ne daulat ka sahaara le kar
Hum gharibon kee mohabbat ka udaaya hai mazaaq
Mere mehboob kaheen aur mila kar mujhse . . .

(An emperor has taken the support of wealth
And mocked the love of the impoverished people
My beloved, meet me somewhere else)

'So, what's new here? The poet–lyric has studiedly garbed it,' revealed Naushad to Dilip Kumar and S. Mukherjee. At that time

'Sahir's sentiment ran radically to Dilip Kumar's grandiloquently Mughalized outlook. Sahir, expediently, had invoked the *Leader* theme (or socialism versus princedom) to go Marxist-Leninist in his anti-Naushad "line" of lyricizing. Sahir's "have not" idea was to annoy, as a "have", that stately composer from the word go. Dilip Kumar, who had been the force behind Sahir's teaming with Naushad, should have known that Sahir's leftism would not wash with a Naushad right there with royalty.'[6]

Naushad retained his favourite Shakeel and the combo of the two 'yielded a music trove'. For the same scene, the two came up with: *Ek shahenshah ne banwa ke haseen Taj Mahal, saari duniya ko mohabbat ki nishani di hai* (By building the beautiful Taj Mahal, a monarch has given the entire world a symbol of love) in Raag Lalit and seven other numbers where

Dilip Kumar glided through the film, serenading the heroine (Vyjayanthimala) and belting out one song after the other, either solo or as duets.

In keeping with the theme and pace of the movie, Naushad 'changed with the times', developing a breezy style in keeping with the demands of the film's situations. Nevertheless, even though disturbed by the entire Sahir episode, the maestro's typical classiest stamp was not missing as attested by the lilting Mohammad Rafi–Lata Mangeshkar duet, based on Raag Lalit. It was all between Shakeel and Naushad, between Rafi and Lata, and between history and fantasy.

The *Leader* collection is made of eight songs: three Mohammad Rafi solos (including one chorus Raag Bhairavi number: *Apni azaadi ko hum hargiz mitaa sakte nahin* (We can never give up our freedom), one Asha Bhosle solo (in which Rafi just chips in with *Aa aa aa . . .*), three Lata Mangeshkar–Mohammad Rafi duets and one Asha Bhosle–Rafi duet.

The Rafi solo selected for mention here is *not* the patriotism-imbued *Apni azaadi ko hum hargiz mitaa sakte nahin* (penned forcefully by Shakeel in the wake of the Indo–China War that took place in late 1962), but a more lively, jaunty and waggish number—*Mujhe duniya waalon sharabi na samjho* (People of the world, don't consider me a drunkard) in Raag Darbari Kanada—picturized on the seemingly tipsy hero during a grand party. It may be worth noting that *Apni azaadi ko hum hargiz mitaa sakte nahin* was originally written and composed for the 1963 Republic Day celebrations when emotions were still running high after the Chinese aggression of 1962. However, the song, soulfully rendered by Mohammad Rafi, unfortunately got washed away by that Kavi Pradeep-penned, C. Ramchandra composed, Lata Mangeshkar number:

Ae mere watan ke logon
Zaara aankh mein bharlo paani
Jo shaheed hue hain unki
Zara yaad karo qurbani

(O people of the homeland
Just fill your eyes with tears
Remember the sacrifices
Of those who became martyrs.)

It turned out to be the piece de resistance. Rafi's number *Apnee azaadi ko hum hargiz mitaa sakte nahin* based on Raag Bhairavi was included in *Leader* as an afterthought.

The racy Mohammad Rafi number that appealed the most begins with the following lines:

Mujhe duniya waalon sharabi na samjho
Main peeta nahin hoon, pilaayee gayi hai
Jahan bekhudi main qadam ladkhaaye
Wohi raah mujhko dikhaayee gayee hai

(People of the world, do not think I am a drunkard
I do not drink but have been forced to do so
Where the feet totter in [a state of] intoxication
That path has been shown to me.)

The song has three stanzas, of which the last one's meaning holds good even today:

Zameen ke yaaron chalan hai niraale
Yahan tan hai ujle magar dil hain kale
Yeh duniya hai duniya, yahan maal-o-zarmein
Diloon ki kharaabi chhupayee gayi hai.

(The ways of the world are strange my friends
The bodies [exteriors] are bright, but the hearts are dark
This world is such, that behind [the veneer] of wealth and affluence
The defects of the heart are hidden.)

Dilip Kumar's antics and capers during the course of this song—in fact, during the course of the entire film—have 'inspired' several later day heroes to follow in his footsteps.

The media reviews were a mixed bag of the good, the not so good and the indifferent. The *Filmfare*, in its edition of 10 March 1964, wrote: 'Dilip Kumar undoubtedly brings to the Indian screen a new concept of graceful comedy. At no stage in the film does he stoop to raise a laugh or two from the groundings. Restrained and natural, subtle and subdued, Dilip's performance is easily his best in the comic genre.'

Ram Aur Shyam (1967)

In 1964, Tapi Chanakya's Telegu language film *Rumudu Bheemudu* was released in the South with the superstar N.T. Rama Rao (NTR; who went on to become the chief minister of Andhra Pradesh in 1980) in the lead. It became a major box-office success and is considered a trendsetting venture which became an inspiration for later films with similar storylines in various Indian languages, including Malayalam, Kannada and Tamil. The Tamil version titled *Enga Veettu Pillai* (1965), had the Tamil superstar M.G. Ramachandran (MGR) in the lead.

Three years later, in1967, Chanakya released *Ram Aur Shyam* in Hindi, with Dilip Kumar in the lead, who kept the audiences regaled with his first double role. The two heroines opposite the superstar were Waheeda Rehman, who came in place of Vyjayanthimala after eight days of shooting, to play the role of an urbanite, and Askari (Mumtaz), who played a village girl. Mumtaz had begun her career as a child artiste in the late 1950s and then acted in a string of what have been called as 'stunt films' with the likes of wrestler-actor Dara

Singh as also some comic roles opposite comedian Mehmood. *Ram Aur Shyam* opened Hindi cinema's floodgates for her and with her acting skills she made it big and even won the Filmfare Award twice. After a long phase when no established actor wanted her as his heroine, *Ram Aur Shyam* lifted her into the so-called 'A' category and every top hero of the day was now waiting for her to be his heroine, including the likes of Dev Anand, Shashi Kapoor, Dharmendra, Jeetendra, Sanjeev Kumar, Amitabh Bachchan and the then superstar of Hindi cinema, Rajesh Khanna, with whom she did six films, all of them huge successes.

Ram Aur Shyam presents Dilip Kumar in entirely two diametrically opposite characters—virtually at the two ends of human personality. As Ram, he appears as a meek, timid, cowardly and a diffident person, while as Shyam, he is outspoken, boisterous, intrepid and a happy-go lucky

Dilip Kumar in a double role in *Ram Aur Shyam* (1967)

personality. The contrast between the two characters is indeed awe-inspiring. In the narrative, Ram is the tragic hero, metaphorizing the growing neurosis in society, where deep insecurity and wretchedness are caused by villainous people by an oppressive environment and a negation of a rightful life. This mental wreck, the inheritor of a rich family, is constantly whipped and beaten by his brother-in-law Gajendra (Pran), who wants him to transfer his inheritance in his name. Shyam, the other character, is an antithesis of Ram. He represents the much-dreamt saviour, omnipresent, a Lord Krishna incarnated.

Looking deeper into these two characters, the film depicted the plight of an inflicted subconscious cured by a positively trained consciousness.

In the film, Gajendra plans to kill Ram after getting him married to a rich girl, Anjana (Waheeda Rehman), in the hope of a big dowry. Ram happens to hear this wicked plan, runs away from home and starts roaming around a temple as a

Dilip Kumar and Waheeda Rehman in *Ram Aur Shyam* (1967)

Dilip Kumar and Mumtaz in *Ram Aur Shyam* (1967)

katha-vachak (storyteller reciting religious texts). However, the village belle Shanta (Mumtaz) sees him and taking him for Shyam, feels that he is up to some mischief, and brings him to the village. In a brilliant piece of comic performance which has the audience in splits, he keeps on telling the village people that he is Ram and not Shyam, while they are convinced that he has been overtaken by a spirit. Finally, when the local *pujari* (priest) starts beating him with a broom full of ash from the holy temple fire so as to get rid of the ghost-spirit sitting inside him, he is left with no choice but to admit, out of sheer necessity, that he is Shyam.

On the other side, the brave and mischievous Shyam, who is in a love–hate relationship with Shanta lands up in the city where everyone, including Anjana, feels he is Ram and informs Gajendra. Through a series of emotional events, Shyam decides to take the place of Ram to face Gajendra. There is a hilarious scene where Shyam makes a funny caricature of the south Indian court staff, who have, at the behest of Gajendra, come to get the property papers signed. Shyam scrutinizes the papers as Gajendra, who thought the papers would be signed without any problem, looks on in utter disdain and refuses to sign his inheritance over, after which Gajendra slaps him. Shyam, in a split-second, retaliates and returns the slap with such force that it shocks Gajendra out of his mind, as the audience is enthralled with this sudden act of justice.

Dilip Kumar as Shyam is undoubtedly brilliant, but it was his performance as Ram that was outstanding and much admired. His scenes where he comes running home, extremely frightful after the mill workers in a function recognize him and garland him much to the anger of Gajendra or that scene, when a nervous Ram, under a perpetual spell of phobia about his brother-in-law, speaks about his tormented state and helplessness in front of the portrait of his parents, is to be seen to be believed. Equally powerful is the scene where Ram reluctantly recalls a childhood event for the family doctor as to why is he always so nervous and fearful, pulling his shirt sleeves again and again.

As Shyam, Dilip Kumar gives a hilarious performance when he is hired as an extra to act as if he is beating some rogues for a film being shot near his village. But he actually beats them up so badly that the director, in his anger, throws him out of the sets. Also, in the scene where Shyam teases his foster mother (Leela Mishra) about his immense but untapped acting talents and starts imitating an old 1953 film *Chacha Chowdhary* song: *Mori chham, chham baaje payal* (My anklets tinkle chamm chamm) sung by Asha Bhosle in Raag Desh.

The huge success of *Ram Aur Shyam* went on to spawn a series of imitators. A beautiful couplet had led to it becoming rhyming poems in the years to come in some form or the other—some good, some downright indifferent. These

included, for example, Ramesh Sippy's *Seeta Aur Geeta*
(1972), Pankaj Parashar's *Chaalbaaz* (1989), Aneez Basmee's
Gopi Kishan (1994), and Rakesh Roshan's *Kishen Kanhaiya*
(1990) and *Karan Arjun* (1995), to name just a few—each one
a box-office success.

Writing in the *New York Times,* Siddhant Adlakha says:

> Ram, a timid, soft-spoken man, and Shyam, a cocksure
> villager whose magnetic aura lends itself to action heroics.
> As Ram, Kumar cowers in the corner of every frame,
> especially in the presence of his violent brother-in-law
> Gajendra (Pran). He elicits pity through posture, often
> lowering himself to the height of his eight-year-old niece,
> while his hands fidget nervously and hover on guard near
> his chest. In contrast, Kumar practically envelops the screen
> as the roguish Shyam, standing tall as he leans against walls
> and pillars. Kumar was known for his immersive Method
> approach, but *Ram Aur Shyam* proves that no matter how
> far inward he drove, he was always aware of the camera's
> gaze and his relationship to it.[7]

Once again, Pran was the villain in *Ram Aur* Shyam, and he
had many scenes with Dilip Kumar. The fights between the two
were brilliantly conceived and the scenes where he as Gajendra
whips Ram are so well done that audiences everywhere would
wince at every whiplash. The result was that Pran, as usual,
succeeded in striking terror in the hearts of the viewers to
such an extent that when Dilip Kumar as Shyam retaliates and
whips the daylights out of Gajendra, the audience would give
a standing ovation.

According to Dilip Kumar:

> Pran and I were friends in the real sense of the term. We met at
> the workplace, and we met informally as often as we could either

at his home or mine since we both lived in the same locality: Bandra in Bombay. At work, we were invariably pitted against each other—our characters were always caught in a conflict. It used to be very amusing for onlookers to watch the change that would come over him when he faced the camera with me in the frame after all the friendliness and affection, they had seen a while ago between us. Well, that's the challenge we actors face all the time.[8]

Here a mention must be made about the fact that wherever needed, Dilip Kumar would himself write, devise and design scenes to improve the quality of the film. Take for example the scene in which Gajendra (Pran) had called a solicitor (Prem Kumar) for signing of the estate papers by Ram in his (Pran's) favour. In the original Telegu superhit *Rumudu Bheemudee,* the scene was very straightforward, with no drama in it. Dilip Kumar spoke to the director Tapi Chanakya as to how he visualized the scene and had designed it by adding drama and comedy into it. Chanakya agreed. The scene is where the munshi (Kanhaiyalal who played the role of clerk) is sent by Gajendra to call Ram:

Munshi: Kumar *babu* (sir).

Ram: (Roughly) *Kya hai **bay***? (What is it?)

Munshi: (Very shocked) *Hain*? (Oh!) Kumar *babu, neeche Gajendra babu bulla rahen hain. Challiye jaldi.* (Kumar sir, Gajendra sir is calling you downstairs. Come fast.)

(Apparently the word 'bay' in Hindi sounds very rough and curt and is an impolite way of talking to anyone. The munshi is taken aback as he has never been addressed in that manner even by the villain Gajendra who always addresses him as munshi *jee*. The word *jee* is respectful. The addition of just

Dilip Kumar and Pran in *Ram Aur Shyam* (1967)

the word '**bay**' apparently, was a spontaneous addition by Dilip Kumar which added a punch to the setting of the entire scene and also set the mood for the audience in terms of what to expect after this. Then there was the entry of Dilip Kumar as Ram who instead of just walking down the staircase decides to wait for a few moments at the top, much to the anger of Pran, and then sit on the banister and slide down into the hall. It was a scene the audience was thrilled to watch. The best was still to come—a scene that was as serious and as funny as it could be.

Dilip Kumar looks at the property papers, reads them and then throws them on the table as an enraged Gajendra watches on, and the surprised solicitor, all along mildly clearing mucus from his nose into his handkerchief) asks in his typical Parsi-Hindi: '*Tu kya tum iss par daskhat nahin karega?* (So, you won't sign these papers?)

Ram: (While copying the tone and pronunciation of the solicitor) *Aap bologey ki khaie mein kood jaaon to kya main kood jaaonga? Aap bologey ki galle mein rassi laga kar ped se latak jaayo to kya mein latak jaaonga? Itna bewakoof samaj rakha hai mujhe?* (If you ask me to jump into a ditch, will I do that? If you ask me to put a rope around my neck and hang from a tree, will I do that? You think I am such an idiot?)

The solicitor is completely baffled. The munshi just can't believe what he is seeing and hearing. Gajendra is seething with rage.

Solicitor: *Yeh log bolta tha ki tum aata hai aur signature karta hai* (These people said you will come and put your signatures on these papers).

Dilip Kumar: (Imitating the tone and voice of the solicitor) *Kya? Kaun log bolta tha?* (What? Which people told you that?)

Solicitor: *Yahi log bolta tha.* (These people told me that.)

Dilip Kumar: *Kya bolta tha?* (What did they say?)

Solicitor: *Ki tum aata hai aur sign karta hai kagaz par.* (That you are coming to sign these papers.)

Dilip Kumar: *Hum aata to hai, par sign nahin karta hai sahib.* (I have come but will not sign the papers sir.)

Solicitor: (All along blowing his nose into his handkerchief) *To sign nahin karta* hai? (So, you won't sign?)

Dilip Kumar: I am sorry...very, very sorry. Very, very sorry, *hain.*

It was a scene that brought the house down.

According to Mumtaz:

I owe my rise in Bollywood as a star and as an actress of consequence to Dilip Saab. Before that I was mostly working in films starring the wrestler Dara Singh, apart from Mehmood, who had recommended me to Dilip Saab. The Dara Singh films came under the 'C' category in commercial terminology. As a result, heroes who were nowhere near Dilip Saab in stature were refusing to work with me. When Mehmood showed tins of reels of a film starring me with him, I was lucky because Dilip Saab liked my work, and he felt that I was ideal for the role of Ram's buxom and vivacious sweetheart. Just imagine the scenario. An actress who had faced the humiliation of being rejected by the A-list lead actors is picked up by the thespian Dilip Kumar to star opposite him. It made sensational news. Life had suddenly turned a full circle. Every top actor was now ready to sign opposite me![9]

Keeping in view such diverse personalities as Ram and Shyam, Naushad had to come up with an appropriate musical score. The film has six songs written by who else but Shakeel Badayuni—two Mohammad Rafi solos, one of which is a chorus number: *Aayeen hain bahaaren mite zulm-o-sitam, pyaar ka zamana aaya dur hue gham* (Spring has come, cruelty and oppression will end, love has come and worries have gone away) based on Raag Pahadi, one Asha Bhosle solo, one Lata Mangeshkar solo, one Lata Mangeshkar–Mohammed Rafi duet and one Asha Bhosle–Mahendra Kapoor duet (a chorus number). For some mysterious reason, the only Lata Mangeshkar solo, a real beauty in Raag Kafi (*Maine kab tumse kahaa tha ke mujhe pyaar karo;* when did I tell you to fall in love with me) was dropped from the movie. Though the songs were (and still are) popular, the element of pure melody was present in just one song (a Rafi solo).

That Rafi solo begins with a sher, set in a lovely, undulating tune, and then comes the mukhda followed by three antaras. In the song, the hero is seen playing the piano (a reliable prop in numerous films) in a party scene. The theme is that the hero (Shyam) is attempting to clear a misunderstanding about his identity as he is mistaken for Ram and treated as an imposter. The mukhda reads:

Aaj ki raat mere dil ki salaami lele
Kal teri bazm se diwaana chala jayegaa
Shamma reh jayegi parwaana chala jayegaa.

(Tonight accept the salutations of my heart
Tomorrow the crazy one will go away from your gathering
The lamp will remain, but the moth will go away.)

It is the second stanza that stands out since it contains the gist of the song:

Maine chaaha ke bata doon main haqeeqat apni
Tune lekin na mera raaz-e-mohabbat samjha
Meri uljhan mere haalat yahan tak pahunche
Teri aankhon ne pyaar ko nafrat samjha
Ab teri raah se begaana chala jayegaa.

(I wanted to tell you the truth about me
But you did not understand the secret of my love
My complications [and] my circumstances reached such a level
That your eyes thought of my love as hatred
Now the stranger will go away from your path.)

Naushad set this stanza in Raag Pahadi—a tune different (in lower notes) from the first and third stanzas, which are in higher notes. He also brought in subtle variations in tone. And, needless to say, Rafi came up trumps.

Before one concludes *Ram Aur Shyam*, here is a little trivia about the words 'shamma' and 'parwanaa'. In Urdu poetry, the *shamma–parwaana* (lamp–moth) imagery is very common and has been used innumerable times. In fact, there is a 1954 Hindi film titled *Shama Parwana* starring Shammi Kapoor and the singing star Suraiya in the lead, with music by Husnlal Bhagatram and lyrics by Majrooh Sultanpuri and Qamar Jalalabadi (born Om Prakash Bhandari). The moth (representing a male) is invariably attracted to the flame of the lamp (representing a female) and keeps on hovering over it until, ultimately, its wings get burnt. In other words, the moth sacrifices its life for the lamp.

Gopi (1970)

A remake of the National Film Award winner, B.R. Panthulu's hit film *Chinnada Gombe* (1964), *Gopi,* directed by A. Bhim Singh, was the first film in which Dilip Kumar was cast with his actress–wife Saira Banu in the lead.

The protagonist Gopi (Dilip Kumar) is a hot-headed, self-willed country bumpkin who is a *bhakt* (devotee) of the Hindu god, Lord Hanuman, and therefore he is a committed *brahamchari* (bachelor). He lives with his foster parents who have brought him up very caringly and lovingly—stepbrother Girdharilal (Om Prakash) and his wife Parvati (Nirupa Roy)—both of whom he loves.

Gopi has the guts to raise his voice against the autocratic zamindar (Pran) of the village. The turning point in the film is when the zamindar refuses to return the money the elder brother Girdharilal had deposited with him as savings for his sister Nandini's (Farida Jalal) wedding. Gopi goes over to the zamindar's mansion and robs the money from the safe at gun point.

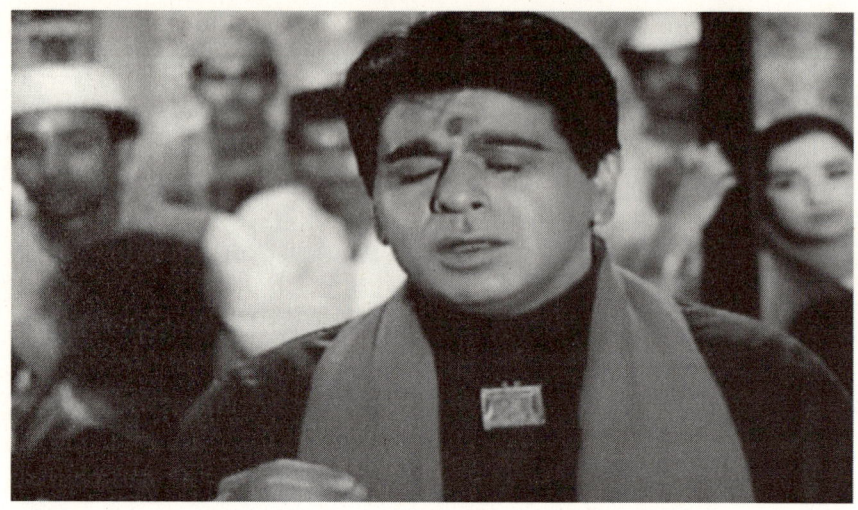

Dilip Kumar singing a bhajan in *Gopi* (1970)

This act of Gopi leads to serious altercation between the two brothers as Girdharilal is a strict moralist. In anger, Gopi leaves home with his sister, Nandini, takes up employment in the city, where he meets Seema (Saira Banu) and returns home to join his brother and sister-in-law, whom he has been missing throughout his separation from them.

The film has some hilarious scenes between Dilip Kumar and Saira Banu, as also between the two brothers. For example, when Nandini, standing between the idol of Lord Hanuman, befools her brother Gopi and orders him to love Seema, who has developed a liking for her bumpkin brother. In all innocence, Gopi goes to Seema and tells her about the order of Lord Hanuman with the directions to follow: '*Seema, Seema main bahut burri tarah se fas gaya hun. Mere saalon ki bhakti ko didhkar diya. Mujhe khub gaaliyan di aur bole ki sab baat main tum se saaf saaf bol dun. Bole ki main tum se prem karoon. Tumse main lagan bhi karunga. Us ka hukum ho gaya hai. Main kya krauun?*' (Seema, Seema, I am badly in a fix now. My years of devotion have been damned. He cursed

Dilip Kumar and Saira Banu in *Gopi* (1970)

me a lot and said that I should tell you everything frankly. He said that I should love you. I will marry you also. These are His orders. What should I do now?)

Then, there is that scene when Gopi returns from the city dressed as a 'gentleman' and starts boasting about his grand urban exposure and talks about his superiority over the 'backward' villagers and sings with much gusto: '*Gentleman, gentleman, gentleman. Main hun babu gentleman*', and later, dressed as a rich man comes to his elder brother and pompously announces that he is no more dependent on him for survival.

However, in spite of the presence of all the shades of histrionics, Dilip Kumar's performance in *Gopi*, unlike in *Ram Aur Shyam*, was very loud and somewhat garish, perhaps because of the influence of the Tamil film style. In the company of his wife, he attempted to establish a hero–heroine relationship based on similar pattern as in *Daag*, *Gunga Jumna* and *Leader*—quarrelsome in the beginning with showdowns galore, the mellowing of the emotions and then the final falling in love.

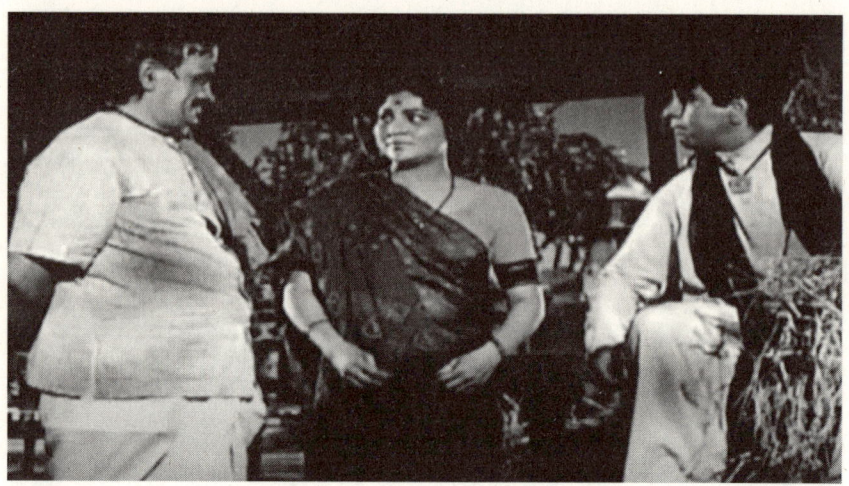

Dilip Kumar with Om Prakash and Nirupa Roy in *Gopi* (1970)

Recalled Dilip Kumar:

On the first day of shooting, after our first shot together as co-stars was canned, a dream which Saira had cherished for years, Rajendra Krishan, the poet and lyricist, who was watching the way Saira was following my brief and performing perfectly, took her aside after all the clapping had died, and told her: 'Beta (child), I think you performed brilliantly. However, I must tell you something in your own interest. You should not try to be Dilip Kumar in your enactment. Be yourself. Be Saira Banu. It is only natural when you have an actor of his stature in the same frame. But don't do it. Try to be yourself.' [It was during the making of *Gopi*] that I began to discover the capacity my wife had for hard work and the pursuit for flawless work. She was receptive to sound advice and was quick to absorb the guidance I gave her.[10]

Farida Jalal, who played Dilip Kumar's sister Nandini in the film, recounts as to how *Gopi* was a great learning experience

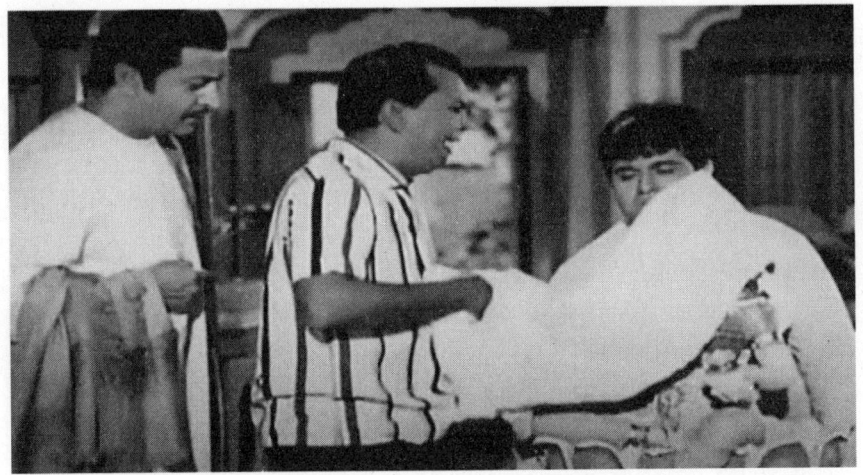

Dilip Kumar with Pran and Johnny Walker in *Gopi* (1970)

for her not only from the work point of view but also on a personal level.

Whatever ego I carried with me about my ability to perform confidently before the camera was dismantled when I witnessed the utter humility with which Dilip Sahab interacted with everybody in the unit and the pains he took to achieve perfection in his work. I was surprised at times when I had to do scenes with him, and he asked for retakes. I mentioned it to an assistant of Dilip Sahab who told me that all those retakes were for me. He wanted my responses to improve and attain the level he desired. I learned from him that a sequence or a scene cannot reach the level of excellence till all the artistes in the sequence or scene gave their best . . . Once during the shooting of *Gopi* at Kolhapur (in Maharashtra), I reached late, and Dilip Kumar was upset. He said: 'Remember success is the most demanding thing in an actor's life. The more success you achieve, the more you have to work and be more responsible, committed and humble. Don't let it go to your head; it can lead to your downfall even before you know it.'[11]

Gopi was a big hit with the audience because first, there was a certain buzz, a certain amount of curiosity about the fact that Dilip Kumar was acting for the first time with his actress–wife Saira Banu. Second was because of Dilip Kumar's performance. The audience enjoyed the entertainment provided by the actor himself as also in the company of Saira Banu, and the interactions with Om Prakash too were delightful indeed.

At the best of times, a bhajan, a prayer or religious chants in any Indian film do become a big attraction for the filmgoers. And *Gopi* had not one but two of them, written by Rajendra Krishan and composed by the Kalyanji–Anandji brother's duo, who gave the proverbial 'lion's share' of songs to Mahendra Kapoor, who by now had become the voice of Dilip Kumar. Mohammad Rafi sang just one bhajan (devotional song). *Sukh ke sab saathi, dukh mein na koi* in Raag Yaman Kalyan. It turned out to be outstanding and Rafi once again displayed his phenomenal range. The setting is a prayer room with many devotees present. Dilip Kumar seemed to excel himself while 'singing' this bhajan. The mukhda is as follows:

Sukh ke sab saathi, dukh mein na koi
Mere Ram tera naam ek saancha, duja na koi.

(All the friends are with you during happy times, there is no one during the bad times
My Lord Ram, your name is pure and there is nobody like you.)

Of the three stanzas that follow, the second one has been chosen:

Na kucchh tera na kucchh mera
Yeh jag jogi waala phera
Raja ho ya runk sabhi ka
Ant ek-sa hoi.

(Nothing is yours nothing is mine
This world is [like] the journey of an ascetic
Whether it is a king or a pauper
The end is the same.)

Mahendra Kapoor sang: *Hey Ramchandra keh gaye Siya se, aaisaa kalyug aaye ga, hans chugayga dana dunka, kaua moti khaiga* (Lord Ramchandra had told Sita, that such a dark age will come, when the swan will pick grain, and the crow will eat pearls), based on Raag Bhairavi. If one were to compare the two numbers, one will realize that although Kapoor sang with gusto, somehow, he just could not create the magic that Rafi's voice had. As Saira Bano mentioned: 'When he [Dilip Kumar] sings a bhajan, as in Gopi . . . no one can believe that Dilip Kumar is a Muslim or that it is Yusuf Khan who is singing this bhajan with such shraddha (reverence) and bhakti (devotion).'[12]

Though the film was a big hit, as far as the music is concerned, besides the two bhajans, which in any case do hit the popularity charts in a country like India, always hungry for new devotional songs, it left the music buffs unimpressed. Kalyanji–Anandji and Mahendra Kapoor could not do what Naushad and Rafi did in a Dilip Kumar film. Clearly something was missing! And that was too obvious.

8

THE CRUSADING HERO

CONSIDERING THE VARIETY OF FILMS IN WHICH DILIP Kumar has acted, his participation in the neo-realistic cinema was largely symbolic. And yet, the undeniable Indianness of his cinematic image propelled many film-makers to utilize his tremendous potential to create very effective realist cinema. Top directors, such as Mehboob Khan, Bimal Roy, Zia Sarhadi, Ramesh Saigal, Amiya Chakravarty, Nitin Bose, B.R. Chopra and later Tapan Sinha, designed some of their films around this image. Even Vijay Bhatt and Guru Dutt had offered him the hero's role in their films *Baiju Bawra* and *Pyaasa*, respectively, both of which he declined.

In fact, it is said that he rejected more films than he accepted, including David Lean's *Lawrence of Arabia*, wherein he was offered to play the character of Sheriff Ali with the likes of Peter O'Toole, Jack Hawkins, Anthony Quinn and several others. The role was finally played by Omar Sharif making him an international star. He was also offered a film by Satyajit Ray and the role of Thakur Baldev Singh in Ramesh Sippy's *Sholay* (1975), which was written by Salim Javed, with Dilip Kumar in mind. However, according to writer Salim Khan, 'He never regretted any of the decisions, except for not having done three films—the title role in *Baiju Bawra* (1952), which was finally played by a relative newcomer Bharat Bhushan, the disillusioned Urdu poet Vijay in *Pyaasa* (1957), a role the filmmaker Guru Dutt did himself, and the role of police inspector Vijay in Prakash Mehra's *Zanjeer* (1973),'[1]—a role that was rejected by several top heroes, including Dev Anand, Dharmendra and Raaj Kumar, to be finally played by Amitabh Bachchan, who too was relatively a newcomer. The rest as they say is history.

In the potpourri of his films, Dilip Kumar showcased his immense talent in creating a high-profile persona of the crusading hero in different socio-political contexts. Here are his films in this category.

Shaheed (1948)

Ramesh Saigal was one of the leading proponents of the neo-realist cinema in the 1940s and 1950s. After making films such as *Khandaan* (1942) and *Ghar Ki Shobha* (1944), he made *Shaheed*, which gave the first-ever glimpse of the highly acclaimed style of Dilip Kumar's acting by which time he was already eight films old, including the highly successful *Mela*. It helped him gain not only a strong foothold in the Hindi film world but also in creating the basic model of an

Dilip Kumar in *Shaheed* (1948)

anti-establishment hero. His performance was marked by an amazing underplay. With tears lingering in his eyes and a smile on his face, he suffered without expressing his pain and used it as a strength to carry out his duty towards the nationalist cause. He negotiated the agony of his lost love with intermittent moments of happiness and self-assurance.

A saga of childhood love, *Shaheed* was told against the backdrop of India's freedom struggle. One of the most passionate love stories ever told on the Indian screen, with a series of highly emotionally charged sequences between Dilip Kumar and Kamini Kaushal, the film deciphered in detail the turmoil caused in the lives of people who opted to sacrifice everything for the cause of the nation.

Shaheed presented Dilip Kumar in the role of a revolutionary, Ram, who leads an armed struggle against the British. It brings a lot of turmoil in the life of his childhood sweetheart Sheela (Kamini Kaushal). Ram's activities are opposed by his father Rai Bahadur Dwarkadas (Chandramohan). The film has some outstanding scenes. For example, Ram showcases a highly inspiring presence in the group song *Watan ki raah mein watan ke naujawan shaheed ho* (In the path of the nation may the youth be martyrs), and the confrontation between the revolutionary son and the father on the side of the law, about the purpose of his life and duties.

Meanwhile, a scheming police officer who is in love with Sheela gets his rival arrested. A brilliant confrontation scene follows and during the trial, Ram refuses to have a lawyer represent him as he calls the court and the law all a farce set up only to perpetuate injustice. The trial court orders Ram to be hanged. There is a very charged conflict scene of Ram in his death cell after his last meeting with his parents.

Dilip Kumar's role had some of the basic ingredients which were to determine the design of his films in his later films: First, a childhood love that was destined to remain unfulfilled.

Dilip Kumar and Kamini Kaushal in *Shaheed* (1948)

Second, living through the contradictions between his love and the external world. Third, the vulnerability of his love caused by misunderstandings, with his heroine. Lastly, the inevitability of death and its arrival as the climax of the film.

The film was hugely successful. The media reviews too lauded it. Baburao Patel of *Filmindia* wrote in the April issue:

> As far as acting is concerned, Dilip Kumar steals the picture with his deeply felt and yet perfectly natural delineation of the main role. Sensitivity and intelligent under-statement are the outstanding characteristics of his acting. Kamini Kaushal is somewhat overshadowed by Dilip and while giving a fairly balanced performance, she fails to rise to any histrionic heights. But the two of them act some of the most tender, most intimate and most moving love scenes that have ever been seen on the Indian screen.

Dilip Kumar explained this chemistry between him and Kamini Kaushal:

> I came out of my shell. I am desperately in love. The void, the vacuum in which I had lived all along, without knowing the meaning of life, was filled with warmth and an exhilarating happiness . . . This is the richest episode of my vaguely troubled existence. It gives me a sense of completeness and a new awareness . . . Years have passed since then. It is the great mystery of human life that old grief passes gradually into quiet tender joy. So, I ask myself: 'Is this enveloped by that subtle beautifying hue which comes with time? Have I slipped into romanticizing?' The answer is 'no'. It is still an understatement which merely indicates the truth without fully reflecting it.[2]

Shaheed also later became an important reference film for many film-makers. It is said that the writers of *Mughal-e-Azam*—Kamal Amrohi, Wajahat Mirza, Aman and Ehsan Rizvi—borrowed heavily from that high-tension conflict between Ram and his father—a civil servant representing the Raj—in sketching out the scenes involving Emperor Akbar and Prince Salim. The scene in which the emperor meets Salim in his army camp where Salim threatens to kill him if Anarkali is harmed in any way, seems to have been inspired by the meeting of father and son in *Shaheed* in which the son asks his father to release his senior revolutionary leader, otherwise he would shoot him.

Dilip Kumar was completely in sync with the character of Ram because of the social and political climate prevailing at that time. He explained it further: 'My own patriotic sentiments were seeking an outlet, which were there for the asking in the well-written scenes and dialogues . . . I had an understanding and facile co-actor in Kamini Kaushal who was very attentive

Dilip Kumar in *Shaheed* (1948)

to the demands of the director and had the intelligence to grasp the intrinsic sensitivity of some of the more poignant situations in the script. She was an artist who could perform with the required authority when needed.'[3]

Shaheeed, laced with a big dose of patriotism, was a stupendous hit at the box office. Besides the patriotic storyline and the performances, it had some superb music by Ghulam Haider with Raja Mehdi Ali Khan and Qamar Jalalabadi writing the lyrics. Mohammad Rafi and Khan Mastana sang, *Watan ki raah mein watan ke naujawan shaheed ho* based on Raag Bhairavi, a superhit that took the nation by storm. That and even the other numbers such as Surinder Kaur's Raag Pahadi-based *Badnam na ho jaye mohabbat ka fasana* (May the story of love not become infamous) and Geeta Dutt's *Aaja bedardi baalma* (Come my heartless lover; based on Raag Kalingada) are still popular, even after seventy-seven years of the film's release.

Aan (1952)

In July 1952, Mehboob Khan released the most splendorous venture of his life which was to become the biggest success story of his—*Aan*. It was released as *The Savage Princess* in the West and was like William Shakespeare's *The Taming of the Shrew*.

It was Mehboob Khan's most ambitious film marked by lavishly mounted sets (by the-then prevailing standards) and sprawling landscapes, replete with palace intrigues and counter intrigues. It was India's first technicolour film, as it was shot in 16 mm in Gevacolour and then blown up to 35 mm at the Technicolour Laboratories in England. It was a film, which some writers, perhaps in a superfluous outburst of enthusiasm, went to the extent of rating as big as Cecil B. DeMille films like *The Ten Commandments*, *Samson and Delilah*, *Cleopatra* and *The Great Show on Earth*. Whatever it be, *Aan* was certainly a spectacle in Indian cinema.

Dilip Kumar and Nadira in *Aan* (1952)

For his star cast headed by Dilip Kumar, Nimmi (born Nawab Bano) and Premnath (Malhotra), Khan brought in the Jewish-born Florence Ezekiel, who made her debut for the silver screen under the name of Nadira, replacing Nargis in the lead role. Nadira, Nimmi and Premnath went on to enact a variety of roles in many films in the years to come.

Khan provided his hero Dilip Kumar with the first-ever opportunity to move beyond his image of the deranged lover to an action hero who had strong convictions and inner strength. Conceived as a tribute to the formation of the Republic of India, this grand costume drama captured the colourful Rajasthani life in full abundance. Its technicolour contributed to the spectacle an exceedingly beautiful countryside, neo-classical décor, expansive gestures and warriors on horseback thundering under the fiery golden-orange skies.

The film, in a powerful narrative, depicted a peasant uprising against the corrupt world of the maharajas of colonial India. The hero Jai Tilak (Dilip Kumar) is the young chieftain of a Rajput clan, the Hadas, who by tradition are bound to serve the royal family headed by the benevolent maharaja (Murad). The villain is the prince, Rajkumar Shamsher Singh (Premnath), the younger brother of the maharaja and his haughty and arrogant sister, Princess Rajeshwari (Nadira). Shamsher tries to usurp power by finishing off the maharaja, who believes in equality for all his subjects and realizes that feudalism has run its course in the newly independent India.

Jai Tilak enters a contest to tame Princess Rajeshwari's horse and after he is successful, Prince Shamsher Singh challenges Jai Tilak to a bout of fencing. Jai Tilak wins again at which the prince is enraged at losing to a poor villager. Highly exalted by his victory in controlling the royal mare, Jai Tilak refuses the monetary award and declares that he will take the mare home as his reward.

Dilip Kumar in *Aan* (1952)

On the other side, Shamsher Singh's plans to kill his brother are unsuccessful and the maharaja manages to escape.

In the true spirit of liberation, Jai Tilak draws up a project to destroy the traditional arrogance and falsehood of the unproductive tyrannical royalty even at the price of his childhood love Mangla (Nimmi). As a courageous and swashbuckling villager, much to the distress of Mangla, he also resolves to tame the haughty Rajeshwari.

One day, Mangla is kidnapped by Prince Shamsher Singh, who tries to molest her, but before he can do so, Mangla takes her own life. Jai Tilak then decides to avenge Mangla's death and asks his mother's permission to wage a war against the tyrannical state.

As the story progresses, Jai Tilak falls in love with Rajeshwari and tries to woo her, but though attracted to him, her arrogance prevents her from revealing her true feelings. He then challenges her that he will destroy her arrogance and transform her into Mangla, an ordinary but culturally well-grounded village woman. He captures Rajeshwari, forcing her to take Mangla's place. Eventually, she realizes that she loves Jai Tilak.

On the other side, it turns out that the maharaja is still alive and on the eve of the final victory of the people over the royal tyranny, when the erstwhile maharaja declares his identity, the people raise slogans: 'Maharaja *ki jai ho*' (May the victory be of the maharaja). However, the maharaja stops them and says, 'No. Not mine! Say Jai Praja,' indicating the changing vision of the colonial Indian royalty to make way for the people's republic.

The long-drawn taming of the arrogant princess by the diligent Jai Tilak seemed to have been inspired by the historical drama *Prithvi Vallabh* (1943) starring the film-maker Sohrab Modi and Durga Khote as the lovers at loggerheads. One interesting element used by Mehboob Khan is the long love call, 'Ooo…Ooo', which Jai Tilak uses to communicate with Mangla, and she too responds with the same call. Apparently, a tribal way of communication, it provided a kind of primitive richness to the romance and also helped in moving the narrative forward.

Aan transformed Dilip Kumar's lovelorn hero into a romantic one, brandishing a sword in hand and a horse to ride. It was a tough act indeed which he pulled off with immense grace and incredible naturalness, without any trace of self-consciousness. This highly charged drama presented a very young-looking actor with a glowing face and sparkle in his eyes, projecting a strange sense of confidence in his style with his acting marked by sharp witty dialogues. For example, he was shrewd enough to tame the shrew in that scene where he pulls her red scarf and hails it as a token of loveful accord between them. And that scene where Jai Tilak in jail, overcomes Nadira's Princess Rajeshwari looks and shows himself teasing her via the sonorous voice of Mohammad Rafi singing *Mohabbat chume jinke haath* (Whose hands love kisses) based on Raag Darbari Kanada. There is another beautiful number when Jai Tilak takes the driver's seat of Rajeshwari's horse carriage and keeps teasing her playfully while rendering joyfully *Dil mein chhupa ke pyaar ka toofan le chale, hum aaj apni maut ka samaan le chale* (Hiding my love in my heart I walk away with a storm, today I take the load of death) based on Raag Desh.

Dilip Kumar's portrayal also had dynamism and an implicit political commitment, ready to prove the irreverence of the royal arrogance in the coming times. And yet, the character concealed in his actions the lingering pain caused by his decision of abandoning his childhood love to execute his project, his goal, of transforming the haughty and arrogant princess Rajeshwari into a humble woman. In this endeavour, he fulfilled Mangla's last wish by leading a mass awakening to make way for establishing people's power and putting an end to age-old royal tyranny.

Aan was the Naushad marquee, a cornerstone. The Naushad–Shakeel Badayuni tapestry comprised ten strands (in the form of songs): four solos by Mohammad Rafi, two by Lata Mangeshkar (one was a chorus with Rafi just singing 'Ooo' in the beginning), coupled with two solos by Shamshad Begum, one Rafi–Lata duet and another Lata–Shamshad Begum duet. It is recorded that Naushad used a 100-piece orchestra while recording the music for this film, both for its songs and background music, something unprecedented in those days. To create the sound effects that could have a better bass, he used special rugs put on the walls of the recording

Dilip Kumar and Nadira in *Aan* (1952)

studio, something he adopted in his later films too, especially in *Mughal-e-Azam*. Eventually, the songs were mixed in a London studio—again unique in those days. Even Naushad's main rival, C. Ramchandra, admitted that Naushad broke new ground in orchestration, 'becoming in the process an example for each one of us . . . In fact, Naushad opened up new vistas for us to explore in the realm of orchestration'.

Of the Lata Mangeshkar numbers, the favourites are *Aaj mere man mein sakhi bansuri bajaye* in Raag Bhimpalasi (Today someone plays the flute in my heart) and *Aag lagi tan man mein dil ko laga thaamna, Ram jaane kab hoga sainya ji ka samna* (With my mind and body on fire, I have to control my heart; God alone knows when I will meet my beloved) in Raag Darbari Kanada.

The four Mohammad Rafi gems that our music wizard proceeded to tune were to equate with Dilip Kumar set to sing such a rare quartet in Raag Yaman: *Man mera ehsaan arey nadaan ki maine tooj se kiya hai pyaar* (Acknowledge my favour you foolish one that I have fallen in love with you), *Mohabbat chume jinke haath, jawani paaon pade din raat* (Whose hands love kisses, youth falls on your feet day and night) in Raag Darbari Kanada and *Takra gaya tumse dil hi to hai, roye na ye kyon ghaayal hii to hai* (It has clashed with you; it is after all, a heart, it does not weep as it is hurt) in Raag Bhimpalasi. The favourite one is the Raag Desh-based *Dil mein chhupa ke pyaar ka toofan le chale, hum aaj apni maut ka samaan le chale* (Hiding my love in my heart, I walk away with a storm, today I take the load of death) because of its quick tempo and catchy rhythm, set to the beat of horse loop—a trend that was later popularized by composer O.P. Nayyar. This number—more in the form of a ghazal—consists of the *matla* (the introductory couplet) as given above and two shers which reflect the eternal clash between ego and love:

Mit-ta hein kaun dekhiye ulfat ki raah mein
Woh le chale hein aan to hum jaan le chale . . .
Manzil pe hoga faisla kismet ke khel ka
Kare jo dil ka khoon ho meheman le chale

(See who is erased in the path of love
If she takes away pride, I take away my life
The decision of fate will be at the destination
Who bleeds the heart takes away the guest.)

Aan went on to win fame internationally with acclaim for Dilip Kumar's performance. It was the first Indian film to have a worldwide release, in twenty-eight countries with subtitles in seventeen languages. Along with Dilip Kumar,

Nimmi as Mangla, though not the heroine, made a big impact on the audiences all over and was promoted as the main star in the French edition, under the title *Mangla, fille des Indes* (Mangla, the Girl of India). In fact, according to Nimmi, after *Aan*, she had received four serious offers from Hollywood, including from the movie mogul, Cecil B. DeMille, who was so impressed with the film that he personally wrote a letter of commendation to Mehboob Khan: 'I believe it is quite possible to make pictures in your great country which will be understood and enjoyed by all nations without sacrificing the culture and customs of India. We look forward to the day when you will be regular contributors to our screen fare with many fine stories bringing in romance and magic of India.'[4]

Shikast (1953)

After two back-to-back 'patriotic' super-hit films—*Shaheed* in 1948 with Dilip Kumar and Kamini Kaushal in the lead and *Samadhi* in 1950, with Ashok Kumar as a soldier in Subhas Chandra Bose's Indian National Army with Nalini Jaywant—Ramesh Saigal turned towards contemporary social realism and came up in 1953 with a black-and-white film titled *Shikast*. He had Dilip Kumar with the sloe-eyed Nalini Jaywant in the lead. In it, once again, as too often in the earlier films like *Jugnu*, *Andaz*, *Deedar* and *Devdas*, Dilip Kumar's love remains unrequited.

This emotional-romantic venture crafted with excellence, relevant more today than ever before, makes a purposeful attempt to extend the social context of *Devdas* by linking the predicament of the characters with a wider social reality. It is 'said' to be based on the famous novel *Garib Samaj* by Sarat Chandra Chattopadhya (though the film credits do not acknowledge it) and loosely based on the famous Bengali film *Palli Samaj* by Niren Lahiri.

Dilip Kumar and Nalini Jaywant in *Shikast* (1953)

Shikast attempts to capture the complexities involved in promoting rural upliftment in a decadent feudal environment in independent India. The narrative is built around a complex love story involving a young zamindar, Dr. Ram Singh (Dilip Kumar), who returns post a seven-year absence to his native village after studying medicine, wanting to sell his land and go back to the city. In the village lives his childhood beloved, Sushma (Nalini Jaywant), whom he could not marry earlier because of the status conflicts between the two families. He soon finds out that Sushma along with her brother, the local landlord, are mistreating the peasants. Though Sushma gets married, her husband dies leaving her with a son to look after.

Ram Singh meets the embittered Sushma outside the village temple and asks her to take pity on the miserable farmers tilling the land. She, in turn, asks him not to sell his land and stay in the village to serve the poor.

In one of the most memorable scenes on interactions with a child, Dr Ram Singh very patiently makes friends with Sushma's son. Unwilling to see the farmers suffer further, Ram Singh decides not to sell his land, instead opens a school and a hospital in the village. One day, he finds Sushma dumbstruck standing outside the school and keeps looking at him as if he is the hope of a new life. Ram Singh too keeps thinking about her much after she hurriedly goes away.

One day, plague breaks out in the village, inflicting death both to the rich and the poor. Sushma's son too gets it. The young doctor Ram Singh organizes medical relief, shaking the people out of the age-old superstitions about the dreaded epidemic. He saves Sushma's son with utmost devotion, indicating *shikast*, the defeat of the old order and the arrival of a new age. It rekindles their flames of love. However, social mores prevent any reunion and when she learns that Ram Singh will soon be leaving the village for the city, she accuses him of his endeavour to serve the villagers as a big farce. She then resorts to further acts of cruelty on the farmers in order to prevent him from leaving. She even goes to the extent of demolishing his school.

A noteworthy scene here is the one when Ram Singh asks Sushma as to why she had the school demolished with the farmers again becoming labourers on her land, she answers that otherwise her zamindari will be in danger. This angers Ram Singh so much that he bangs the thali in which she had served him sweets on the floor and quickly leaves her house. Meanwhile, Sushma's brother stirs up hostility against the two leading to Sushma's death, which gives us a heartrending scene of Ram Singh grieving over the dead Sushma, killed in the heavy deluge even though he had tried to save her.

Dilip Kumar, once again, used his patented natural underplay to portray the complex character of Dr Ram Singh, who wants to undo his feudal past represented by the

Dilip Kumar in *Shikast* (1953)

widowed Sushma, who still holds feudal values, as is expected of her and is cruel to her people. Transcending the agony of lost love, Ram Singh interprets his pain in the wider social context, and against all odds created by his family and, by Sushma, initiates a series of endeavours for the upliftment of the poor villagers.

Nalini Jaywant worked with Dilip Kumar in only two films, the other being *Anokha Pyar*, which had Nargis too in the cast. She gave an incredible performance, where her silences spoke volumes. With her superb but complex portrayal of a widow whose forbidden love for Ram Singh leads to high tragedy won the audiences. Her emotional scenes between Dilip Kumar are 'said to be the most celebrated moments with the histrionic jugalbandi of the two attaining unsealed heights'.[5]

The songs have been composed by Shankar–Jaikishan and penned by Shailendra and Hasrat Jaipuri. The solo number on Dilip Kumar in this film (written by Shailendra) has been rendered movingly by Talat Mehmood. The setting is a large hall with a garden in the background. Dilip Kumar is shown playing a *tanpura* (a stringed instrument resembling a sitar). Needless to say, he enhances the melody with his range of emotional expressions. Here is the mukhda:

Sapnon ki suhani duniya ko aankhon mein basaana mushkil hai
Apno se bataana mushkil hai ghairon se chhupaana mushkil hai.

(It is difficult to fit in the world of dreams in one's eyes
It is difficult to tell the near and dear ones [about the world of dreams]
and it is difficult to hide from strangers.)

Of the three following stanzas, it is the second one where the hero is apparently referring to his beloved:

Ehsaan tera kaise bhoolun, tere gham ke sahaare zinda hoon
Varna in jaati saanson ko phir lautke aana mushkil hai.

(How can I forget your kindness, I am alive with the support of the sorrow you have given me
Otherwise, it is difficult for the breaths that are going away to come back.)

Naya Daur (1957)

After the success of *Ek Hi Rasta* in 1956, with which producer–director B.R. Chopra (Baldev Raj) had launched his own banner B.R. Films, he went on to produce forty-six more films and twelve television serials, including the *Mahabharta*, based on the epic by Vyasa, in a total of ninety-four episodes, in a period of fifty-two years, which made him one of the big and influential names in the Hindi film industry. In 1957, he launched *Naya Daur*, with Dilip Kumar and Vyjayanthimala in the lead.

Naya Daur was a unique film even in world cinema. It took up, perhaps for the first time on celluloid, the academic debate of high technology vis-à-vis traditional technologies for promoting rural development and how an alienated high technology can affect the socio-economic life of the poor. In a highly innovative plot, B.R. Chopra deals with the theme in the Schumacherian framework of 'Small Is Beautiful' and raises the question of technological choice for a developing society— whether to go or not for the new advanced technologies.

Dilip Kumar in *Naya Daur* (1957)

Dilip Kumar and Jeevan in *Naya Daur* (1957)

Naya Daur validates the proposition that the threat of private ownership of the means of production for the sake of modernization would play havoc with the livelihood of the poor and this threat can only be overcome by the people's collective power.

The film starts off with a series of idyllic scenes, punctuated with songs, of a village whose people are peace-loving, friendly and hard-working. The melodrama begins when Kundan (Jeevan) introduces an electric saw in the local mill and then a motorized bus for public transport. While the electric saw threatens the livelihood of many woodcutters, the bus creates insecurity amongst the local *tonga* (horse-carriage) drivers. The economic, caste and religious divisions in the rural society of the isolated sylvan village are woven in to the main story of the rivalry between Shankar (Dilip Kumar), a tonga driver, and Krishna (Ajit), the village carpenter, both of whom are eagerly vying for the attention and love of the

Dilip Kumar and Johnny Walker in *Naya Daur* (1957)

heroine, Rajni, played by Vyjayanthimala (who incidentally had replaced Madhubala in the film after an ugly and an unfortunate, highly publicized spat with B.R. Chopra—a case which Madhubala lost souring the love relationship between her and Dilip Kumar).

The narration reaches a dramatic high point when Shankar, despite initially facing tremendous odds, mobilizes the entire village community facing the threat of mechanization to build a road through that traditional rocky and inhospitable terrain to prove the community's belief that traditional technology is no less efficient in meeting the people's needs. The collective initiative by the village gets massive publicity in the media, thanks to the comedian Johnny Walker, who plays a newspaper reporter in the film, as a unique experiment in harnessing people's power for the community's benefit.

After a few twists and turns, a race takes place between the bus driven by Kundan on the main road and the tonga by

Shankar, who takes the route of the newly built road. Shankar eventually wins the race, and the film ends when the benevolent father figure, Seth Mangal Das, hopes that a humanist attitude towards new technology will abolish the class divisions. Shankar argues for collectivization as the proletarian way of managing technology.

One interesting aspect of the narrative is that it is the villain Kundan who advances the policy of technological modernization being pursued by the country. His clash with Shankar is basically due to differing viewpoints. For example, that powerful scene where Shankar argues with Kundan, the new entrepreneur, on the issue of modern technology and the plight of the poor being caused by it: '*Tumhara dharam to paisa hai Kundan babu, paisa! Par hum daya ke bekhari nahin hain*' (Your religion is only money Kundan sir, money! But we are not beggars of compassion).

Dilip Kumar's performance was exceptional. He had worked hard to get into the role. In scene after scene, he stole the show. He essayed the role of the tonga driver with aplomb. Many scenes from the film stand out indelibly etched in every aficionado's memory even today. There are many tonga scenes in the film, but that final one where in the race sequence, Shankar, highly confident but tense, keeps on urging his horse to run faster and faster to help him win, is to be seen to be believed! Also, that scene where Shankar exhibits tremendous zeal and energy in the inspirational song, *Saathi hath badaana* (Friends keep on lending a hand), is unforgettable.

In his company was Vyjayanthimala, who too did a superb job. She recounts:

In 1957, *Naya Daur* was offered to me by B.R. Chopra, with Dilip Saab in the lead. Having worked with him earlier in *Devdas*, I was fully aware as to how much he worked to get into a role. When he had to ride a tonga, I remember how hassled he was. And how much he practised to ride it. In those days, realism was something you couldn't compromise with and that's why it was the most glorious phase of Indian cinema. By the way, the story of *Naya Daur*, written by Akhtar Mirza, apparently was turned down by both Mehboob Khan and Raj Kapoor. Chopra saab liked it immensely and did great justice to the theme.[6]

According to producer–director Yash Chopra, who assisted his elder brother B.R. Chopra on the film:

Once Dilip Saheb accepted to do *Naya Daur*, he spent an entire month with the writer Akhtar Mirza, and Chopra Saheb. He took up each scene with the dialogue and enacted it bringing in drama, sentiment, humour, pathos and deep emotion that would dazzle us all and render us speechless. He would show us variations in the enactment that would enthral us. He not only dwelt on the moulding of his character but also that of Ajit to see that Ajit's part was equally strong and sensitively written. The same measure of sensitivity went into the delineation of Vyjayanthimala's role.[7]

Dilip Kumar as the good-hearted and moralist Shankar made the viewers fall in love with him. Because of him, and his on-screen chemistry with Vyjayanthimala, the film remains a brilliant, and a very entertaining one. And he had a great supporting cast with him. No wonder, as mentioned above, he had worked so hard with Akhtar Mirza and B.R. Chopra on the script. Dilip Kumar knew the importance of a good ensemble cast. Look at the performances of Ajit, Johnny Walker, Chand Usmani, Jeevan and even child artist Daisy Irani. Each stood out. As veteran actor Amrish Puri mentioned: 'The hero is like a concrete floor and character actors are like the pillars. If the pillars are weak, the entire floor would crumble. The film would fall apart. The hero has to be supported by character actors to bring out the different shades in the film.'[8]

Naya Daur is a complete film, one that stands out as an important milestone in Dilip Kumar's career.

Naya Daur was a mega hit at the box office. While audiences all over praised the film, critics too gave it a thumbs-up in a big way. In the Sunday edition (18 August 1957), the *Times of India* wrote: 'It's a picture with a purposeful distinctive impressive theme from almost the beginning to the end.' The Bombay daily *Bharat Jyoti* described it as: 'One of the most ambitious and unusual subjects ventured in India.' The weekly *Screen* in its edition of 23 August 1957 said: 'One of the most important films made in this country.'

As was to be expected, at the fifth Filmfare Awards (19 April 1958), Dilip Kumar, already caressingly in love with that black beauty, once again bagged it for the third consecutive year—after *Azaad* (1955) and *Devdas* (1956)—for the Best Actor, while Akhtar Mirza walked away with the Award for Best Story. However, that evening there was another Filmfare Award waiting for *Naya Daur*. O.P. Nayyar, who was signed by B.R. Chopra to compose the music for the film to the lyrics of Chopra's favourite Sahir Ludhianvi, had come up with an undoubtedly unmatchable musical score, which won him the Best Music Director Award. As he held the novel black statuette in his hands, who knew then that it was the beginning of his advancing on the greasy pole of Hindi film music world where he would come like an avalanche to soon grab the number three position, just a little behind Shankar–Jaikishan, but far behind the number one uno of the time, Naushad.

And what a musical score had Nayyar composed. Each of the eight songs was a super-duper hit, with Asha Bhosle and

Shamshad Begum in their true elements. And Mohammad Rafi was just incredible, for who else could have sung those songs but Rafi, and Rafi alone, for Dilip Kumar, and a number for a hermit outside the temple: *Aaana hai to aa raah mein kuch der nahin hai bhagwan ke ghar der hai andher nahin hai* (If you have to come, do so for in the house of God, there may be delay but not darkness) based on Raag Bhairavi. There was another song—ninth—sung by Asha Bhosle, but it was edited out and is not even in the film's soundtrack.

Unfortunately, that was the first and last association of Nayyar with Chopra. Once the film became a big hit and with the Filmfare black beauty in his hands, Nayyar, known for his over-bloated ego, started announcing openly that the massive success of *Naya Daur* was because of his music alone—a fact that the rest of B.R. Films team could not chew. True, Nayyar was very innovative, but the loaves and fishes of *Naya Daur* were a combined effort of one and all in that team, right from the story to its performances to direction.

Dilip Kumar and Vyjayanthimala in *Naya Daur* (1957)

However, one has to give full credit to Nayyar for that rhythmic and melodious musical score and that too without using the voice of Lata Mangeshkar even for a single song in the film, a film where he used Mohammad Rafi to the hilt on Dilip Kumar who, in turn, brought in so much life, an immense high feel, that he sung every song with great passion much to the enjoyment of the public. That was Dilip Kumar's speciality. Once he grasped the lyrics to go with the mood of the song, he would be a dazzling public mood swinger. The two most lively song sequences are the ones where Rajni and Shankar sing *Mang ke saath tumhara maine maang liye sansar* (By asking for your companionship, I have asked for the world) based on Raag Kafi and that highly entertaining Punjabi dance sequence *Ude jab jab zulfen teri, kunwarioon ka dil machle* (Whenever your hair flies, the heart of the unmarried girls beats fast) based on Raag Yaman and of course *Reshmi salwar kurta* composed in Raag Bhairavi.

Unfortunately, in this film, there is no solo song picturized on Dilip Kumar except possibly for the Rafi number *Dil leke dagha denge, yaar hai matlab ke* (Friends will win your heart and then betray you, they are selfish). This number has been picturized separately on both Dilip Kumar and his co-actor Ajit (real name: Hamid Ali Khan).

Paigham (1959)

Hailed as the Cecil B. DeMille of India, by film historian Randor Guy, S.S. Vasan, a movie and print mogul from south India, was known for the grandiose film sets and innovative techniques that he introduced, particularly for his four-million-rupee (Rs 4 crore) extravaganza *Chandralekha* (1948). It stands out as his unique contribution to the genre of Indian spectacles. He specialized in creating the classic,

Dilip Kumar and Vyjayanthimala in *Paigham* (1959)

exotic, oriental narrative and also intense message-centred melodrama around a social problem.

Vasan's *Paigham* is a tribute to the working class which shows Ratan Lal (Dilip Kumar), a student of engineering and a highly talented technician (a la K.L. Saigal in Nitin Bose's *President*, 1937), who impresses the owner, Seth Sewakram (Motilal) and the workers of the mill where his poor elder brother, Ram Lal (Raaj Kumar) also works, by repairing a state-of-the-art machine. Impressed with his acumen, Seth Sewakram offers Ratan Lal a job in his mill, where he falls in love with a typist, Manju (Vyjayanthimala).

While working in the mill, Ratan Lal discovers that Seth Sewakram has been defrauding the mill employees and he decides to form an employees' union, a move that is opposed by his elder brother Ram Lal, who as an old employee of the mill, is devoted and loyal to Seth Sewakram. In a powerful scene from the film, Ratan Lal addresses the workers and

Dilip Kumar and Raaj Kumar in *Paigham* (1959)

explains as to how the mill owner does not care for human life and suggests the need for formation of a labour union.

After the union is formed, there is a call for strike of the workers to demand their rights. It is a flashpoint that results in relations being soured not only with Seth Sewakram but also between the two brothers. Finally, it leads to a confrontation between Ratan Lal and his elder brother on the non-payment of bonus to the mill workers. It is a highlight of the film, as also the scene where, as an opponent of the elder brother, Ratan Lal, as the union leader, delivers a highly charged and dramatic speech at the mill gate about the rights of the workers. And there is also the discourse by Dilip Kumar when he meets Seth Sewakram and talks about the need for building cordial and humanistic relations between the mill workers and the owners.

The twist in the story however is when Seth Sewakram's daughter, Malti (B. Saroja Devi), falls desperately in love with Ratan Lal, knowing fully well that he is in love with the office typist, Manju. Later, in another twist, it is discovered that Manju too is the daughter of Seth Sewakram, who, many years earlier, had discarded her mother.

In the end, *Paigham*, like *President*, stresses the importance of concrete employer–employee relations as a major key to economic and industrial growth.

According to Dilip Kumar:

S.S. Vasan was a genial, unassuming gentleman. We liked each other and became friends in no time. He was the boss of the sprawling studio and a respected figure in the South Indian film industry. He liked chatting with me and telling me tales that may or may not have anything to do with his own life . . . He was a great storyteller and I remember listening to him in rapt attention. If you ask me about the most successful film-makers in India or anywhere in the world, it is men and women who know how to tell stories without letting the listeners' mind stray for a split second. Vasan Sahab had great knowledge about everything and an imagination that came to the fore when we discussed scenes for *Paigham*.[9]

Dilip Kumar recalled that once when he was travelling by train with Vasan to Madhurai, he was told by the film-maker of not being very sure about the development of the scene they were to shoot the next day as it was a tricky one where the heroine would muster up all her feminine guile to find out the hero's feelings for her.

'I told him that I had seen a foreign film in which the hero and heroine meet on the terrace of a building when they hope to share some quiet moments. The heroine asks the hero if he had dated any girls or desired anyone before he met and befriended her . . . Her hair keeps falling over her face and

Dilip Kumar and Johnny Walker in *Paigham* (1959)

he leans forward and moves her back to see her face clearly. Then he begins to tell her about a girl.... He sees the colour recede on her face and her eyes betray her anxiety. She is almost in tears. He then tells her that the girl he was describing and talking about was none other than the girl sitting infront of him.

'I suggested that the scene be done differently where the hero would do all the talking and the heroine would respond with expressions. He would go on telling her about the woman he is in love with and arouse her envy and anxiety. She would try and hide her reactions, but the audience can see that she is getting edgy and jealous from the expressions that flit across her face involuntarily.'

That night, Dilip Kumar wrote the lines for the scene, rehearsed them and was ready to face the camera the next morning. The scene was shot and became the highlight of the film, something that many a film-maker has copied over the years in many a film, for example, David Dhawan in *Kyon Kii . . . Main Jhuth Nahin Bolta* (2001), with Govinda and Sushmita Sen in the lead.

The music of *Paigham* was by C. Ramchandra, by which time he was not the composer of any standing that he had been till just a couple of years earlier. That sheen of his had evaporated and besides *Paigham,* he had only one other 'biggie', if one could call it that, to score for—V. Shantaram's musical *Navrang.* Though *Navrang*, with V. Shantaram's muse, Sandhya, turned out to be a dragged silver jubilee success and was dismissed by the industry as an inhouse Maharthian show at best, Asha Bhosle scored eight of the dozen songs, which were quite successful. On the other hand, *Paigham*, a blockbuster at the box office, had Asha Bhosle, a participant in six of the songs, with not one hitting the success charts. Thus, *Paigham* turned out to be a no C. Ramchandra music show. The only song that worked was the Raag Bagaeshree-based title number by lyricist Kavi Pradeep (Ramchandra Narayanji Dwivedi) sung by Manna Dey:

Insaan ka insaan se ho bhaichara
yahi paigham hamara
Naye jagat mein hua purana
Ho batwara

(May all humans live in brotherhood
This is our message.
In this new universe, its divisions are old.)

Gunga Jumna (1961)

A legend of Indian cinema, a classic entertainer with a powerful story, outstanding performances and riveting music, *Gunga Jumna*, written and produced by Dilip Kumar, is considered a classic to this day—a spectacular dacoit drama that kept the audiences all over glued to their seats. With it, the actor made his final contribution to realist cinema. The film, which had a strong social underpinning, enforced with excellent directional and technical support, presented the actor completely integrated with the theme of the film and his relationship with the rest of the cast. The film also signified a unique linguistic breakthrough, as it used the local rural dialect, Bhojpuri—a dialect of Hindi spoken in parts of Uttar Pradesh, Bihar and Nepal—and yet had big stars and the associated large-scale sets and finery.

Directed, officially at least, by Nitin Bose and shot in technicolour by the veteran V. Bala Saheb, the film narrated the tale of two brothers on opposite side of the law: Gunga (Dilip

Dilip Kumar in *Gunga Jumna* (1961)

Dilip Kumar and Vyjayanthimala in *Gunga Jumna* (1961)

Kumar) and Jumna (played by Dilip Kumar's younger brother Nasir Khan). Gunga works as a farm labourer in a village where a rich but a wicked zamindar is the domineering force. One day, he is wrongly accused by the wicked zamindar—played by Anwar Hussain—for a crime he did not commit. When pursued by the police, he meets Dhanno (Vyjayanthimala), his sweetheart, and cries his tale of woe to her: '*Ram kasam, yeh sab kuttey ki tarah mere pichha kiya, Dhanno. Main bhooku mar gaya, Dhanno. Main ghar se beghar ho gaya, Dhanno*' (By God, all of them followed me like a dog. I died of hunger, Dhanno. I have become homeless, Dhanno). What makes the scene exemplary is the raw, unfiltered portrayal of his sadness. His genuine tears and heart-wrenching expressions with a voice that conveys an immense sense of loss of everything that he possessed in life—his pride and the few possessions that he had. It is a scene that is more than just a scene on the screen. It was to become more than just a story.

Dilip Kumar and Nasir Khan in *Gunga Jumna* (1961)

They both flee to a remote area, where he joins a gang of dacoits and soon becomes their leader. Living in the ravines he marries Dhanno.

For his part, Jumna, whom Gunga had sent to the city for education, becomes a police officer.

When Gunga is about to become a father, he decides to return to the village to ask for people's forgiveness, but his righteous brother Jumna (who has been posted in that area) asks him to surrender to the police. Dhanno intervenes and tries to take her husband away. In prison, Gunga's gangmates arrive to free him. In the ensuing gun battle, Dhanno dies in the crossfire and later, Jumna shoots his rebel brother dead.

The film is studded with some of the most humorous and light-hearted, as well as the most poignant, gripping and dramatic sequences ever to be filmed in Hindi cinema. And Dilip Kumar's performance is to be seen to be believed. For example, the *kabbadi* (a contact sport) match where the hero virtually, single-handedly wins for his team; that seemingly unending street quarrel when Gunga collides with Dhanno

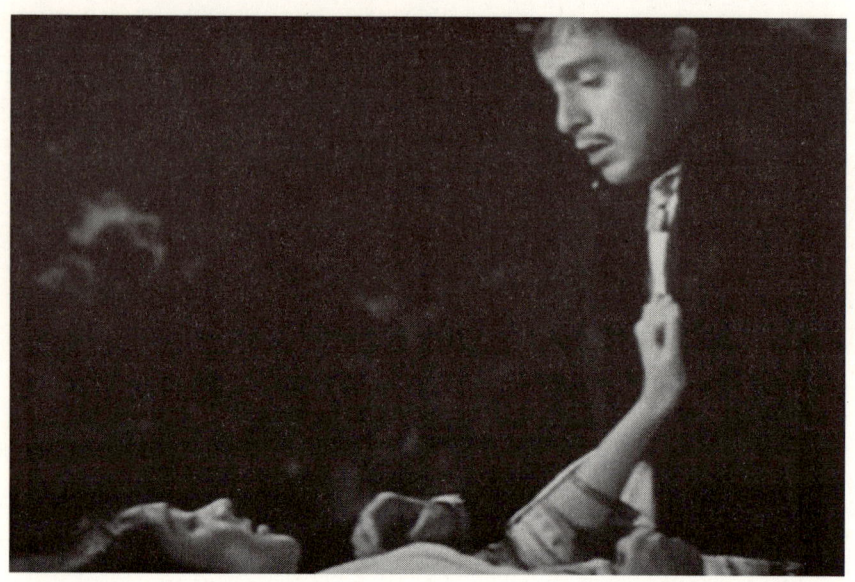

Dilip Kumar and Vyjayanthimala in *Gunga Jumna* (1961)

while going home after buying a fountain pen for his brother Jumna. There is also the mind-boggling dance performed by Gunga while singing *Nain lad jaiye* (Our eyes have met) in a village gathering. The most heart-rending scenes are the death of Dhanno in the gun battle between the police and the dacoits, after which Gunga, boiling with anger, starts putting the village on fire, even when Jumna tries his best to stop him.

And ultimately, the death scene in which Jumna shoots his brother, who dies in Jumna's arms, at the feet of the deity his mother worshipped so trustingly and devotedly. It shows a victory for the law when Gunga succumbs to the bullet wounds. Says Dilip Kumar: 'I wanted to tell the audience that it was Gunga who had achieved a bigger triumph—the moral victory God has given him by fulfilling his objective of establishing his poor mother's innocence and restoring her reputation in the village.'[10]

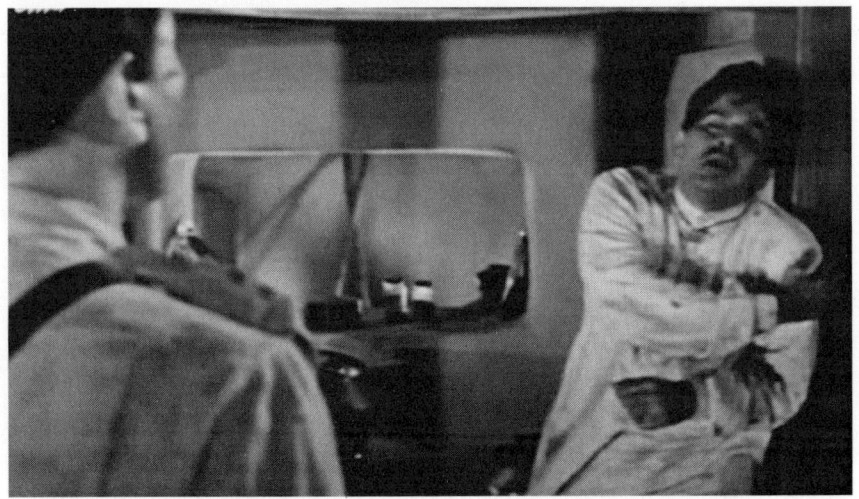

Dilip Kumar and Nasir Khan in *Gunga Jumna* (1961)

Vyjayanthimala personally loves the scene 'where Gunga breaks down over his wife Dhanno's death and the pathos that comes through. Dilip Kumar's performance is amazing. His forte is the painstaking study that goes into the characters. The perfection he seeks in each scene cannot be described in words.' The scene is as real as it could get. The fear in Dilip Kumar's eyes, the expressions on his face, the blood-curdling voice, isn't just acting. It is an outstanding visceral, a Pavlovian reaction on the situation.

Gunga Jumna drew some of its inspiration from the great saga *Mother India* by Mehboob Khan. Although Khan provided the basic model of the *baghi* (the rebel) in the form of the angry rural youth Birju (Sunil Dutt), it was in *Gunga Jumna* that he redesigned the character, with far more depth and insight.

The dacoity problem had also been dealt with by Raj Kapoor in his 1960 film *Jis Desh Mein Ganga Behti Hai* and later by Sunil Dutt in *Mujhe Jeene Do* (1963), influenced by the dedicated reformer Jayprakash Narayan's (JP) famous crusade for eradicating the problem of dacoity in rural India. JP's efforts to win over the people gone astray by peaceful Gandhian means enthused these film-makers. However, *Gunga Jumna* turned out to be the most authentic in portraying the root of the dacoity problem: rampant exploitation of the rural poor by the zamindars and the inhuman response of the state. The failure of the law-enforcing machinery to address the grievances of the honest labourer-turned-rebel, Gunga, and his eventual killing by his upright brother, showed the omnipresent nature of the state, which refuses to look into the actual causes of human suffering and exploitation and has a stock response: crush the non-conformist.

Though, as mentioned above, Dilip Kumar had played a rustic young lad in *Insanyiat* and *Naya Daur*, in *Gunga Jumna*, he came up with a few innovations: He completely changed his body language to liberate himself from his usual restrained postures, while, at the same time, he revelled in his new spontaneity. He totally declassified his image from his earlier characters (which were mostly set in the aristocratic or middle-class milieu) and presented on screen a typical rustic rural youth, rambunctious but down to earth and strongly rooted in the sociocultural milieu. The metamorphosis of this youth into a dacoit was one of the high points of the film, which also depicts a distinct class attitude against which the protagonist rebelled and had to face the grim consequences.

Though the film's direction was credited to Nitin Bose, it was Dilip Kumar who not only wrote and produced the film but directed it too as per his vision of the story. In fact, he had started working on the story idea of the film when he was shooting for *Naya Daur* and opted to make it in Bhojpuri, along with a smattering of other dialects such as Awadhi and Purvi. Apparently, as the story goes, he was fascinated when he heard Bhojpuri spoken by a *maali* (gardener) and his wife during his growing up years in Deolali (a small town now in the western state of Maharashtra). He records: 'Recently . . . Amitabh Bachchan mentioned to me that he had repeatedly viewed *Gunga Jumna* as a student to understand how a Pathan was effortlessly playing a rustic character and speaking the dialect with such ease . . . This Pathan from Peshawar (now in Pakistan) did it by instinct, careful study [and] untiring rehearsals, and a temperament to succeed even in those ventures that were new.'[11]

As for the cast, he says:

> It was during the making of *Naya Daur* that I noticed Vyjayanthi's ability to feign a rustic character's mannerisms with conviction. As I was scripting *Gunga Jumna*, I felt that she would fit the role of Dhanno if she took pains to render the Bhojpuri dialect (used in the film) with the right accent and inflexions . . . I decided that if I went ahead and made *Gunga Jumna*, I would cast her in the lead and carry forward the professional understanding and bonhomie we had developed during *Devdas* to the six films we worked in thereafter. She had emerged as a capable artiste and a quick learner . . . She had made considerable progress in her rendering of scenes and dialogues. She was diligent and took pains to grasp the pace and complexity of the situations, especially when the surrealistic and metaphysical scenes and situations were given to her for study before we went before the cameras to film Madhumati.[12]

Dilip Kumar would record Vyjayanthimala's dialogues on tape and give it to her to study, as he knew that it would be hard for her to speak the Bhojpuri dialect. For every scene, he would have her study the dialogues first and then deliver them for her simultaneously showing her how to articulate each word and how to give facial expressions.

Vyjayanthimala recalls:

Gunga Jumna was a very rustic film with typical portrayal of a village girl. It was a tough call, as the phonetic sounds of Bhojpuri threw the real challenge . . . But I would never forget how much Dilip Saab helped me with the diction needed for the film. He was always guiding. He would be there for every scene, always behind the camera—totally dedicated and meticulous. When you have a competent co-star, you derive a lot of strength, and it becomes a mutual source of inspiration. I could portray the role of Dhanno with fluent bantering and raucous arguments in colourful Bhojpuri dialect because of Dilip Saab. Being a very strong actor, he helped me express and convey, act and react, accordingly. Of course, the character, the script, the direction comprises the support system, but the co-star is very important for that support, especially, when you have a rapport like two batsmen at the crease. *Gunga Jumna* became a special movie for me, my best! I found myself working extra hard. The role had a lot of depth, the linguistic coding was used so artfully, with rural life celebrated in exuberant songs and carefree dancing.[13]

When Dilip Kumar was writing the story and the screenplay of the film, even his brother, Nasir, felt that he was making a mistake, as people would not like to see their favourite actor as a bandit and a law breaker. However, after much thought, he decided to go ahead without making any changes. He felt that 'though his hero is on the wrong side of the law, he had the audience sympathy with him and the conflict in the story was not so much between the brothers as it is between the law of the country and the moral freedom of a human being to fight injustice and corruption and take the world forward.'

'*Gunga Jumna* was a blockbuster at the box office. The audience loved it to the hilt. The critics lauded it endlessly. According to the American author, Philip Lutgendorf, who is Professor Emeritus of Hindi at the University of Iowa: 'Linguistic coding is artfully used, with Gunga and Dhanno's raucous arguments in colourful Bhojpuri dialect contrasted with Jumna's carefully measured pronouncements in Khari-boli or "high" Delhi speech. Rural life is also celebrated in exuberant songs and dances.'[14]

Dilip Kumar once again proved that he is indeed unmatchable.

Dilip Kumar, as the captain, chose his team judiciously and roped in his favourite duo of the composing czar—Naushad and the lyricist poet par excellence, Shakeel Badayuni—as the composer and lyricist, respectively. Needless to say, Naushad's musical score was memorable and became a major highlight of the film, as it brought alive the rural rhythms, the rustic beats and the earthy fragrance of the soil. With it Naushad hit the jackpot—a stunning hat-trick—with each song of each of the three films—*Mughal-e-Azam*, *Kohinoor* and *Gunga Jumna*—without exception, being a massive hit and on top of the music charts for a long, long time. Badayuni's lyrics were in perfect harmony with Naushad's tunes, which was only to be expected.

Of the eight songs, Lata Mangeshkar accounted for four solos, which includes the lovely Raag Desh-based number *Jhanan ghoongar baaje* (*Jhanan* the anklets ring), where Mohammad Rafi chips in towards the end with just 'O oh ho', which thus, cannot strictly be called a solo; Asha Bhosle for one solo, Mohammad Rafi for one solo (plus chorus), Rafi and Asha Bhosle for one duet and Hemant Kumar—a rare choice on Naushad's part—for one solo. One of Lata's most popular numbers from the film is *Dhoondo dhoondo re saajna dhoondo re saajana, more kan ka baala* in Raag Pilu (Find my beloved, find my beloved, my ear-ring) with Naushad providing the notes through the sitar of Abdul Halim Jaffer Khan, 'which left the mere male in the audience groping for the missing ear-ring of Dhanno; and that *Do hanson ka jooda bichhod gayo re* in the Naushadian Raag Bhairavi (the two swans have got separated), as contrastingly tinted held the ear'.[15] According to Naushad, 'The beauty of Bhairavi lies in the fact that you are going back to this raagini even while you are indulging in the merry delusion of thinking that you are taking it forward! How do you take *forward* such an exemplary set traditional song form adorning the rich vocabulary of our music?'[16]

No less euphoniously envisioned upon the provocatively rangy Vyjayanthimala were those Naushadian Pilu notes of *Na maanoon na maanoon na maanoon re* were well articulated by Lata Mangeshkar.

The Mohammad Rafi chorus-backed solo, picturized on Dilip Kumar and a large bunch of male and female dancers, upholds in the form of a folk song with a medley of intertwined tunes; just when one thinks the song is over, Naushad springs a surprise and comes up with a new tune, which is totally different from the earlier lot. The song consists of a two-line prelude, three antaras and the additional lyrics for the new tune. The mukhda is:

Nain lad jaiye to manva kasak hoibe kari
Prem ka chut hai pataakha to dhamak hoibe kori

(When the eyes [of lovers] meet, there is bound to be heartache
When the cracker of love goes off, there is bound to be pounding [of the heart].)

The third antara of the song is the favourite one for its boisterous lyrics:

Aankh mil jayen sajaniya se to nashan lagi hain
Pyaar ki mithi gajal manwa bhi gaavan lagi hai
Jhaanjh baji hain to kamrya ma lachak hoibe kari

(When my eyes meet those of my beloved, they dance
A sweet ode of love my heart sings
When cymbals clash, the waist is bound to[begin] swinging.)

Dilip Kumar's rustic flamboyance was very much apparent in this peppy number.

Gunga Jumna, considered a cult film of Dilip Kumar, went on to bag several awards, deservingly at that.

Sunghursh (1968)

If *Sunghursh* was a narrative of a conflict between two families on screen, it also became a story of conflict off screen too. First, the romantic and one of the most successful screen pairs of the times over a period of thirteen years and seven films, Dilip Kumar and Vyjayanthimala, after giving hits or blockbusters, parted ways, never again to work in a film together. In fact, by the time *Sunghursh* could be completed, their relations had soured to such an extent that they were not even on talking terms. Second, Dilip Kumar and his most favourite duo of composer–lyricist, Naushad–Shakeel Badayuni, respectively, too parted ways after fifteen films with mesmerizing evergreen music, never again to work in tandem on a film project. All in all, a sad and an unfortunate loss indeed for the world of Hindi cinema.

Yet, much tortured and delayed in the making, the film had great performances by the star-cast which producer–director

Dilip Kumar and Vyjayanthimala in *Sunghursh* (1968)

H.S. Rawail, who was basking in the huge glory of his multi-starrer *Mere Mehboob* (1963), collected—Dilip Kumar, Vyjayanthimala, Balraj Sahni, Sanjeev Kumar, Durga Khote, Jayant, Devan Verma amongst others. The film, depicting a historical saga set in nineteenth-century Banaras (Varanasi), gave Dilip Kumar a rare opportunity to reaffirm his acumen in a narrative set in an authentic historical setting.

Based on a Bengali short story by the Jnanpith Award winner, Mahasweta Devi, the film narrates the vendetta between two families against the background of thuggee, a cult perpetrated by bandits from the medieval central and northern India. For generations they practised the tantra of Goddess Kali, looting the pilgrims to Kashi (Banaras), and then indulging in human sacrifice by waylaying them and taking them to the underground sanctum sanctorum of the temples for the rituals. The plot, quite complicated, encompasses three generations.

The story of the film is about Bhawani Prasad (Jayant), who heads a family of bandit priests whose own relatives have threatened to destroy him. He initiates his grandson, Kundan Prasad (Dilip Kumar), against the wishes of his wife into the ancestral profession. In a superbly acted scene, at the beginning of the film, one sees that the grandfather wants Kundan to join the traditional bloodshed occupation of the family, but he expresses much disdain for this occupation: '*Janasheen bhi aapne banaya hai Dada aur shatru bhi. Saab aap ki hi den hai. Aapka yeh dharam, jis mein na jaane kitne masoomon ke khoon ki aahooti deni paadi, main is dharam ko savikaar nahin kar sakta*' (You made me the vicegerent successor and an enemy also. This is all your giving. This religion of yours, in which so many innocent lives have been sacrificed, I cannot accept). Another example of superb histrionics is Kundan's reaction of anger and disgust when his grandfather prevails upon him to kill him (grandfather) so as to make him as his first *bali* (human sacrifice) to join the old family profession of killing and thuggee, followed by the delirious condition in which Kundan moves around the house with his sheet of cloth shed with his father's blood: *Baap dada ki nishani hai yeh. Ek ka punya, dusre ka paap. Dono is rang mein range hain . . . Woh paap jo tum is duniya main chod gaye ho, Dada, uska prayashchit main karunga.* (This is an emblem of my father and grandfather. One's uprightness is another's sin. Both are mixed in this colour . . . The sins that you have left behind in this world, Grandfather, I will do penance for them).

Kundan, however, grows up into a pacifist, virtually a peace activist, whose mission is to completely replace the doctrine of hate with love and brotherhood (a la Raj Kapoor in *Jis Desh Mein Ganga Behti Hai*). In essence, Kundan attempts to end the long-standing feud between the two warring families. When his cousins, Ganeshi Prasad and Dwarka Prasad (Balraj Sahni and Sanjeev Kumar, respectively) try to kill him, a mysterious singer-cum-dancer, Laila-e-Aasmaan played by Vyjayanthimala,

Dilip Kumar and Sanjeev Kumar in *Sunghursh* (1968)

who was Kundan's companion during childhood, saves him. He falls in love with her and tries to woo her through romantic melodies.

In the end, Kundan wins the heart of his senior cousin Ganeshi Prasad by serving him, in disguise as Bajrang, his servant, thus pleasing him, but perpetuating much suffering on himself and his love. The younger cousin, Dwarka Prasad, becomes a victim of his own plot to poison Kundan.

Given the kind of inputs that went into the making of *Sunghursh*, the film had a great potential to emerge as a classic during a time when this genre was being not so earnestly attempted. However, the film got marred because of several reasons, particularly due to an overemphasis on the romance angle of the lead pair. Dilip Kumar, with his characteristic overlap of underplay and overplay, meticulously built up an intense character who suffers due to the ancestral burden of guilt and wants peace to reign over the two families. However,

Dilip Kumar and Balraj Sahni in *Sunghursh* (1968)

for whatever reasons, in the latter part of the film, the focus entirely shifts to the love triangle involving Kundan, the dancer Laila and the senior cousin, Ganeshi Prasad, in which Dilip Kumar (as seen in his earlier films like *Shaheed* and *Dil Diya Dard Liya*) gets obsessed with winning over his enemy, sacrificing his own love. The result is that the basic spirit of the story failed to come through. The film was rated 'below average' at the box office. This even though Dilip Kumar's performance, as usual, was master class.

The main beneficiary of *Sunghursh* was Sanjeev Kumar (Harihar Jethalal Jariwala) who, in his first major role, provided a glimpse of his formidable potential. In their scenes together, he did give the stalwart a run for his money. No wonder, soon after this film, he carved a niche for himself in Hindi cinema in an impressive manner.

For the music and melodies, Rawail brought in his old team from *Mere Mehboob,* the 1963 Muslim social multi-starrer in which Naushad and Badayuni had created magic with its nine outstanding beauties, which occupied top position on the music charts and are often heard even today, sounding as fresh as ever. In *Sunghursh,* the line-up comprised seven songs: three Mohammad Rafi solos (including a breezy folk-music based chorus number), three Lata Mangeshkar solos and one by Asha Bhosle. Of the Rafi solos—*Haay, mere pairon mein ghunghroo bandhaa de to phir meri chaal dekh le* (Tie anklets on my feet and then look at my gait) in Raag Desh, *Jab dil se dil takrata hai* (When the heart clashes against the heart) in Raag Yaman, and *Ishq deewana husn bhi ghayal* (Love is crazy and beauty wounded), one would opt for the second one for its underlying amorous overtones, but platonic in nature.

In it, the mukhda and three antaras give shape to *Jab dil se dil takrata hai,* a very slow-paced melody intricately tuned by the composer, and put across equally tenderly by the *gulukaar* (singer). The mukhda is:

> *Jab dil se dil takrata hai*
> *Mat poochiye kya ho jaata hai*
> *Jhukti hain nazar rukti hai zubaan*
> *Maathe pe pasina aata hai*

> (When one's heart clashes against the heart
> Do not ask what happens
> The eyes look down and one becomes tongue-tied.
> Sweat breaks out on the forehead.)

But it is the last antara that one can choose for the dainty usage of imagery and metaphor by the poet:

Mukhda na chhupa yoon haaton se
Din ko na badal aab raaton se
Gulshan mein bikharne de naghme
Tu pyaar ki meethi baton se
Ah husn ki devi aankh mila
Apnon se koi sharmata hai

(Do not hide your face with your hands
Do not convert the days into nights
Let songs be spread across the garden
By your sweet speech
O goddess of beauty look into my eyes
One should not feel shy of one's own folks.)

Of the three Lata Mangeshkar solos—*Mere paas aao nazar toh milao* (Come near me meet my gaze) based on Raag Bhairavi, *Chedo na dil ki baat abhi, tum nashe mein ho* (Don't broach matters of the heart, you are high), and *Agar yeh husn mera pyaar ke sholyon mein dhal jaye* (If my complexion gets burnt in the flames of love), are indeed beguiling, but the single Asha Bhosle solo in Raag Miyan ki Todi—*Tasveer-e-mohabbat thi jis mein, humne woh seesha tod diya* (I have broken the glass in which was the portrait of love)—is nothing short of effervescent.

For the film, Naushad used the music from the regions of Awadh and eastern Uttar Pradesh. However, the music failed to create the magic that the Naushad–Badayuni duo was known for. It was labelled as 'below average' by music critics and film music buffs alike. It was Naushad's third film in a row whose music had failed to click, the other two being S.U. Sunny's *Palki* (1967) and A. Bhim Singh's *Aadmi*.

As the film music historian Raju Bharatan wrote: 'Imagine Dilip Kumar singing *Haay, mere pairon mein ghunghroo bandhaa de to phir meri chaal dekh le*. By 1968, he was no longer the Gunga of *Gunga Jumna* to do a *Nain led jaiye* in 1961. A near quarter-century in films (as 1968 drew to a close) had not treated thespian Dilip Kumar too kindly by way of his looking well preserved.'[17]

By the early 1970s, Naushad faced a possible career crunch because his only film to succeed was B. Nagi Reddy's *Ram Aur Shyam*. According to Bharatan:

> The same Naushad who always instinctively struck the right note, why does he falter now? was the question. In the scene in which Vyjayanthimala and Dilip Kumar meet beyond the temple steps, why, in such a situation, a contextually inapt tune like *Jab dil se dil takrata hai*? Lady luck, as an old flame by then, no longer glowed so bright in Naushad's life and times rapidly transforming the film's landscape.
>
> 'However, Naushad denied that his music during this period was a failure: 'Everyone looks upon late sixties as fatal years for me. Yet, the fact is that I composed some of my better music in a clutch of films like *Gunga Jumna*, *Mere Mehboob*, *Leader*, *Dil Diya Dard Liya*, *Ram Aur Shyam*, *Aadmi*, *Sunghursh* and *Saathi*. My work was far more mature, and my orchestration was even better ordered. My singers were seasoned enough to perform at their finest. My recordings were designed to take full advantage of the vastly improved technology. In short, my work now was better rounded in every way.'[18]

If *Sunghursh* was the last film together of Dilip Kumar and Vyjayanthimala, it was also a final goodbye between Dilip Kumar and the Hindi film music's tried-and-tested first trio—Naushad, Shakeel Badayuni and Mohammad Rafi. 1968 was the benumbing year in which Naushad all but met his Waterloo, with three failures, in a highly demoralizing

41-week period. It reminded one of the words of the British actor Richard Burton: 'You reach the top of the heap, but it's a circle and you slip off the downside, maybe for years. You get scarred.'

How true! The world of films is indeed a capricious one!

Sagina Mahato (1970; Bangla)

Though some mention that Tapan Sinha's *Sagina Mahato* was an Indianized version of Elia Kazan's *Viva Zapata!* starring Marlon Brando, it was claimed to be based on a true Bengali story by Gour Kishore Ghosh, a well-known Bengali writer and journalist associated with *Anandabazar Patrika*. Starring Dilip Kumar and Saira Banu, it is all about the labour movement of 1942–43, told through fictional characters.

Sagina Mahato is the only thematically strong film of the actor during the post-classical phase, presenting him in a role which was located in a definite social context. The film is a critique of the extremist radical politics in the country,

Dilip Kumar and Saira Banu in *Sagina Mahato* (1970, Bangla)

Dilip Kumar in and as *Sagina Mahato* (1970, Bangla)

represented here by Aniruddha, played by the renowned Bengali actor Anil Chatterjee, who is in pursuit of power by manipulating oppressed people. For him, the 'wretched of the earth' are merely fools to be employed for establishing the supremacy of his ideological thought.

The film is set in the north-eastern region of India during the colonial period, where a tea estate factory labour leader, Sagina Mahato (Dilip Kumar) is a leader of the workers, who has learnt early in life that an underdog has to snatch his rights to survive in this harsh and cruel world. A rebel, he defies the authority of the British owners and managers of the factory who are brutally exploitative. Sagina comes to the rescue of his fellow factory workers and challenges the high-handed bosses. He declares a strike when an old-time worker of the factory, Gurum (Om Prakash), is removed from service for refusing to supply girls to the management and when one factory officer rapes Sagina's friend's fiancée.

In Calcutta, Aniruddha comes to know about this unusual natural leader of the workers. He sends two representatives of his party—Aparna Sen playing the role of the secretary

Visakha and Swaroop Dutta representing the management—
to the labour colony to meet Sagina and make him a party
member. They begin indoctrinating him, telling him about the
fall of Bastille and the gains of the Russian revolution only to
find the latter snoring lustily, a sarcastic comment on the lack
of understanding of the city-bred revolutionaries, about the
reality at the grassroots and the attitudes of the downtrodden
about them and their viewpoints.

Paranoiac Aniruddha, however, gets unnerved by the
growing political stature of Sagina among the workers and
the party members. He lays a trap and Sagina is made the
welfare officer in the factory. The workers now see him as
a stooge of the management. In the end, after much intrigue
and counter-intrigue, melodrama and elaborate theatrics,
Aniruddha is exposed as a ruthless power seeker, while Sagina
is rehabilitated in the colony as a symbol of the hope of the
working class.

Shot on locations in Kurseong, near Darjeeling, the film
was a display of histrionics all the way. Dilip Kumar took his
acting to an entirely new domain and exhibited once again
his deep understanding and handling of a character through
excellent intuitive gestures and interaction with the events, as
they unfold. He simply 'lived' through the character, depicting
by his style and crisp dialogues, the ideological influences on
his thinking and actions. The way in which he improvises his
mannerisms when he is officially made the trade union leader,
intoxicated with newly acquired power and status, and when
he argues his forthright down-to-earth understanding of the
class relations and the Left politics, is truly amazing—to be
seen and studied to be believed. The Sagina in Ghosh's novel
gets sucked into the actor and virtually emerges as a true
incarnation of the original.

Look at the scenes in which Sagina presents to the visiting
activists his own grassroots version of politics and says

'*Yahi to saala hamari takkat hai ki hamare pass kuch bhi nahin*' (Our strength is that we have nothing on us). And that scene where in his indigenous style, he explains to his fellow workers about their constant exploitation by the British factory owners. And, of course, those last scenes where a shocked Sagina rushes to a fatally injured activist and takes him in his arms after the fascist Aniruddha shoots the comrade, and then after chasing him down thrashes him: '*Hum bhuke-nange goli bandook mein vishwas nahin rakhte. Inhi haaton se hum roti-rozi kamatey hain aur is duniya ka muqabala karte hain*' (We the hungry and naked do not trust the gun and the bullet. With these hands we earn our daily bread and also face the world.)

And yet the complex theme of the film is largely negated by the formula's packaging and overemphasis on Sagina's love affair. As in other films of this period, Dilip Kumar's histrionics overpowered everything else in the film, including its political context.

The political evolution of Sagina, the illiterate, unindoctrinated worker, and his subsequent disillusionment with the wider working-class movement in Bengal, looked too defused to make the film a memorable document on the struggles of the working class of the country. According to Dilip Kumar:

> I was fascinated by the character of Sagina—his complete lack of guile in dealing with critical issues and convincing people, his perceptions and instinctive abilities, his maverick behaviour at times, his love for Lalita and, above all, his chequered destiny. There was depth and realism in the way Tapanda had created the character of Sagina on paper and he told me that I was free to improvise if I wished . . . He had long academic discussions with me about the backdrop and the period of the story and he

urged me to read some literature he had compiled about the pre-Independence labour union movements and about the birth and spread of Naxalism in certain parts of east and north-east India. Such literature was very helpful to me in understanding the characters and their vulnerabilities against the backdrop of the revolutionary political scenario that had surfaced there.[19]

Sagina Mahato was a great success, creating box-office records in Bengal. The media too was unanimous in its praise, particularly Dilip Kumar's performance. The film critic of the *Statesman* in its edition of 19 April 1970 wrote: 'Perhaps the most memorable distinction is Dilip Kumar's performance as the hero . . . I can hardly recollect any Hindi film in which he was as impressive as he is in his first appearance in the Bengali cinema. It is a power of great and professional assurance.'

The *Anandabazar Patrika* of the same date said: 'The film has for its outstanding feature, excellent acting by Dilip Kumar, the likes of which is rarely seen on the Bengali screen.'

And, according to the *Amrit Bazar Patrika*:

It would be impossible to imagine a more finished [sic] performer than Dilip. His chief virtue, which takes him higher than any living actor on the Indian screen (and I mean 'any'), is that his art lies in [the] complete concealment of art and in the submergence of his personal self under the forces of the role . . . The nuances of his expressions, his vocal artistry in both high and low pitches are marvels of acting that any of our high and mighty actors have to see and hear to believe.

Sagina (1974; Hindi)

The success, the praise, the accomplishments, the triumph of *Sagina Mahato*, all got washed away as a remake of the film came out in its Hindi avatar under the title *Sagina*, after a long, long wait in the wings of four years, in 1974. The cast, the technicians, the unit hands, the producers and the director, all were the same as in the Bengali version. If there was a difference, it was in its music department. While the Bengali film had music by Anup Ghoshal, for the Hindi version, ace composer S.D. Burman was brought in with lyrics by Majrooh Sultanpuri.

And, in a wonder of wonders, a generation that had grown up listening to Mohammad Rafi in film after film (and in

Dilip Kumar and Saira Banu in *Sagina* (1974, Hindi)

certain cases Mukesh too), as Dilip Kumar's voice, had to now tolerate Kishore Kumar on the thespian. For example, listen to the song *Chhote chhote sapne hamare* (Small, small, dreams of ours) or that *Uparwala dukhiyon ki nahin suntan re* (He does not listen to the poor) or even that boisterous chorus *Saala main to sahaab ban gaya* (I have become a sahaab) and one can clearly make out the difference. And this despite the fact that Kishore Kumar tried his best to blend his voice adeptly with that of Dilip Kumar as he sang with his characteristic verve and elan, but somehow that Rafi enchantment was missing. And the audience soon realized that Kishore Kumar, even with four numbers to himself, going on Dilip Kumar, was a damp squib. No wonder, Kishore Kumar's voice was used on Dilip Kumar only a decade later by Hridaynath Mangeshkar in *Mashaal*, again to not much positive results. Kishore Kumar was undoubtedly a great singer, but Rafi was Rafi. Period.

Apparently, the song situations were inserted in *Sagina* to provide some relief in the original narrative since it was moving at a slow pace. There is that number by Lata Mangeshkar and Kishore Kumar: *Tumhre sang to raen bitayee kahaan bitaaun din?* (I spent the night with you where should I spend the day?) choreographed in the most unconventional manner with Dilip Kumar and Saira Banu's personal inputs in the movements. It was forced into the film suggesting the intimacy between Sagina and Lalita the previous night, in much the same way that *Dhoondo dhoonda re sajna more kaan ka bala* (Find, find, my love my ear-ring) suggesting the consummation of the relationship between Gunga and Dhanno after their hurried wedding in *Gunga Jumna*. And see the difference between the two. Need one say anything more?

Whatever be the case, the film sank without a trace. As the film magazine *Star & Style*, dated 13 September 1974, wrote in its review: 'The last really good and successful film Dilip Kumar had was *Ram Aur Shyam*. That was in 1967, which makes it seven years ago! And seven years is hell of a long time, for nowhere is the proverbial shortness of public memory more cruelly manifest than in show business . . . The whole film was one long and continuous crescendo. *Sagina* has turned into an ear-splitting and dreary movie . . . The thespian's performance is not vintage Dilip Kumar.'

Yet, *Sagina* had some great Dilip Kumar moments. One such scene was the telephone scene and the other where Dilip Kumar delivers a speech on the hillside. And one still remembers the scene where Sagina (Dilip Kumar) confesses to Vishakha (Aparna Sen) the loneliness and poverty of his childhood, which made him what he was. What a performance that was? Dilip Kumar, and only a Dilip Kumar, could have done those scenes.

Kranti (1981)

After three back-to-back failures at the box office—*Dastaan*, *Sagina* and *Bairaag*—Dilip Kumar's sheen seemed to be wearing off and he needed to relook at his subsequent career moves. True, the danger of sinking into oblivion in the harsh and unpredictable, the cruel and callous world of showbiz, should not affect a confident and secure artiste, but the hard fact is, it does. And affects badly. Here, the life of an artiste is as long as the last Friday was—the day when a film is released, and verdict given on its fate. In this world of showbiz, it's all about winning, for here everyone is looking for winners. No one has time to look back at losers, in a world where 'the glam-sham maxim' is for today, not for the morrow. The film world where many have come and many have disappeared, in a world where many rose and then went down the greasy pole, unsung and uncared for, uncelebrated and unacclaimed, overlooked and unremembered, ignored, neglected and relegated to the backwaters of the Arabian Sea!

Dilip Kumar in *Kranti* (1981)

In 1976, Dilip Kumar decided to take a sabbatical and waited in the wings to rediscover his lost space in Hindi cinema. And when he came back in 1981, with Manoj Kumar's multi-star historical costume drama *Kranti*, written by Salim Javed, he proved to one and all that age had not forsaken or withered his talent nor custom staled his infinite variety. Time had been kind to him as he was at the cusp of his second innings. He had grown into a senior, leaving behind his most dependable composer Naushad, whom Manoj Kumar had replaced with Laxmikant–Pyarelal. And in place of his favourite lyricist Shakeel Badayuni, who had passed away much earlier, in April 1970, Manoj Kumar was romancing with his most dependable Santosh Anand. In this extensive paraphernalia and gloss, typical of a Manoj Kumar film, it had besides Manoj Kumar himself as the actor, producer–director, Hema Malini, Shashi Kapoor, Parveen Babi, Shatrughan Sinha, Nirupa Roy, Prem Chopra, Pradeep Kumar and others. Dilip Kumar played the role of Sangha, a senior revolutionary leader in the people's struggle against the British rule, and Manoj Kumar as who else but Bharat, his revolutionary son.

Dilip Kumar and Manoj Kumar in *Kranti* (1981)

Apparently, there were two reasons that inspired Manoj
Kumar to offer the lead role to Dilip Kumar. One, having
made his place among the most successful film-makers in the
late 1960s and early 1970s, Manoj Kumar wanted to pay
a tribute to the senior who had been the main inspiration
for him to become an actor. Second, Manoj Kumar had a
cherished desire to match his acting style with his guru, but
unlike in *Aadmi*, on his own ground. However, the result
was indifferent. The rapid-fire dialogues in some scenes
between the two and Manoj Kumar's ponderous exchange
of looks looked rather contrived without much substance
or impact.

This was the most expensive film Manoj Kumar ever made,
and it went on to become one of the highest-grossing Hindi
films of the 1980s. Dilip Kumar proved once again that a
diamond is a diamond, whichever angle you look at it from,
under whatever light you see it in, it will only shine.

Set in nineteenth-century British India, *Kranti* presents the
highly inspiring crusades of the father-and-son revolutionaries,
who are both hailed by their people as krantikari

Dilip Kumar and Shashi Kapoor in *Kranti* (1981)

(revolutionary), in their fight against the British between 1825 and 1875. Sangha (Dilip Kumar) is an honest and dedicated employee of Raja Laxman Singh of Ramgarh (P. Jairaj), whose allegiance and loyalty are to no one except for his raja, who conditionally permits the British to use the port of Ramgarh for trading purposes. However, the British use the port for taking out gold and bringing in ammunition instead.

When Sangha goes to report this outrage to the raja, he finds that the ruler has been killed. Sangha is charged with treason and of murder by the new ruler, Raja Shamsher Singh (Pradeep Kumar) and his stooges, including the villainous Shambu Singh (Prem Chopra). Sangha, who is sentenced to death, manages to escape from prison and forms a group of revolutionaries, whose only aim is to drive the British out of the country. These revolutionaries carry out their campaign under the slogan 'Kranti' (revolution—one India).

Kranti was yet another example of the underutilization of the legendary actor because of weak characterization, a meandering storyline and excessive melodrama, which was naturally aimed at the front-benchers. For example, there is a ferocious and burning with vengeance Sangha, who cuts off the arm of Shambu Singh when he touches his pregnant wife; or when Sangha is accused of treason in the court, he demolishes the accusation: '*Main mulzim hoon par aap ka nahin. Mulzim hoon apni matrabhoomi ka. Is desh ki sarzamin ka. Mulzim hoon uska, jiska zrra zrra mujhe lalkarta hai, kehta hai dhikaar hai Sangha tum par. Tum aaj tak in videshi bhediyoon ko desh se bahaar nanin nikal sake!*' (I am guilty, but not of yours. I am guilty of my motherland, of this land of my country. I am guilty of the one whose every bit is calling me . . . saying that may you be cursed Sangha. To this day you have not been able to throw these foreign wolves out of this country!)

The film is replete with such patriotic dialogues—heavy, melodramatic, emotionally exaggerated—and theatrical scenes, which made the film very appealing to the masses. One recalls that during the initial few minutes of screening of the film when Sangha thunders: '*Humein Hindustan ke khoon ki saugandh hai, aapne is khoon se hum aasman par inqilab likh denge. Kranti likh denge*' (We swear in the name of the blood of Hindustan. With our blood we will write revolution in the sky. We will write revolt), the front-benchers went delirious with excitement, shouting, screaming, wolf-whistling and the back-benchers clapping loudly and heavily.

Manoj Kumar, as a film-maker, was known for adopting a populist slogan-mongering approach to theme in all his films. And *Kranti* is no different. The critics, of course, panned the film. But whatever they may have written, the public was not complaining and Manoj Kumar, with his feel on the pulse of the movie-goers, was as happy as he could be. The film was a blockbuster. And, the most important fact remained, that though it was said that Dilip Kumar's role was 'cut down' a great deal at the editing stage, the actor had reinvented himself and nobody could stop him now.

Manoj Kumar (born Harikrishan Goswami) was a man of many parts—actor, producer, director, screen writer, lyricist and editor known for making patriotic films with the name Bharat in every film, thus nicknamed Bharat Kumar. One of the strong points of his films as always was the music score. Take any of the films that he made; music was the main scoring point which went on the hit charts.

For *Kranti*, Laxmikant–Pyarelal wrote the music score to the lyrics of Santosh Anand, and used Lata Mangeshkar, Mahendra Kapoor, Nitin Mukesh, Minoo Purshottam, Manna Dey, Shailendra Singh with Kishore Kumar and Mohammad Rafi in just one number, the Raag Desh-based: *Chana jor garam babu* and that too just as a part of the chorus, singing for Dilip Kumar, where his powerful and resonant vocals stole the show. Every song was a big hit and contributed to the success of the film.

9

THE ANTI-HERO

DILIP KUMAR'S ANTI-HERO PRESENTED A CRITIQUE OF A dehumanized society. The hero exhibited a curious obsession with the sensuous female form. This self-destructive syndrome was characterized by mortgaging oneself for unreciprocated love, carrying the dilemmas of an ugly past, and often overblown sadism causing distrust and hate in his relationship with the heroine. In a sense, this anti-hero stance of the protagonist was a protest against the dominant social system articulated through self-denial of what he desired. This self-isolated bitter man erased from his mind all the notions of goodness and love and these features became the basis of his 'negative' roles in the classical phase in films such as Mehboob Khan's *Andaz* and later in *Amar*, where he is shown as a successful and upright lawyer who was trapped in unbearable self-denial after he had raped a poor girl. In Amiya Chakravarty's *Daag*, he was a creative artisan but denied respect and love because of his incurable addiction to alcohol and Zia Sarhadi's *Footpath*, presented him as an ambitious slum youth inspiring to be rich by unfair means.

This was followed in the post-classical phase such as A.R. Kardar's *Dil Diya Dard Liya* (1966) and A. Bhim Singh's *Aadmi*. In senior roles he depicted with immense precision and in high scale the persona of a vengeful patriarch, for example in Ramesh Talwar's *Duniya* and Yash Chopra's *Mashaal* (both in 1984), K. Bapaiaah's *Izzatdaar* (1990) and in two films by Subhash Ghai—*Vidhaata* (1982) and *Saudagar* (1991). In these roles, this anti-hero was cast in a different mould. He was a noble innocent human being to start with, and in the social milieu an upholder of strong moral values and courage. But as he fell prey to cruel and crude social forces, he rose to be extremely vengeful, setting on a course to teach his enemies a lesson, using his suppressed anger and single-mindedness.

In such characterizations, Dilip Kumar seemed to be greatly influenced by the two nineteenth-century classical novels: *Wuthering Heights* by Emily Bronte and Charlotte Brontë's *Jane Eyre*. Some authors like Trinetra Bajpai and Anshula Bajpai have claimed that 'Heathcliff was Dilip Kumar's favourite character whom he attempted to portray in a number of his films. He fancied Heathcliff and was able to effectively bring out the anguish of the novel's protagonist time and again, albeit in toned down romanticized versions, minimizing the negative traits in the beastly character.'[1]

Andaz (1949)

The ambitious romantic drama *Andaz* was the first film Dilip Kumar did with Mehboob Khan, the producer–director known for giving blockbusters. And this time he was in the company of Nargis and Raj Kapoor. The film, which was a huge success at the box office, presented Dilip Kumar in the archetype of a desperate singer–lover. Located in the affluent urban society setting of the post-colonial period, the film raises the issue of the modern identity of Indian womanhood vis-à-vis the traditional values enshrined in Indian womanhood. It also attempted to examine the contradictory propositions that the newly independent India should value, that is, capitalist modernization, while retaining feudal family and moral values.

Dilip Kumar and Nargis in *Andaz* (1949)

The heroine, Neena (Nargis), is a modern, pampered and spoilt young woman whose lifestyle is more Western than Indian. One day, out riding, she loses control of her horse, which goes amok. A dashing young man Dilip (Dilip Kumar) saves her life and the two become good friends. Neena's father tries to caution his daughter that her meeting Dilip that often is not wise as he may misconstrue their friendship as love. Dilip, under the illusion of apparently reciprocated love of Neena, communicates his feelings through his songs so as to win her love.

After Neena's father's sudden death, Dilip comforts her during her moments of grief. Neena soon makes him a partner in the flourishing business left behind by her father.

Dilip tries to confide in Neena about his feelings for her, but before he can do so, her fiancée, Rajan (Raj Kapoor), returns from overseas and the two get married. Dilip's managerial efficiency disintegrates under the pressure of his frustrated desires, while the infantile Rajan begins to suspect his wife's fidelity. Eventually, the tensions erupt into a violent clash between the two men in which Dilip is seriously hurt. He recovers but, in his desperation, triggered by a long ungratified love, the disgruntled lover keeps saying to Neena that she is his and only his. And as he makes advances on Neena and tries to embrace her, she shoots him and is jailed for murder.

The ensuing trial establishes that the root cause of the tragedy was the excessively liberal lifestyle of Neena, which in a male-dominated world is full of danger and a source of her family's unhappiness. The shooting, in fact, represents the stereotype, self-preserving image of the Indian woman, no matter how modern she may seem in her conduct.

In *Andaz*, Dilip Kumar demonstrated his newly acquired style of agonized and disillusioned lover. The film, along with Sunny's *Babul*, also helped him establish the image of an intensely romantic hero who conveys to his love his dreams through his songs.

According to television director and author Nasreen Munni Kabir:

> Mehboob's *Andaz* is a most extraordinary film, and one of the first Hindi films to ever deal with the psychology of emotions. One major underlying theme of the work juxtaposes the behavioural nuances of the westernized, liberal middle class against the traditional Indian expectations of how men and women are supposed to relate to each other . . . Instead of the usual outcries of the broken-hearted lover, Dilip Kumar's anguish is expressed through soft and ghostly singing that floats through the room as Neena (Nargis) stands by the window on her wedding night. The subconscious voice expressed in the form of the song runs through her heart: *Kya paaya hai loot ke tumne is gareeb ka pyaar* (What did you gain by robbing a humble man of his love.)[2]

It certainly created Hindi cinema's most stirring moments.

Dilip Kumar and Raj Kapoor in *Andaz* (1949)

Already nine films old, Dilip Kumar's performance came in for much praise. Baburao Patel of *Filmindia,* who in the earlier films had shred Dilip Kumar's performances to bits, wrote in its April 1949 edition:

Andaz Draws Crowds
DK gives his Greatest Performance

Dilip Kumar improves beyond recognition under Mehboob Khan's direction. He casts off his usual mannerisms and becomes versatile in the role of the frustrated lover. The way he portrays his struggle of suppressed emotions is a time piece of histrionic art. This is easily Dilip Kumar's best performance so far.

Clare Mendonça's review in the *Times of India* dated Saturday, 26 March 1949 said:

Dilip Kumar runs away with acting honours in the central role, which he portrays with an inimitable grace of which

Nargis, Raj Kapoor and Dilip Kumar in *Andaz* (1949)

his entire naturalness and spontaneity are the chief
ingredients. He does not act but lives the role, displaying
the rare genius of the born actor, who is unaware that he
is acting. He will go far if he retains this priceless gift for
spontaneity which characterizes him today.

And far he did go!
According to author–journalist Bunny Reuben:

Just look at Dilip Kumar's performance. That scene, where
after her father's death Nargis is dazed and dumb with
shock, so much so that she cannot weep. Dilip Kumar
knows that she has to be jilted out of her numbness; she
needs to be made to weep. And how he does it, how he
compels her to cry, the manner in which he uses his voice
to achieve this dire imperative. Incredible indeed!
. . . *Andaz* will always stand very high amongst the
greatest films ever made in India. Aside from the superb

Dilip Kumar and Nargis in *Andaz* (1949)

performances by Nargis, Dilip Kumar and Raj Kapoor, apart from the Hollywoodian gloss and the spellbinding telling of the story, in *Andaz* the story escaped from the hands of the teller and went galloping away down into the depths of the human heart and its secret and dark complexities.[3]

In *Andaz*, Dilip Kumar lip-synched four solo songs rendered by Mukesh, whereas Raj Kapoor had only one song in the voice of Rafi, a duet with Lata Mangeshkar. Later on, Mukesh went on to become the established voice of Raj Kapoor and Rafi that of Dilip Kumar. The songs have been composed by Naushad and penned by Majrooh Sultanpuri (real name: Asrar ul-Hassan Khan), who went on to become a prolific songwriter.

Naushad's music for *Andaz* was a huge success, with each song, particularly the four Mukesh nuggets—quintessential quartet—all played on the piano by Sonny Castelino, are remembered and played to this day. The four songs are given below, recreating a snatch each: *Hum aaj kahin dil kho baithe, yun samjho kisike ho baithe* in Raag Jaijaiwanti (I have lost my heart somewhere today, just think I have become somebody's), *Toote naa dil toote naa, saath hamara chootey naa* in Raag Bhairavi (May the heart not break, may we never separate) and *Jhoom jhoom ke nacho aaj gayo khushi ke geet* in Raag Shivrangani (Swing, swing and dance today, sing songs of joy).

The last number is: *Tu kahe agar jeevan bhar main geet sunata jaoon, main been bajata jaoon* in Raag Kirwani (If you say so, I will keep singing for you throughout, play the *been* in my heart). It is worth discussing it in a little more detail for its subtle variations in tone and tune and the stirring lyrics (which may appear bland in the English translation). The song has been picturized on Dilip Kumar playing the piano in a party, with Nargis watching him playfully and the danseuse Cuckoo (Moray) prancing in a lively manner. Even while sitting throughout, Dilip Kumar's facial expressions convincingly portray a variety of emotions as per the different moods of the song. Here is the mukhda:

> *Tu kahe agar jeevan bhar main geet sunaata jaaon*
> *Main been bajaata jaaon*
> *Aur aag main apne man ki*
> *Har dil mein lagaata jaaon*
> *Dukh dard mitaata jaaon.*

(If you say so, I shall keep singing for you throughout my life
I shall keep on playing the *been* [a wind instrument used by snake charmers] of my heart
And shall ignite each heart with the fire in my heart
I shall eradicate all worries and sorrows.)

Of the two following stanzas, it is the first one that brings out the everlasting relations between the instrument and the musical notes:

Main saaz hoon tu sargam hai
Deti jo sahaare mujhko
Main raag hoon tu beena hai
Jis dum tu pukaare mujhko
Awaaz mein teri hardam
Awaaz milaata jaaon
Akaash pe chhaata jaaon
Tu kahe agar ...

(I am the instrument and you are the range of musical notes
That support me
I am the *raag* [a melodic pattern] and you are the *beena* [a large string instrument]
Whenever you beckon me
I shall blend my voice with yours
I shall make my presence felt across the sky.)

Such is the spell cast by Dilip Kumar that we forget that there are six other songs too, including four solos by Lata Mangeshkar, a duet with Shamshad Begum tuned in Raag Kafi: *Darr na mohabbat kar le, ulfat se jholi bhar le* (Don't be scared to love, fill your lap with it) and another with Mohammad Rafi in Raag Bhairavi: *Yun to aapas mein bigadte hain khafa hote hain milne wale kahin* (Like this they fight among themselves and get angry, those who come together in love do not get separated). The Lata solo *Meri ladli, re meri ladli* (My favourite, oh my favourite) was in Raag Bilawal Thaat and that pensive *tod diya dil mera* (broke my heart) based on Raag Pahadi. However, the favourite is Lata's *Uthaey jaa unke sitaam* in Kalyan Thaat—a scale of seven notes from which any number of raags take birth.

Naushad teaming with the lyricist Majrooh Sultanpuri, Mukesh toning with Dilip Kumar; the dream piano, played by Sonny Castelino, synthesizing his piano notes with the geriatric, nostalgic vocalizing of Mukesh, were tuned for the listeners of various generations. What sensitivity, what subtlety of Naushad's touch it was! What delicacy, what impressionability of Mukesh it was! And, what grace, what elegance of Dilip Kumar's singing on the screen it was. Only Dilip Kumar could have sung them the way he did. To this day 'we sway to the musical feast that is the mood amalgam of the quartet. Is there anything more will-of-the-wisp in the song history of the motion picture of India? The lyrics of Majrooh Sultanpuri, written ever so feelingly, going so arrestingly on Dilip Kumar wooing Nargis, as he had never wooed her before'.[4]

No wonder *Andaz* and Dilip Kumar, Dilip Kumar and *Andaz*, became a screen fantasy of two generations.

Babul (1950)

Director S.U. Sunny, who had earlier made the highly successful *Mela* with Nargis and Dilip Kumar, retained the same star cast for his new venture *Babul* with the addition of Munawar Sultana. It is perhaps the most curious and tragic love story ever depicted in Hindi cinema.

Here, Dilip Kumar is the lover in pursuit by two equally demanding women—Bela (Nargis), the retired postman's simple, vivacious daughter and Usha (Munnawar Sultana), the haughty daughter of the local zamindar (landlord)—with neither of whom is he able to lead a happy life.

The new local postman Ashok (Dilip Kumar) teaches Usha music until Bela, in a fit of jealousy, lies to Usha that Ashok has already confessed his love for her and warns her to keep

Dilip Kumar and Nargis in *Babul* (1950)

away from 'her' man. Usha, in a surprising show of class-transcending compassion, renounces her love for Ashok in favour of Bela's, and accepts a pending proposal from a well-to-do crony of her father. However, at this stage, Bela, in a fit of guilt, intervenes, revealing to Usha her own misguided belief that Ashok has professed his love for her.

Ashok is devastated when the zamindar tells him about settling Usha's marriage with a friend's son and requests Ashok to convince Usha to marry the groom selected for her to save the family's honour. A sequel of close-ups shows the perturbed Ashok's grief with figures hammering his forehead. As the wedding approaches, both Usha and Ashok lapse into depression, while Bela exults, despite recurring nightmares of a black-veiled rider approaching to carry her away. A happy ending appears increasingly unlikely, and the director makes no last-minute attempt to manufacture one.

In this unusual plot, the film attempts to locate the hero and the two heroines in three distinct spaces, where each of them becomes finally incommunicable. The hero, indecisive and confused as he is about true love, is charmed by the aristocratic lifestyle of Usha and flirts with her, making her feel that he loves her. But he lacks conviction about love for her and fails to win her hand before she is married off.

The climax builds up into a quick sequence of tragedies. Bela watches Usha's wedding procession and in a deranged condition falls off a tree and is seriously injured. In her last moments, she desires, as a sort of last wish, in her delirious state, that Ashok marry her. In the end, a tearful Ashok dresses Bela as a bride and marries her rendering in Talat Mahmood's voice a stanza from the popular song *Chhod babul ka ghar mohe pi ke nagar* (Leaving my father's home I had to go to my husband's) tuned in upbeat Raag Pilu.

Bela's death portrays a medieval horseman descending from the skies to receive her as the smoke from the cremation pyre merges with the clouds.

The anti-hero character in *Babul* seemed to be in quest of a new world of passionate love and music in abundance so that he could move above his ordinary past and the present, symbolized by the low status of the heroine and her family. His quest is lost in the end! And he has to finally accept his reality by marrying the dying heroine.

In this peculiar role, Dilip Kumar effectively juxtaposes his moments of silence with occasional outburst of emotional articulation of his innermost feelings.

Babul too, like Dilip Kumar's other films during those years, was a big success at the box office, in fact, a 'golden jubilee', and came to be lauded by the audience and the press alike. Wrote Baburao Patel in his mouthpiece *Filmindia* of November 1949 issue:

Dilip Kumar and Munnawar Sultana in *Babul* (1950)

Babul—The Role of His Life

Dilip Kumar, now a master in portraying morbid characterizations of a spineless, frustrated hero, lives the role of Ashok, the postmaster. Even his natural humour takes the hue of his helpless sex and soul starvation, and he strides through the picture with a pathetic poverty of a licked spineless lover who has neither the courage to love nor the guts to ask and take what he wants. It is a great work and the ease with which Dilip Kumar portrays the role makes one wonder whether the man himself has lived through similar moments of pathos and frustration in his private life.

Clare Mendonça's review in the *Times of India* of Saturday, 14 October 1949, commented: 'Dilip Kumar also acts extremely well as the Dak-Babu—kind, honest, blunt and dignified even in the moments of his keenest pain and sorrow. He has shed most of his irritating mannerisms, and if he would only enunciate clearly—a primary consideration in an actor—he would be near perfect.'

However, in its December 1950 issue, *The Motion Picture Magazine*, in a hard-hitting review, said: 'Dilip Kumar as a postmaster looked rather befogged and stunned throughout the picture. His oft-repeated mannerisms and style of speaking is (sic) fast losing its effect.'

Both the music composer Naushad and lyricist Shakeel Badayuni were in their elements and came up with some outstanding melodies sung by Shamshad Begum and the man with a golden voice, Talat Mahmood, who has given us that memorable Raag Bhairavi-based *Mera jeevan saathi bichhod gaya, lo khatam kahani ho gayi* (My life partner has separated, the story has come to an end). The scene (in a huge hall) here depicts Dilip Kumar's beloved (Munnawar Sultana) about to get married to someone else. As expected, the thespian displays quiet dignity and self-control while rendering this touching song. The song begins with a sher (couplet) as a prelude:

Khushi ke saath duniya mein hazaaron gham bhi hote hai
Jahan bajti hai shehnai wahan maatam bhi hote hai.

(Along with joys, in this world, there is also a lot of sorrow
Where the shehnai* can be heard, there is also mourning.)

*Shehnai: A wind instrument resembling a clarinet, usually played during wedding ceremonies

After that comes the mukhda:

Mera jeevan saathi bichhad gaya
Lo khatm kahaani ho gayee.

(My life companion has been separated from me
The story has ended.)

Of the two stanzas that follow, the second one tellingly describes the anguish of a tormented heart:

Dil deke yahan sab haar gaye, duniya mein kisiki jeet kahan
Hoton pe shikwe qismat ke, woh pyaar bhare ab geet
kahan?
Jab khel hi duniya ka bigad gaya, har baat puraani ho
gayee.

(After giving away the heart [to one's beloved], one loses everything
Nobody wins anything in this world
On the lips are complaints against destiny, where are those love-filled   songs?
When the game of the world has been ruined, everything becomes old.)

Two other beauties are the Shamshad Begum–Talat Mahmood Raag Pahadi-duet *Milte hi aankhen dil hua dewana kisi ka,* *afsana mera ban gaya afsana kisi ka* (As eyes met, the heart was mad for someone else, my story has become a story of someone else) with Dilip Kumar on the piano romancing Munawar Sultana and the heart-rendering Raag Miyan Ki Sarang-based duet, *Duniya badal gayi, meri duniya badal gayi, tukde hue* *jigar ke, churi dil pe chal gayi* (The world has changed, my

Dilip Kumar and Nargis in *Babul* (1950)

world has changed, the heart broke into pieces as the knife pierced it). However, the most popular number from the film is the powerful rendering of *Chhod babul ka ghar, mohe pi ki nagar aaj jaana pada* (Leaving my father's home I had to go to my husband's)—a song that to this day is played at the *bidai* (farewell) ceremony that takes place at an Indian wedding.

Daag (1952)

Amiya Chakravarty, the man who was the director of Dilip Kumar's debut film *Jwar Bhata*, cast the actor once again, nearly a decade later, in his new film *Daag*. It was to become one of the most memorable films of the actor for which he won his first Filmfare Award for Best Actor, in the inaugural year of the awards, in 1953. It also prepared him for his forthcoming film, *Devdas*.

Dilip Kumar in *Daag* (1952)

Daag, like other films by Amiya Chakravarty—*Badal* (1951), *Patita* (1953), *Seema* (1955) and *Kathputli* (1957)—dealt with a burning social problem: alcoholism. Conceived as a tribute to the Gandhian theme of prohibition, the film projected an excellent narrative through its alcoholic protagonist. It brings to light the creativity of a village artisan who seeks momentary release from the prevailing social oppression through the bottle. In a scene, Shankar (Dilip Kumar), in a drunk state, talks to the friendly bar-owner, Raghu, as to why he is so fond of alcohol: *... aur main pee leta hoon, Raghu, to mujhe yeh duniya itni buri nahin lagti. Tab mein ek lakdi ke tukde mein bhi jaan dal sakta hoon* (When I have a drink, this world doesn't seem that bad, Raghu. Then I can put life into a piece of wood also).

For the poor toymaker, alcohol is a vehicle that takes him beyond the vagaries of life's cruelties to a world where he can

Dilip Kumar and Nimmi in *Daag* (1952)

create his art. But in society, he is looked down upon as a die-hard drunkard, beyond any reformation. He spends all his earnings and even the money for his ailing mother's medicine on drink. The bottle also separates him from his sweetheart Parvati aka Paro (Nimmi), whose family, headed by her stepbrother, Jagatnarayan (Kanhaiyalal), suddenly gains a higher status in society through an inheritance left behind by a relative.

After a quarrel with his mother, repentant Shankar gives up drinking and leaves for the city to make money so that he can ask for Paro's hand. He returns home just in time to pay off his mortgage to the moneylender. But Jagatnarayan throws him out of the house when he goes with a proposal for Paro. Shattered, he starts drinking again. Finally, Shankar reaches the venue where Paro is being forcefully married off to a well-to-do person and pleads before Jagatnarayan to save his love. He is thrashed by Jagatnarayan's goons. But now, after what he witnesses, the bridegroom's father refuses to go ahead with the wedding of his son. Finally, Jagatnarayan agrees to marry

Dilip Kumar and Lalita Pawar in *Daag* (1952)

Paro to Shankar. In the last scene, where a reformed Shankar is married to Paro and his old drinking buddy brings him a bottle to celebrate the event, he takes it, looks at it for a long, long time, with sheer disdain, and to the great delight of Paro, breaks it.

Daag offered Dilip Kumar an opportunity of a lifetime to demonstrate his histrionics in full abundance. He perfectly articulated that toymaker's creative restlessness caused by perpetual deprivation through his drinking bouts, mood swings and highly charged dialogues written by Rajinder Singh Bedi. He shouts out his frustrations, but his helplessness soon takes him into deep silence as if the alcoholic is talking to his inner self. For example, when he sings to himself: *Hum dard ke maaron ka itna hi faasana hai, peene ko sharab-e-gham, dil gham ka nishana hai* (Just this much is the story of those in the grip of pain, to drink we get the wine of sorrow and our heart is the target of anguish). And, when his mother dies, Shankar goes into a state of shock, announcing the loss by repeating in a sad, monotonous voice to Paro: '*Meri maa mar gayi, Paro, meri maa mar gayi'* (My mother has died, Paro, my mother has died). That's all he says but with each repetition the vocal inflections are subtly varied. Look and study that very emotional scene where his mother lies dead and 'he realizes, sitting by her bedside, that she is no more. There is no ranting and raving. No facial contortions. No crying, no tears. One doesn't even see Dilip Kumar's face much of the time, because he chooses to play it with his back to the camera, using only nuances to enhance deep sorrow'.[5]

And there is that enduring scene in which Shankar, when he is angry with everyone and with himself too, in a long protestation to God, accuses Him of hypocrisy and helping only the rich. He asks his mother: *'Kisne likha hai mere bhaag mein. Usne likha hai jis ke samne tu haath jod-jodkar roti rehti hai?'* (Who has written [this misfortune] in my fate. He, in front of whom you keep on weeping with folded hands?) Finally, he breaks down realizing his helplessness. The helpless sufferer, in desperation, becomes an iconoclast and standing in front of God's idol says: *'Kan khol kar sun le. Aaj se tu is ghar mein nahi rahega, samjah? Yeh bhudiya to sathiya gayi hai, par Shankar nahi sathiyaya. Woh tujhe aachi tarah se janta hai. Main isko galli mein fenk doonga. Main iske tukde-tukde kar doonga. Dekhunga ki yeh mera kya bigaad sakta hai'* (Hear me with open ears. From today onwards you will not stay in this house. Understood? This old woman has gone mad. But Shankar has not. He knows you well. I will throw Him into the streets. I will break it to pieces. I will see what damage He can do to me).

These scenes by far are the most compelling pieces of acting on Indian celluloid. It is not all make-believe. Sometimes what you see on screen is shockingly real—scenes of raw emotions that undoubtedly go far beyond what a viewer could have even imagined, which reminds one of the French phrase 'Les larmes sont les gouttes du coeur (Tears are indeed the drops of the heart).

According to author and film critic Nikhat Kazmi:

> It is the same world which must be eschewed in films like Bimal Roy's *Devdas* and *Daag*, where alcoholism is the only way out. In *Devdas*, when the hero is unable to transcend class barriers and marry a low-caste beloved Parvati (Suchitra Sen), he finds succour with a prostitute Chandramukhi (Vyjayanthimala) and chooses to drown his sorrow in liquor. In *Daag*, he is unable to cope with separation and hits the bottle when he is parted from his sweetheart (Nimmi). *Aye mere dil kahin aur chal, gam ki duniya se dil bhar gaya, dhoond le ab koi ghar naya* (Dear heart, lets depart for distant lands. This world of pain doesn't interest me any more. Let's find a new home), drones the dipsomaniac and walks away from a world that holds no allure for the disheartened, disillusioned soul.

In *Daag*, Amiya Chakravarty, as in some of his other films, used extensively white clouds spread on a clear sky as a metaphor to express the hope of a beautiful world. The film, in fact, opens with the famous 1833 English hymn by Saint John Henry Newman, in the poem titled 'The Pillar of the Cloud':

> Lead, kindly light, amid the enriching gloom
> Lead, Thou me on.
> The Night is dark. And I am far from home
> Lead Thou me on

appearing in the sky with the hero standing on a boulder watching the clouds.

In his style, Chakravarty followed the typical formalistic and generic convention of Bombay Talkies, whose illustrious alumni he was. He relied heavily on constricted spaces to develop and interpret the drama, often realizing the tension in the vast outdoors, particularly using open sky full of white clouds to symbolize freedom.

The noted film writer Partha Chatterjee observes:

> The song *Aye mere dil kahin aur chal, gham ki duniya se dil bhar gaya* (Oh my heart let's go somewhere else) sung by the alcoholic toy maker walking briskly across an unyielding landscape, was shot in extreme long, long, mid-long and mid-shots. The spiritual despair of a good man held prisoner by an addiction could have scarcely been filmed by V. Babasaheb with greater empathy. A curious dichotomy is achieved in the picturization as if to mirror ordinary people's ambivalent attitude towards helping alcoholics in a positive way. Nature, photographed in semi-silhouette, seems to embrace and reject the hapless toymaker at one and the same time.

Filmfare while reviewing the movie noted that 'in essence the film had come to Indian audiences with a refreshing newness, at a time when most producers were not daring to experiment with different subjects but merely trying to play safe with the formula and failing.'

If the film was a big hit at the box office, so was its music by Shanker (Singh Raghuvanshi) and Jaikishen (Dayabhai Panchal) to the lyrics by Shailendra (Shankardas Kesarilal Shailendra) and Hasrat Jaipuri (real name: Iqbal Husain). It was once again the ghazal superstar Talat Mahmood, whose voice by now had been distinctly identified upon Dilip Kumar. *Ae mere dil kahin aur chal,* in Raag Bhairavi, was a stupendous melodic triumph in two versions by Talat—one fast and one slow—and one by Lata Mangeshkar, more in the form of a ghazal than a song, on a moping Nimmi. Here, one must admit that Lata's version, though well rendered, somehow suffers in comparison to Talat's on Dilip Kumar. 'His hypnotic vocals do expose the sole (tandem) chink in Lata's otherwise formidable singing armour.'[6] And, of course, Dilip Kumar piteously singing (lip-synching) it the way he did makes all the difference—immensely heart-wrenching! Unforgettably agonizing! Let us take up the slow Talat Mehmood version. In this song sequence, Dilip Kumar walks around the town (in which he resides) depicting a range of emotions keeping in mind the diverse moods of the melody. The mukhda sums up the essence of the song:

> *Ai mere dil kahin aur chal*
> *Gham ki duniya se dil bhar gaya*
> *Doondle ab koi ghar naya.*

(O my heart let's go somewhere else
My heart is fed up with this world of sorrow
Search now for a new home.)

Of the two stanzas in the song, the first one reflects the underlying theme of the song:

> *Chal jahan gham ke mare na hon*
> *Jhooti asha ke taaren na hon*
> *In bahaaron se kya faayda*
> *Jisme dil ki kali jal gayi*
> *Zakhm phir se hara ho gaya.*

(Go to a place where there are no sad people
There are no stars of false hope
What is the use of that springtime
In which the blossom of the heart is burnt
The wounds have become raw again.)

If the highlight of some of Shankar–Jaikishan films of that period like *Barsaat, Badal, Awaara* was Peter Monsorate—the Henry James of India—on the trumpet, it was Sebastian D'Souza, that Goan arranger, who came in with *Daag* into the Shankar–Jaikishan camp. Along with him was Goody Seervai, the unusually bright accordion player who gave the background music for *Ae mere dil kahin aur chal,* which was the highlight of the film's music. Even today, seventy-three years later, as soon as the prelude of the song on the accordion starts, a film music buff can easily associate it with Dilip Kumar singing *Ae mere dil kahin aur chal.*

What a phenomenal and significant feat indeed!

Sangdil (1952)

> It was full of long hallways, plenty of rooms—mostly unused, belonging to the troubled owner. It housed a terrible secret in the attic. When Jane Eyre arrived at the isolated mansion, she noticed that a very chill, vault-like air pervaded the stairs, and the gallery of unspecified size, and the hall's gloominess expressed and amplified the sense of Rochester's depression and malaise before he fell in love with Jane, suggesting cheerless ideas of space and solitaire. And every midnight, there's a great deal of weird, ghostly and awfully frightening laughter. In contrast, the grounds surrounding Thornfield are sublime and healthful, thus serving as a backdrop to happier scenes.

The above extract is from Charlotte Brontë's famous classic *Jane Eyre,* published in 1847, in which Thornfield Hall was the home of the protagonist Edward Rochester. It was the inspiration for the setting of *Sangdil* which, once again, had Dilip Kumar in a true anti-hero role. Once again, after Ram Daryani's *Tarana* (1951), it brought together Dilip Kumar as

Dilip Kumar and Madhubala in *Sangdil* (1952)

Shankar in the company of two heroines: Madhubala (born Begum Mumtaz Jehan Dehlavi) and Shammi (born Nargis Rabadi; not to be confused with hero Shammi Kapoor). Shankar and Madhubala as Kamla, are childhood friends who get separated at a young age.

A young flamboyant aristocrat, Shankar, living under the shadow of a mentally challenged wife (Kuldip Kaur), is torn between his ugly past and the promise of a bright and joyous future offered by the love of Kamla, a *devadasi* (an artist who is dedicated to the worship and service of a deity or a temple). Kamla had lost her rich father when she was just a child. Before dying, her father had handed her upbringing, and all his wealth too, to his close friend, Thakur with the promise that the child will be brought up well, and her inheritance would be kept safe till she grows up. However, her evil foster mother throws her out of the house when some sadhus pick

Dilip Kumar in *Sangdil* (1952)

her up and take her with them to an ashram dedicated to the worship of Lord Shiva.

Years later, Shankar meets the devadasi and follows her to Lord Shiva's Nataraja idol where he looks at it in a strange way. Then in a conversation with her, Shankar shares his strange feeling which he has been nurturing for years, as if someone from his childhood, as if some old companion who had drifted away to another shore, is calling him. Soon they rekindle their romance. Lighter moments follow. In one scene, Shankar renders a ghazal at a social gathering: *Yeh hawa yeh raat yeh chandani.* (This breeze, this night, this moonlight). In another, Shankar, in the disguise of an astrologer, reveals to Kamla his love for her and asks her to reveal her identity so as to light up his world. We also come across the head priestess of the math questioning Shankar and Kamla about the purity and purpose of their love.

Dilip Kumar and Shammi in *Sangdil* (1952)

Just when they are about to tie the knot, the dark secret comes out and it is revealed that Shankar is already married. Apparently, many years earlier, his mother, in a bout of greed, tricked him into 'marrying' the mentally challenged daughter of a rich man. He keeps her locked up in the mansion. Shankar grows up to be an unhappy man and turns vindictive because of life's wrongdoings. Kamla is hurt and decides to leave. In a long emotional conversation, Shankar pleads with her not to leave him when she accuses him of concealing his married status.

Meanwhile, during one of the routines of the ashram, Kamla, along with the other *pujarin*s (female worshippers), is invited to stay in the mansion where she, every night hears eerie howls and screams. Gradually, she realizes that Shankar's marriage to a mentally challenged woman, now kept imprisoned in the mansion, has destroyed him. She also discovers that this anguished man was her friend in their childhood days.

Finally, when she returns to Shankar's mansion, Kamla learns that it was accidentally reduced to ashes by the insane wife, who herself became a victim in the accident. She goes in search of Shankar, only to realize that he lost his eyesight in the fire.

The film was not a big success at the box office and got mixed reviews in the press. Baburao Patel, the editor of *Filmindia* (November 1952) who called it 'a dull, boring and stupid picture', had high praise for Dilip Kumar's performance: 'Dilip Kumar puts to good use that famous face of his with its fixed tragic expression. He is quite faithful to the role, and we certainly do not mind his whispers for a change in this loud industry.'

Film writer Madhulika Liddle observes:

Sangdil was an interesting blend of romance, suspense and tragedy, and a fairly decent adaptation of *Jane Eyre*, especially the more Gothic elements and the tormented hero trope. Dilip Kumar's acting is—as always—brilliant. He manages to very effectively portray the turmoil and angst of a man who harbours a deep-rooted bitterness towards those who have reduced him to these circumstances. Yet, too, a man who is capable of love, and that too a deeply passionate, affectionate love. This is a well-etched character, a good Indian equivalent of Edward Rochester in the original story, and Dilip Kumar plays the role well, without any melodrama.

Here, the composer was the talented Sajjad Husain and the songwriter Rajinder Kishen. Of all the songs in this movie, the ghazal picturized on Dilip Kumar and rendered gracefully by Talat Mehmood stands out. The setting is a large room with a breeze blowing and one of the heroines (Shammi) playing a sitar. Dilip Kumar 'sings' this ghazal for her in a carefree, romantic and lively manner. The opening sher is as follows (which is rather difficult to translate into English):

Yeh hawa yeh raat yeh chandni teri ek ada pe nisaar hai
Mujhe kyoon na hon teri arzoo teri justju mein bahaar hai.

(This breeze this night this moonlight will sacrifice themselves upon your elegance
Why should I not desire you [even] the springtime is looking for you.)

Of the two couplets that follow, I have chosen the second one:

Teri baat baat hai dilnashin koi tujhse badhke nahi hasin
Hai kali kali mein jo mastiyaan yeh teri nazar ka khumaar hai.

(Everything about you is heartwarming there is nobody more beautiful than you
The merriment in every blossom is [due to] the intoxication of your gaze.)

One of the most underrated composers in Hindi cinema, Sajjad Hussain, composed some powerfully lilting musical score to the lyrics penned by Rajendra Krishan. The most outstanding, evergreen beauty from the film is the above one through the velvety vocals of Talat Mahmood in Raag Jaunpuri, which perhaps ranks as the greatest romantic ghazal ever heard on the Indian screen through the lips of Dilip Kumar, undoubtedly his most romantic number ever, and the way he sang it on the screen, that weak smile, the expressions on the face going to his forehead which could melt any woman, went straight into the heart, the mind, the entire body to create a sensation never felt before by any music lover:

Yeh hawa, yeh raat, yeh chandani
Teri ik ada pe nissar hai
Mujhe kyon nah o teri arzoo
Teri justajoo mein bahar hai

(This breeze this night this moonlight will sacrifice themselves upon your elegance
Why shouldn't I keep yearning for you?
You are my springtime,
Ever fresh, evergreen, ever new.)

Does one need to listen to anything more?

Footpath (1953)

A gifted writer, film-maker Zia Sarhadi was an important figure of the classical period known for his strong political stances. Although he was a product of Mehboob Khan's school of film-making, he was greatly influenced by IPTA (Indian People's Theatre Association), which was formed in 1943, to promote themes related to the Indian freedom struggle. Khan had also cast him in his romantic tragedy *Manmohan* (1936), a film inspired by Sarat Chandra Chattopadhyay's *Devdas*, with Bibbo and Surendra in the main cast, for which he also wrote the script, dialogues and lyrics. After scripting three films—*Jagirdar* (1937), *Bahen* (1941) and *Anokha Pyar* (1948)—for Khan, he became a noted scenarist and writer and later a film-maker. His best-known trilogy—*Hum Log* (1951), *Footpath* (1953) and *Aawaz* (1956)—designed as part of IPTA's efforts

Dilip Kumar and Meena Kumari in *Footpath* (1953)

in film-making in the 1950s, established this unusual film-maker among the top names of the classical era. Apart from his own projects, he scripted nearly a dozen films from 1937 to 1952, when he also wrote the dialogues of Vijay Bhatt's blockbuster *Baiju Bawra*. Unfortunately, after Partition, he migrated to the newly created Pakistan.

Footpath brought together for the first time the 'Tragedy King' Dilip Kumar with the 'Tragedy Queen' Meena Kumari—a pair that went on to give three more unforgettable films: *Azaad*, *Yahudi* and *Kohinoor*—all three big box-office successes.

Footpath, an offbeat film, is the only film of Dilip Kumar which falls in the category of neo-realist cinema. Set during the Second World War, it foretold the development of a new class, which is expanding its economic base at the expense of the poor and how. In this process, the educated middle class gets lured into becoming an equal

Dilip Kumar and Anwar Hussain in *Footpath* (1953)

partner in acquiring ill-gotten wealth. The film, therefore, took up a serious debate on the responsibility of the educated people towards society.

The film depicts the moral crisis of an upright but poor writer, Noshu (Dilip Kumar), who is attracted to a girl in the neighbourhood and wants to woo her. Soon, he comes into contact with black marketeers hoarding medicines in a famine-stricken area and joins them in their nefarious activities. As he begins to amass wealth, he not only abandons his erstwhile principles but also his doting elder brother Bani (Ramesh Thapar) and the love of his life Mala (Meena Kumari). In his arguments with his brother on morality vis-à-vis becoming rich by unfair means, Noshu expresses his deep disdain for being poor. Similarly, in the arguments between Noshu and

Mala, she asks him to reveal the source of his wealth and why people call him a thief and why has his elder brother Bani left him. There is that outstanding scene where Noshu tells Mala that he enjoys befooling people to make money and how now money has fallen in love with him and chases him. She is repulsed by his very thinking.

Later, when Bani is in need of monetary help, he refuses any from Noshu because his money is tainted. It leads to an angry outburst by Noshu on the ill-treatment by all those dear to him just because he has become rich. Bani tells him clearly that he is no more a human being because he sells food and medicines meant for the poor in the black market. To this, Noshu, in much distress, says that he still loves his people. The two go their separate ways. So also his poor but honest friends.

Awakening comes with the outbreak of an epidemic among the starving poor and when he sees people agonize and die for lack of food and drugs. When Noshu comes to know that his Bani too is very unwell, he rushes to be with his elder brother only to reach just as Bani breathes his last. Noshu is devastated and realizes that his path is wrong. Denouncing his companions in crime, he hands himself over to the police, which is shown in a long sequence of Noshu repenting for his evil deeds.

Footpath reaffirmed Dilip Kumar's reputation as a sensitive actor, signifying the possibility of his valuable participation in the parallel Indian cinema or the 'new wave' cinema, which had started taking shape at that time with its serious content, realism and naturalism. However, this possibility was never explored by the actor or his film-makers, except for Satyajit Ray who, in 1962, did approach him through Waheeda Rehman, who was working with Ray at that time for *Abhijan*, and later personally too for a film he had in mind, an idea Ray believed was perfect for the actor. However, Dilip Kumar politely declined the offer.

With lyrics by Majrooh Sultanpuri and Ali Sardar Jafri, the music for *Footpath* was composed by Khayyam (Mohammed Zahur Khayyam Hashmi), that composer of abiding class and calibre, a veteran of fifty-five films who gave us that Raag Kafi-based evergreen hypnotic number by the 'Ghazal King' Talat Mahmood, which sent many a dejected lover, waiting for his unrequited love, into a mood of melancholy or downturn. In the initial phase of this song, the hero is shown sitting in a chair in a large room. Later on, he moves into a garden. As expected, Dilip Kumar's expressions deftly reflect the various moods of the melody. The mukhda is fairly long:

Sham-e-gham ki kasam
Aaj ghamgin hai hum
Aa bhi jaa, aa bhi jaa
Aaj mere sanam
Dil pareshaan hai raat veeran hai
Dekh jaa kis tarah
Aaj tanha hai hum.

(I swear on this evening of sorrow
Today I am anguished
Please come, please come
Today my beloved.)
The heart is troubled
The night is desolate
Come and see
How lonely I am today.)

Of the two stanzas that follow, the first one subtly captures the melancholic mood of the protagonist:

Chain kaisa jo pehlu mein tu he nahin
Maar dale na dard-e-judaai kahin
Rut haseen hai to kya
Chandni hai to kya
Chandni zulm hai aur judaai sitam.

(There is no comfort when you are not by my side
Let not the pain of separation kill me
What if the season is beautiful
The moonlight is cruel and the separation is oppressive.)

The dream singer, the singer who gave, at his ghazal pinnacle, every other male singer a complex, Talat Mahmood's voice, soft as Dhaka muslin, at that time had been recognized and established on Dilip Kumar. It suited the 'Tragedy King' to the T. The moviegoers, the music listeners, all thought that it was Dilip Kumar singing himself and they resonated with his voice, his mood, the feeling he was going through on the screen. In fact, our sweetest Talat songs going on Dilip Kumar 'are those that tell the saddest thoughts'—the Percy Shelley stream of thought. How tenderly Khayyam created this number, how sensitively Talat sang it and how romantically Dilip Kumar lip-synced it. It is sheer magic, and this magic is all there and can be felt even today.

Amar (1954)

Mehboob Khan's *Amar* provided a down-to-earth analysis on the question of morality in the man–woman relationship and probed a three-way relationship. The film depicts the moral crisis of an aristocrat, Amarnath (Dilip Kumar), a well-known

Dilip Kumar and Madhubala in *Amar* (1954)

upright lawyer, held in high esteem, who is in love with his fiancée Anju (Madhubala), an educated, socially conscious young girl who believes in aiding the poor. In a moment of weakness, Amarnath seduces Sonia (Nimmi), a simple-minded village milkmaid, and rapes the ignorant and helpless girl whom he does not even consciously like. Tormented by feelings of guilt, he is unable to solve his dilemma, unable to come to a decision that will be fair to all concerned. Amarnath watches silently as Sonia suffers the consequences of his lustful moments with her while the villain, Sankat (Jayant), offers her help and comfort.

Meanwhile, Anju, completely unaware as to what is going on, and yet vaguely troubled by his long silences and varying moods, tries to draw him out, but all in vain. When

Dilip Kumar and Nimmi in *Amar* (1954)

Sankat comes to know that it is Amarnath, the lawyer, who is responsible for Sonia's suffering, he attacks Amar but is killed with his own knife in the fight. However, as events turn out, it is Sonia who is arrested for murder and, while defending her in the court, Amarnath reveals the truth. Devastated, Anju walks out of his life, while Amarnath reluctantly puts the necklace, returned to him by his wronged fiancée, around Sonia's neck.

The title of the film, *Amar*, implies immortal love that can have its basis in sacrifice and suffering. The melodramatic theme, combined with some unusually surreal imagery, made the film an oddity in the genre. The film had an average run at the box office which was attributed to its controversial subject as also the fact that the audience could not accept their favourite Dilip Kumar in an extremely negative role of a rapist. However, the actor exhibited immense skill in underplay, living through his guilt with a chilling silence, as he is unable to express his feelings to his fiancée. In the entire film, he uses

Dilip Kumar in *Amar* (1954)

his intense, stark facial expressions to share his pent-up guilt
with the audience. And, in this discourse in silences, he enacted
the dilemma of self-preservation vis-à-vis the moral position
of meting out justice to his own victim.

The film is a great study of the art and craft of Dilip
Kumar's unlimited and extendable abilities. First, the scene
that depicts the gradual flow of seductive expressions on his
face as he succumbs to the impulse of the moment on viewing
a rain-drenched, shivering Sonia on that rain-washed night
with her wet, sensuous and curvaceous body lit up in the light
of the lamp that he holds. Second, that long self-interrogatory
sequence about the conflict between his guilt and his love for
his fiancée, Anju. Third, the entrancing build up to the film's
climax in the song sequence *Jaanewale se mulakaat na hone
paie* (Couldn't meet the one who went away) based on Raag
Yaman Kalyan sung by Anju, an indecisive Amarnath is unable
to hand over the letter to his fiancée in which he has confessed

his guilt. Fourth, when Amarnath in a pensive mood is walking back home as he listens to the song sung by the helpless Sonia in the nearby temple *Khamosh hai khevanhar mera* (My rower is silent). Fifth, the scene where Amarnath confesses his act of sexually exploiting Sonia on that fateful night.

However, the most heart-wrenching scene is which shows a temple at the top of a lengthy flight of steps. A young woman waits with her eyes eloquent with the pain of the loss of her beloved. If only those eyes could speak, if only her heart had a little tongue, what would they say to the young man approaching her with dragging feet? And he, silently expressing his inner turmoil and reluctance to go inside the temple. But 'no words are spoken, there is no reproach as she takes his hand and closes it over the gold chain he had pledged her with. She swallows and turns away to walk down those interminable steps alone',[7] the steps she had walked up with him holding her hand a little while back. In the background, we hear Mohammad Rafi singing that evergreen number based on Raag Bhairavi:

> *Insaf ka mandir hai yeh*
> *Bhagwan ka ghar hai*
> *Kehna hai jo keh de*
> *Tujhe kis baat ka darr hai?*

> (This is the temple of justice
> And the house of God
> Say whatever you want to
> What are you scared of?)

Amar was much ahead of its time. Its theme was way too bold back then, when the audience of the times was far too immature and conservative in its thinking, to appreciate the film. However, the critics appreciated it. Baburao Patel of *Filmindia* reviewed it in the issue of October 1954, as 'a brilliant picture with a gripping human story superbly directed and acted with flawless perfection. A masterpiece of film craft. Dilip Kumar performs with his usual polish and confidence though his role cried for some cogent psychological development. He is, however, the best amongst the three principal artistes'.

Writing in *The Hindu*, Deepak Mahaan lauded the film for its characterization of strong female characters and photography of the rape scenes without any nudity. 'The black and white canvas lent the story a quiet dignity, appropriate to the ethical tussle between truth and desire, moral turpitude and justice.'

Discussing the film, author and director Khalid Mohamed wrote that it is a Thomas Hardy-esque story of guilt and redemption: 'The motivation and behaviour of the characters are so psychologically precise that the film appears to have been made in consultation with a therapist. Good people essentially, the two women and the lawyer still have their human weaknesses, a truism far too bold for the Indian cinema which unfailingly flaunts heroes and heroines as snow-white protagonists of virtue.'

The *Filmfare* review of 29 October 1954 said: '*Amar* which puts Mehboob among the greatest directors on the Indian screen, is embellished with finely sympathetic and powerful portrayals by Dilip Kumar, Madhubala and Nimmi, highlighted by a rich musical score by Clare-winning maestro Naushad . . . *Amar* is a brilliant as well as an absorbing and entertaining picture with everything it takes to make one, from story to screen.'

The songs of *Amar* were super hit. 'The lion's share' of the ten songs went to the distaff side, i.e., to Lata Mangeshkar and Asha Bhosle. The trilogy of three heart-tugger Lata songs were simply outstanding. My first pick from these would be that song-lyric in which the lyricist Shakeel Badayuni just soars our imagination with that heart-tugger *Na milta gham to barbadi ke afsaane kahan jaate?* (If one didn't get sorrow, where would the talks of devastation go?) in Raag Yaman; *Na shikwa hai koi, na koi gila hai, salammat rahe tu yeh meri dua hai* (There is no complaint, nor any protest, may you live long is my prayer for you) also in the same raag, and *Janewale se mulaqaat na hone pai, dil ki dil mein rahi baat na hone pai* (I could not meet the one who left, matters of the heart remained there as no conversation was possible), in Raag Yaman Kalyan, or in Raag Shudh Kalyan as some purists claim. Mohammed Rafi was summoned by Naushad for just one song, no, not on Dilip Kumar, who went songless in the film, but just on an extra with our actor only in the background. But what an impact it made! The knowledgeable readers would have guessed the song, but for youngsters who may not be familiar with the 'oldies', it is in the form of a bhajan: *Insaaf ka mandir hai yeh Bhagwaan ka ghar hai* penned commendably by Shakeel Baduyuni.

The bhajan (set in the ever-popular Raag Bhairavi) consists of the mukhda and four antaras. Here is the mukhda:

> *Insaaf ka mandir hai yeh Bhagwaan ka ghar hai*
> *Kehna hai jo kehde; tujhe kis baat ka dar hai?*

(This is a temple of justice and the house of God
Say whatever you want; what are you afraid of?)

It is the first antara that one has chosen as it succinctly sums up the predicament of the hero:

> *Hai khot tere man mein jo Bhagwaan se hai door*
> *Hain paaoon tere phir bhi tu aane se hai majboor*

Himmat hai to aa ja: yeh bhalai ki dagar hai.
Insaaf ka mandir hai yeh Bhagwaan ka ghar hai.

(The vice/flaw in you keeps you far away from God
Even though you have feet, you are helpless and
cannot walk
If you have the courage, come, this is the road of virtue.
This is a temple of justice and the house of God.)

The other three stanzas also are profound and meaningful,
and underline Baduyuni's ability to not only write for the
occasion but also to project the philosophical aspects of life
within a limited frame.

Naushad's tunes for the antara and the mukhdas swing
from low notes to high notes and vice versa and Rafi takes
everything in his musical stride—as expected!

Insaaf ka mandir hai yeh strikes a chord even with the
captious listener despite more than seven decades having
flown by.

According to Madhubala's biographer, Khatija Akbar:

Apparently, the songs of *Amar* which were superhits,
appealed greatly to Madhubala. When she first heard *Na
milta gham to barbadi ke afsaane kahan jaate,* she went to
Naushad and asked him to write down the words for her.
Khamosh hai khevanhar mera and *Naiyya meri dhobi jaati
hai* in Raag Bhairavi (my boat is sinking) were her other
favourites, but it was *Janewale se mulaqaat na hone pai, dil
ki dil mein rahi baat na hone pai,* that had a special place in
her heart. In fact, when it was first played on the sets, she
burst into tears, which brought about a spell of crying by
the others present, recalled Naushad.

Dil Diya Dard Liya (1966)

Immediately after Ram Mukherjee's *Leader*, written by Dilip Kumar, 'underperformed' at the box office, A.R. Kardar's *Dil Diya Dard Liya* released in 1966, which was conceived by the actor to write off the failure of the upbeat comedy role and to resurrect his time-tested image of a tragedian—a persecuted man in pursuit of his childhood love. Deriving its basic plot from the 1941 Nitin Bose-directed *Lagan*, which had K.L. Saigal and Kanan Devi in the lead, coupled with his own Shaheed Latif-directed *Arzoo* in 1950 and S.K. Ohja's *Hulchul* (1951), he borrowed again the characters from the English novelist Emily Brontë's classic *Wuthering Heights*, which was first published in 1847.

The film, which had Waheeda Rehman and Pran as his co-stars, it seems, was doomed from the start itself.

Though the story, screenplay and casting were completed in early 1960, the film took nearly six years to reach the cinema halls, after many disagreements and much animosity, many

Dilip Kumar and Waheeda Rehman in
Dil Diya Dard Liya (1966)

tensions and much stress between Dilip Kumar and A.R.
Kardar on the making of the film which also led to a court
battle which the actor won. Finally, Dilip Kumar reportedly
took over the direction to complete the film. According to
author and film journalist Bunny Reuben, 'The story and
screenplay of the film were by Dilip Kumar, and although the
film's producer A.R. Kardar was supposed to have directed it,
it was Dilip Kumar's creative inputs that often exceeded those
of the credited director.'[8]
According to Dilip Kumar:

> It was also the time when a lawsuit that was slapped on me
> by A.R. Kardar was coming up for repeated hearings
> and I was determined to fight it tooth and nail to prove
> the falsehood of his charges. The irony was that the
> confrontation was provoked by an individual for whom I
> had done all that I could do as a star to redeem his ship
> from sinking into abject penury . . . I worked tirelessly to
> hone the film and make it a memorable one so that I could
> give the man a place among the successful film-makers of
> the country and end his hardships. In return, he perfidiously
> framed me on the basis of false allegations and accusations.[9]

The film tells the story of a tyrannical Ramesh (Pran), son
of a feudal chief, Thakur (Sapru), who is a kind-hearted man
and had rescued a child Shankar (Dilip Kumar) from a sinking
ship and adopted him. Ramesh grows up to hate Shankar
and mistreats him regularly. Shankar, who bears it all, loves
Ramesh's sister Roopa (played by Waheeda Rehman) and
vows to earn enough to win her hand. However, when Ramesh
learns of this, he has him severely beaten up by his goons and
taking Shankar to be dead, they throw him off a cliff.

However, as fate would have it, Shankar survives and later,
as luck would have it, is discovered to be the long-lost son

Dilip Kumar and Pran in *Dil Diya Dard Liya* (1966)

of a wealthy raja of the kingdom of Belapur and the heir to the kingdom. Now rich and well settled, Shankar goes to compromise with Ramesh to let bygones be bygones and asks him for the hand of his sister Roopa, who by now is engaged to be married to Satish (Rehman). Ramesh literally degrades and pours all sorts of insults on Shankar and asks him to get out of his house or he would have him thrown out. He leaves but not before announcing to Ramesh his plans to avenge the brutal treatment meted out to him all along: '*Tumse tumhaare ek ek julm ka hisaab maangunga. Un zakhamon ki jalan mita raha hoon jo is ghar ne mujhe diye the* (I will take you to task for each and every act of cruelty done by you. I am erasing the burn of the wounds which this house gave me).

A dejected Shankar begins to suspect Roopa of betraying him and makes it his life's ambition to destroy her—the very woman whom he loved all along. In front of the same idol of Lord Shiva, Shankar, burning with despise and anger, accuses

Roopa of double standards, of claiming to love him and deceiving him at the same time.

In spite of the anti-hero characterization of Dilip Kumar (in the latter part of the film) and impressive performances by all members of the cast, particularly by Dilip Kumar and Pran, both of whom got nominations for the Best Actor and Best Supporting Actor Award, respectively, in the 14th Filmfare Awards in 1967, the film was a massive dud at the box office. *Dil Diya Dard Liya* turned out to be nothing more than a contrived melodrama with Dilip Kumar having a commanding presence by being present virtually in the entire footage. Though the narrative sought to highlight the erosion of human expression caused by excessive harassment and a series of disappointments, it failed to leave a strong impression on the audience. Moreover, the overall environment was typically feudal and the rebel hero's preoccupation with his love depicted within this framework appeared illogical as also soulless in the film that carried on and on for a tiring three-hour duration.

Dilip Kumar adopted a curious blending of underplay with respect to the victimized hero in the first half of the film, with overplay of vengeance in the latter half. But neither his normally reliable histrionics, nor the 'clash scenes' with Pran, could salvage the film, simply because Dilip Kumar, who had started to face audience rejection by then, was out of depth. Pran, however, was very impressive and his acting came in for much praise. The Pran and Dilip Kumar rivalry was stupendous, with Pran terming his role in the film as one of the strongest 'bad man's' roles that he played in his career:

Even though the film didn't do well at the box-office, I had an outstanding negative role in it, and it remains one of my best performances and also one of the favourite films of my career. But I must admit that my performance was good because of Dilip Saab. . . . In most films I never laugh loudly. But in *Dil Diya Dard Liya*, the role demanded it. This is the only film in which I used malicious laughter to heighten the villainy and Dilip Kumar helped me a lot with my performance. He was always of the opinion that 'the scene should stand in its entirety, only then will it come out good. Until all the artistes in the scene have not given their best, the scene cannot come off well'. Dilip Saab has been a real master of his profession.[10]

However, any creative process is one of give and take. And just as Pran said that he had benefited from Dilip Kumar's help, Dilip Kumar too benefited from Pran's mastery over the medium. This was clearly visible when, after giving a particular shot, Dilip Kumar would look at Pran to ascertain whether he had done the scene perfectly.

For those acquainted with Emily Brontë's *Wuthering Heights*, it was Dilip Kumar who played Heathcliff, Waheeda Rehman played Catherine Earnshaw and Pran was cast as Hindley Earnshaw.

True to form, composer Naushad and lyricist Shakeel Badayuni did not slacken their efforts in any manner and the duo's efforts were up to, if not beyond, expectations. Yes, the music did not quite achieve the glory it was expected to. That apart, let us focus on the songs, as they certainly are hummable.

Dil Diya Dard Liya comprises eight songs: three Mohammed Rafi solos, two solos each by Lata Mangeshkar and Asha Bhosle, and one Mohammed Rafi–Asha Bhosle duet. By this stage, Asha Bhosle was gaining ground in Naushad's domain.

All the three Rafi solos—*Dilruba maine tere pyaar mein kya kya na kiya?* (Beloved, what haven't I done while in love with you?) in Raag Yaman, *Koi saagar dil ko behlaata nahin* (No

Koi saagar dil ko behlaata nahin . . . Dilip Kumar in
Dil Diya Dard Liya (1966)

goblet brings pleasure to my heart) and *Guzren hain aaj ishq
mein hum us maqaam se/nafrat-si ho gayee hai mohabbat ke
naam se* (I have gone through that phase in love/[that] I have
developed a sort of hatred for love) in Raag Gara/Darbari—do
make a profound impact and it is very difficult to choose just
one. Nonetheless, one feels that the dainty number *Koi saagar
dil ko behlaata nahin*, which is a ghazal, is the most melodious
of the three. Set in Raag Kalawati, it follows the traditional
pattern: It is made up of the matla and three more shers, with
the second sher in a different tune from the first and third shers.
Through the matla, the shayar brings out the predicament of the
protagonist who cannot derive peace of mind despite indulging
in the age-old habit of hitting the bottle (a trend that needs to
be reversed once and for all). The matla reads:

*Koi saagar dil ko behlaata nahin
Bekhudi mein bhi qaraar aata nahin.*

(No goblet brings pleasure to my heart
Even in a state of intoxication, I cannot find solace.)

Of the three shers, one has opted for the second one, which underscores the loneliness and frustration of the hero:

Kal to sab the kaarwaan ke saath saath
Aaj koi raah dikhlaata nahin.

(Yesterday, all were together with the caravan
Today, there is no one to show me the way.)

The speciality here is that Rafi dips his voice to almost a whisper while intoning the first line of this couplet: a treat for the connoisseur of music and poetry. One of the other Rafi solos—*Guzren hain aaj ishq mein hum us maqaam se*, which is also a ghazal, set in Raag Darbari Kanada, also makes a powerful impact on the listener as he has rendered it with full-throated gusto.

One cannot refrain from making references to another Lata Mangeshkar-rendered heart-touching ghazal from the film: *Phir teri kahaani yaad aayee, phir tera fasaana yaad aayaa* (Once again I remembered your story: once again I remembered your tale), which was written, rewritten, and re-re-written to be finally set in Raag Maand, and also to the Rafi–Bhosle duet *Saawan aaye ya na aaye* (Whether saawan [the month associated with the monsoon] comes or not), set in that afternoon raag—Brindavani Sarang. In the former, Lata Mangeshkar's dulcet vocals in consonance with Naushad's nostalgia-tinted *tarz* (tune) and Shakeel's shayiri (in the same mood) cast a lingering spell. In the latter, Mohammed Rafi and Asha Bhosle's vocals literally glide through the song with finesse and grace, engendering a dreamy environment.

Aadmi (1968)

The traumas of A.R. Kardar's *Dil Diya Dard Liya* it seemed, were to linger on not only for Dilip Kumar but also for composer Naushad and the poet Shakeel Badayuni. Producer P.S. Veerappa's *Aadmi*, who originally wanted to sign the whimsical Raaj Kumar but finally settled for Manoj Kumar, took so long to mount after the customary trade announcement that at one stage, it seemed it had been shelved. However, once the shooting started, the progress was so slow that one was not sure if it would ever be completed to hit the screens. As Dilip Kumar mentioned:

> Although shooting for this film began long before *Ram Aur Shyam* mounted the sets, its pace slowed down halfway through the production because the cash flow came in dribs and drabs. While I was shooting some hilarious scenes for *Ram Aur Shyam*, I had to agree to dub for certain poignant

Dilip Kumar and Waheeda Rehman in *Aadmi* (1968)

scenes with Waheeda for *Aadmi* because Veerappa would send word that some funds had come in and they were in a position to hire a dubbing studio and pay the technicians. Likewise, the editor of *Aadmi* [A. Paul Doraisingam] used to invite me to take a look at the edited reels and I spent many evenings (after pack-up at B. Naggi Reddy's *Ram Aur Shyam*) in the suites where *Aadmi* was being edited.

Once again, Dilip Kumar's preoccupation with the anti-hero image found expression in *Aadmi*, directed by A. Bhim Singh. It was a grim theme—the extent to which a friend, who has been the recipient of a millionaire's largesse, goes to repay that generosity and kindness, even at the cost of his own happiness. The hero Rajesh/Raja Sahab (Dilip Kumar), who belongs to a very affluent family, has been living with a guilty conscience for years because he had killed his friend, Babu, over a doll about which he was very possessive, during his childhood. At the start of the film there is a monologue by Rajesh: 'You are not worthy of friendship. Like a ghost, the mistake of childhood will never give me *mukti* (release).' And his friend Babu's voice comes in the background: 'You cannot find mukti in exchange for all your wealth. One day you will kill your friend Shekhar also.'

Shekhar (Manoj Kumar) is undoubtedly his closest friend. Rajesh has supported him all along financially and otherwise to help him get an education and become a doctor—an act to assuage his guilt by helping the downtrodden financially. After a chance encounter, he falls in love and gets engaged to Meena (Waheeda Rehman), whose family is one of his many beneficiaries, who in turn is in love with Shekhar.

One day when Rajesh comes to know that his closest friend Shekhar is involved with his fiancée, he becomes extremely jealous and his compulsive childhood obsession of acquiring everything he desires even at the cost of destroying the other

Dilip Kumar and Manoj Kumar in *Aadmi* (1968)

person/s, instantly resurfaces. He begins to torment both his fiancée and his friend, but again the feeling of guilt becomes so overwhelming that the devil in him resurfaces and prevails upon him to kill Shekhar. Failing in his attempt to do so, he also realizes that he was all wrong regarding his suspicions about his friend Shekhar and his fiancée Meena. He attempts suicide but is saved by the temple priest, whom he had helped in the past. Rajesh then laments to God that a criminal like him does not have the right to live and when he wants to die, he is saved. Finally, he regains his equanimity.

According to Manoj Kumar, 'Though Bhim Singh was the director, it was Dilip Sahab who was actually shaping the film and was keenly helping with its editing too.'[11] Dilip Kumar pointed out:

Aadmi was essentially a psychological drama and I tried to give it the edge and slickness it deserved on the editing table. Those days, the French new-wave directors, especially

Jean-Luc Godard, had created an interest in our editors to employ the jump-cut unnecessarily. Although I was not formally trained in the job of editing, I had a fair idea of the contribution an editor could make to engage a viewer in the storytelling process. The subject of *Aadmi* was such that it needed imaginative editing.

As an actor, I was struck by the promise that the character I played in *Aadmi* held. I had to bring out the protagonist's cerebral struggle to leave his past behind and move on. The basic conflict in the story, which had the external appearance of a common love triangle, was unusual in the sense that it was not so much a conflict between the two men over one woman as is common in film stories. The friction was in the minds of the characters.

The character I played was to be explored from a psychological angle and that intrigued me. From my experience and understanding, I concluded that the film had to have a mood and an ambience that would go with the vicissitudes in the protagonist's life and the Freudian thought process he gets into. So, I got involved in two vital aspects of its making, besides the writing. I took a keen interest in the camera movements and lighting and also in the selection of the shots on the editing table.

Film-making, unlike some other art forms like painting or writing poetry, for instance, has a great deal to do with communication. I mean the communication between the actor and the director, between the director and the cameraman and the art director, between the director and the editor, between the artiste and the cameraman and so on. If the coordination is well orchestrated, it shows in the final product. If not, it shows equally in the frayed look of the product.[12]

Aadmi was a success at the box office. Besides being noted for Dilip Kumar's acting, it was speckled with some dramatic scenes and emotion-filled dialogues by the award-winning Akhtar ul-Iman, the man who wrote the dialogues for some of the most successful films of the period and trick photography by the award-winning Faredoon A. Irani.

The media reviews, however, were mixed, with some being rather harsh. According to writer–author Raju Bharatan: 'Dilip Kumar, enacting Rajesh, looked astoundingly undecided about his approach to essaying a role performed with such empathy by Shivaji Ganeshan in the Tamil version, K. Shankar's *Aalayamani*, in the cosy company of B. Saroja Devi . . . Waheeda Rehman too, as Meena, came through as appearing to be none too certain opposite Dilip Kumar. So much so that it looked as if Waheeda Rehman had already rehearsed—in the April 1966 *Dil Diya Dard Liya* itself—to look as bewildered on the screen, opposite Dilip Kumar, as she now did in *Aadmi*.'[13]

Naushad's *Aadmi* music outcome may have suffered in the process, but it was still pretty well-honed to the theme. According to a film critic, 'Lata Mangeshkar's solos were at the best pleasing to the ear, but it was Mohammad Rafi who lost out for no vocal fault of his, as Dilip Kumar sent the already perplexed audience into a further fit of depression through the three numbers—*Main tooti hui ik naiyya hoon* (I am a broken boat), *Aaj puraani raahon se koi mujhe awaaz na de* (Let not anyone call me from the old paths), both based on Raag Bhairavi and *Na aadmi ka koi bharosa* in Raag Bhimpalasi (No man is trustworthy).'[14]

Whatever the views of music critics, the fact remains that for the film music buffs, Naushad seemed to have regained

Aaj puraani raahon se koi mujhe awaaz na de . . .
Dilip Kumar in *Aadmi* (1968)

his form to some extent and his six creations for *Aadmi* provided ample testimony! There are three Mohammed Rafi solos, two Lata Mangeshkar solos and one 'odd' duet. The old-song aficionados would have guessed the duet by now—*Kaisi haseen aaj bahaaron ki raat hai* (How beautiful today is the springtime night) based on Raag Desh—which was originally recorded in the voices of Mohammed Rafi and Talat Mahmood. In fact, the music company, HMV (His Master's Voice), now known as Saregama, even released a 78-rpm (revolutions per minute) record. Apparently, Manoj Kumar was not too happy to be singing on the screen in the voice of Talat, by then a fading voice whom no music director was signing, against the evergreen voice of Mohammad Rafi going on Dilip Kumar. 'Manoj Kumar was conscious of the vocal beating that he would have to take in the softer tones, at the hands of Rafi–Dilip Kumar combine hitting the apt notes.'[15] As Naushad recounted: 'There was not a day when Manoj Kumar did not ring me up, with just twelve weeks to go for the release of the film. The burden of Manoj Kumar's song was straight forward, "get for my visage a voice with which I can hold my own against Dilip Kumar already giving me the willies".'[16]

Naushad resisted. Manoj insisted! At the end of it all, Manoj Kumar, 'in sheer desperation carried his urgent urgings to the producer P.S. Veerappa himself. Finally, Naushad was left with no choice but to bring in, entirely predictably, Mahendra Kapoor, who had already been a voice over for Manoj Kumar in his own directorial debut *Upkar*, a year earlier, and that too successfully.' Talat Mahmood was dropped overnight. It's another matter that the *Aadmi* song was no shakes on the music charts.

Of the three unforgettable Rafi solos, all picturized on Dilip Kumar, the one that stands out is *Na aadmi ka koi bharosa*, through which Badayuni highlights the fickleness of human relationships. The song begins with a two-line prelude followed by the mukhda and two antaras. Here is the mukhda:

Na aadmi ka koi bharosa, na dosti ka koi thikaana
Wafa ka badla hai bewafaee, ajab zamaana hai yeh zamaana.

(No man is trustworthy, [and] friendship has no direction [cannot be relied upon]
The reward for loyalty is disloyalty, this world is a strange world.)

It is the second antara that brings out the turmoil and agony of the protagonist who has trusted his friend and his fiancée:

Dava ke badle mein zehr dedo, utaardo mere dil mein khanjar
Lahoo se seencha tha jis chaman ko, uge hai sholay usike andar
Mere hi ghar ke chiragh ne khud jala diya mera aashiana.

(In place of medicine give me poison, pierce my heart with a dagger
Flames have erupted from the garden that I nourished with my blood
The lamp of my house itself has burnt my nest.)

The other two Rafi solos are contrasting in nature. Whereas *Main tooti hui ek nayya hoon* (I am a broken boat) is mellow and melancholic (set in low notes), *Aaj puraani raahon se koi mujhe awaaz na de* (Let no one call me from the old paths) begins on a high note with Rafi's *Oh ho ho . . .* (somewhat like *Khoya khoya chaand, khula aasmaan*: the lost moon and the clear sky, from the 1960 film *Kala Bazar*) and then settles into a rhythmic pattern. The tunes in the former number are quite complex in nature, but Rafi, as to be expected, handled them adroitly.

With a formidable star cast and despite a not too compelling musical score, *Aadmi* was successful at the box office.

Dastaan (1972)

If there was one film that sent shock waves through the otherwise reliable and stable B.R. Films banner, it was *Dastaan*. This author recalls B.R. Chopra once telling him that *Dastaan*, based on his earlier hit film *Afsana*, which had Ashok Kumar, Veena and Pran in the cast, in 1951, was the biggest box-office 'disaster' in his fifty-nine-year film career (1949–2008), in which he made forty films

Dilip Kumar and Sharmila Tagore in *Dastaan* (1972)

and ten TV serials, including the ninety-four-episode epic
Mahabharat in 1988.

   Dastaan, which had, for the first time, Sharmila Tagore with
Dilip Kumar in the lead 'is certainly not a chapter from which
to start the curriculum of a course of the work', of B.R. Chopra,
who had given fifteen box-office hits at a stretch like *Afsana*
(1951), *Ek Hi Raasta* (1956), *Naya Daur* (1957), *Kanoon*
(1960; India's first film without songs), *Gumrah* (1963), *Waqt*
(1965) and *Hamraaz* (1967), to name a few. Written by actor–
director I.S. Johar, the film is a gory tale of suspicion, greed,
deceit, dénouement and revenge built on the entirely different
experiences of two separated twins. The story is of a simple-
hearted judge, Vishnu Sahay, who is betrayed by his wife
(Bindu), who is in an illicit relationship with his best friend
Rajan (Prem Chopra). By a sheer coincidence, the lookalike
of the judge, a playboy (whom the judge has befriended),

Prem Chopra, Bindu and Dilip Kumar in *Dastaan* (1972)

gets killed in a road accident and the judge takes his place and devises a plan of revenge. He stages a play to expose his two tormentors.

One of the most unimaginative productions under the B.R. Films banner, the film also contained a number of sequences that looked like shoddy imitations of certain scenes lifted straight from old Hollywood masterpieces such as the Roman thriller *Random Harvest* (1942) by Mervyn LeRoy which was nominated for seven Academy Awards, Fritz Lang's *The Woman in the Window* (1944) and Alfred Hitchcock's *Spellbound* (1945), starring Ingrid Bergman and Gregory Peck. The film was so weak that one can't even remember a single scene that stood out in a Dilip Kumar film. If one were forced to stress upon their memory, what comes to mind is the scene, by which time we are well into half the film, when the judge discovers the illicit relationship of his wife with his best friend and keeps wandering in the wild in an utterly shocked state. And second, when his wife commits suicide, he asks God: '*Main kaise yeh tera insaaf samju ya insaan ka inteqam. Kya teri yeh duniya begaair paap ke nahin chal sakti?*' (How

Dilip Kumar in *Dastaan* (1972)

can I consider this to be your justice or a man's revenge. Can this world of yours not run without sin?)

Was there any redeeming factor in the film? Certainly *not*, except perhaps for, if at all, Dilip Kumar's innate ability in succinctly capturing the distinction between the two characters. It seems he partly designed his two roles—the judge and the flamboyant imposter—on his resounding portrayals in *Azaad* and *Leader*.

As was to be expected, if the audience totally ignored the film, the press blew it to bits. Film journalist and author Bunny Reuben raised a question: 'After the collapse of *Dastaan*, which follows closely on the heels of A.R. Kardar's *Dil Diya Dard Liya*, A. Bhim Singh's *Aadmi* and H.S. Rawail's *Sunghursh* (both 1968), two years ago both *Sagina* and *Bairaag* were virtually ready. Yet, *Sagina* took another two years to get released and *Bairaag* is in the process of being remade for the umpteenth time. Why? Is the thespian, the greatest actor of the

Indian cinema, tired? More important, is he still where he has always been, right on the top?'[17]

Reuben answered it himself: 'Quite unconsciously, what had happened to him was that he had been functioning on one histrionic graph since *Gunga Jumna*, embellishing it with farce and comedy (as he did in A. Bhim Singh's *Gopi*) and with special overtones (as he did in Tapan Singh's *Sagina*), but essentially, giving no other performance through his last few movies other than the one which he subconsciously thinks displays his histrionic prowess best. Where are the subtleties gone?'

The music of *Dastaan* too failed to create any buzz whatsoever. This despite the fact that Laxmikant–Pyarelal had been brought in to join hands with B.R. Chopra's favourite and most dependable lyricist Sahir Ludhianvi. The only thing to remember, if at all any, is that Mohammad Rafi, who by now had decided never to sing again for Dilip Kumar, *did* sing for the actor in an otherwise Mahendra Kapoor song scope in addition to a Raag Madhmad Sarang-based duet with Asha Bhosle: *Maria my sweetheart*. The Rafi-rendered Raag Yaman-based ghazal *Na tu zameen ke liye hain na aasmaan ke liye* (You are neither for the earth nor for the skies) reverberated only in the background as Dilip Kumar emoted in a tragic manner. Sadly, both the compositions are not even remembered nowadays, not even by a handful of aficionados. Perhaps it could be because B.R. Chopra had by now switched over to the duo from his favourite composer Ravi.

Vidhaata (1982)

Subhash Ghai's *Vidhaata* recounted on screen a gruesome tale of an ordinary man's violent fight against the evil forces that have created havoc in his life. In the process, he becomes Vidhaata—a ruthless mafia don seeking vengeance against the tormentors—something like what one saw in Francis Ford Copolla's *Godfather* (1972).

Shamsher Singh (Dilip Kumar) starts off as a nondescript railway engine driver with his friend Gurbaksh Singh (Shammi Kapoor). Shamsher Singh's son Pratap Singh (Suresh Oberoi), an upright police inspector, is killed by the villain Jagawar Chaudhary (Amrish Puri). Enraged, Shamsher kills Jagawar's men and escapes with his pregnant daughter-in-law on a goods train, where she dies after giving birth to a boy Kunal (Sanjay Dutt). Shamsher is now landed with the job of bringing up his grandson, a job he entrusts to his loyal employee Abu Baba (Sanjeev Kumar) so as to keep his grandson away from the world of crime

Dilip Kumar in *Vidhaata* (1982)

Dilip Kumar and Shammi Kapoor in *Vidhaata* (1982)

Meanwhile, Shamsher is preoccupied with writing his own destiny and that of his grandson. After joining Sir Miziya (Shriram Lagoo), a powerful underworld don, he takes on a new identity as Sir Shobraj and soon becomes a Vidhaata (a la Godfather)—a wealthy and powerful smuggler who gets sucked into many encounters with the notorious Jagawar Chaudhary.

Kunal, whose upbringing has been done under the strict supervision of Abu Baba, falls in love with a beautiful girl, Durga (Padmini Kolhapure), who is the only daughter of an employee of Shamsher and also from a poor family. Because of the vastly different backgrounds, the Vidhaata refuses to let the two marry and orders Durga's mother to leave the city with her daughter or face his wrath. While leaving on a ship, there is an attempt to rape Durga. Abu Baba comes to her rescue but in the ensuing fight loses his life. Kunal is devastated on seeing his foster father's dead body and there and then decides to take revenge.

After a series of action-packed scenes and pithy dialogues, Kunal's investigations into Abu Baba's death lead him

Dilip Kumar and Sanjeev Kumar in *Vidhaata* (1982)

to the true identity of his grandfather as also his father's killers. Shamsher is morally humbled by his grandson, who questions his grandfather's right to write his destiny. In the final fight between Shamsher and Jagawar, the latter is killed and Shamsher mortally wounded. He dies in the arms of his grandson and his friend Gurbaksh, who eventually gets Kunal and Durga married.

While Shammi Kapoor pitched in with an energetic performance, playing a happy-go-lucky engine driver friend of Dilip Kumar, it was all-in-all a Dilip Kumar film and he did not let the viewers down. As was to be expected, he gave a powerful performance. Some of his outstanding scenes included the one in which he grieves over his dying police inspector son and where he goes to the police station and shouts at the cops for not taking any action regarding his son's murder. There were two other outstanding scenes—one, in which Shamsher announces his transformation into a vengeful man to avenge the death of his son; second, in the final death scene in the temple, where Dilip Kumar repents and asks God to forgive him for taking destiny in his own hands. He is certainly at his best in the scenes where he emotes anger. As writer Salim Khan once said: 'A large number of self-proclaimed stars have projected anger, but compared to Dilip Saab, they look like paper tigers.'[18]

According to Dilip Kumar:

> Subhash Ghai came to meet me with the story of *Vidhaata*. He impressed me with his credentials and his sincerity. He was honest that his previous film [*Krodhi*, 1981, which had an ensemble cast of Dharmendra, Shashi Kapoor, Hema Malini, Zeenat Aman, Moushumi Chatterjee, Pran and Amrish Puri] was not successful and that he hoped to make that setback the stepping stone to his future success. I liked his optimistic enthusiasm and his passion. The subject was interesting and offered the actor in me the scope to do some good work. What was more, like my role in *Kranti*, the role in *Vidhaata* was of an earthy character, a railway engine driver, who becomes the axis of the screenplay as a protagonist.[19]

Though the music of *Vidhaata* was composed by Kalyanji–Anandji, with lyrics by Anand Bakshi, it was nothing to write home about—something rather surprising for a Subhash Ghai film. There was a duet picturized on Dilip Kumar and Shammi Kapoor. (It would not be an exaggeration to state that in the years gone by, Mohammad Rafi and Shammi Kapoor were made for each other.) In Rafi's absence, it was Suresh Wadkar who sang for Shammi Kapoor and Anwar (Hussein), whose voice was quite a good copy of Rafi's, for Dilip Kumar in the vibrant *Haaton ki chand lakeeron ka* (A few lines on the hands) based on Raag Miyan Ki Malhar. However, the number just did not work for the film music buffs. It left us all rather unaffected.

The film was a hit at the box office. Seeing its tremendous success, it was later remade in Kannada as *Pithamaha* (1985) by K.S.L. Swamy, in Malayalam as *Alakadalinakkare* (1984) by Joshiy, and in Tamil as *Vamsa Vilakku* (1984) by R. Krishnamoorthy. In each of the three languages too it was a super hit.

Mashaal (1984)

The year 1984 saw two Dilip Kumar films—Yash Chopra's *Mashaal* and *Duniya* by Ramesh Talwar, a long-time assistant of Yash Chopra. Both were designed in the same vein as Subhash Ghai's *Vidhaata*. Both were written by Javed Akhtar. Both were lauded by the critics for Dilip Kumar's acting. And both were big failures at the box office thus adding to the thespian's short list of failures. Though *Mashaal* had the advantage of having Waheeda Rehman in the female lead

Dilip Kumar and Waheeda Rehman in *Mashaal* (1984)

Dilip Kumar and Amrish Puri in *Mashaal* (1984)

and Anil Kapoor as the young journalist—a role that was apparently refused by both Amitabh Bachchan and Kamal Haasan—who won the Filmfare Award for Best Supporting Actor for it, it did not work.

Based on the well-known Marathi play *Ashroonchi Zhali Phule* by Vasant Shankar Kanetkar, *Mashaal* essentially followed the plot structure of *Vidhaata*. This time, Dilip Kumar played the role of a senior journalist, Vinod, committed to upholding the social role of media in exposing those sinister deeds of the anti-people forces. As he leads a spirited campaign against the mafia lord S.K. Vardan (Amrish Puri) through his small newspaper, the villain starts harassing him, leading eventually to the death of his wife Sudha (Waheeda Rehman) under tragic circumstances. Vinod Kumar is hit hard by the

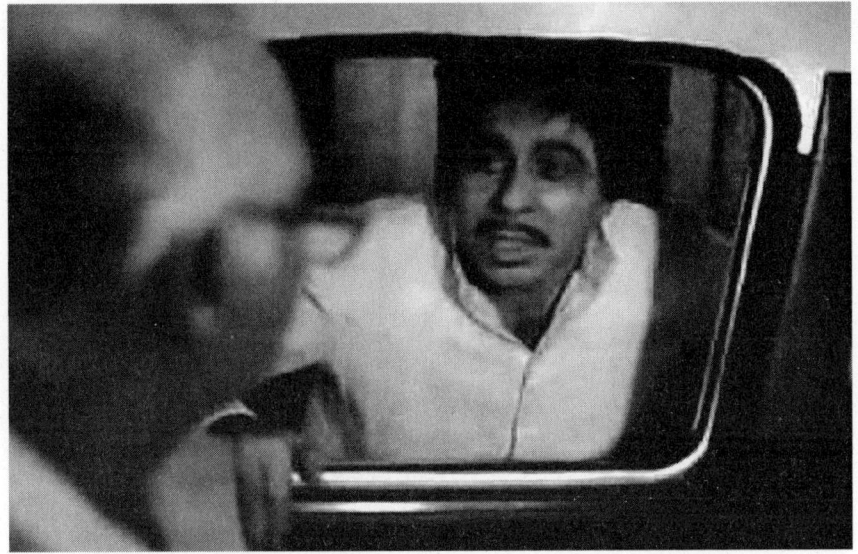

Dilip Kumar in *Mashaal* (1984)

apathy of the justice delivery system and the indifference of the people around him and opts to become a powerful mafia don himself so that he can seek revenge against the tormentor.

The anti-establishment stance is juxtaposed with the burning idealism of a young journalist, Raja (Anil Kapoor), whom the senior had earlier resurrected from the ghettos of crime. However, soon Raja finds out that Vinod is now himself a big criminal don. He starts writing about Vinod and Vardhan's criminal deeds.

One day, in the course of the confrontation between the two dons, Vardhan kidnaps Raja, but Vinod saves him and kills Vardhan, putting him in the wheels of the printing press. However, when a henchman of Vardhan aims to shoot Raja, Vinod comes in between and gets fatally shot and the mentor dies in his protégé's arms.

Though it was a Dilip Kumar film all along, both Anil Kapoor and Waheeda Rehman were superb in their respective

Dilip Kumar, Waheeda Rehman and Anil Kapoor
in *Mashaal* (1984)

roles. One still remembers that scene, in the beginning of the
film, in which Vinod laments in front of his wife the utter
lack of comforts in their lives: '*Tum ne kis faatichir aadmi
se shaadi ki? Aathara saalon mein tumhe kuch nahin mila*'
(Which ragged man have you married? In these eighteen years,
you got nothing). And that scene where the extremely biased
Vinod gives his opinion on Raja to his wife: '*Naali ke kidae
ko duniya bhar ke saare sabun ikhata kar ke dho liya jaaya to
bhi woh gandah hi rahega*' (An insect from the gutter, even if
washed with all the soap collected from around the world will
remain dirty). Then there is that scene where Anil Kapoor asks
Dilip Kumar, in the name of his dead wife, whether he too has
become a don. Vinod, very reluctantly, accepts his allegation:
'*Tum jo kasam de rahe ho, uske baad mein jhoot nahin bol
sakta*' (The oath under which you have asked me to swear by,
after that I cannot lie).

However, the highlight of the film is that bone-chilling, one
of the widely remembered scenes of Indian cinema in which
Vinod's wife, seriously ill, is about to die in the dead of the

night, on a rain-swept street of Bombay and Vinod is begging, desperately seeking help, by trying to stop every vehicle that comes from either side of the road, by trying to wake people sleeping in their homes, but no body stops, no body wakes up, nobody cares for them. It is a scene which no film buff can ever forget, for it's etched in our memory, a scene every teacher, every student and every critic ought to observe, a scene that needs to be minutely watched just to study the art and craft of the great master. A scene only Dilip Kumar could have done! It added an unexpected layer of intensity making it a memorable tale in Indian cinematic history. It has become 'a symbol of achieving the near impossible thus illustrating the heights of Dilip Kumar's potential and perseverance' on screen.

Talking about the shooting of the scene, Dilip Kumar narrated:

> . . . it was typical of (father) to pretend to be unemotional and detached. His warmth and concern surfaced only once when Amma had a serious attack of asthma, and she was choking and gasping for breath. He began yelling for someone to rush and fetch the doctor who lived across the street. His face was then a picture of helpless alarm, and I can still recall the tall strapping figure bending to hold my frail Amma in his arms . . . I must tell you that, while going through my rehearsals, I drew my emotions for rendering of the scene, shot over four nights in a row, from the memory of that episode and the agony of Aghaji in his urgency to get instant medical help . . . where images surfaced from my subconscious to spur me.
>
> Few know that the entire scene was rendered in one shot once the cameras rolled. When we completed the work, it was pretty late in the night, and I could see moist eyes all around me and there was an eerie silence. For a second or two it disturbed me. Then Yash came up to

me and I could see that he was unable to say whatever he wanted to because he was choked with emotion. After a while everybody relaxed, and the admiration surfaced. There is no greater award for an actor than the genuine appreciation of his colleagues.[20]

According to actor Anil Kapoor, Dilip Kumar's contribution to his acting career is immensely valuable and if he is still working in films at the age of sixty-seven (with two National Film Awards, seven Filmfare Awards and over a hundred films in his kitty), it is only because of what he learnt from Dilip Kumar indirectly, and what he was taught from his first lead role in *Mashaal*.[21]

From my impressionable years, I was literally breathing Dilip Kumar, and my sole desire was to grow up and find an opportunity to observe him at work. And that came with *Mashaal*. In a rehearsal shot, Dilip Sahab walked sturdily into the canteen and began on his dialogue. I kept ignoring him when suddenly he shouted: 'Cut, cut, cut. Why are you not facing me when I am talking to you?'

I said, 'Sir, my character is one that of an impudent chap, ill-mannered so that I should not be looking straight at you while you are addressing me.'

Dilip Sahab immediately turned to Yash Chopra and said: 'Okay, let's do the scene that way. I walk into the canteen, walk straight to Anil, pull him by the scruff of his shirt collar, make him turn to me and then start talking.'

Both Yash Chopra and I thought that was just right. He requested if we could go straight for the take. Pin-drop silence followed. Dilip Sahab walked in briskly, pulled me up by the collar with his strong Pathani hand while I was choking and trembling as I looked into his piercing eyes, genuinely fighting for breath. The take was okayed. There was a wild applause because it was a superb shot, and my expression could not have been more real. But I was still sweating and choking. Dilip Sahab noticed by predicament and took me to a quiet corner and said he was sorry, but sometimes it helped if the action got slightly real. 'When you see the shot on the screen and get kudos for it, you will know what I mean,' he said.

And he was right. All through the making of *Mashaal*, I had the privilege to observe the dedication and painstaking preparation he put into his work. He became my institution, my textbook, my encyclopaedia.

Mashaal reminds one the words of the legendary Method actor Marlon Brando: 'To grasp the full significance of life is the actor's duty, to interpret it his problem, and to express it his dedication.'[22] However, unarguably, Dilip Kumar, in many ways, was far ahead in the development of his art and craft than Marlon Brando.

The audience did not appreciate *Mashaal*, and it failed at the box office. So did its music by Hridaynath Mangeshkar. However, film critics were unanimous in their praise. Critic Khalid Mohamed wrote:

Dilip Kumar is masterly: the very nakedness of acting. His journalist is not a beaming hero but a battered veteran, stubborn and shambling. Caught in a corner, his voice is as tormented as the neigh of a battle-maddened charger. Truly, he is one of the few living actors who has shown us the mystery and power of which cinema is capable. All the grand unplayable parts should be open to him after this: as long as you see that great jaw sag, those lion eyes search for solace.

The film critic of the *Indian Express* commented in the Sunday issue of 12 February 1984: 'Yash Chopra's *Mashaal* is a brilliant, marvellously watchable, melodrama in the first half—the best thing Yash Chopra has ever done . . . there are interesting touches—Dilip shooting goal, playing with the gang et al—the old throwaway humour, the flashes of fury, are back. There is something new—helpless, beaten, vulnerable, pleading—an unbearably poignant scene with Dilip, lost and desolate in the heart of Mumbai at night, fighting to save Waheeda's life.'

Duniya (1984)

Ramesh Talwar, a long-time assistant of Yash Chopra and director of seven independent films and four television serials, released his most ambitious film, *Duniya*, with Ashok Kumar, Dilip Kumar, Rishi Kapoor and Amrita Singh in the lead. It was written by Javed Akhtar and had music by R.D. Burman.

As mentioned above, *Duniya* too was designed in the same vein as *Vidhaata* and presented Dilip Kumar (playing Mohan Kumar) again as a vengeful man who had to settle scores with the villainy of the world. The film presented the saga of an honest and conscientious man turning into a single devastating apparatus of vengeance.

Mohan Kumar (Dilip Kumar) is sentenced to life imprisonment for the murder of his boss which was not committed by him but by the villain trio (Pran, Amrish Puri and Prem Chopra), who also arrange the killing of his wife in an accident. After his release from prison, Mohan makes a long search of the three and kills them one by one in cold blood.

Duniya brought Dilip Kumar and Ashok Kumar together after a gap of thirty-three years. They had earlier acted in Nitin Bose's *Deedar* (1951), when Ashok Kumar had advised his junior, 'You are a handsome man, and I can see you are

Dilip Kumar and Ashok Kumar in *Duniya* (1984)

eager to learn well. It's very simple. You just do the scene given to you as you would behave in a real-life situation, if you were really in it. Be natural. If you try to act it out, it will look silly.'[23]

As also already mentioned above, the film was a flop at the box office and there is nothing much to write about it except for Dilip Kumar's intensity of performance. One remembers the scene when talking to the old don R.D. Puri (Ashok Kumar) about his desperate search for his three tormentors who destroyed his life, he says: '*Yeh teen aadmi nahin, teen saroon-wale rakshash hain jis ne meri zindagi ko pairon taale kuchal diya*' (They are not three men, but a three-headed demon, who has crushed my life under his feet.) And Mohan Kumar explains to R.D. Puri about the three unlit diyas in front of the portrait of his wife, Sumitra (Saira Banu), killed by the three villains: '*Maine yeh teen diye raakhen hain par jalayen nahin hain. Ek ek kar ke in zaalimoon ke diye bujtey jayenge aur mein ek ek kar ke yeh teen diyon ko roshan karunga*' (I have kept three lamps which have not been lit. One by one, the lamps of these three tyrants will be extinguished, and I will light one by one these three lamps).

Like the film, R.D. Burman's music to the multifaceted Javed Akhtar's lyrics was a washout. He used Kishore Kumar on Dilip Kumar in three solos, one duet each with Lata Mangeshkar and Asha Bhosle, each one of which failed to create an impact and were forgotten as soon as one stepped out of the theatre hall

Izzatdaar (1990)

Once again, like in *Vidhaata*, *Mashaal* and *Duniya*, in K. Bapiah's film *Izzatdaar*, Dilip Kumar emerged as the angry, ageing man replaying with a renewed vigour the dominant drama of vengeance initiated in the Hindi cinema by him in films such as *Gunga Jumna*. This genre could boast of many additions to its kitty by the young contender, Amitabh Bachchan, mainly in the 1970s and the early 1980s. These films

Dilip Kumar and Govinda in *Izzatdar* (1990)

Anupam Kher, Raghuvaran and Dilip Kumar in *Izzatdaar* (1990)

depicted the transformation of an ordinary upright man into
a vengeful dispenser of natural justice, beyond the purview of
the institutionalized legal system.

Izzatdaar was an attempt to capture the painful moral
decline in society vis-à-vis the unshakeable ethics of a few
strong-willed individuals. Recounted as a flashback by the
protagonist, Braham Dutt (Dilip Kumar), a wealthy upright
man, in the form of a book, the film depicts the upheaval
caused in his life by a young unscrupulous upstart Indrajeet
(Raghuvaran), who has designed his success in life by trapping
the judge's daughter Swapna (Sonu) in a love affair. On
discovering that Sonu has come to know about his various
nefarious activities and also about his attempt to rape her
friend Mohini (Madhuri Dixit), he kills her. Eventually,
Braham, falsely convicted in a murder, himself turns into a
powerful don and avenges the death of his daughter Sonu and
the years spent in prison.

Dilip Kumar exhibited his formidable capacity to innovate and improvise. His portrayal, extremely credible and forceful, was executed with perfect timing and precision. His presence infused a certain gravitas to the film, which was badly needed. However, as was the case with some of his recent films, his characterization tended to overshadow everything else—Govinda, Madhuri Dixit notwithstanding. Thus, *Izzatdaar* too proved to be of no serious consequence even within the broad standards of commercial films. The actor virtually repeated in this run-of-the-mill film lacking any serious purpose, except of course to keep the money coming in.

As for the music by Laxmikant–Pyarelal, the less said, the better. It was a nonstarter. It was obvious that by this stage, Dilip Kumar, so very particular about his music scope in film after film at one stage of his career, after having lost his favourite trio of Naushad, Shakeel Badayuni and Mohammad Rafi, had lost all interest in this important and essential department of Indian films too.

A pity indeed!

Saudagar (1991)

Subhash Ghai, after having given two blockbusters with Dilip Kumar—*Vidhaata* and *Karma*—now launched the most ambitious film of his career, *Saudagar*. It had a huge star cast headed by Dilip Kumar and the whimsical Raaj Kumar, starring together after a gap of thirty-two years. Earlier they had done S.S. Vasan's *Paigham* in 1959. It was labelled as the 'Clash of the Titans', which generated a great deal of media coverage. Raaj Kumar, who had a gravelly voice, was known for his powerful and unique delivery of dialogues which were especially written for him, and which he would at times even improvise or rewrite as the need be. All this helped him

Dilip Kumar in *Saudagar* (1991)

steal scenes, which would amply substantiate his otherwise mediocre acting abilities.

With feet of clay and insecurity writ large, even the top stars of the time would normally thick twice, even thrice, before signing on a project with him, for he was almost always sure to walk away with the film, and the honours, whatever his role be, whosoever be acting with him in it. On the other hand, so confident would he be that he was always ready to sign with anyone pitied against him. Apparently, it is said that when Ghai went to talk to him about the *Saudagar* project and informed him that he was thinking of casting Dilip Kumar against him, Raaj Kumar said, 'Yes, that's correct. After Raaj Kumar, if there is any actor, it is Dilip Kumar.'

Yes, Raaj Kumar was eccentric to the core and had mood swings, quirky habits and unpredictability—an impenetrable carapace that made him somewhat of an enigma. At the best of times, he remained aloof, and no one could fathom his thoughts—his colleagues, his friends, his staff, not even his family.

Manisha Koirala and Vivek Mushran in *Saudagar* (1991)

Saudagar introduced two new actors to Hindi cinema—Vivek Mushran and Manisha Koirala—the later was to become an 'A' lister, acting with almost every top banner, director and hero of the times. Influenced by Shakespeare's famous play *Romeo and Juliet*, with Anupam Kher playing a parallel role to that of Friar Laurence, *Saudagar* was a huge success and was the highest grosser of the 1990s.

The film is about the rivalry between two ageing patriarchs. Bir Singh (Dilip Kumar), a local farmer aka Veeru, and Thakur Rajeshwar Singh (Raaj Kumar), a rich landlord, were close friends in their youth. Bir Singh, who was to marry his friend's sister, is compelled to marry another woman, whose marriage is disrupted due to her in-laws' demand for dowry. Veeru steps in to save the face of the girl and her parents by marrying her. While Rajeshwar Singh is shocked on getting this news, his sister, who loved Veeru, commits suicide. This makes the two childhood friends bitter enemies for life.

With these developments, the two have their territories marked and come to an unwritten understanding that no one will kill anyone living in the other's territory, but anyone entering the other person's territory will be doing so at his own peril. One day, when Rajeshwar Singh's private plane makes an emergency landing in the area of his arch-rival, Bir Singh, he spares his life, saying: '*Jahan tu khada hai, us dharti par anaaj boya jaata hai aur faasl kati jaati hai. Nihate aadmi ka khoon bahana theek nahin hai*' (Where you stand, we plant food grains and harvest our crops. It will not be proper to shed the blood of a defenceless person there). Veeru's elder son, Vishal (Jackie Shroff), takes up the initiative to make peace between the two friends but is killed by Chunia (Amrish Puri), the brother-in-law of Rajeshwar, who wants to take away the wealth of Rajeshwar by keeping the two sides at war.

Meanwhile, Rajeshwar Singh's granddaughter Radha (Manisha Koirala) and Veer's grandson Vashu (Vivek Mushran) meet each other by chance and fall in love, totally unaware of the enmity between the two families. When Mandhari (Anupam Kher) comes to know about it, he reveals the truth of the two families to the lovers and to end the enmity makes Vashu and Radha infiltrate in each other's homes. Through certain twists and turns, it is the innocence of the love of Vashu and Radha which eventually brings the warring families together but not before Chuniya is exposed and in a gun battle that follows is killed by the two friends, who by now have come together once again. In this battle, the two are also fatally wounded and breathe their last in each other's arms.

Saudagar was a show of histrionics, dialogue delivery by Raaj Kumar's powerful voice against Dilip Kumar's, who lent a colloquial shade to his character by speaking the Haryanvi dialect. It was an out and out Dilip Kumar–Raaj Kumar film and certainly designed for the two. The rest of the cast were mere appendages. Though in comparison to Dilip Kumar, Raaj Kumar was a mediocre actor but with a scene-stealing voice

Anupam Kher and Dilip Kumar in *Saudagar* (1991)

that helped him in rendering his dialogues powerfully and authoritatively, like royal commands, he certainly matched Dilip Kumar, scene by scene, dialogue by dialogue. He looked regal and certainly acted so. As Ghai once said: 'Raaj Kumar is a king. He walks like one, talks like one, behaves like one and lives like one.'[24] Recalls Anupam Kher: 'He was a natural in the role of Rajeshwar Singh . . . it was his everyday personality with all the quirks and eccentricities.' Once during the course of a shoot in Manali, I said: '*Bhook lagi hai Sir, bahoot zyada. Aap ko bhi lagi hai*? (I am feeling very hungry Sir. Are you also hungry?). His reply was: "*Jaani, hamesha to sirf janwaroon ko bookh lagti hai*" (Jaani, only animals are always hungry). That made my day. He had finally called me his favourite word "jaani". It was my Raaj Kumar moment.'[25]

Amrish Puri reminisced:

The script did not give me that much importance as the characterization of Dilip Kumar and Raaj Kumar. This is how I felt, but I also understood that they were senior actors and the audience expected much more from them . . . much more dominating. The story of the film was written and built around them. I was always conscious that my performance had to be made stronger vis-a-vis those two. I felt that it could have been made stronger, but then I couldn't have claimed it. I managed to go beyond the script, though I was not making any conscious or unconscious attempt to make it strong and performed to the satisfaction of my director. The role has to be taken purely in the spirit of the role, and one should not complain but surrender to the director and focus. The attention paid to an actor's role is as much as it deserves, what the role demands and how popular the actor is.[26]

The music of *Saudagar*, composed by Laxmikant–Pyarelal to the lyrics of Anand Bakshi, is just about passable. It did not create any impact except perhaps for the two-part Raag Miyan Ki Todi-based song *Imli ka boota beri ka paed, imli khatti meethe ber* (The tamarind shrub the jujube tree/The tamarind is bitter the jujube sweet), sung by Mohammed Aziz, Sudesh Bhosle, Sadhana Sargam and Udit Narayan.

10

MAN OF THE LAW

IT IS SAID THAT 'THE WORLD OF ART IS NOT A WORLD of immortality; it is a world of metamorphosis'. Today metamorphosis is the very life blood of a work of art. Post 1980, Dilip Kumar reinvented himself keeping in mind the ever-changing taste of the cinemagoers and thus the face of cinema itself. Though always choosy about the roles he played, subtle and restrained, bringing in dignity and intensity to the art of acting, he started selecting, at this juncture, roles that offered him satisfying pivotal role in the scripts. If Manoj Kumar's *Kranti* was signed without even reading the script to pay back a debt to Manoj Kumar (which was an unheard-of exception), the other films were picked, according to Dilip Kumar himself, 'because they had themes that celebrated the courage of the central character to stand up to [the] odds. I was drawn to the characters, and I felt I could make them inspiring and unforgettable if I applied myself to rendering them with conviction and realism.'[1]

In the films of this era, Dilip Kumar exhibited his formidable capacity to innovate and improvise. His portrayals, extremely credible and forceful, were executed with perfect timing and precision. His presence imposed a certain gravitas to these films, which they severely needed. However, the minus point was that his characterizations tend to overshadow everything else. Hence, leaving aside films such as Ramesh Sippy's *Shakti* and, to a lesser extent, B. Gopal's *Kanoon Apna Apna* (1989), most of his films during this period proved to be of hardly any serious consequence, even with the broad standards of commercial films.

Shakti (1982)

In 1982, producer–director Ramesh Sippy, who was still reeling from the phenomenal success of his multi-starrer *Sholay* (1975), and failure of *Shaan* in 1980, came up with a Dilip Kumar–Amitabh Bachchan combination, in the company of Rakhee and Smita Patil, *Shakti*. Like his other box-office successes, *Andaz* (1971) and *Seeta Aur Geeta* (1972; a female version of Tapi Chanakya's *Ram Aur Shyam*), this film too was written by Salim–Javed. If *Andaz* brought a fading Shammi Kapoor back into the cinema limelight, and *Seeta Aur Geeta* got Hema Malini her first and only Filmfare Award for Best Actress in 1973 and pushed her career to the top, Ramesh

Rakhee and Dilip Kumar in *Shakti* (1982)

Dilip Kumar, Rakhee and Amitabh Bachchan in *Shakti* (1982)

Sippy gave Dilip Kumar his first real breakthrough in a senior role in *Shakti*, notwithstanding Manoj Kumar's *Kranti*.

A well-crafted affair on the conflict between family affinities and societal responsibilities, *Shakti*'s strong storyline offered Dilip Kumar the most valuable opportunity to validate, once again, his unquestionable supremacy in film acting.

Shakti was not an original script in terms of its plot and characterizations. Inspired by Gyan Mukherjee's film *Sangram* (1950) to which Salim–Javed managed to add their own flavour, it was, in many ways, a remake of K. Asif's classic, *Mughal-e-Azam*, mounted in a modern setting, like Yash Chopra's *Deewar* was a rework of Nitin Bose's *Gunga Jumna* in a new avatar. In fact, Dilip Kumar's character as an upright police officer (deputy commissioner of police), Ashwini Kumar, was created by combining three of the most powerful characters one has seen down the years in Hindi cinema: Mohammad Jalaluddin Akbar, the third Mughal emperor (Prithviraj

Kapoor) in K. Asif's magnum opus *Mughal-e-Azam*, Radha (Nargis) in Mehboob Khan's epic *Mother India* (1957) and Jumna (Nasir Khan) in Nitin Bose's unforgettable *Gunga Jumna*. It too has no clear blacks and whites. Dilip Kumar and Amitabh Bachchan, as father and son, were on the opposite sides of the law.

The character, following the Machiavellian theory of the state, strives to prove that the state is omnipotent, and in fact, he represents the state itself. It also indicates that there is an inbuilt vulnerability in the state apparatus, and its overpowering presence is made possible by operational cruelty in its functional system. For this, the state builds into the mental state of its upholders (in this case, Dilip Kumar as the police officer) an uncompromisable sense of commitment to live for the state even at the cost of his personal life and emotional attachments. Thus, Dilip Kumar becomes the patriarch representing the state apparatus whose own rigidly lawful conduct results in greater alienation of its prospective victims.

However, the character of Dilip Kumar in *Shakti* is far more multidimensional and complex than that of Emperor Akbar in *Mughal-e-Azam*. In it, if the emperor says to his wife Maharani Jodha Bai: '*Aap ma hain, sirf ma*' (You are mother, only a mother), to which she answers: '*Aur aap shahenshah, sirf shahenshah*' (You are an emperor, only an emperor), here, the police officer is not only a mere symbol of the state but also a human being who has internalized the ensuing conflict between his professional imperatives and family obligations. This makes the character not only uphold his convictions but also live through the conflict itself. The father is so sure of his doctrinal moral precepts and idealism that he expects to infuse them in his son, Vijay Kumar (Amitabh Bachchan), and thus build the latter's personality on his own model. The son has his own ideas and beliefs, which run counter to his father's lofty principles.

Dilip Kumar and Amrish Puri in *Shakti* (1982)

In the film, Vijay, as a small boy, is kidnapped by a bunch of
gangsters, whose leader, J.K. Verma (Amrish Puri), threatens
to kill him unless the police officer releases one of the gang
members who is in police custody. The ethically-minded police
officer refuses to accept this demand. The son overhears his
father telling the gang leader on the phone that protecting the
law is more important than his son's life. The son is shocked
and in his young mind are sown the seeds of antagonism against
his father. The son manages to escape from his kidnappers
with the help of one of the goons—K.D. Narang (Kulbhushan
Kharbanda), who takes pity on the young lad.

As time moves on, the predictable conflict between the
father and the son becomes one between the past generation
of moral uprightness and the present-day generation, alienated
and vulnerable, looking for security in material success by
any means, even at the cost of destroying delicate family
relationships and giving up one's ethics and morality. While
the police-officer father ignores personal emotions as a result

of his duty-bound conduct, his son, Vijay, plans the course of his life in response to his deep-rooted animosity for his father's idealism.

Vijay teams up with the well-known smuggler K.D. Narang, the one who had once saved him and has now moved 'up' the greasy pole in life and hit the big time in the world of vice. Vijay now takes the short-cut to earning wealth, somewhat reminiscent of *Deewar*. The narrative depicts very effectively the lack of communication or rather a mutual transgression between the old ethics and the germination of new unhealthy values, which inspire unending pursuits for self-gratification and short-cut success between the two generations despite the mutual affection between the father and the son. Although the two do make attempts to understand each other, they only end up creating friction between themselves. It is eventually Sheetal (Rakhee Gulzar), Ashwini's wife, who has to bear the brunt of antagonism between the father and the son.

Dilip Kumar interpreted his character through an extremely well-inducted sensitivity in his portrayal. In fact, with *Shakti*, he virtually rediscovered his immense histrionics, which helped him in re-establishing once again his indisputable status of numero uno, beyond the constraints of age and the changing film milieu. Through his typical sense of underplay as seen in his earlier films, Dilip Kumar in *Shakti* internalized the dilemma posed by his son and progressively builds into his character an unusual emotional intensity. In the climax, the father is compelled to shoot his son, who refuses to surrender to the police.

The character of the rebel son, Vijay, as portrayed by Amitabh Bachchan, on the other hand, was far less effective in its design and execution than of Prince Salim in *Mughal-e-Azam*, Birju (Sunil Dutt) in *Mother India*, Gunga in *Gunga Jumna* and the anti-hero character played by Ashok Kumar opposite Nalini Jaywant in *Sangram*, as early as 1950, wherein

Dilip Kumar and Amitabh Bachchan in the climax scene in
Shakti (1982)

the hero is finally shot dead by his retired police-officer father
for his links with the city's mafia.

For example, see the very opening scenes of the film, which
can be a great lesson for any student of cinema, where Dilip
Kumar, as the police officer, now old, narrates his painful life
experiences to his grandson (Anil Kapoor); and the scene
where the father faces his son after coming to know of his
nefarious activities. And, of course, the scene in which Dilip
Kumar, in a deep sense of desperation, breaks down before
his wife after his rebel son leaves home. However, the show
stealers are two scenes: first, at Rakhee's death when Amitabh
Bachchan comes in and sits down near his father, holds his arm,
first with one hand, then with both, but does not look him in
the eye, as he does not have the courage to do so. Instead, he
turns his face towards the left. Both have tears in their eyes as
the son tries to console his father without saying a word. Yes,

not a word is said in the entire scene. Their expressions say it all. Second, the last few minutes when the father shoots his son on the tarmac of the airport, and the latter breathes his last in his father's arms. What a scene it is—the composition, the setting, the photography and beyond it all the agony and the strain, the paroxysm and deep pain in the eyes of the father as he listens to the emphysematous and stertorous voice of his dying son, is all par excellence.

This scene was later copied by American film director and screenwriter Michael Mann as a long-drawn-out sequence in his film *Heat* (1995), where Neil McCouley (Robert De Niro) flees on to the tarmac of the airport, pursued by Lieutenant Vincent Hanna (Al Pacino). The two stalk each other and Hanna shoots McCouley. The only difference between the two scenes from the two films being that while Dilip Kumar shoots his fleeing son in his back and then takes his dying son in his arms, Al Pacino shoots Robert De Niro in the chest and holds the hand of the dying man.

According to Dilip Kumar:

[He] was intrigued by the basic premise of *Shakti*, which evoked on the wisdom of ordinary individuals practising the moral principles of dharma. The question was raised provocatively in the script through the character of one of the two heroes—a police officer, who places his duty to be honest and gritty above his duty to rescue his young son who is kidnapped by criminals. The plot had a deceptive simplicity at the service level, yet its power to move the audience emanated from several forceful sequences that bared the emotional wounds of the police officer endured as a consequence of his adherence to his principles of dharma.[2]

The media reviews were mixed as also the response of the audience. Some critics claimed that Dilip Kumar completely overshadowed Amitabh Bachchan. Some others said Bachchan was underplaying. According to one critic, 'Shakti alone in the long decades of decline had promise of immortality, a film which had once-in-a-lifetime kind of star combination and performances.'

According to film journalist and author Bunny Reuben:

> One remembers the kind of craze that had [been] spontaneously generated for this film before its release. But *Shakti* turned out to be a frustrating film for any connoisseur of histrionics to watch, frustrating to watch two accomplished actors trying to desperately out-act each other, frustrating to watch a film that never really took off into dizzy heights of splendour nor could smash a fist into you, grab your heart and squeeze the tears out of your eyes ... Ask other perceptive fans of this remarkable artiste: Do the hairs on your body stand on end like mine do when you sit again and again through umpteen reruns of *Andaz* and *Daag* and *Mughal-e-Azam* and *Gunga Jumna* and all those magnificent Dilip Kumar starrers of the 1950s? They still do, don't they? Yes. And how do you feel to sit through the [later] era starrers?[3]

That is the tragedy of the cycle of life because the *wheel* of life goes turning upwards, and then inevitably it has to go downwards again. Up-down, up-down is the law of nature. The trick, of course, is to get off the wheel while it's got you up like Greta Garbo did. And nearer home, like Nargis and Vyjayanthimala, Nimmi and Asha Parekh did. But that's easier said than done. Perhaps the indurated fact is that it's very tough to 'get off' and just a handful of them do because there are, and will always be, two opinions about this. Because the fact remains that there are times when this author, like numerous others, too feels that Hindi cinema without Dilip Kumar would lose its raison d'etre. It would be like Shakespeare's *Hamlet* without the Prince of Denmark!

Mazdoor (1983)

As already mentioned, in 1972, B.R. Chopra had made *Dastaan* with Dilip Kumar and Sharmila Tagore in the lead. It was a total dud at the box office. Eleven years later, he made *Mazdoor*, which was directed by his son, Ravi Chopra, with Dilip Kumar and Nanda supported by Raj Babbar, Padmini Kolhapure, Rati Agnihotri and others. It turned out to be another big disaster. If there was a redeeming factor, it was the performances of Dilip Kumar and Nanda, and for the latter, it turned out to be her final screen appearance, for she went into retirement soon after.

Dilip Kumar takes up a realist character of Dinanath Saxena, an elderly foreman in a textile mill, who is revered by the fellow workers for his goodwill as well as expertise in

Raj Babbar, Iftekhar, Nanda and Dilip Kumar in
Mazdoor (1983)

Suresh Oberoi and Dilip Kumar in *Mazdoor* (1983)

managing the technical operations of the mill. Inspired by an enlarged business vision much beyond his financial abilities, he thus represents the inane grassroots entrepreneur capability of the country's industrial workers.

The mill owner, Hiralal (Suresh Oberoi), wants to bring in numerous changes so as to maximize profits, which brings him into conflict with his employees, including Dinanath, on several issues. He finally resigns to build a modern industrial enterprise in collaboration with a young struggling textile engineer Ashok Mathur (Raj Babbar). After much struggle, they do eventually succeed and build up a good reputation in the market with their products. Dinanath, impressed by the young Ashok, gets his daughter, Meena (Padmini Kolhapure), married to him. However, Smita (Rati Agnihotri), the daughter of a multi-millionaire, who had an affair with Ashok earlier, concocts a scheme along with Hiralal to bring in a discord between Dinanath and Ashok. It results in his workers going against him, and in an ensuing violence, his son gets killed.

The highlights of the film are the scenes where Dinanath expresses his frustration to his wife Radha (Nanda) over the non-payment of bonus to the mill workers by the management. And the scene where Dinanath grieves over the dead body of his son. And, of course, the scene where Dinanath, as a mill owner, vehemently presents his highly discomfiting viewpoint about the mistrust between him and the workers in a meeting with them and accuses his enemies of destroying the exemplary harmonious relations between them. In the end, Dinanath pronounces his vision on the need for truly cordial industrial relations: '*Sabko miljul ke hi rehna hoga. Is naye daur ka sapna hum pa sakte hain. Mazdoor-maalik ekta zindabad*' (We all need to stay together. We can achieve the dream of this new age. Long live the employer–employee unity).

Karma (1986)

Having won wide public applause at the box office and critical acclaim for his roles in *Kranti* and *Shakti*, Dilip Kumar was now all set to storm the Hindi film world in a big way. The quick succession of films that he signed, it seems, was perhaps due to a sense of urgency on his part to resurrect his career and consolidate his position at the top. And he was successful at that. They say nothing succeeds like success and he was ruling the box office. Roles were being especially written for him which presented him as a patriarch, towering high over the rest of the cast. His cine persona now embarked upon two distinct tracks as influenced by the current preoccupations of cinema: the agonized man as the upholder of the law or the vengeful veteran.

Dilip Kumar in *Karma* (1986)

The first such film was Subhash Ghai's *Karma* in 1986, with an ensemble cast and his first-ever appearance with the veteran actress Nutan.

Karma was a rehash of V. Shantaram's award-winning classic *Do Ankhen Barah Haath* (1957), which in turn was based on the core plot of Hugo Fregonese's *My Six Convicts* (1952), (inspired by a real-life experiment conducted by the Gandhian Maurice Frydman), Robert Aldrich's hugely successful film *The Dirty Dozen* (1967) and nearer home, *Sholay*.

It presented Dilip Kumar as the upright benevolent jail superintendent Rana Vishwa Pratap Singh (aka Dada Thakur), whose family has been massacred by Dr Michael Dang (Anupam Kher), the dreaded kingpin of an international terrorist organization. Only his wife, Rukmini (Nutan), who turns deaf with shock, and his youngest son (Jugal Hansraj) are saved. Like the protagonist from Donald Powell Wilson's autobiography *My Six Convicts: A Psychologist's Three Years in Fort Leavenworth*, Rana, the jailer, also holds the view that hardened criminals in prisons can be transformed by showing

Nutan and Dilip Kumar in *Karma* (1986)

them the right direction, thus enabling them to become socially useful persons.

Rana selects three persons—Baiju Thakur (Jackie Shroff), Jhonny (Anil Kapoor) and Khairuddin (Naseeruddin Shah), all condemned to death—to constitute a special anti-terrorist squad under his leadership. With his human approach as well as an aggressive stance of nationalism, the jailer transforms them into his committed allies and the quartet eventually destroy the villain Dr Dang's heavily guarded, high-tech military hideout located in a remote border area.

Karma, like *Sholay*, thus justified the role of extra-constitutional interventions in the nation's affairs. Dilip Kumar in an awe-inspiring performance was his usual self, masterfully internalizing the agony of the victim. Using his trademark histrionics, he once again captured the undercurrents of inseparable loss and transformed his anguish into a posture that exuded strength. His soulful relationship with his wife was a major highlight of the film as also the scene where Rana comes to the cell of Dr Dang and humiliates him for his arrogance by slapping him.

Dilip Kumar and Anupam Kher in *Karma* (1986)

Though much comparison has been made between *Karma* and *Do Ankhen Barah Haath*, where V. Shantaram himself played the role of the humane jail warden, Adinath, it was, besides its storyline, the music that set it apart. That gentle giant composer, Vasant Desai, who has the distinction of bringing in Ustad Amir Khan and Ustad Bismillah Khan to perform in Vijay Bhatt's *Goonj Uthi Shehnai* (1959), whose grip on folk forms, coupled with the depth of his knowledge on classical music, made him sound at once thematic and authentic. In *Do Ankhen Barah Haath*, he tuned with the creator to give us that sublime number *Aye malik tere bande hum, aise hon hamare kadam* (God, we are your beings, may our steps be such), written by Bharat Vyas, that to this day is 'the prayer anthem' of the nation.

Unfortunately, no such thing happened with *Karma*. Laxmikant–Pyarelal could come nowhere close to Vasant Desai. The closest they came to are the twin patriotic numbers:

Aye watan tere liye (O homeland for you) by Mohammad Aziz and Kavita Krishnamurthy and *Aye sanam there liye* (O beloved for you) in which Dilip Kumar also pitches in with Aziz and Kavita.

Dharm Adhikari (1986)

Down South, there is one K. Raghavendra Rao, known in the film industry as 'the man with the Midas touch'. Producer, screenplay writer, actor and choreographer, he has directed an unbelievable 108 films in Telegu and Hindi languages across multiple genres, such as romantic, comedy, fantasy, melodrama, action thriller and biographical films in addition to television serials. Known for his strict discipline and tight working schedules to finish a film in record time, he works on multiple films in a year—most of them highly successful.

Dilip Kumar in *Dharm Adhikari* (1986)

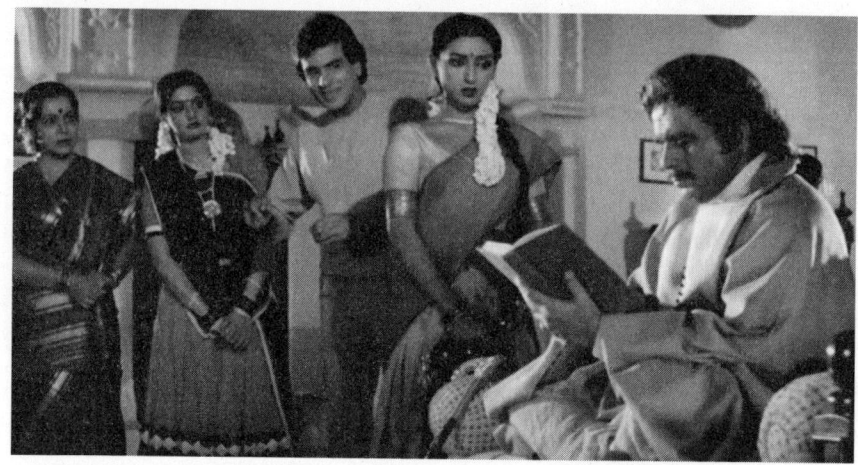

Rohini Hattangadi, Sridevi, Jeetendra and Dilip Kumar
in *Dharm Adhikari* (1986)

In 1985, he directed a record eight films and in 1986 seven, with one of them being *Dharm Adhikari* with Dilip Kumar and the favourite actor of South film-makers, Jeetendra (Ravi Kapoor) with Sridevi, Pran and others. However, what made Dilip Kumar do this film will remain a mystery.

Based on his Telegu superhit *Bobbili Brahmanna* (1984), *Dharm Adhikari* was intended to project a journey back in time to depict virtues of the traditional institution of justice in Indian rural society and to highlight its virtues beyond the pale of the state.

Dilip Kumar personified the classical sage figure of Dharamraj, the traditional law officer who is revered by the people for his virtually divine sense of justice which is accepted as God's judgement. The court of this crownless king is a desolate ground where the poorest of the poor can get immediate access to justice, where his very name instils fear among the wrongdoers.

In an opening scene, when his daughter Aarti (Anuradha Patel) asks him the reason for him to hold the holy book Gita

Rohini Hattangadi, Dilip Kumar and Pran in
Dharm Adhikari (1986)

with much devotion before going to his court, he replies:
'*Gita mere man main satya ki jyoti jagakar mujhe marg
dikhlati hai*' (The Gita lights up the truth in me and leads me
on the path of righteousness) and a little later in the village
dharam-sabha, (religious assembly) he brings forth the role of
dharma, righteousness, in upholding the true sense of justice
for the welfare of society. However, this judge becomes a
victim of the village politics as also his exceptionally rigid
values on justice, which does not distinguish between the
rich and the poor, between his own blood and anyone else in
the village.

Aarti falls in love with Arun, the son of a widow who is
under the care of Dharamraj. However, he in his judgement
pronounces that his daughter must marry a poor villager who
had lost his eyesight in a freak accident when Aarti's swing
had fallen on him. Dharamraj's younger brother Prakash
(Jeetendra) disagrees with this verdict and gets the two lovers
married. When Prakash brings the young couple home to

seek the blessings of Dharamraj, the man of justice announces: '*Jis din meri putri ne vivaah kiya, usi din se mera bhai aur putri mar gaye. Yeh ghar nahin, shok-grah hai. Yahan kisi ko aashirwad nahin milta*' (The day my daughter got married, that day she and my brother were dead for me. This is not a home but a house of mourning. No one gets any blessings here).

Later, when Dharamraj's wife, Savitri (Rohini Hattangadi), decides to go to Aarti's house to perform the ceremonies for her daughter's baby shower, Dharamraj orders her, too, to leave his house. A long discourse follows between the upholder of the law and his humane counterpart, which is shown being carried out on a chessboard drawn on the floor and the use of dear ones as the pawns.

This is the moment the villainous duo of Chaudhary (Pran) and Shastri (Kader Khan), who are jealous of Dharamraj's popularity, had been waiting for—to bring Dharamraj down from his seat of justice. They now charge him with having an illicit relationship with Arun's mother, the widow who lives under his charge. In the end, as Chaudhary and Shastri try to kill Arun and his mother, Prakash reaches the spot as also Dharamraj, who joins hands with his younger brother, and saves them.

Dharm Adhikari was a downright platitudinous film, something even Dilip Kumar, known for selecting his scripts very carefully and with a lot of thought, regretted having done: 'The film had Sanskritized dialogues and I even made the effort of learning Sanskrit, just for this role. The producers had promised me that the film would not have any vulgar comedy. But they went back on their word. Other than my scenes, the film had much obnoxious comedy.'

Kanoon Apna Apna (1989)

Directed by B. Gopal, this Dilip Kumar starrer, despite an intense and outstanding performance by the actor, failed to click at the box office. This despite the fact that it had for its star cast besides Dilip Kumar, Nutan, Sanjay Dutt, Madhuri Dixit, Anupam Kher and a host of others.

Dilip Kumar as Jagatpratap Singh portrayed an upright district collector who has to uphold the law of the land amid the challenges of two other ideologies—first, a mob leader, who thrives on public sentiments, and second, a pro-people militant activist. Here, Dilip Kumar, once again, as in Ramesh Sippy's *Shakti*, opted for a highly sophisticated underplay. For example, in one of the early scenes he, with much passion and forcefulness, can be seen describing to his son his viewpoint about the importance of maintaining the sanctity of law. Clearly, he is a hard taskmaster but in conflict with his son Ravi (Sanjay Dutt), who believes that sometimes illegal means need to be adopted to punish the villainous characters in society.

Dilip Kumar and Sanjay Dutt in *Kanoon Apna Apna* (1989)

Dilip Kumar and Kader Khan in *Kanoon Apna Apna* (1989)

Kailash (Gulshan Grover) and Prakash (Tej Sapru), the sons of the two corrupt ministers, Bhushannath Bhadboli (Kader Khan) and Kabza Kanhaiyalal (Anupam Kher), respectively, rape and kill Jagatpratap's maid servant as also Ravi's friend. Though arrested, they are acquitted by the court because of the fake alibis given to them. To punish these two murderers, Ravi joins the police force, as he has different ideas about the meaning of justice which only widens the rift between the father and the son. The film 'rips through the machinations of the corrupt local politicians and we have three interpretations of the law of the land: the upright administrator's understanding of the law; it's manipulation by the mob leader; and the (morally justified) violation of law by the militant activist, who also happened to be the collector's son'.[4] The film was not much appreciated by the public. However, Dilip Kumar's performance came in for much praise by the media.

According to the *Indian Express* of 29 October 1989:

The era of escapism is temporarily dead in mainstream Hindi cinema [and the film] even offers a plausible solution to the problems and the confusion which have besieged the modern Indian state. In a powerful, hard-hitting statement, the film also offers an alternative to the now routine celluloid war for justice by the lone ranger . . . Director B. Gopal's film makes perhaps the most critical comment (in the Hindi cinema) on the new breed of the populist, unscrupulous, criminalized politicians we have seen emerge during the last decade. The film quite naturally revolves around the intense but grand conviction of the honest administrator . . . and Dilip Kumar turns out a marvellously intricate display of voice modulation and dialogue delivery. It is a performance that compares with the great actor's best, and the barriers of age are easily undone by him.

The weekly *Screen* of 3 November 1989 wrote: 'The performances are generally good or very good. Dilip Kumar naturally dominates the screen with his stature. His typical nuance and style are difficult to equal. But Kader Khan, who also wrote the film's dialogues, is able to muster up interesting encounters with Dilip. The dialogues have the usual punch and occasionally sound sophisticated when Dilip Kumar speaks them.'

Qila (1998)

Way back in 1953, one F.C. Mehra launched a production house under the banner of Eagle Films, which went on to get established in the top names of the Hindi film industry with many a hugely successful film, including Raaj Kumar, Shammi Kapoor, Mala Sinha's *Ujala* (1959); Shammi Kapoor, Kalpana, Parveen Chaudhary's *Professor* (1962); *Amrapali* (1966) with Sunil Dutt and Vyjayanthimala; Raaj Kumar,

Dilip Kumar in *Qila* (1998)

Hema Malini, Rakhee and Vinod Mehra's *Lal Pathar* (1971); and the Shammi Kapoor-directed *Manoranjan* (1974), to name just a few.

After F.C. Mehra, his son Umesh took over the direction of films under the banner and in 1998, released *Qila*, in which he brought back an aged Dilip Kumar, after a gap of nine years. And the actor, opting for a double role and drawing diverse elements from many of his previous portrayals, appeared to be cashing on his earlier charisma. Rekha was in the female lead.

The film was intended to show allegorically the inevitable transition of society from its feudal moorings to a democratic form in which the decadent feudal order is sought to be corrected by a new world view.

It was Dilip Kumar, once again in a double role—his third after *Ram Aur Shyam* and *Dastaan*. He portrayed two brothers—Jagannath Singh, a tyrannical feudal lord, an anti-hero, who has played havoc with the people in his domain, and Amarnath Singh, an upright professional, a judge, who is pained by the deeds of his evil brother. One fine morning, it is discovered that the cruel Jagannath Singh is murdered and the democrat brother, Judge Amarnath Singh decides to investigate. The prime suspect, Jagannath's son, Amar Singh (Mukul Dev), confesses to killing his father but reveals that he accidentally shot his father while trying to fight him off when he held Amar and his mother at gunpoint. This murder mystery also involved Yamini (Rekha), who claims that she was raped by Jagannath.

A couple of scenes stood out and one of them was when the judge brother, Amarnath Singh, very affectionately advises his nephew, Amar Singh, who has refused to light the pyre of his dead father: '*Yeh khoon ke rishte hain, Amar. Insaan inhaen banata hai aur na todtha hai. Tumhe ek bete ke naate apna kartavya pura karna chahiye*' (These relationships are of blood. A man doesn't make them, nor can he break them. You, as a son, must carry out your obligation). The other one being when Dilip Kumar as an extremely perturbed judge brother says: '*Ek judge ki hasiyat se farz aur kanoon mein bandha hoon. Bhai ke qatal ne insaf ki dagar par aisi bedardi se khincha, jaise ki main khud se bhaaga hua mulzim hoon*' (As a judge, I am bound by my duty and the law. My brother's murder has been committed so heartlessly that it seems, I am myself a fugitive running away).

However, for nostalgia's sake, here is the last screen dialogue rendered by Dilip Kumar in his glorious film career, in the scene in which he describes the virtue of the justice system:

Yahi to kanoon ki ruh hai ki un hazooron ko uski saaza miley aur bekasooroon ko rehaii.

(This is the spirit of the law that thousands be punished, and the innocent be freed.)

The film was a non-performer in all respects and was forgotten in no time. As a critic put it: 'This is a completely ridiculous murder mystery.' After ridiculing the film right through, the *Times of India* review published on Sunday, 12 April 1998, remarked that 'it was unfortunate that Dilip Kumar's style of acting was no longer in consonance with the present era'.

Dinesh Raheja, author and columnist, in his review for *Sunday Mid-Day* of 19 April 1998, said: 'Since Dilip Kumar had chosen to act in *Qila* after a break of nine years, everybody's expectations had been high. However, he has failed to impress in his double role, resulting in double disappointment.'

According to Bunny Reuben:

What most people found difficult to accept was that the two Dilip Kumars spoke two different lingos—one speaking in chaste Urdu and the other rattling off his dialogues in Bhojpuri, while the son Mukul Dev spoke in Punjabi . . . One thing definitely stands out—the thespian's heart was not in his performance. Perhaps he had grown weary—weary of constantly trying to keep up his image. His histrionic prowess was absent, and the subtleties gone. *Qila* will always regrettably stand as a turning point in an otherwise illustrious career. It will stand out as the turning point . . . In reverse.[5]

Yes, what could have been a grand finale to a career spanning fifty-four years, which started in 1944, with Amiya Chakravarty's *Jwar Bhata*, ended with a giant disaster at the box office. This is one film Dilip Kumar ought never to have done, for *Qila* is certainly not a film on which to end the curriculum of the course of 'The Art and Craft of Dilip Kumar', of the unique Method acting of the actor, of the sui generis film career of a legend— 'the greatest actor of Indian cinema'—the one and only Dilip Kumar.

Quel dommage—A pity indeed!

A question that has often been asked was as to why Dilip Kumar did such indifferent films in the latter part of his career. He once answered the question himself:

Selectiveness has been my hallmark from the beginning, and it is this that has enabled me to survive for so long. Today you cannot choose between good and bad films. You have to choose between bad and horrible films. So, can you blame me for choosing the bad films? I cannot say that the new style of functioning suits my temperament. Our films are also becoming like fast food and this breakneck pace is taking us nowhere. There is no time to concentrate, no atmosphere to imbibe, absorb and deliver, which is why I have decided to give up acting.[6]

11

REJECTING HOLLYWOOD AND THE UNRELEASED, UNFINISHED FILMS

MUCH HAS BEEN WRITTEN ABOUT DILIP KUMAR REJECTING David Lean's film *Lawrence of Arabia*, but few know that there were other offers too—all of which he refused. When David Lean was casting for his *Lawrence of Arabia* some time in early 1960, he offered him the role of Sherif Ali ibn el Kharish, that was later played by Omar Sharif. But Dilip Kumar did not want to play the second lead. Instead, he wanted the title role, which Peter O'Toole played. David however had his own calculations.

There had been some other offers too. The Hungarian-born British film director Sir Alexander Korda, who had made many a successful film, had approached Dilip Kumar to play the role of the fifth Mughal emperor Shah Jahan in his dream project *Taj Mahal*. After a series of meetings with Korda, the project could not materialize. Similarly, sometime in mid-1955, Dilip Kumar was approached to work in *The Rains of Ranchipur*—a drama-disaster film made by Jean Negulesco for 20th Century Studios. It was to be a remake of the film *The Rains Came* (1939) by Clarence Brown, based on Lois Broomfield's novel. However, Dilip Kumar felt that the Western market may have a novelty value but one couldn't think of a permanent career in Hollywood.

Through the years 1944, when Amiya Chakravarty's *Jwar Bhata* was released, to 1998, when Umesh Mehra's *Qila* hit the screens, Dilip Kumar acted in a total of fifty-seven films in a career of fifty-four years. Besides these, there were six films in which he made a 'guest' or 'special' appearance: Vijay Anand's *Kala Bazar* (1960) opposite the three Anand brothers—Chetan, Dev and Vijay—with Waheeda Rehman, Nanda and Kishore Sahu in the cast; Jagannath Chatterjee's *Paari* (1966) in Bengali, with Dharmendra in the lead; A. Bhim Singh's *Sadhu Aur Shaitan* (1968) with Mehmood and Bharati; Jagganath Chatterjee's *Anokha Milan* (1972) with Dharmendra; Gulzar's *Khoshish* (1972) with Sanjeev Kumar and Jaya Bhaduri; and Hrishikesh Mukherjee's *Phir Kab Milogi* (1974) with Biswajeet and Mala Sinha in the lead.

The biggest surprise was the non-release of his fifty-eighth film—the 1991 *Aag Ka Dariya*, which had Rekha, Rajiv Kapoor and Padmini Kolhapure in it, with Dilip Kumar playing the role of Air Marshal Arjun, who was on a crusade against corrupt capitalists haemorrhaging the Indian air force. Directed by S.V. Rajendra Singh Babu, it was not only completed but also passed by the censors with a 'U' certificate. It still remains unreleased even on any of the television channels. A mystery indeed! But such are the ways and methods, twists and turns of the show world.

There were as many as fourteen films which were announced but were either shelved, for whatever reasons, or were partly shot and dropped at various stages of production. Of these, as many as six were shelved including K. Asif's *Taj Mahal* and *Aakhri Mughal* as also *Mera Watan* and *Samandar*, of which no details are available. There was also K. Asif's third project, which was launched with a great deal of optimism—*Janwar*, with the singing-star Suraiya opposite Dilip Kumar. This time shooting too started but history repeated itself for once again, as with his previous two projects, *Janwar* was shelved despite having shot extensively.

There was also B.R. Chopra's ambitious project *Chanakya Chandragupt* for which extensive preparations were completed in 1986 itself with set designs, costumes, wigs including the wild cape in which Dilip Kumar was to be seen as Chanakya opposite Dharmendra as Chandragupt. Hema Malini and Parveen Babi too were in the cast. However, after all the pre-production work, the project was dropped.

In 1950, Mahesh Kaul announced *Haar Shingaar* with Madhubala opposite Dilip Kumar. Shooting began in all earnest but after eight shooting schedules and a few reels canned, for some reason, the film was shelved.

Three years later, in 1953, P. Rajendra Jain announced *Shikwa* with Nutan opposite Dilip Kumar. It too was shelved after shooting a few reels.

There was also Nasir Hussain's untitled film with Dilip Kumar and Asha Parekh, which strangely got shelved after the mahurat shot itself.

In 1992, film producer Sudhakar Bokade launched a film which was to be Dilip Kumar's debut as a film director, officially. It was the ambitious *Kalinga* which had Raj Babbar, Meenakshi Sheshadri and Amjad Khan in the cast. Extensive shooting was underway with few reels already canned but once again, unfortunately, as with his previous films, Dilip Kumar shelved *Kalinga* too. It was a regret every cinema buff would have, for it was a film one was so looking forward to, a film about which, those who saw the rushes spoke highly about its emotional impact and its hair-raising scenes, a film that Dilip Kumar himself was very enthusiastic about.

Similar was the fate of Kuku Kohli's project in 2001, *Asar*, which was shelved after some shooting with Dilip Kumar, Ajay Devgn and Priyanka Chopra.

In the list of Dilip Kumar's shelved projects is also R.C. Talwar's *Bank Manager*, in which Dilip Kumar and Meena Kumari came together again. And believe it or not, music composer Madan Mohan—whose music is a class apart and who was extolled as the 'Ghazal Ka Shahzaada' (Prince of Ghazals) by none other than Lata Mangeshkar herself—was brought in for the first time for a Dilip Kumar film. In the *shayraana sohbat* (poetic company) of Sahir Ludhianvi, Kaifi Azmi or Raja Mehdi Ali Khan, he always seemed to excel himself. His euphonious compositions in film after film still linger in the memories of ghazal aficionados. Apparently, he had written some music for the film in which his phenomenal creativity dovetailed perfectly with the theme of the movie. However, most unfortunately, the film was shelved. One wonders whatever happened to that music.

'Good night, sweet prince,
And flights of Angels sing thee to thy rest.'

—William Shakespeare, *Hamlet*,
[Act 5, Scene 2]

FILMOGRAPHY
(ARRANGED IN ALPHABETICAL ORDER)

Aadmi 1968
Director (D): A. Bhim Singh
Music (M): Naushad
Cast (C): Dilip Kumar, Waheeda Rehman,
Manoj Kumar, Simi Garewal and Pran

Aan 1952
D: Mehboob Khan
M: Naushad
C: Dilip Kumar, Nimmi, Premnath and
introducing Nadira

Amar 1954
D: Mehboob Khan
M: Naushad
C: Dilip Kumar, Madhubala, Nimmi and
Jayant

Andaz 1949
D: Mehboob Khan
M: Naushad
C: Dilip Kumar, Raj Kapoor and Nargis

Anokha Pyar 1948
D: M.I. Dharamsey
M: Anil Biswas
C: Dilip Kumar, Nargis and Nalini
Jaywant

Arzoo 1950
D: Shahid Latif
M: Anil Biswas
C: Dilip Kumar, Kamini Kaushal, Gope and
Shashikala

Azaad 1955
D: S.M.S. Naidu
M: C. Ramchandra
C: Dilip Kumar, Meena Kumari, Pran and
Om Prakash

Babul 1950
D: S.U. Sunny
M: Naushad
C: Dilip Kumar, Nargis and Munnawar
Sultana

Bairaag 1976 (first triple role)
D: Asit Sen
M: Kalyanji–Anandji
C: Dilip Kumar, Saira Banu, Leena
Chandavarkar and Prem Chopra

Daag 1952
D: Amiya Chakraborthy
M: Shankar–Jaikishan
C: Dilip Kumar, Usha Kiran, Nimmi, Lalita
Pawar and Kanhaiyalal

Dastaan 1972 (second double role)
D: B.R. Chopra
M: Laxmikant–Pyarelal
C: Dilip Kumar, Sharmila Tagore, Prem
Chopra and Bindu

Deedar 1951
D: Nitin Bose
M: Naushad
C: Ashok Kumar, Nargis, Dilip Kumar
and Nimmi

Devdas 1955
D: Bimal Roy
M: S.D. Burman
C: Dilip Kumar, Suchitra Sen,
Vyjayanthimala, Johnny Walker and Pran

Dharm Adhikari 1986
D: K. Raghavendra Rao
M: Bappi Lahiri
C: Dilip Kumar, Jeetendra, Sridevi,
Anuradha Patel, Pran, Kader Khan and
Shakti Kapoor

Dil Diya Dard Liya 1966
D: A.R. Kardar
M: Naushad
C: Dilip Kumar, Waheeda Rehman, Pran,
Rehman and Johnny Walker

Duniya 1984
D: Ramesh Talwar
M: R.D. Burman
C: Ashok Kumar, Dilip Kumar, Saira
Banu, Rishi Kapoor, Amrita Singh, Prem
Chopra, Amrish Puri and Pran

Footpath 1953
D: Zia Sarhadi
M: Khayyam
C: Dilip Kumar, Meena Kumari and
Kuldip Kaur

Ghar Ki Izzat **1948**
D: Ram Daryani
M: Gobindram
C: Dilip Kumar, Mumtaz Shanti and
Jeevan

Gopi **1970**
D: A. Bhim Singh
M: Kalyanji–Anandji
C: Dilip Kumar, Saira Banu, Om Prakash,
Pran, Johnny Walker, Nirupa Roy and
Farida Jalal

Gunga Jumna **1961**
D: Nitin Bose
M: Naushad
C: Dilip Kumar, Vyjayanthimala, Nasir
Khan, Azra, Kanhaiyalal and Nazir
Hussain

Hulchul **1951**
D: S.K. Ojha
M: Mohd. Shafi and Sajjad Husein
C: Dilip Kumar, Nargis and Balraj Sahni

Insaniyat **1955**
D: S.S. Vasan
M: C. Ramchandra
C: Dilip Kumar, Dev Anand and Bina Rai

Izzatdaar **1990**
D: K. Bapaiah
M: Laxmikant–Pyarelal
C: Dilip Kumar, Bharati, Govinda and
Madhuri Dixit

Jogan 1950
D: Kidar Sharma
M: Bulo C. Rani
C: Dilip Kumar and Nargis

Jugnu 1947
D: Syed Shaukat Hussain Rizvi
M: Feroz Nizami
C: Noor Jehan, Dilip Kumar and
Shashikala

Jwar Bhata 1944
D: Amiya Chakrabarty
M: Anil Biswas
C: Dilip Kumar, Mridula, Agha Jan and
K.N. Singh

Karma 1986
D: Subhash Ghai
M: Laxmikant–Pyarelal
C: Dilip Kumar, Nutan, Jackie Shroff,
Anil Kapoor, Naseeruddin Shah, Sridevi
and Poonam Dhillon

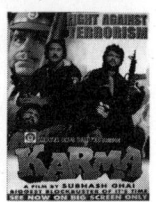

Kanoon Apna Apna 1989
D: B. Gopal
M: Bappi Lahiri
C: Dilip Kumar, Nutan, Sunjay Dutt,
Madhuri Dixit, Kader Khan and Anupam
Kher

Kohinoor 1960
D: S.U. Sunny
M: Naushad
C: Dilip Kumar, Meena Kumari, Jeevan
and Kumkum

Kranti **1981**
D: Manoj Kumar
M: Laxmikant–Pyarelal
C: Dilip Kumar, Manoj Kumar, Hema Malini, Shashi Kapoor, Parveen Babi, Shatrughan Sinha and Nirupa Roy

Leader **1964**
D: Ram Mukherjee
M: Naushad
C: Dilip Kumar, Vyjayanthimala, Motilal, Jayant and Nazir Hussain

Madhumati **1958**
D: Bimal Roy
M: Salil Chowdhury
C: Dilip Kumar, Vyjayanthimala, Pran and Johnny Walker

Mashaal **1984**
D: Yash Chopra
M: Hridaynath Mangeshkar
C. Dilip Kumar, Waheeda Rehman, Rati Agnihotri, Anil Kapoor and Amrish Puri

Mazdoor **1983**
D: Ravi Chopra
M: R.D. Burman
C: Dilip Kumar, Nanda, Raj Babbar, Padmini Kolhapure, Rati Agnihotri and Raj Kiran

Mela **1948**
D: S.U. Sunny
M: Naushad
C: Dilip Kumar, Nargis and Jeevan

Milan 1946
D: Nitin Bose
M: Anil Biswas
C: Dilip Kumar, Meera Mishra, Ranjana
and Pahari Sanyal

Mughal-e-Azam 1960
D: K. Asif
M: Naushad
C: Prithviraj Kapoor, Dilip Kumar,
Madhubala, Ajit and Durga Khote

Musafir 1957
D: Hrishikesh Mukherjee
M: Salil Chowdhury
C: Dilip Kumar, Usha Kiran, Kishore
Kumar, Suchitra Sen and Nirupa Roy

Nadiya Ke Paar 1948
D: Kishore Sahu
M: C. Ramchandra
C: Dilip Kumar, Kamini Kaushal and
Maya Banerji

Naya Daur 1957
D: B.R. Chopra
M: O.P. Nayyar
C: Dilip Kumar, Vyjayanthimala, Ajit,
Chand Usmani, Jeevan and Johnny
Walker

Pratima 1945
D: P. Jairaj
M: Arun Kumar
C: Dilip Kumar, Swarnalata, Jyoti and
Mumtaz Ali

Qila 1998 (third double role)
D: Umesh Mehra
M: Anand Raj Anand
C: Dilip Kumar, Rekha, Mukul Dev and
Mamta Kulkarni

Ram Aur Shyam 1967 (first double role)
D: Tapi Chanakya
M: Naushad
C: Dilip Kumar, Waheeda Rehman,
Mumtaz, Pran and Nirupa Roy

Sagina Mahato 1970 (Bengali)
D: Tapan Sinha
M: Tapan Sinha
C: Dilip Kumar, Saira Banu and Aparna
Sen

Sagina 1974 (Hindi)
D: Tapan Sinha
M: S.D. Burman
C: Dilip Kumar, Saira Banu, Om Prakash,
Aparna Sen, Anil Chatterji and Kader
Khan

Sangdil 1952
D: R.C. Talwar
M: Sajjad Husein
C: Dilip Kumar, Madhubala and Leela
Chitnis

Sunghursh 1968
D: H.S. Rawail
M: Naushad
C: Dilip Kumar, Vyjayanthimala, Balraj
Sahni, Sanjeev Kumar and Jayant

Saudagar **1991**
D: Subhash Ghai
M: Laxmikant–Pyarelal
C: Dilip Kumar, Raaj Kumar, Jackie Shroff, Manisha Koirala, Vivek Mushran, Deepti Naval, Anupam Kher and Amrish Puri

Shabnam **1949**
D: Bibhuti Mitra
M: S.D. Burman
C: Dilip Kumar, Kamini Kaushal and Jeevan

Shaheed **1948**
D: Ramesh Saigal
M: Ghulam Haider
C: Dilip Kumar, Kamini Kaushal, Chandramohan and Leela Chitnis

Shakti **1982**
D: Ramesh Sippy
M: R. D. Burman
C: Dilip Kumar, Amitabh Bachchan, Raakhee, Smita Patil, Kulbhushan Kharbanda and Amrish Puri

Shikast **1953**
D: Ramesh Saigal
M: Shankar–Jaikishan
C: Dilip Kumar, Nalini Jaywant and Om Prakash

Tarana **1951**
D: Ram Daryani
M: Anil Biswas
C: Dilip Kumar, Madhubala, Jeevan and Gope

Uran Khatola 1955
D: S.U. Sunny
M: Naushad
C: Dilip Kumar, Nimmi, Surya Kumari,
Jeevan and Agha

Vidhaata 1982
D: Subhash Ghai
M: Kalyanji–Anandji
C: Dilip Kumar, Sanjeev Kumar, Shammi
Kapoor, Sanjay Dutt, Padmini Kolhapure,
Sarika and Amrish Puri

Yahudi 1958
D: Bimal Roy
M: Shankar–Jaikishan
C: Dilip Kumar, Sohrab Modi, Meena
Kumari and Nigar Sultana

SPECIAL APPEARANCES

Anokha Milan 1972
D: Jagannath Chatterjee
M: Salil Chowdhury
C: Dharmendra, Pranoti Ghosh, Abhi
Bhattacharya and Dilip Kumar

Kala Bazaar 1960
D: Vijay Anand
M: S.D. Burman
C: Dev Anand, Waheeda Rehman,
Nanda, Vijay Anand, Chetan Anand,
Kishore Sahu and Dilip Kumar

Paari 1967 (Bengali)
D: Jagannath Chatterjee
M: Salil Chowdhury
C: Dharmendra, Abhi Bhattacharya and
Dilip Kumar

Phir Kab Milogi 1974
D: Hrishikesh Mukherjee
M: R.D. Burman
C: Mala Sinha, Biswajeet, Deven Varma
and Dilip Kumar

Sadhu Aur Shaitan 1968
D: A. Bhim Singh
M: Laxmikant–Pyarelal
C: Mehmood, Bharati, Kishore Kumar,
Om Prakash, Pran and Dilip Kumar

Koshish 1972
D. Gulzar
M. Madan Mohan
C: Sanjeev Kumar, Jaya Bhaduri, Om
Shivpuri, Asrani and Dilip Kumar

UNRELEASED FILM

Aag Ka Dariya (Completed and censored by the Central Board of
Film Certification (CBFC) in 1995 but unreleased)
D: S.V. Rajendra Singh Babu
C: Dilip Kumar, Rekha, Rajiv Kapoor, Padmini Kolhapure

INCOMPLETE FILMS

Bank Manager (shelved)
D: R.C. Talwar
M: Madan Mohan
C: Dilip Kumar and Meena Kumari

Taj Mahal and *Aakhri Mughal* (planned/shelved)
D: K. Asif
C: Dilip Kumar

Chanakya Chandragupt (shelved after extensive preparation)
D: B.R. Chopra
M: Naushad
C: Dilip Kumar, Dharamendra, Hema Malini, Parveen Babi, Helen and Vijayendra

Haar Singaar (1950) (shelved after a few reels)
D: Mahesh Kaul
M: Anil Biswas
C: Dilip Kumar, Madhubala, Kuldeep and Baby Zubeida

Janwar (shelved after a few reels)
D: K. Asif
C: Dilip Kumar and Suraiya

Shikwa (launched in early 1950s; shelved after a few reels)
P: Rajendra Jain
C: Dilip Kumar and Nutan

Mera Watan (shelved)

Samandar (shelved)

Kala Aadmi (after much research, shelved)
D: Ramesh Saigal and Dilip Kumar
C: Dilip Kumar

Untitled venture (shelved after *mahurat*)
P: Nasir Hussain
C: Dilip Kumar and Asha Parekh

Kalinga (1995) (incomplete)
D: Dilip Kumar
C. Dilip Kumar, Raj Babbar, Amjad Khan and Meenakshi Seshadri

Asar (2001) (shelved after mahurat and some shooting)
D: Kuku Kohli
M: Nadeem Shravan
C: Dilip Kumar, Ajay Devgan and Priyanka Chopra

ACKNOWLEDGEMENTS

Mera sapna sajaane ka tera shukriya
(Thanks for embellishing my dream)
—**Sahil Nawaz**

I AM PROFOUNDLY GRATEFUL TO ASHOK RAJ, A RESEARCH coordinator and author who wrote a sixteen-part series on cinema, for generously allowing me access to his research notes on Hindi filmland and permitting me to use them freely. I also owe a deep debt of gratitude to my former colleague of over three decades, K.J. Ravinder. His encyclopaedic knowledge, unwavering passion for Hindi film music and remarkable memory have been invaluable in shaping this volume, particularly through his inputs on the songs listed here. Without the help of these two altruistic individuals, this book would not have been possible. In a way, both can be called co-authors of this book.

A heartfelt thank you to the insightful Gaurav Srinagesh, who leads the Penguin Random House family in India; my ever-smiling and sharp-witted publisher, Milee Ashwarya; and my assiduous editor, Manali Das, whose patience and meticulous care breathed fresh life into this work. Coupled with her is Manisha Sobhrajani, who ran a fine wooden comb through the typeset pages to remove all those lice-like typos which have a knack of creeping into even the cleanest of page proofs.

I am equally indebted to my wonderful and ever-helpful colleagues—Rakesh Kumar, Raghav Khattar, Aditya Jarial, Sonali Pawar, Nupur Hirani, Riya Sharma and Ravi Grover—whose timely inputs, even at short notice, were invaluable.

Lastly, I remain deeply beholden to the many authors whose works on the silver screen I have published, read or engaged with over nearly five decades. Many of them are no longer with us, but each one enriched my understanding of cinema in general—and Hindi movies in particular—in ways that continue to shape my perspective today.

Notes

Kabhi aankhen kitab main gum hain
Kabhi gum hain kitab aankhon mein
—Mohammad Alvi

(At times the eyes are lost in the book
At times the book is lost in the eyes.)

Author's Note

1. Ashok Chopra, *A Scrapbook of Memories: My Life with the Rich, the Famous and the Scandalous*, New Delhi: HarperCollins Publishers India, 2015.

Chapter 1: The Legend

1. Dilip Kumar, *The Substance and the Shadow: An Autobiography*, New Delhi: Hay House Publishers India, 2014.
2. Nikhat Kazmi, *The Dream Merchants of Bollywood*, New Delhi: UBS Publishers Distributors, 1998, p. 81.
3. Ibid., p. 83.
4. Ibid.
5. Kumar, *The Substance and the Shadow*, p. 439.

Chapter 2: Unlocking the Craft

1. Dilip Kumar, *The Substance and the Shadow: An Autobiography*, New Delhi: Hay House Publishers India, 2014, p. 12.

2. Anupam Kher, *Lessons Life Taught Me, Unknowingly: An Autobiography*, New Delhi: Hay House Publishers India, 2019, p. 225.

3. Kumar, *The Substance and the Shadow*, p. 358.

4. Kher, *Lessons Life Taught Me*, p. 231.

5. Kumar, *The Substance and the Shadow*.

6. Ibid.

7. Ibid., p. 348.

8. Kumar, *The Substance and the Shadow*, p. 387.

9. Naseeruddin Shah, *Indian Express*, 10 July 2021.

10. Amrish Puri with Jyoti Sabharwal, *Bonding: A Memoir*, New Delhi: Steller Publishers, 2013.

11. Uta Hagen, *Respect for Acting*, New Jersey (US): John Wiley & Sons, 2008, p. 240.

12. Elia Kazan, *A Life*, London: Andre Deutsch Ltd, 1988, p. 151.

13. Kher, *Lessons Life Taught Me*, pp. 228–29.

14. Marlon Brando, *Songs My Mother Taught Me*, New York: Random House, 1994.

15. Stevan Riley, *Listen to Me Brando*, a documentary, 2015.

Chapter 3: Birth of a New Art, New Craft

1. Kher, Anupam, *Lessons Life Taught Me, Unknowingly: An Autobiography*, New Delhi: Hay House Publishers, India, 2019, p. 225.

2. Ibid., p. 227.

3. Dilip Kumar, *The Substance and the Shadow: An Autobiography*, New Delhi : Hay House Publishers, 2014, p. 295.

4. Ibid., p. 443.

5. Ibid., p. 437.

6. Sergei Eisenstein, *Film Form: Essays in Film Theory*, New York: Mariner Books, 2014.

Chapter 4: His Music Makers

1. Rishi Kapoor with Meena Iyer, *Khullam Khulla: Rishi Kapoor Uncensored*, New Delhi: HarperCollins Publishers India, 2018, pp. 119–21.
2. Raju Bharatan, *A Journey Down Melody Lane*, New Delhi: Hay House Publishers, 2010, p. 124.
3. Amrish Puri with Jyoti Sabharwal, *The Act of Life: An Autobiography*, New Delhi: Steller Publishers, 2013, p. 247.
4. Javed Akhtar in a talk at Jashn-e-Rekhta, the world's largest Urdu language literary festival, 5 March 2018.
5. Bharatan, *A Journey Down Melody Lane*, p. 124.
6. Ibid.
7. Raju Bharatan, *Naushadnama: The Life and Music of Naushad*, New Delhi: Hay House Publishers, 2013, p. 231.
8. Raju Bharatan, *Lata Mangeshkar: A Biography*, New Delhi: UBS Publishers Distributors, 1995, p. 129.
9. Here, one must point out that much is lost in translation. Hence, please note that the translations here and elsewhere in the book are neither literal nor perfect; the aim is to give the readers, especially those who are not familiar with Hindi/ Hindustani/Urdu, a general idea of the original work/s. No wonder the term 'lost in translation' has been coined!
10. Nasreen Munni Kabir, *Bollywood: The Indian Cinema Story*, London: Channel 4 Books, Pan Macmillan Ltd, 2001.
11. Bharatan, *Naushadnama*, p. 231.
12. Anupam Kher, *Lessons Life Taught Me, Unknowlingly: An Autobiography* New Delhi: Hay House Publishers, 2019, p. 227.

Chapter 5: Many Faces, Many Hues, Many Shades

1. *Filmindia*, January 1945.
2. Free Press Journal, Bombay, 16 December 1944.

3. Dilip Kumar in an interview with Udaytara Nayar, *Screen*, 5 October 1984.

4. *Filmindia*, October 1945.

5. Dilip Kumar, *The Substance and the Shadow: An Autobiography*, New Delhi: Hay House Publishers, 2014, p. 147.

6. Ibid., p. 124.

7. *Filmindia*, October 1948.

8. Trinetra Bajpai and Anshula Bajpai, *Dilip Kumar: Peerless Icon Inspiring Generations*, New Delhi: Bloomsbury India, 2019.

Chapter 6: Negotiations with Grief

1. Trinetra Bajpai and Anshula Bajpai, *Dilip Kumar: Peerless Icon Inspiring Generations*, New Delhi: Bloomsbury India, 2019, p. 32.

2. Meghnad Desai, *Nehru's Hero: Dilip Kumar in the Life of India*, New Delhi: Lotus Books, 2017, p. 76.

3. Raju Bharatan, *Naushadnama: The Life and Music of Naushad*, New Delhi: Hay House Publishers, 2014.

4. Dilip Kumar, *The Substance and the Shadow: An Autobiography*, New Delhi: Hay House Publishers, 2014.

5. Ibid.

6. B.D. Garga, *The Art of Cinema: An Insider's Journey Through Fifty Years of Film History*, New Delhi: Penguin Books India, 2005, p. 42.

7. Nitin Bose, Interview with Udaytara Nayar in *Screen*, 16 March 1985.

8. Garga, *The Art of Cinema*, p. 42.

9. Kumar, *The Substance and the Shadow*.

10. Ibid., p. 120.

11. Ibid., p. 121.

12. Ibid, p. 29.

13. Ibid.

14. Ibid.

15. Raju Bharatan, *A Journey Down Melody Lane*, New Delhi: Hay House Publishers, 2010, p. 15.

16. Kumar, *The Substance and the Shadow*, p. 118.

17. B.K. Karanjia, *Blundering in Wonderland*, New Delhi: Vikas Publishing House, 1990, p. 93.

18. Bharatan, *Naushadnama*, p. 13.

19. Ibid., p. 219.

20. Ibid., p. 220.

21. Garga, *The Art of Cinema*, p. 87.

22. Nasreen Munni Kabir, *Bollywood: The Indian Cinema Story*, London: Channel 4 books, Pan Macmillan Ltd., 2001, p. 132.

23. Dilip Kumar, *The Substance and the Shadow: An Autobiography*, New Delhi: Hay House Publishers, 2014, p. 174.

24. Vyjayanthimala Bali and Jyoti Sabharwal, *Bonding: A Memoir*, New Delhi: Steller Publishers, 2013, p. 174.

25. Kumar, *The Substance and the Shadow*, p. 443.

26. Ibid.

27. Ibid.

28. Adlakha Siddhant, 'Lasting Legacies of a Towering Bollywood Star', *New York Times*, 12 July 2021.

29. Kumar, *The Substance and the Shadow*, p. 406.

30. Ibid., p. 407.

31. Suraiya in an interview with the *Illustrated Weekly of India* in December 1974.

32. Garga, *The Art of Cinema*, p. 56.

33. Kumar, *The Substance and the Shadow*, pp.175–76.

34. Bali and Sabharwal, *Bonding: A Memoir*, p. 84.

35. Raju Bharatan, *Naushadnama: The Life and Music of Naushad*, New Delhi: Hay House Publishers, 2013, p. 123.

36. Kabir, *Bollywood*, p. 132.
37. Siddhant, Adlakha, 'Lasting Legacies of Towering Bollywood Star', *New York Times*, 12 July 2021.
38. Kumar, *The Substance and the Shadow*, pp. 174–75.
39. Kabir, *Bollywood*, p. 114.
40. Shankar in an interview with *Filmfare*, April 1998.
41. Kumar, *The Substance and the Shadow*, p.167.
42. Khatija Akbar, *'I Want to Live': The Story of Madhubala*, New Delhi: Hay House Publishers, 1997, p. 63.
43. Ibid., p. 168.
44. Kumar, *The Substance and the Shadow*, p. 202.
45. Bharatan, *A Journey Down Melody Lane*, p. 122.

Chapter 7: The King of Comedy

1. Khatija Akbar, *'I Want to Live': The Story of Madhubala*, New Delhi: Hay House Publishers, 1997, p. 16.
2. Dilip Kumar, *The Substance and the Shadow: An Autobiography*, New Delhi: Hay House Publishers, 2014, p. 156.
3. Ibid.
4. Raju Bharatan, *Naushadnama: The Life and Music of Naushad*, New Delhi: Hay House Publishers, 2013, page 186.
5. Kumar, *The Substance and the Shadow*, p. 239.
6. Bharatan, *Naushadnama*, p.113.
7. Siddhant Adlakha, 'Lasting Legacies of a Towering Bollywood Star', *New York Times*, 12 July 2021.
8. Kumar, *The Substance and the Shadow*, p. 239.
9. Ibid., p. 403.
10. Ibid., p. 203.
11. Ibid., p. 380.
12. Ibid., p. 15.

Chapter 8: The Crusading Hero

1. Dilip Kumar, *The Substance and the Shadow: An Autobiography*, New Delhi: Hay House Publishers, 2014, p. 397.

2. Ibid., p. 140.

3. Ibid., p. 113.

4. Reuben, Bunny, *Mehboob . . . India's DeMille: The First Biography*, New Delhi: HarperCollins Publishers, 1994.

5. Trinetra Bajpai and Anshula Bajpai, *Dilip Kumar: Peerless Icon Inspiring Generations*, New Delhi: Bloomsbury India, 2019, p. 74.

6. Vyjanthimala Bali with Jyoti Sabharwal, *Bonding : A Memoir*, New Delhi : Steller Publishers, 2013, p. 81.

7. Kumar, *The Substance and the Shadow,* p. 358.

8. Amrish Puri with Jyoti Sabharwal, *The Act of Life: An Autobiography*, New Delhi: Steller Publishers, 2013, p. 224.

9. Kumar, *The Substance and the Shadow,* p. 181.

10. Ibid., p. 174.

11. Ibid., p. 198.

12. Ibid.

13. Bali with Sabharwal, *Bonding*, p. 182.

14. Philip Lutgendorf, *The Life of a Text: Performing the Ramcaritmanas of Tulsidas*, US: University of California Press, 1991, p. 236.

15. Raju Bharatan, *Naushadnama: The Life and Music of Naushad*, New Delhi: Hay House Publishers, 2013, p. 303.

16. Ibid.

17. Ibid.

18. Ibid, p. 293.

19. Kumar, *The Substance and the Shadow*, p. 260.

Chapter 9: The Anti-Hero

1. Trinetra Bajpai and Anshula Bajpai, *Dilip Kumar: Peerless Icon Inspiring Generations*, New Delhi: Bloomsbury India, 2019, p. 49.

2. Nasreen Munni Kabir, *Bollywood: The Indian Cinema Story*, London: Channel 4 Books, Pan Macmillan Ltd, 2001, p. 127.

3. Bunny Reuben, *Dilip Kumar: The Definitive Biography*, New Delhi: HarperCollins Publishers, 2004, p. 117.

4. Raju Bharatan, *Naushadnama: The Life and Music of Naushad*, New Delhi: Hay House Publishers, 2013, p. 259.

5. Nikhat Kazmi, *The Dream Merchants of Bollywood*, New Delhi: UBS Publishers' Distributors, 1998, p. 84.

6. Bharatan, *Naushadnama*, p. 167.

7. Khatija Akbar, *'I Want to Live': The Story of Madhubala*, New Delhi: Hay House Publishers, 1997, p.125.

8. Bunny Reuben, *. . . and Pran: A Biography*, New Delhi: HarperCollins Publishers, 2011, p. 113.

9. Dilip Kumar, *The Substance and the Shadow: An Autobiography*, New Delhi: Hay House Publishers, 2014, p. 293.

10. Reuben, *. . . and Pran* p. 113.

11. Dilip Kumar, *The Substance and the Shadow: An Autobiography*, New Delhi: Hay House Publishers, 2014, p. 398.

12. Ibid., p. 204.

13. Bharatan, *Naushadnama*, pp. 150–51.

14. Ibid.

15. Ibid.

16. Ibid.

17. Reuben, *Dilip Kumar*, p. 416.

18. Kumar, *The Substance and the Shadow*, p. 396.

19. Ibid., p. 296.

20. Kumar, *The Substance and the Shadow,* p. 303.

21. Ibid., p. 383.
22. There is a possible ambiguity regarding the origin of this quote. Though widely attributed to the actor Marlon Brando, many believe that it is by the American actor James Dean, though the original source or publication is not specified.
23. Kumar, *The Substance and the Shadow*, p. 117.
24. Subhash Ghai in a TV interview.
25. Anupam Kher, *Lessons Life Taught Me, Unknowingly*, New Delhi: Hay House Publishers, 2019, p. 232.
26. Amrish Puri with Jyoti Sabharwal, *The Act of Life: An Autobiography*, Stellar Publishers, 2013, p. 247.

Chapter 10: Man of the Law

1. Dilip Kumar, *The Substance and the Shadow: An Autobiography*, New Delhi: Hay House Publishers, 2014, p. 301.
2. Ibid., p. 302.
3. Bunny Reuben, *Dilip Kumar: The Definitive Biography*, New Delhi: HarperCollins *Publishers*, 2004, p. 436.
4. *Indian Express*, 29 October 1989, New Delhi.
5. Reuben, *Dilip Kumar*.
6. Trinetra Bajpai and Anshula Bajpai, *Dilip Kumar: Peerless Icon Inspiring Generations*, New Delhi: Bloomsbury India, 2019.

The moving finger writes; and having writ,
Moves on: nor all thy Piety nor Wit
Shall lure it back to cancel half a Line,
Nor all thy Tears wash out a word of it

—Omar Khayyam in *Rubaiyat**

* Edward FitzGerald (Tr.), 1859, London: Single Hall & Co, 1910.

Scan QR code to access the Penguin
Random House India website